ICONS OF ROCK

ICONS OF ROCK

An Encyclopedia of the Legends Who Changed Music Forever

VOLUME 1

Scott Schinder and Andy Schwartz

Greenwood Icons

GREENWOOD PRESS
Westport, Connecticut · London

Library of Congress Cataloging-in-Publication Data

Schinder, Scott.
   Icons of rock: an encyclopedia of the legends who changed music forever / Scott Schinder and Andy Schwartz.
      p.   cm.—(Greenwood icons)
   Includes bibliographical references and index.
   ISBN-13: 978-0-313-33845-8 ((set) : alk. paper)
   ISBN-13: 978-0-313-33846-5 ((vol. 1) : alk. paper)
   ISBN-13: 978-0-313-33847-2 ((vol. 2) : alk. paper)
   1. Rock music—History and criticism.   2. Rock musicians.   3. Rock groups.   I. Schwartz, Andy.   II. Title.
   ML3534.S336 2008
   781.66092'2—dc22
   [B]   2007040132

British Library Cataloguing in Publication Data is available.

Library of Congress Catalog Card Number: 2007040132
ISBN-13: 978-0-313-33845-8 (set)
          978-0-313-33846-5 (vol. 1)
          978-0-313-33847-2 (vol. 2)

First published in 2008

Greenwood Press, 88 Post Road West, Westport, CT 06881
An imprint of Greenwood Publishing Group, Inc.
www.greenwood.com

Printed in the United States of America

The paper used in this book complies with the Permanent Paper Standard issued by the National Information Standards Organization (Z39.48-1984).

10 9 8 7 6 5 4 3 2 1

Contents

List of Photos

Elvis Presley (page 1). "The King of Rock & Roll" on stage at a Tampa, Florida armory in July 1955. The picture, taken by local photographer William V. "Red" Robertson, was later cropped for use on the cover of Elvis' self-titled debut album, released on RCA Records. Courtesy of Photofest.

Ray Charles (page 27). "The High Priest" of Rhythm & Blues in the late 1950s. Courtesy of Photofest.

Chuck Berry (page 55). Singer, songwriter, guitarist, and founding father of rock & roll. Courtesy of Photofest.

Buddy Holly (page 77). A rock & roll auteur, ahead of his time and gone too soon. Courtesy of Photofest.

The Beach Boys (page 101). "Summer Days & Summer Nights" circa 1964 with (L. to R.), Carl Wilson, Dennis Wilson, Mike Love, Al Jardine, and Brian Wilson. Courtesy of Photofest.

James Brown (page 131). "The Godfather of Soul," "The Hardest-Working Man in Show Business," and much more—on stage in the mid-Sixties. Courtesy of Photofest.

The Beatles (page 159). (L. to R.) Paul McCartney, George Harrison, Ringo Starr, and John Lennon in the velvet-collared stage suits they wore during the Beatles' debut North American tour of 1964. Courtesy of Photofest.

Bob Dylan (page 185). An early performance at Gerde's Folk City, New York, 1961. Courtesy of Photofest.

The Rolling Stones (page 209). "The World's Greatest Rock & Roll Band" in rehearsal at the Empire Pool in London before the BBC telecast of the *Ready Steady Go!* "Mod Ball" on April 8, 1964. L. to R. Brian Jones

U2 (page 565). During the European leg of their "Vertigo" tour in 2005, performing before a crowd of 60,000 fans at the Arena AufSchalke in Gelsenkirchen, Germany. L. to R. Larry Mullen Jr. (drums), The Edge (guitar), Bono (vocals), and Adam Clayton (bass). © AP/World Wide Photos.

Nirvana (page 589). (L. to R.) Krist Novoselic, Kurt Cobain, and Dave Grohl. Courtesy of Photofest.

Preface

It's now been more than half a century since rock and roll's official birth, although the music's roots stretch back much further. In that time, the genre has produced a rogues' gallery of memorable performers who've made essential contributions to rock's development as a major American art form, while emerging as fascinating, bigger-than-life figures in their own right.

It's common for historians to point to July 5, 1954—the evening that Elvis Presley recorded his debut single, "That's All Right, Mama" at Sun Records' Memphis studio—as the Night That Rock and Roll Was Born. But rock's birth cycle was messier and more complicated. The mongrel synthesis of black and white musical forms—blues, jazz, gospel, country—was the product of the convergence of an unruly mass of musical, cultural, and social forces that had been percolating for longer than anyone could remember. Presley's significance lies largely in the fact that in addition to being a brilliant and riveting performer, he was a charismatic young white man whose music could be marketed to Caucasian audiences at a time when musical tastes were as racially segregated as the rest of American society.

Those musical divisions began to break apart in the years following World War II. Postwar posterity created the first generation of American teenagers with sufficient disposable income to make them a potent economic force. Not coincidentally, that generation became the first to forge its own musical tastes; prior to the rock and roll era, kids more or less listened to the same music as their parents.

Beginning in the early 1950s, substantial numbers of white kids, who found little to relate to in the white-bread pop hits of the day, had begun to embrace the energy and immediacy of black rhythm and blues. While legal, social, and economic boundaries could prevent the races from mixing in public, they couldn't keep white teens from listening to the black R&B discs that could be heard on the radio in most cities, spun by hipster disc jockeys of both races.

One of the most prominent was Alan Freed, whose combination of patter and platters captivated teens in Cleveland and New York, and who's generally credited as the man who popularized the term "rock and roll."

Almost immediately, rock and roll became the subject of outrage and derision from various moral guardians, authority figures, and bigots, who decried the music as an inducement to sexual abandon and race mixing. The critics, of course, were correct, and the music would play an integral, if gradual, role in breaking down racial barriers. In rock's early days, though, it was standard practice for hits by African American artists to be covered, in watered-down form, by white artists in order to make them palatable to white listeners. Thus, Little Richard's raucous, sexually charged "Tutti Frutti" became a jaunty, nonthreatening nonsense ditty in the hands of clean-cut Pat Boone, while the Penguins' passionate doo-wop anthem "Earth Angel" was whitewashed by the Crew-Cuts' version. But teenagers were too savvy to be fooled for long; most of the neutered cover versions, even the popular ones, were soon forgotten, while the originals were permanently enshrined in listeners' hearts.

But the view of rock and roll as a matter of whites co-opting and diluting black music is simplistic and inaccurate. For example, the multitude of rockabilly artists who followed in Elvis's wake, most of them Southerners of humble means, brought their own personalities and experiences to the mix, as evidenced by the dynamic work of Elvis's Sun Records labelmates Jerry Lee Lewis, Carl Perkins, and Johnny Cash, and that of such lesser-known iconoclasts as Charlie Feathers, Sonny Burgess, and Billy Lee Riley.

The first flowering of rock and roll in the 1950s produced a rich and diverse array of black and white performers. Many of the latter—like Bill Haley, the Everly Brothers, Buddy Holly, Eddie Cochran, and Gene Vincent—were steeped in country and rockabilly yet equally enamored of rhythm and blues. New Orleans, the city that had given birth to jazz, spawned jazz-rooted hits by Fats Domino, Huey "Piano" Smith, Lloyd Price, Lee Dorsey, Ernie K-Doe, and Clarence "Frogman" Henry. In Chicago, the seminal blues label Chess entered the rock and roll market by introducing two of rock's preeminent auteurs, refined wordsmith Chuck Berry and primitive genius Bo Diddley. Various urban centers spawned a biracial wave of doo-wop vocal groups. And innovative, forward-thinking African American artists Ray Charles, Sam Cooke, Jackie Wilson, and James Brown worked to lay the foundations of modern soul music.

It's a widely accepted truism that the years between the 1959 plane crash that killed Buddy Holly, Ritchie Valens, and the Big Bopper and the arrival of the Beatles in early 1964 were fallow ones for rock and roll. But that notion is refuted by the sheer volume of magnificent music that was made during that period—by such one-of-a-kind voices as Roy Orbison and Del Shannon, by a wave of urban girl groups, by visionary producer Phil Spector, by surf-music overachievers the Beach Boys, and in the early stirrings of Motown, Stax and numerous other R&B labels.

For an America whose idealism had just been shattered by the assassination of its youthful president John F. Kennedy, the Beatles' arrival was welcomed as a desperately needed dose of optimism. The Beatles' influence was so pervasive that their success opened the doors for a massive influx of British acts, who dominated the American charts until the social and cultural upheavals of 1967's Summer of Love. Although the idealism of the Woodstock era didn't last, that period's musical changes did, pushing rock in a heavier, more self-consciously serious direction, and shifting the music industry's emphasis from hit singles to long-playing albums.

The 1970s saw rock diversify and fragment into diverse subgenres, which enriched and deepened the music's stylistic range, even if it limited its potential to spawn mass movements as it had in the 1950s and 1960s. As mainstream rock grew increasingly bloated and impersonal, blowback arrived in the form of the do-it-yourself rebellion of punk rock. Punk was both a mass movement and an influential commercial phenomenon in Britain, but it remained a cult item in America, where it spawned a vibrant independent underground that would eventually inspire the commercial alternative-rock boom of the 1990s.

In America, mainstream rock grew moribund in the 1980s, with the rise of style-obsessed MTV seeming to signal the death of the music's potential for provocation and transcendence. But the stasis of mainstream rock helped to fuel an increasingly vibrant underground circuit of left-of-center bands, scrappy independent labels, and small regional clubs. The built-in limitations of airplay, distribution, and media exposure conspired to keep American indie-rock underground for years, until the long-simmering groundswell exploded in the major-label success of Nirvana in the early 1990s.

As of this writing, the massive influence of the Internet, downloading, and affordable home recording has democratized music making and redrawn the parameters of the music industry. The long-term effects of these changes are still in the process of revealing themselves, but the music itself remains as integral to American life as ever.

In *Icons of Rock*, we examine the lives, music, and long-term influence of two dozen of rock's most prominent and influential bands and solo artists. Although each left an indelible mark on rock's development, we chose this combination of acts in effort to provide a representative cross-section of rock's rich panoply of sounds, styles, and stances. Indeed, rock's history is so broad and varied that we could just as easily have chosen twenty-four other acts and provided an equally representative selection. While history is written by the winners, it's worth noting that the rock's foundation owes as much to obscure visionaries, forgotten geniuses, and one-hit wonders as it does to superstars. But the twenty-four artist profiles featured in *Icons of Rock*—accompanied here by a variety of related features—offers a useful introduction for new listeners while providing additional insight for committed fans.

—Scott Schinder

Acknowledgments

The authors wish to acknowledge Kristi Ward for her consistent professionalism and patience beyond the call of duty, and to thank the following individuals for their invaluable contributions to this book: Leslie Rondin, Drew Wheeler, Jesse Jarnow, Keith Lyle, Sue Wilson, Randy Haecker, Rob Santos, Bob Irwin, Tim Livingston and Ira Robbins.

Photographer: William V. "Red" Robertson.

Elvis Presley

Scott Schinder

THE BOY WHO INVENTED ROCK AND ROLL

Actually, no one person can claim to have invented rock and roll. The fundamentally mongrel genre arose from a long-simmering cross-pollination of
black and white musical styles, an evolution that was fueled by the increasing
pervasiveness of music radio broadcasting in America beginning in the 1930s.
The cross-pollination of black and white music had already begun long before

the term "rock and roll" (originally African American slang for sexual intercourse) was ever applied to music, with blues and jazz elements turning up frequently in white country music, and vice versa.

But if one were to narrow down the birth of rock and roll to a specific time and place, the most logical choice would be the informal recording session that took place on the evening of July 5, 1954, in the modest studio of Sun Records on 706 Union Avenue in Memphis, Tennessee. It was there that Elvis Presley, a poor teenaged country boy from Tupelo, Mississippi, merged disparate strands of blues, country, and gospel into a fiercely dynamic sound that ignited a musical and cultural explosion whose reverberations are still being felt today. The track that Presley cut that night, "That's All Right, Mama," would quickly emerge as the cornerstone of a revolution.

Elvis Presley is the single most significant figure in rock and roll history, and it's hard to imagine rock and roll without his contributions. In addition to revolutionizing the way popular music sounded and looked, he forever changed the way young people relate to music. Emerging from the racially segregated South in the mid-1950s, Elvis, consciously or not, struck an important blow for racial harmony by making African American music accessible to millions of white teens who wouldn't have been exposed to it otherwise. And in popularizing rock and roll for a worldwide audience, Elvis almost single-handedly altered the parameters of the entertainment industry. By many estimates, he remains history's biggest-selling recording artist.

Elvis certainly wasn't the first white man to perform black music. But he was the first to fuse elements of rhythm and blues, country, and gospel into a distinctive, charismatic package that held consistent appeal for white kids, without sanitizing the music or sacrificing its essential grit.

Charismatic and cocky yet humble and polite, generous and charitable yet paranoid and tyrannical, Elvis embodied the contradictions of his country, his time, and his genre. If his life and career would take a darker turn and end in tragedy and dissipation, his best music remains as compelling as ever. His original status as the King of Rock and Roll has never been seriously challenged, and he's remained a bottomless source of inspiration for the generations of rock and rollers who've taken up the cause in the decades since that July night in Memphis.

"When I first heard Elvis's voice, I just knew that I wasn't going to work for anybody, and nobody was going to be my boss," Bob Dylan once said. "Hearing him for the first time was like busting out of jail."[1]

"Before Elvis," commented Keith Richards, "everything was in black and white. Then came Elvis. Zoom, glorious Technicolor."[2]

"Before there was Elvis, there was nothing," John Lennon declared.[3]

"It was like he came along and whispered some dream in everybody's ear, and somehow we all dreamed it," rhapsodized Bruce Springsteen.[4]

The basic elements of Elvis Presley's history have been so thoroughly documented, retold, and mythologized that it can be a challenge to separate fact from legend. But even the most circumspect reading of his story reveals a quintessential American saga that's both a heroic saga and a cautionary tale.

THE BOY KING

Elvis Aaron Presley was born just before dawn on January 8, 1935, in a two-room house in rural Tupelo, Mississippi, to Vernon and Gladys Presley. Like many of their home region, Vernon and Gladys struggled amidst the lingering effects of the Great Depression, with Vernon taking various odd jobs to make ends meet. Elvis's twin brother, Jesse Garon, was stillborn, leaving Elvis an only child. When Elvis was three years old, Vernon began serving a nine-month sentence at the infamous Parchman Farm prison camp for forging a check; his father's extended absence contributed to the closeness that he would maintain with his mother for the rest of her life.

Although Vernon and Gladys were poor, they were protective and indulgent of their son. At age ten, Elvis made his first known public appearance, singing "Old Shep" (a song he would record after becoming famous) in a youth talent contest at the Mississippi-Alabama Fair and Dairy Show, which was broadcast over local radio station WELO. That event prompted his parents to buy him a guitar for his eleventh birthday.

When Elvis was thirteen, the family relocated to Memphis, in search of a better life. Memphis was a cultural crossroads that, despite institutionalized racial segregation, played host to a vibrant melting pot of black and white musical traditions. The Presleys lived in public housing, and in the poor neighborhoods of the city's north side. Their attendance of a white Pentecostal church instilled Elvis's lifelong affinity for gospel music. He also developed a passion for country, blues, and bluegrass, as well as the work of mainstream white pop vocalists (he often cited Dean Martin as one his favorite singers).

As a teenager attending all-white L.C. Humes High School, Elvis was shy, quiet, and something of a misfit. A highlight of those years was his prize-winning performance at a school talent show. He absorbed black music through regular trips to Memphis's bustling Beale Street, where he purchased slick hipster threads that belied his family's humble economic circumstances. He cultivated a nonconformist personal style, with sideburns and a slicked-back haircut that was scandalous by the standards of the time.

After graduating from high school on June 3, 1953, Elvis took a job working at Parker Machinists Shop, moving to a better-paying position driving a delivery truck for the Crown Electric Company in the fall. During the summer, he had visited the Memphis Recording Service, home of the Sun Records label, and paid about $4 to record a pair of pop ballads, "My Happiness" and

"That's When Your Heartaches Begin," onto a ten-inch acetate disc as a present for his mother.

The Memphis Recording Service had been founded in early 1950 by Sam Phillips, a former disc jockey from Alabama who paid the bills by hiring out his services to make tape recordings of local weddings, bar mitzvahs, and community events. But Phillips's real passion was music, and he drew from the region's rich regional talent pool to record blues, R&B, and hillbilly musicians, licensing the results to such independent labels as Chess in Chicago, Duke-Peacock in Houston, and Modern and RPM in Los Angeles. Among the notable African American musicians who recorded for Phillips were Howlin' Wolf, Rufus Thomas, Rosco Gordon, Little Milton, Bobby Blue Bland, and a young B.B. King. Eventually, Phillips started his own label, Sun, and began releasing his recordings himself.

One of Phillips's early successes was 1951's "Rocket 88," credited to Jackie Brenston and His Delta Cats but actually the work of a young Ike Turner and his band the Kings of Rhythm. That song is considered by many to be the first rock and roll record, thanks to its driving backbeat and raw, distorted electric guitar.

Although Phillips had had considerable success recording and releasing music by black artists, he realized that the racial divisions that governed the entertainment industry at the time limited his sales potential. "If only I could find a white man (with) the Negro feel," Phillips had been quoted as saying, "I could make a billion dollars."[5]

Phillips wasn't present when Elvis came to Sun to record the acetate disc for Gladys. But Marion Keisker, Phillips's secretary and right-hand woman, was impressed enough to make a tape copy of the tracks to play for her boss. Phillips wasn't immediately impressed when he heard the tape the next day. In January 1954, Elvis showed up at Sun again to cut another two-sided acetate. This time, Phillips was in attendance, but still wasn't ready to invite Presley to make records for his label.

In June 1954, Phillips took a liking to a demo of a ballad titled "Without You" and decided to record the tune for Sun. After an unsuccessful attempt to find the vocalist on the original demo, Keisker suggested getting "the kid with the sideburns" to take a crack at it, and called Elvis to Sun for his first chance at making a real record. But the inexperienced singer had trouble connecting with the song, and nothing usable arose from the session. Despite the fruitless recording attempt, Phillips was intrigued by Presley's voice and presence, and tested the newcomer by asking him to run through every song he knew. Elvis responded to the challenge by regaling Phillips with a broad array of country, blues, gospel, and pop material.

Phillips was sufficiently impressed with the breadth of Presley's musical knowledge to decide to invest some effort into developing the unseasoned youngster into a recording artist. Toward that end, Phillips teamed the nineteen-year-old with a pair of older local musicians, twenty-one-year-old guitarist

Scotty Moore and twenty-seven-year-old bassist Bill Black. Moore and Black were members of the local country and western outfit the Starlight Wranglers, which had done some recording at Sun, but Phillips felt that Elvis might fare better with spare, stripped-down backing than a full band. For a few weeks, Presley, Moore, and Black met daily to run through songs and work on developing a sound.

In an era when most records were made quickly and within tightly controlled session timeframes, Sam Phillips was an early proponent of keeping the tape rolling and allowing the musicians to experiment. Since Phillips owned the studio, Sun artists had the luxury of recording in informal, open-ended sessions, minus the usual deadline pressures. That method would play a key role in the development of Elvis's musical persona.

On July 5, Presley, Moore, Black, and Phillips gathered at Sun to cut some tracks, including a hopped-up version of the Bill Monroe bluegrass standard "Blue Moon of Kentucky." After they'd spent several hours running through various material with unsatisfying results, Elvis spontaneously broke into "That's All Right, Mama," a 1946 number by Mississippi bluesman Arthur "Big Boy" Crudup. As the legend goes, Moore and Black picked up the accelerated tempo, Phillips got the tape rolling, and the rest is history.

It's fair to say that no one had ever heard anything like "That's All Right, Mama" before. The combination of Elvis's playful, forceful vocal, Moore and Black's spare, fiery support, and Sun's trademark slapback echo combined to create a sound that was completely new.

As spirited as the performances were, the tape-delay echo that Phillips used on "That's All Right, Mama" was equally integral to the track's appeal. Thereafter, echo would become a key component in the sound of early rock and roll.

Phillips loved the track's manic energy, but when Sun released Presley's debut single two weeks later, "That's All Right, Mama" (listed on the label as "That's All Right") was initially relegated to the B-side. The designated A-side was "Blue Moon of Kentucky," but it was the flip that would put Elvis—and rock and roll—on the map.

A couple of nights after "That's All Right, Mama" session, Sam brought a test pressing of the single to his friend Dewey Phillips (no relation), a manic white disc jockey who spun black rhythm and blues platters on his show *Red Hot and Blue* on local station WHBQ. The show was broadcast from the station's headquarters at the Chisca Hotel in downtown Memphis, and maintained a large biracial audience. The motor-mouthed DJ played "That's All Right, Mama" several times in a row, and the station's switchboard was reportedly flooded with requests to hear it again. Dewey phoned the Presley home to get Elvis to the station for his first-ever live interview. By the end of the week, Sun had advance orders of 7,000.

Released on July 19, just two weeks after it was recorded, "That's All Right, Mama" became a local hit in Memphis. Presley promoted the release with some informal local performances; on some of those, he was backed by Moore and Black's band the Starlight Wranglers, whose other members reportedly resented Scotty and Bill's moonlighting with Elvis.

In an effort to generate interest outside of their hometown, Elvis, Scotty, and Bill (sometimes billed as "the Blue Moon Boys") hit the road as a touring act. The three musicians and their gear crammed into a Chevrolet Bel Air, with Black's doghouse bass strapped to the roof, and worked at a grinding pace, regularly driving hundreds of miles between shows around the South. They often worked as a warmup act for such established country stars as Slim Whitman, Minnie Pearl, and the Louvin Brothers, whose fans had never before experienced anything like Elvis's volcanic vocals and hip-swiveling, leg-shaking stage moves.

"The first time that I appeared on stage, it scared me to death," Presley later asserted in the 1972 documentary *Elvis on Tour.* "I really didn't know what all the yelling was about. I didn't realize that my body was moving. It's a natural thing to me. So to the manager backstage I said, 'What'd I do? What'd I do?' And he said, 'Whatever it is, go back and do it again.' "[6]

It wasn't long before Elvis's stage moves were regularly evoking hysterical responses from female audience members. One such instance was a pair of Webb Pierce concerts on August 10, 1954, at Overton Park in Memphis, at which Presley appeared as an unbilled opening act. For the early show, he played a set of country ballads to a lukewarm response. But for the late performance, he concentrated on up-tempo material, and whipped the crowd into such a frenzy that headliner Pierce—then one of country's biggest stars— refused to perform. Such occurrences generated hostility toward the young upstart in some quarters of the conservative country music community, but they also hastened Elvis's rise to headliner status.

Presley delivered another savage performance on his second Sun single, "Good Rockin' Tonight," a reworking of a 1948 hit by New Orleans rhythm and blues shouter Roy Brown. The disc was released in September 1954, and maintained Sam Phillips's strategy of combining a "black" R&B song with a "white" country ballad (in this case "I Don't Care If the Sun Don't Shine"), in order to broaden airplay potential. "Good Rockin' Tonight" became another regional hit.

The same month, Elvis performed on Nashville's *Grand Ole Opry*, the wildly popular Saturday-night radio show that was a bastion of mainstream country and western music. As the story goes, he was not well received, with Opry manager Jim Denny famously telling the singer that he should go back to driving a truck.

While he may have been too unruly to be embraced by the staid Opry, Presley was more warmly received by the show's less hidebound competitor the *Louisiana Hayride*, which originated on Shreveport's KWKH. He made his first *Hayride* appearance in October 1954 and soon won a one-year contract, becoming popular enough with listeners that his regular slot was expanded to twenty minutes. His presence on the *Louisiana Hayride* would play a significant role in winning Elvis new fans across the South.

Presley's own live shows continued to draw larger concentrations of young female fans, with the performances growing progressively wilder and more provocative. The more raucous direction was aided by the addition of *Louisiana Hayride* house drummer D.J. Fontana to Presley's touring band.

Elvis's rising popularity, and his musical progress, would continue with four more Sun singles. Most were interpretations of material recorded by other artists, but to call them cover versions hardly does them justice. By the time Presley was done with Kokomo Arnold's "Milkcow Blues Boogie," Arthur Gunter's "Baby, Let's Play House," and Junior Parker's "Mystery Train," they were his, and his versions would forever eclipse the originals. "Mystery Train," with its foreboding lyrics and general aim of enigmatic dread, is one of Presley's finest and most resonant moments.

By mid-1955, it had become obvious that Elvis had superstar potential. But his popularity was still limited to the South, and it was apparent that a boost to national fame would require more money and clout than Sam Phillips—or Bob Neal, the Memphis DJ who'd become Presley's manager—could muster. His association with the *Louisiana Hayride* had put Presley in contact with Colonel Tom Parker, whose résumé included managing country stars Eddy Arnold and Hank Snow. A savvy huckster who'd picked up the rudiments of show business while touring with a traveling carnival, Parker recognized Elvis's untapped earning potential, and officially took over as his manager in August.

Parker—who'd received the honorary title of colonel in 1948 from Louisiana governor and country singer Jimmie Davis—claimed to have been born in Huntington, West Virginia. But in later years, it would emerge that Parker had constructed an elaborate persona to mask his real history. Apparently born Andreas Cornelis Van Kuijk in Breda, Holland, on June 26, 1909, he was actually a native of the Netherlands who'd fled his homeland, under shadowy circumstances, in May 1929 and later served in the U.S. Army before being discharged for "psychosis, psychogenic depression (and) emotional instability."

The colonel's relationship with Elvis, and the many questionable decisions that he would make on his client's behalf, would become the subject of much speculation and criticism in the future. But there can be little doubt that Parker was instrumental in engineering Presley's initial rise from regional phenomenon to international sensation.

Parker's first major move was to secure a new record deal. In November 1955, Elvis signed with RCA Records, in an arrangement that involved a buyout of his Sun contract and recordings. Sam Phillips received the then-record sum of $35,000, plus an additional $5,000 in back royalties owed to Presley.

Sun Records Beyond Elvis

The seismic impact of Elvis Presley's success made him the brightest star in the galaxy of Sun Records. But Sam Phillips's matchless ear for original talent and his deceptively casual style of production brought forth several more major artists in the period 1954–57 including three Rock and Roll Hall of Fame inductees: Johnny Cash, Jerry Lee Lewis, and Carl Perkins.

Johnny Cash grew up to become one of the most important artists in American music—one whose popularity and influence extended well beyond the country field. The 1956 Sun release "I Walk the Line," was the singer's first number one country song. It established the immediately identifiable sound of Cash's resonant baritone voice; the sparse but propulsive accompaniment of his band, the Tennessee Two (later Three), and songs that blended primal strains of American folk, blues, and gospel music.

Louisiana singer/pianist Jerry Lee Lewis combined a precarious emotional volatility with effortless musical versatility. He shot to international stardom in 1957 with the landmark Sun hits "Whole Lotta Shakin' Goin' On" and "Great Balls of Fire."

Carl Perkins, the son of poor Tennessee sharecroppers, was a fine electric guitarist with a warm, inviting vocal style and a knack for writing catchy, country-flavored songs set to a rock and roll beat. In early 1956, Perkins's second Sun single, "Blue Suede Shoes" (which he wrote), became the label's first million-seller when it reached number one on the country charts and number two on both the pop and R&B lists.

Andy Schwartz

In hindsight, it's easy to view Phillips's willingness to relinquish Presley as folly. But $35,000 was an unprecedented payoff by 1955 standards. Phillips also pointed out that he didn't possess the financial wherewithal to promote Elvis nationally, and that Sun was in need of an influx of cash to expand the company and promote new artists like Jerry Lee Lewis and Carl Perkins.

Parker, meanwhile, set up music publishing companies to oversee the songs Elvis would record for RCA. Shrewdly realizing the commercial value of having a composition cut by Presley, the colonel was able to demand that songwriters give up a piece of their publishing royalties in return for the privilege (which explains non-writer Presley's name occasionally turning up in the credits of several of the tunes he recorded). While this practice would generate additional income, it would also limit the range of material that Presley had access to.

To further maximize his client's profitability, Parker licensed Presley's name and likeness for a dizzying array of products, from toy guitars to phonographs to wallets to cologne to stuffed hound dogs and teddy bears, unleashing a torrent of Elvis-related trinkets that continues to this day. Such commercial tie-ins demonstrated the colonel's knack for sniffing out profits, but they were also symptomatic of his tendency to go for the quick buck, with little consideration of those moves' long-term affect on Elvis's image or credibility.

Parker's schemes would generate considerable income for Presley—and for Parker, whose hefty 25 percent commission would later rise to an unprecedented 50 percent. For better or worse, the colonel would exercise control over most of Elvis's business and creative decisions for the remainder of his career.

ELVISMANIA

Elvis's first RCA session took place on January 10, 1956—two days after his twenty-first birthday—at the company's Nashville studio. Recording was overseen by Steve Sholes, head of RCA's country division, who'd signed Presley to the label. Moore, Black, and Fontana were augmented by legendary guitarist Chet Atkins and noted session pianist Floyd Cramer, plus the gospel vocal quartet the Jordanaires, who would continue to play a prominent role in his recordings.

That date yielded "Heartbreak Hotel," a stark, seething, sexually charged manifesto that proved to be the perfect calling card to introduce Elvis to a national—and international—audience. Released in late January as his RCA debut, the song justified the company's investment by becoming Presley's first national hit, rising to the number one slot on *Billboard*'s pop chart and selling over 300,000 copies in its first three weeks.

Two months later, the label released Presley's first full-length LP, *Elvis Presley*, which combined new RCA recordings with some previously unheard leftovers from his Sun days. Despite containing none of his hits, the collection spent ten weeks at the top of *Billboard*'s pop LP chart, earning Elvis his first gold album award.

Elvismania briefly simmered down on April 23, 1956, when Presley made his Las Vegas debut with an extended engagement at the New Frontier Hotel. But Elvis (billed as "the Atomic Powered Singer") wasn't well received by the gamblers and tourists who comprised most of the New Frontier audience, and the gig was cut short after two weeks.

Although his first Vegas trip had been a failure, one good thing did come out of it. During their visit, Elvis and band heard Freddie Bell and the Bellboys performing a flamboyant version of "Hound Dog," a song penned by the up-and-coming duo of Jerry Leiber and Mike Stoller, and originally recorded by Big Mama Thornton in 1953. Elvis worked up his own raucous reading of the song, which would become one of his signature hits three months later.

A key factor in Elvis's rise to household-name status in 1956 was a series of high-profile prime-time TV appearances which Parker cannily booked. Between January and March, he performed on six episodes of Tommy and

Jimmy Dorsey's CBS variety show, followed by a pair of guest spots on Milton Berle's NBC program. His June 5 performance of "Hound Dog" on the Berle show generated a storm of controversy over the singer's gyrations—and simultaneously established Presley as a top ratings draw.

When Elvis performed "Hound Dog" on Steve Allen's Sunday night ABC show three weeks later, Allen had an uncomfortable-looking Elvis trussed up in a tuxedo and singing to a basset hound. That night also marked the first time Allen had beaten Ed Sullivan's wildly popular variety hour in the ratings, and the shrewd Sullivan—who had initially vowed that he'd never allow Presley onto his stage—responded by booking Elvis for three appearances in September, October, and January, for which Colonel Tom was able to extract a hefty $50,000 performance fee.

The Sullivan shows were instrumental in launching Elvis Presley as a national phenomenon, raising his public profile while amplifying the moralistic furor over his scandalous movements. The controversy was such that, for the last of his Sullivan spots, the camera operators were instructed to only shoot Elvis from the waist up, even when he performed the gospel standard "There'll Be Peace in the Valley for Me." The mild-mannered camera work aside, Sullivan, at the time one of the most powerful men in television, did his part to defuse the controversy by assuring his audience that Presley was a fine, decent boy.

While the TV appearances helped to ratchet up the air of fan hysteria that surrounded Presley, the real evidence of Elvismania was in his riotous live concerts, which attracted teenage ticket buyers in record numbers. Reports of his fans literally tearing the clothes off of their idol's back arose on more than one occasion. When he performed at the Mississippi-Alabama Fair in 1956, 100 National Guardsmen were recruited to keep fans from storming the stage.

In its May 15, 1956, issue, *Time* magazine offered an adult perspective on the live Elvis experience: "Without preamble, the three-piece band cuts loose. In the spotlight, the lanky singer flails furious rhythms on his guitar, every now and then breaking a string. In a pivoting stance, his hips swing sensuously from side to side and his entire body takes on a frantic quiver, as if he had swallowed a jackhammer."[7]

As his popularity rose, Elvis was increasingly the target of various media observers and moral guardians who decried him as a corruptor of the nation's youth. As the most visible figurehead of the new youth culture, he was an inviting target for those eager to blame him and his music for a litany of social ills, from juvenile delinquency to teen promiscuity.

The groundswell of anti-Elvis outrage was such that, when he performed in Jacksonville, Florida, in August 1956, juvenile court judge Marion Gooding threatened to arrest the singer if he shook his body while on stage. Presley remained still for the entire set, wiggling a single finger in protest.

"Rhythm is something you either have or don't have," Elvis commented, "but when you have it, you have it all over."[8]

Although he was still treated with trepidation, condescension, or downright derision by many mainstream commentators, the adult world's skepticism strengthened Elvis's credibility with teenagers. Thanks to post–World War II prosperity, those teens now comprised a powerful economic force that was essential in fueling rock and roll's birth.

Much of the criticism leveled at Elvis carried a thinly veiled—and sometimes not so thinly veiled—air of racism. While some religious and community leaders condemned him for playing the Devil's Music, others castigated his style as "nigger music."

Much as they tried, the critics couldn't stop Presley, or the legion of rock and roll stars—both black and white—who followed in his wake. Elvis's success created an eager audience for such African American performers as Chuck Berry, Little Richard, Fats Domino, and Bo Diddley, as well as white rockers like Jerry Lee Lewis, the Everly Brothers, and Buddy Holly, who shared his background in country and western music.

Presley's example, particularly the homespun, do-it-yourself vibe of his Sun recordings, also launched an explosion in rockabilly, with countless young white boys, mostly but not exclusively in the South, picking up guitars and delivering high-energy variations on Elvis's sound. Some of them, like Lewis, Carl Perkins, Johnny Cash, and Roy Orbison, would launch their careers at Sun. Some, like Eddie Cochran, Gene Vincent, and Presley's high school classmate Johnny Burnette, would gain major-label deals, while hundreds more would record for small independent regional labels.

The Rockabilly Explosion

Rockabilly hitched the driving beat of early black rhythm and blues artists like Fats Domino and Little Richard to the guitar-based instrumentation of "hillbilly," as the industry dubbed the country sounds of Hank Williams and Lefty Frizzell. Although it lasted only from about 1954 to 1958, the sound and style of rockabilly touched every region of the United States. Its popularity expanded the overall music market through an outpouring of raw talent, the likes of which would not be repeated until the Beatles-inspired rock explosion of the mid-1960s.

A great rockabilly record didn't require much in the way of musical sophistication or technical ability. The songs were just three or four chords, and the singers privileged excitement over enunciation. If the recording engineer could apply enough echo to the tracks, a cardboard box might even substitute for real drums. Many confirmed country performers attempted to jump on the new trend, often recording big-beat numbers under pseudonyms: George Jones as "Thumper Jones," Buck Owens as "Corky Jones," Webb Pierce as "Shady Walls."

By contrast, both the Everly Brothers and Ricky Nelson were more sincere in their commitment to the new music and more inventive in their approach.

The roots of Don and Phil Everly lay deep in the country and bluegrass styles of their native Kentucky, but beginning in 1957 they incorporated pop, blues, and R&B in a dazzling series of discs including the number ones "Wake Up, Little Susie" and "Cathy's Clown." In that same year, Ricky Nelson released his first single—a cover of Fats Domino's "I'm Walkin'"—and promptly became the second most famous rock and roller in the country (after Elvis), thanks to a featured musical segment on his family's weekly television series *The Adventures of Ozzie & Harriet.* In his first five years as a recording artist, Nelson scored seventeen Top Ten hits, most featuring the peerless lead guitar work of James Burton.

Gene Vincent placed five songs on the Hot 100 in 1956–57 (including the masterful "Be-Bop-A-Lu-La") and never had another hit. But his initial impact was sufficient to sustain the troubled singer's performing career until his death in 1971, especially among the dedicated Vincent cultists of Britain and France. Two brothers from Memphis, Johnny and Dorsey Burnette, formed the Johnny Burnette Trio with guitarist Paul Burlison. Their lone album, *Rock 'n' Roll Trio* (1957), is an all-time rockabilly classic that includes "The Train Kept A-Rollin'," a song later recorded by the Yardbirds and Aerosmith. In 1960, Wanda Jackson's "Let's Have a Party" was a spirited late entry in the rockabilly sweepstakes, although she soon returned to a straight country repertoire.

For every hopeful with a record on the national charts, there were a halfdozen whose songs found only local or regional success. "Everybody's Got a Baby but Me" by Warren Miller and "Rockin' by Myself" by Sammy Gowans are just two rockabilly classics by artists who were barely acknowledged even in their own time.

A. S.

Records weren't the only things that Elvis was helping to sell. Sales of transistor radios and record players boomed in the wake of his rise to fame, while the rock and roll explosion that he set off helped to build the fledgling record business into a major industry. Teenagers around the United States emulated his dress sense and adopted his "ducktail" haircut.

One example of Elvis's ubiquitous fame was the publicity that accompanied the brief, informal jam session on December 4, 1956, by the one-off super group that came to be known as the Million Dollar Quartet. That event transpired when Presley dropped in to visit Sun Records while Carl Perkins was recording, with Jerry Lee Lewis playing piano on the session and Johnny Cash also in attendance. They ran through an improvised array of gospel, country, R&B, and pop material. One highlight was Elvis's admiring description of Jackie Wilson, then lead singer of Billy Ward's Dominoes, singing his version of the recent Presley smash "Don't Be Cruel," followed by Presley's imitation of Wilson's delivery.

Sam Phillips had the presence of mind to keep the tape rolling. The publicitysavvy Phillips also called the local newspaper the *Memphis Press-Scimitar.*

Bob Johnson, the paper's entertainment editor, came by to document the event, bringing a photographer who took the famous shot of Presley at the piano surrounded by Lewis, Perkins, and Cash (Elvis's girlfriend Marilyn Evans was cropped out). Bootleg tapes of the sessions circulated for years before being officially released in 1990.

While some observers quibble that Presley's early RCA releases lacked some of the raw edge and primal power of his Sun sessions, it's hard to argue with the quality of his early RCA releases. The impassioned "I Want You, I Need You, I Love You" (backed by another Arthur Crudup cover, "My Baby Left Me") was a number one follow-up to "Heartbreak Hotel," while the subsequent "Hound Dog"/"Don't Be Cruel" was a double-sided smash that became one of the biggest-selling singles the music industry had ever seen. While less rootsy and more polished than his Sun work, they're still first-rate vehicles for Presley's talent and charisma.

The holiday LP *Elvis' Christmas Album*, was also released in 1957, which combined bucolic seasonal fare, serene gospel material, and bluesy Yuletide tunes like "Santa Claus Is Back in Town," "Santa, Bring My Baby Back (to Me)," and the hit "Blue Christmas."

GOING HOLLYWOOD

Despite his massive record sales, Presley's—and Parker's—aspirations extended beyond music. Offers of movie roles began to pour in during the 1956 media assault, and in April Elvis signed a seven-year movie contract with producer Hal Wallis and Paramount Pictures. His studio screen test was a scene from the upcoming A-list Burt Lancaster/Katharine Hepburn production *The Rainmaker*. But rather than appearing in that prestigious project, Elvis made his big-screen debut with a star turn in *Love Me Tender*, a hokey Civil War–era drama that allowed him to croon four songs. It was dismissed by critics, but became a box office smash.

Love Me Tender was followed in 1957 by Presley's first color feature *Loving You*, a slick but stale showbiz romance which riffed on Elvis's early experiences touring the rural country and western circuit. *Jailhouse Rock*, released later that year, offered a slightly darker take on his rise to fame, with Presley demonstrating genuine acting ability as an ex-con turned arrogant, amoral rock and roll star. In 1958 with *King Creole* Elvis rose to the challenge of a complex role in a serious drama, holding his own alongside such serious thespians as Carolyn Jones, Vic Morrow, and Walter Matthau, under the guidance of *Casablanca* director Michael Curtiz.

Indeed, Presley's early performances demonstrated that he possessed immense natural screen presence, and his early directors and co-stars consistently described him as hard working and serious about developing his acting skills. But the colonel's fondness for the easy payoff—and his client's apparent inability to stand up to intimidating father figure Parker—would ultimately crush Elvis's dream of establishing a reputation as a dramatic actor.

By 1957, Elvis Presley was arguably the world's most famous musical entertainer. Bill Haley (the first American rocker to tour overseas) had been instrumental in popularizing rock and roll in Europe, but Elvis triggered a massive shift in musical tastes around the world. Other countries began to spawn their own answers to Elvis, like England's Cliff Richard, France's Johnny Hallyday, and Italy's Adriano Celentano, who offered homegrown (if watered-down) variations on the Presley style.

Elvis's popularity even extended behind the Iron Curtain. On February 3, 1957, the *New York Times* ran a story under the headline "Presley Records a Craze in Soviet Union." The paper reported that, although not officially released in the Soviet Union, bootleg recordings of his music were being pressed on discarded X-ray plates and sold on the black market in Leningrad for the equivalent of about $12.

In March 1957, Elvis purchased his soon-to-be-famous mansion Graceland in Memphis. The following month, he made his first Canadian appearances, playing concerts in Toronto and Ottawa. A performance in Vancouver that August would mark the last time he would perform outside of the United States.

Presley's music and film careers were still on the upswing when Elvis received his draft notice in December 1957. By the time he reported to Fort Chaffee for induction (and his much-publicized GI haircut) three months later, he'd left enough unreleased tracks in the can that RCA was able to continue releasing new material to keep him a steady chart presence during his two-year army stint. The fan furor surrounding his induction would inspire the successful 1960 Broadway musical *Bye Bye Birdie*, which would also be adapted into a film.

After completing six months of basic training in Fort Hood, Texas, Presley was stationed in Friedberg, Germany, for eighteen months. Although he maintained an off-base residence in nearby Bad Nauheim, Elvis was reportedly a model soldier who requested and received no special treatment from his superiors. On August 12, 1958, Gladys Presley suffered a heart attack; Elvis flew back to Memphis to be with her, and she died two days later.

While in Germany, Elvis met fourteen-year-old Priscilla Beaulieu, step-daughter of Army Captain Joseph Beaulieu. She would become Presley's wife on May 1, 1967. On February 1, 1968, exactly nine months after the wedding, Priscilla would give birth to their only child, Lisa Marie Presley.

Although he'd worried that his fans would forget him during his absence, Elvis Presley returned to civilian life in March 1960 to find his popularity intact. The following month saw the release of *Elvis Is Back!*, a solid collection of rockers, ballads, and blues that seemed to bode well for his musical future. It was followed by *His Hand in Mine*, the first of his several gospel albums; while that disc was mild-mannered rather than impassioned, it offered credible evidence of Elvis's sincere and deep-rooted affinity for gospel.

The next few years would see Elvis release a handful of memorable singles, including the catchy novelty "Return to Sender" (written by Otis Blackwell, author of several Presley hits), the moony ballad "Can't Help Falling in Love," and the tough rockers "Little Sister," "I Feel So Bad," and "(Marie's the Name) His Latest Flame." But by 1963, just as rock was preparing to enter a new era as an agent of social change, Elvis had more or less walked away from his hard-won status as the King of Rock and Roll.

Elvis had initially been enthusiastic about becoming a serious actor, and his work in *Jailhouse Rock* and *King Creole* demonstrated that his natural screen presence could, with proper support and the right material, translate into substantial performances.

But the Colonel had other ideas. Elvis gave sincere performances in the flawed but heartfelt Don Siegel–directed 1960 western *Flaming Star*, playing a pensive half-breed confronting racism, and in the soap-operatic *Wild in the Country*, which incongruously cast him as an aspiring novelist. But instead of following in the footsteps of his heroes Marlon Brando and James Dean, Elvis would spend much of the 1960s starring in a series of mind-numbingly innocuous b-movies that neutered his dangerous edge into soft-centered cuddliness.

Two or three times a year between 1960 and 1968, Elvis dutifully walked through such creatively bankrupt exercises as *G.I. Blues, Blue Hawaii, Girls! Girls! Girls!, It Happened at the World's Fair, Fun in Acapulco, Kissin' Cousins, Viva Las Vegas, Roustabout, Girl Happy, Tickle Me, Harum Scarum, Paradise Hawaiian Style, Spinout, Easy Come Easy Go, Double Trouble, Clambake, Speedway,* and *Live a Little Love a Little*, which demanded little more of Elvis than that he show up. The formula was so predictable—cast Elvis as a rakish lifeguard/helicopter pilot/race car driver, place him in an exotic location, surround him with pretty girls and cartoonish comic complications, and have him sing enough mediocre songs to fill the accompanying soundtrack album—that the films were virtually interchangeable. But most of them were huge money makers, and the colonel saw no point in messing with a winning formula.

While America was caught up in the political, social, and musical upheavals of the 1960s, Elvis seemed encased in a show business bubble, out of touch with his own talent and oblivious to the changes afoot in the outside world. Although he remained immensely popular with millions of fans, it was hard to believe that this was the same restless revolutionary who had single-handedly altered the face of Western culture just a few years before.

When John F. Kennedy was assassinated in Dallas in 1963, Elvis was busy cavorting in *Fun in Acapulco*. In 1965, while the Beatles and Bob Dylan were leading rock into provocative new areas of personal discovery and sonic experimentation, Elvis was singing "Do the Clam" amidst carefree spring-break hijinks in *Girl Happy*. In 1967, as the Vietnam War, the civil rights movement, and the summer of love were forcing Americans to reexamine their most deeply held beliefs, Elvis was starring in *Clambake*.

"The only thing worse than watching a bad movie," Presley reportedly said, "is being in one."[9]

Elvis made little effort to disguise his contempt for his 1960s movies, refusing to watch them and deriding them as glorified travelogues. By all accounts, he was deeply resentful that the colonel had steered him toward such lightweight fare and away from more credible projects. For instance, he was the first choice of the producers of *West Side Story* for that film's male lead, but Parker passed. *West Side Story* became one of the decade's biggest blockbusters, and Presley apparently held it against Parker for the rest of his life. Elvis certainly had the clout to put his foot down and demand better scripts and bigger budgets, but he never did.

The colonel also reportedly kept Elvis from auditioning for roles in such edgy, culturally important films as *Cat on a Hot Tin Roof*, *The Defiant Ones*, *Thunder Road*, and *Midnight Cowboy*. In the mid-1970s, long after his box office appeal had been decimated by too many lousy movies, Presley was offered an attractive comeback vehicle in *A Star Is Born*, but the colonel apparently wouldn't hear of his boy sharing star billing with Barbra Streisand.

By the time the Beatles usurped his status as the world's biggest rock and roll act in 1964, Elvis's musical career had become little more than a half-baked sideline. His film commitments kept him from performing concerts, and most of his record releases were throwaway soundtrack albums, loaded with trivial film tunes and often padded with old studio outtakes.

Although his recorded output gave little indication that he'd been keeping up with musical trends, Elvis actually played host to the Beatles in his Bel Air home in August 1965, while the Fab Four were on tour. The four-hour visit, according to John Lennon, included an informal jam session, on which Elvis played piano and drums.

One of the few bright spots of his largely forgettable soundtrack album output was a 1966 reading of Bob Dylan's "Tomorrow Is a Long Time" that proved that Presley was still capable of delivering sensitive, compelling performances when presented with quality material. But such instances were few and far between, and the fact that this meeting of generational icons was buried on the *Spinout* soundtrack LP is indicative of how far out of touch Elvis and his handlers were with the seismic changes that were occurring in music and popular culture at the time.

THE COMEBACK

The generally appalling quality of his movie-era music made Elvis's subsequent musical rejuvenation seem all the more miraculous. By 1968, the King's prestige was at an all-time low. Even his most patient fans had stopped turning out for his films, which by now were often consigned to the lower half of double features, and which often didn't receive play dates in major cities at all. Whether due to artistic inspiration or career necessity, Presley's long-dormant musical instincts stirred back to life in the late 1960s, spawning a brilliant new body of work that instantly reestablished him as a creative force.

Presley's return to rock and roll was signaled by a pair of tough, rootsy singles, the Jimmy Reed blues classic "Big Boss Man" and the Jerry Reed–penned "Guitar Man." Released in September 1967 and January 1968, respectively, those efforts found him sounding more focused and engaged than he had in nearly a decade, weaving his blues and country influences into an updated sound that was effortlessly contemporary without pandering to trends.

They were followed in October by "If I Can Dream," an idealistic anthem whose acknowledgment of the era's social ills marked something of a milestone for Elvis. In other hands, the song might have felt naive or simplistic, but Presley tore into it with such passionate belief that one couldn't help but be uplifted by its hopeful message. "If I Can Dream" reached number twelve in *Billboard*, his best chart showing in years.

Those releases could only hint at the full-on resurrection that would occur with Presley's upcoming NBC-TV special. Commonly referred to as "the 1968 comeback special" but officially titled *Elvis*, the show—shot in late June but not broadcast until December 3—decisively re-embraced Elvis's rocking roots, and in the course of one hour managed to reestablish the tarnished icon as a contemporary artist.

Although the colonel had originally envisioned the show as a bucolic Christmas-themed trifle, the show's producer/director Steve Binder had something more substantial in mind. He saw the special as an opportunity for Presley to reassert his performing prowess and reclaim his credibility. Elvis, frustrated after the years of forgettable films and mediocre music, stood up to his manager for a change. Actually, he and Binder conspired to keep the colonel placated and distracted while they went ahead with their plans to do the show their way.

Presley and Binder's instincts proved correct. The NBC special reestablished Elvis as a vital musical force virtually overnight, showing his talent and magnetism intact after nearly a decade of aesthetic neglect. The show opened with a trim, leather-clad Elvis delivering the *King Creole* chestnut "Trouble" with a swagger that immediately announced that he was back with a vengeance. An informal jam session segment in which Elvis traded songs and stories with a circle of musical pals including Scotty Moore and D.J. Fontana, showed him to be loose, confident, and firmly in control.

Another highlight was an extended, athletic production number built around "Guitar Man." The piece follows its protagonist through his journey from struggling musician to successful star, through his eventual realization that his dream has been achieved at the expense of his original passion. In the end, he abandons the trappings of stardom to return to his humble musical roots. It would be hard to miss the reference to Elvis's own travails.

Although the colonel had originally insisted that the program end with a rendition of "Silent Night," the actual finale of "If I Can Dream" ended the show on an inspirational note. Standing alone on stage, Elvis delivered the song's idealistic lyrical message with an intensity that made it one of the most galvanizing moments of his career.

Suddenly, the thirty-three-year-old Elvis, long considered an anachronism, was relevant again. As critic Greil Marcus observed in his 1975 book *Mystery Train*, one of the first serious tomes to attempt to unravel Presley's mythical appeal, "It was the finest music of his life. If ever there was music that bleeds, this was it."[10]

The NBC special set the stage for a remarkably productive period during which a reenergized Elvis returned to music-making in earnest. In January and February 1969, he entered American Studios in Memphis for his first hometown sessions since 1955. Working with noted producer Chips Moman and a crack assortment of Southern session players, Presley took a proactive role in marathon all-night sessions, and the result was *From Elvis in Memphis*, considered by many to be the best album of his career.

The American Studios recordings found Presley shaking off the boredom and complacency that had set in during his movie years, and taking a hands-on role in leading the band, putting together the arrangements and running the sessions, just as he had in the old days.

As veteran producer/engineer Bones Howe, who'd served as music producer on the NBC special, told author Jerry Hopkins in his 1971 book *Elvis, A Biography*, "Elvis produced his own records. He came to the session, picked the songs, and if something in the arrangement was changed, he was the one to change it. Everything was worked out spontaneously. Nothing was really rehearsed. Many of the important decisions normally made previous to a recording session were made during the session."[11]

From Elvis in Memphis introduced a punchy new sound that imbued Elvis's country and blues roots with funky country-soul grooves that were well suited to the songs' more mature attitude. There was no mistaking the level of emotional commitment that he brought to the material, which spanned the breadth of his interests and influences. The songs ranged from contemporary soul hits like Jerry Butler's "Only the Strong Survive" and Chuck Jackson's "Any Day Now" to such venerable country tunes as Hank Snow's classic "I'm Movin' On" and Eddy Arnold's "I'll Hold You in My Arms," as well as the recent Glen Campbell hit "Gentle on My Mind."

From Elvis in Memphis spawned a major hit in the Mac Davis composition "In the Ghetto." It was the closest Presley would ever come to singing a protest song, and its socially conscious message carried a particular resonance in an America torn by racial and economic injustice. If the song was somewhat simplistic and melodramatic, the fact that it was delivered by a figure of Elvis's stature carried much weight in the divisive atmosphere of 1969.

Meanwhile, with box office receipts dwindling, Elvis closed out his acting career with some relatively offbeat projects that made some token attempts to break away from the established formula. *Charro!* was a poorly executed faux–spaghetti western in which Presley played it straight as a scruffy, non-singing gunfighter. *Change of Habit* was a well-intentioned but ill-conceived stab at social relevancy, with Elvis as a guitar-slinging inner-city doctor who may or may not be in love with nun Mary Tyler Moore.

With Elvis having finally freed himself of his Hollywood commitments, the next logical step in his resurrection was a return to live performance. Rather than bother with the rock audience that had expanded and diversified during the 1960s, Colonel Parker booked a much-ballyhooed four-week, fifty-seven-show engagement at the newly constructed International Hotel in Las Vegas beginning on July 31, 1969 (eleven days after Neil Armstrong became the first man to walk on the moon). Those performances introduced Presley's powerful new live band, an expanded ensemble that included the peerless rockabilly guitarist James Burton.

At the center of the lavish presentation was the lean and hungry Elvis, performing with the fire of a man given a second lease on life. The International Hotel run was an unmistakable triumph, winning rave reviews and breaking Las Vegas attendance records. It would be followed by a series of massively successful national tours and Vegas engagements. Presley would give over 1,000 sold-out Vegas performances between 1969 and 1977, and would be the first act to sell out New York's Madison Square Garden for four shows in a row.

The Vegas comeback coincided with Elvis's biggest hit since 1962, the number one smash "Suspicious Minds," recorded during the *From Elvis in Memphis* sessions but not included on the album. "Suspicious Minds" was a perfect distillation of his soulful new sound, and would remain one of his most popular numbers (and its subject matter resonated strongly with rumors of troubles in the Presley marriage). Two more songs cut during the American Studios sessions, "Don't Cry Daddy" and "Kentucky Rain," also became hits in late 1969 and early 1970, respectively.

Three months after "Suspicious Minds" was released, the song turned up in a live version on the double album *From Memphis to Vegas/From Vegas to Memphis*, which combined an LP of performances from the closing week at the International with a disc of leftovers from the American Studios sessions. The live half (the first installment in a steady stream of live Elvis material that RCA would continue to grind out through the 1970s) offered a persuasive document of Presley's return to the stage. The studio half underlined what a bountiful creative purging the Memphis sessions had been.

When Elvis returned to the silver screen, it was as the focus of a pair of successful feature documentaries that documented his return to the live stage, 1970's *Elvis: That's the Way It Is* and 1972's *Elvis On Tour*. In January 1973, he'd score a massive small-screen success with *Aloha from Hawaii*, the first-ever worldwide live satellite broadcast of a musical event, seen by over a billion viewers worldwide.

As it happened, Hawaii would be the furthest Elvis would ever travel to perform. Many have speculated that the colonel turned down lucrative offers of overseas tours because he was an illegal alien whose status would have been discovered had he attempted to travel abroad. It has also been theorized that Parker kept Elvis performing in Vegas in order to cover Parker's massive gambling debts.

ELVIS: WHAT HAPPENED?

The reestablished superstar of *Aloha from Hawaii* was a very different animal from the comeback kid of the NBC special and the 1969 Vegas gigs. By this point, Elvis concerts had ballooned into overblown extravaganzas that often felt less like musical performances than opportunities for the faithful to worship at the Elvis altar. While there was no denying the undiminished energy of his performances or the ongoing magnificence of his voice, many considered the spectacle—along with the King's bejeweled, jumpsuit-clad stage persona—to be gauche and overly grandiose.

By then, Priscilla had left Elvis (their divorce would become final on October 9, 1973) and troubling rumors of drug use and unpredictable behavior had begun to swirl around the singer.

On December 21, 1970, a reportedly drug-impaired Presley paid a visit to President Richard M. Nixon at the White House, after writing Nixon a six-page letter suggesting that he be made a "Federal Agent-at-Large" in the Bureau of Narcotics and Dangerous Drugs. The meeting yielded a famous photo of an uncomfortable-looking Nixon shaking hands with Presley, clad in a dark cape, open-collared shirt, and garish belt buckle. Elvis brought the soon-to-be-disgraced president the gift of a World War II commemorative Colt .45 pistol (which the Secret Service seized), and Elvis was eventually sent a "specially prepared" badge from the Bureau of Narcotic and Dangerous Drugs.

During a 1975 show at the Las Vegas Hilton, Elvis spontaneously addressed recent rumors in a bizarre onstage outburst in which he denied using drugs and threatened severe physical harm to those who'd suggest that he did. Despite such unpredictable behavior, Presley would continue touring successfully for the remainder of his life, playing for large, adoring crowds in Vegas and in arenas around the United States.

In 1972 "Burning Love" became Presley's final Top 10 hit, and, for all intents and purposes, his last stand as a rock and roller. Thereafter, he settled into a comfortably middle-of-the-road country-pop style that yielded some catchy, well-crafted music, but nothing approaching the intensity of his best work.

But Elvis had bigger issues than musical direction. He had grown increasingly isolated, rising at sunset and rarely venturing outside of Graceland when he wasn't on tour. He'd become increasingly dependent on a number of prescription drugs, and his prodigious consumption took a heavy toll on his health. His weight fluctuated wildly and his performances could be distracted and incoherent, further raising concerns among fans and the press.

His fans' worst suspicions were confirmed with the 1977 publication of *Elvis: What Happened?*, a book that drew upon interviews with Red West, Sonny West, and Dave Hebler, former members of the cadre of Elvis cronies and gofers commonly known as the Memphis Mafia. The tawdry tome painted a disturbing portrait of the artist as a volatile drug addict obsessed with sex, death, religion, and firearms, with his most irrational whims (like plotting to have his estranged wife's lover killed) indulged by his posse of yes-men. In those days before twenty-four-hour news channels and Internet gossip, the book shocked fans who still thought of Elvis as the humble, polite country boy who gave generously to friends and charities, and purchased Cadillacs for needy strangers.

On the evening of August 16, 1977, mere weeks after the publication of *Elvis: What Happened?*, Elvis Presley died at Graceland at the age of forty-two. He was found lying on the floor of the bathroom adjoining his bedroom by girlfriend Ginger Alden, who had been asleep in his bed. He was taken to Memphis's Baptist Memorial Hospital, where doctors pronounced him dead at 3:30 P.M. While the official cause of death was heart failure, lab reports detected fourteen different drugs in his system and strongly suggested that his drug use played a role in his demise. His remains were initially buried at Forest Hill Cemetery in Memphis, next to his mother. After an attempted theft of the body, Elvis's and Gladys's graves were moved to Graceland.

Elvis Presley's death precipitated a massive outpouring of mourning from fans around the world. It also spawned an industry of posthumous Elvis-related commerce, from all manner of memorabilia to a variety of musical, literary, and cinematic tributes.

One measure of the public's ongoing Elvis obsession is the persistence of theories that he didn't actually die in 1977, but faked his demise to escape the pressures of the spotlight. Another curious manifestation of Presley's iconic status—and of the public's desire to hang on to some vestige of the departed star—is the proliferation of Elvis impersonators. Acts appropriating the King's likeness and performing style began to spring up almost immediately after his death and have continued to prosper, with several annual Elvis impersonator festivals hosting multiple tribute artists.

In the decade following his death, Elvis's recorded legacy was treated by RCA Records and Colonel Tom Parker with the same capriciousness with which they handled his catalog while he was alive. The company churned out a stream of carelessly assembled, blatantly exploitive releases, with little regard for historical perspective and musical quality. Elvis's body of work finally began to receive respectful repackaging in the CD era.

Graceland was opened to the public in 1982 as a monument to Presley's memory and continues to be a major tourist destination, attracting over

600,000 visitors per year. It was designated a National Historic Landmark on March 27, 2006.

In 1986, Elvis was one of the first group of inductees into the Rock and Roll Hall of Fame. He was added to the Country Music Hall of Fame in 1998 and the Gospel Music Hall of Fame in 2001. In 1993, the image of the young Elvis was featured on a U.S. postage stamp. As of this writing, the Sirius Satellite Radio service features an all-Elvis channel.

In October 2005, when the entertainment trade journal *Variety* named the top 100 entertainment icons of the twentieth century, Elvis was in the top ten, along with Louis Armstrong, Lucille Ball, the Beatles, Marlon Brando, Humphrey Bogart, Charlie Chaplin, James Dean, Marilyn Monroe, and Mickey Mouse. A week later, *Forbes* magazine named Elvis, for the fifth straight year, the top-earning dead celebrity.

More than a quarter century after his death, Elvis remains the best-selling solo artist in popular music history, according to the RIAA, with worldwide sales estimated at one billion as of 2006. His classic recordings continue to attract new listeners, as evidenced by the 2002 chart success of Junkie XL's remix of the obscure "A Little Less Conversation" (originally from the 1968 film flop *Live a Little Love a Little*) and the following year's Paul Oakenfold remix of "Rubberneckin' " (from *Change of Habit*).

Like the country and culture that spawned him, Elvis Presley was a tangled mass of contradictions. If he was ultimately brought down by his inability to fully understand his own talent or grasp the larger implications of the changes that he wrought, his accomplishments speak for themselves.

TIMELINE

January 8, 1935
Elvis Aaron Presley is born to Gladys and Vernon Presley in a two-room cabin in East Tupelo, Mississippi.

July 18, 1953
Elvis Presley goes to the Memphis Recording Service, home of Sun Records, and pays $3.25 to record two songs, "My Happiness" and "That's When Your Heartaches Begin," as a present for his mother. Office manager Marion Keisker makes a note to alert her boss Sam Phillips to the eighteen-year-old's talents as a ballad singer.

June 27, 1954
In an effort to help Presley find his style, Sam Phillips teams him with two local musicians, guitarist Scotty Moore and bassist Bill Black, and has the trio begin rehearsing and learning songs together.

July 5, 1954
During a recording session at Sun, Elvis spontaneously breaks into "That's All Right, Mama," a blues number by Arthur "Big Boy" Crudup. The next day, Elvis, Scotty, and Bill cut a similarly energetic reworking the Bill Monroe bluegrass tune "Blue Moon of Kentucky."

July 19, 1954
Sun Records releases "That's All Right, Mama" and "Blue Moon of Kentucky" as Elvis Presley's first single, bearing the catalog number Sun 209.

July 20, 1954
Elvis makes his first public appearance, performing on a flatbed truck in Memphis.

October 2, 1954
Elvis appears on Nashville's Grand Ole Opry for the first and only time. His performance of "Blue Moon of Kentucky" receives a polite audience response.

October 16, 1954
Elvis makes the first of many appearances on the *Louisiana Hayride* radio show, broadcast from Shreveport, Louisiana.

August 15, 1955
Elvis Presley signs a management contract with Colonel Tom Parker.

November 20, 1955
After Parker fields an offer from RCA Records, Sam Phillips sells Elvis's recording contract to RCA for $35,000.

January 27, 1956
Elvis Presley's RCA debut, "Heartbreak Hotel," is released. It will be the first of Presley's seventeen number one hits, spending eight weeks at the top of the charts and establishing Elvis as a national sensation.

January 28, 1956
Elvis Presley makes his first network TV appearance on bandleaders Tommy and Jimmy Dorsey's *Stage Show*.

September 9, 1956
Elvis makes the first of three appearances on TV's *Ed Sullivan Show*, drawing an estimated 82.5 percent of the viewing audience.

November 15, 1956
Elvis's first film, *Love Me Tender*, premieres at the New York Paramount.

December 4, 1956
Elvis and his former Sun label-mates Jerry Lee Lewis, Carl Perkins, and Johnny Cash gather at Sun for an informal jam session, performing gospel standards and R&B hits around the piano. Sam Phillips dubs the one-time aggregation the Million Dollar Quartet.

December 20, 1957
Elvis Presley is served with his draft notice while home at Graceland for Christmas.

March 24, 1958
Elvis is sworn in as a private in the U.S. Army. The Memphis draft board had granted him a deferment to allow him to complete filming on *King Creole*.

October 1, 1958
Elvis begins his army service.

March 2, 1960
Elvis returns to the United States after completing his army service. He is honorably discharged at the rank of sergeant.

May 12, 1960
Elvis is featured in *Welcome Home Elvis*, a Frank Sinatra–hosted TV special.

August 27, 1965
Elvis hosts the Beatles for an evening of music and conversation at his house in Bel Air, California.

May 1, 1967
Elvis Presley marries Priscilla Beaulieu at the Aladdin Hotel in Las Vegas.

February 1, 1968
Elvis and Priscilla's only child, Lisa Marie Presley, is born, exactly nine months after her parents' wedding.

December 3, 1968
NBC airs *Elvis*, a prime-time TV special that serves notice of Presley's resurrection as a rock and roll performer.

January 13, 1969
Elvis enters American Sound in Memphis for his first hometown recording sessions since leaving Sun in 1956. The American sessions mark Elvis's revitalization as a recording artist, and spawn such hits as "Suspicious Minds" and "In the Ghetto."

July 31, 1969
Elvis ends an eight-year hiatus from live performance, beginning a four-week engagement at the International Hotel in Las Vegas. He will continue to perform regularly in Vegas, and on tour, for the rest of his life.

October 9, 1973
Elvis and Priscilla Presley divorce.

June 26, 1977
Elvis Presley performs his last concert, at Market Square Arena in Indianapolis.

July 16, 1977
"Way Down" enters *Billboard*'s pop chart, becoming the last of 105 singles by Elvis Presley to reach the Top Forty during his lifetime.

August 16, 1977
An unconscious Elvis Presley is rushed to Memphis's Baptist Memorial Hospital and subsequently pronounced dead.

July 1982
Graceland is opened to the public. It will become a popular tourist destination.

January 8, 1993
The U.S. Post Office's Elvis Presley postage stamp goes on sale.

June 2002
A remix of the 1968 Presley non-hit "A Little Less Conversation," by Junkie XL, becomes a number one hit in twenty countries.

March 27, 2006
Graceland is officially designated a National Historic Landmark.

SELECTED DISCOGRAPHY

Elvis Presley, 1956
Elvis, 1956

Elvis TV Special, 1968

From Elvis in Memphis, 1968

In Person at the International Hotel, 1969

The King of Rock 'n' Roll: The Complete 50's Masters, 1992

From Nashville to Memphis: The Essential 60's Masters, 1993

Elvis 56, 1996

Sunrise, 1999

Suspicious Minds: The Memphis 1969 Recordings, 1999

That's the Way It Is, 2000

NOTES

1. wikipedia.cas.ilstu.edu/index.php/Elvis_Presley.
2. wikipedia.cas.ilstu.edu/index.php/Elvis_Presley.
3. wikipedia.cas.ilstu.edu/index.php/Elvis_Presley.
4. www.elvis.com.au/presley/article_thenightspringsteenjumpedthefence. shtml.
5. www.time.com/time/magazine/article/0,9171,135845,00.html.
6. www.elvis.com/elvisology/quotes/byelvis.asp.
7. www.time.com/time/magazine/article/0,9171,808428,00.html?iid=chix-sphere.
8. quotations.about.com/od/stillmorefamouspeople/a/elvispresley2.htm.
9. quotations.about.com/od/stillmorefamouspeople/a/elvispresley2.htm.
10. Greil Marcus, *Mystery Train: Images of America in Rock-N-Roll*, 4th ed. (New York: Plume, 1997).
11. en.wikiquote.org/wiki/Talk:Elvis_Presley.

FURTHER READING

Carr, Roy and Mick Farren. *Elvis: The Illustrated Record*. New York: Harmony, 1982.

Floyd, John. *Sun Records: An Oral History*. New York: Avon Books, 1998.

Guralnick, Peter. *Last Train to Memphis: The Rise of Elvis Presley*. New York: Little, Brown, 1994.

Guralnick, Peter. *Careless Love: The Unmaking of Elvis Presley*. New York: Little, Brown, 1999.

Marcus, Greil. *Mystery Train: Images of America in Rock-N-Roll*, 4th ed. New York: Plume, 1997.

Marsh, Dave. *Elvis*. New York: Rolling Stone Press/Warner Books, 1982.

Nash, Alanna. *The Colonel: The Extraordinary Story of Colonel Tom Parker and Elvis Presley*. Chicago: Chicago Review Press, 2003.

Courtesy of Photofest.

Ray Charles

Andy Schwartz

SATURDAY NIGHT AND SUNDAY MORNING

The weather in Atlanta, Georgia, is damp and breezy on the night of May 29, 1959. Despite intermittent rainfall, a crowd of 9,000 people has filled the stands of a minor league ballpark called Herndon Stadium for a long evening of live rhythm and blues. The Drifters, Ruth Brown, Jimmy Reed, Roy Hamilton, and B.B. King all have performed to an enthusiastic response; now the crowd is enraptured by the show's headline attraction, whose set has reached a peak of controlled frenzy.

Wearing dark sunglasses and rocking from side to side in his seat at an electric piano, the singer stomps his right foot to count off a mid-tempo blues called "(Night Time Is) The Right Time." He hits the first chord and one of his accompanists, saxophonist David "Fathead" Newman, swoops in with eight bars of searing tenor. The singer bears down hard on the lyrics—exhorting, pleading, commanding—as he rides the relentless rocking-chair rhythm of bass and drums: *You know the night time . . . is the right time . . . to beeee . . . with the one you love.*

On the opposite side of the stage, a harmonizing trio of female backup singers echoes his secular sermon with wordless syllables *("bah-doo-day")* until he calls forth one of them with a gruff shout: "Sing the song, Margie!" The piercing voice of Margie Hendricks emerges from the group for a fiery solo turn until the leader reenters, soaring into top of his vocal range with a hair-raising wail. At the end of his last chorus, the band thunders to a close and the entire audience leaps to its feet for a standing ovation that lasts nearly ten minutes.

The organizer and MC of the show, a local disc jockey named Zenas Sears, races onto the stage and grabs the microphone. "The great Ray Charles!" he shouts deliriously over the roar of the crowd. "The High Priest! The High Priest! *Ray Charles—What a show*!"

EARLY YEARS

Ray Charles Robinson was born in Albany, Georgia, in 1930. Because he never possessed a birth certificate, the exact date of birth can't be verified. Most but not all sources state September 23, the date observed by Ray. His mother Aretha (known as Retha) was a teenage orphan who'd been adopted by Bailey Robinson and his wife Mary Jane and lived with them in the small north Florida town of Greenville. When Retha became pregnant, word spread that Bailey was the father; the girl was sent to stay with relatives in Albany to have the baby. Shortly after the birth, Ray and Retha returned to Greenville where they lived in a shack in the impoverished black neighborhood known as Jellyroll. Bailey Robinson remarried, moved to a nearby small town, and had little involvement in Ray's upbringing.

Ray's brother George was born less than a year later; as toddlers, the two boys were inseparable. Retha was a strict mother who assigned regular chores to her sons when they were just five and six years old. Every Sunday, she brought them with her to the New Shiloh Baptist Church where the reverend preached fiery sermons, gospel singers wailed and shook tambourines, and parishioners "fell out" in spasms of devotional ecstasy.

Outside the church, young Ray's important musical influence came from Wiley Pitman, the owner of a local general store and café called the Red Wing. Pitman was a talented stride and boogie-woogie pianist who sat Ray on his knee for his first lessons at the piano. The boy also listened avidly to the Red Wing jukebox with its selection of guitar blues, piano boogies, and swing tunes.

One afternoon in 1935, the Robinson boys were splashing around in a large washtub outside the café. When George suddenly began to panic in the water, Ray wasn't big or strong enough to rescue him. George's accidental drowning, before his brother's own eyes, was the first of two tragedies that scarred Ray's early childhood. The second followed later that same year when mucus began to ooze from his eyelids and his sight began to fail. (Years later, doctors speculated that the cause was congenital juvenile glaucoma.)

Retha was determined that her nearly sightless son be able to make his own way in the world. She refused to lighten Ray's load of chores or allow him to just hang around the house. Again and again, his mother reminded Ray that she wasn't going to live forever: He had to do everything he could to prepare himself for independent life as an adult.

"The woman never let me get away with anything just 'cause I was blind," Charles told co-author David Ritz in his autobiography *Brother Ray*. "I was treated like I was normal. I acted like I was normal. And I ended up doing exactly the same things normal people do."[1]

By the fall of 1937, Ray had lost his sight. Over his tearful protestations, Retha put her son on the train to St. Augustine, Florida, where she had enrolled him in the Florida School for the Deaf and Blind. For the next eight years, Ray remained a boarding student at this racially segregated state institution, where he became known as RC to his friends and fellow students.

Despite facilities and materials inferior to those bestowed upon the school's white pupils, the mostly poor black students and underpaid black faculty of D&B forged a powerful bond. The children learned to read Braille, play sports, and make handicrafts in addition to their academic subjects. At the Christmas break and the end of the school year, Ray would return to Retha's dilapidated home in Greenville.

RC was an avid radio listener from adolescence. He tuned into the sounds of country and western music and the big bands of Benny Goodman, Artie Shaw, and Tommy Dorsey; he was astounded by blind jazz pianist Art Tatum's flawless technique and unending flow of musical ideas. The hardcore down-home blues of the Mississippi Delta and Chicago was almost never heard on radio in the years before World War II but Ray heard Tampa Red and Lonnie Johnson on jukeboxes as well as local blues players in cafés or on the street.

By the age of thirteen, Ray had picked up a second instrument, the clarinet. When not attending D&B, he played piano for a Tallahassee jazz band led by guitarist Lawyer Smith that worked weddings, proms, dances, juke joints, and fraternal organization affairs. Ray was still in school in the spring of 1945 when his mother, still in her early thirties, died suddenly of an undiagnosed illness. Retha's death was a crushing blow to her only surviving son. But he was comforted by Rebecca Bea aka Ma Beck, a healer and midwife widely admired in the Greenville black community who herself had given birth to at least nineteen children.

In October 1945, Ray was expelled from D&B—a place he felt he'd outgrown already—and moved in with some family friends in Jacksonville, Florida. He scuffled for gigs on the local music scene while honing his piano chops and learning the pop standards required for all-occasions entertainment. The singer and alto saxophonist Louis Jordan was approaching the peak of his national stardom with bouncy hits like "Caldonia" and "Choo Choo Ch'Boogie." Ray enjoyed Jordan's witty R&B style but was more deeply enamored of Nat King Cole, a virtuoso jazz pianist and vocalist, and of Johnny Moore's Three Blazers, whose massive 1946 hit "Drifting Blues" featured the mellow vocal and piano of Charles Brown.

"By the time I hit the streets of Jacksonville," Ray later recalled, "I'd been schooled on all these different sounds way 'fore I ever heard the word school; it was part of my natural upbringing. And at school, of course, I'd been exposed to Bach, Beethoven, Mozart, Sibelius, Chopin, and all the other big names."[2]

Ray traveled to Orlando with a band led by saxophonist Tiny York; when work ran out and the group broke up, he stayed on. Blind, broke, and alone in a city where he knew almost no one, RC literally went hungry on many occasions while trying to hustle gigs on the competitive local music scene. Yet he never gave up and seems never to have asked for charity—only for the chance to play and be paid for his music.

Gradually, RC found work on the bandstands of the black community in west Orlando. In early 1947 he was hired to play piano with Joe Anderson's fifteen-piece big band and later to write original arrangements for the group. Ray's confidence rose as he began teaching himself to play alto saxophone. Soon he'd earned enough to buy his first record player and a treasured handful of 78 rpm jazz discs by Charlie Parker, Dizzy Gillespie, and other jazz innovators.

Later that year, Ray relocated to Tampa and was quickly recruited by two different groups. The Honeydrippers, led by Charlie Brantley, were an all-black "jump blues" band in the mode of Louis Jordan's Tympani Five; the Florida Playboys were an all-white country band playing the songs of Hank Williams, Eddie Arnold, and other Grand Ole Opry favorites. In a segregated city like Tampa, it was surprising that the Playboys would enlist a blind black pianist. But RC could play country music with as much ability and feeling as any white musician—he even sang lead on a couple of tunes. Heeding the suggestions of friends, he also began to wear the heavy-rimmed dark sunglasses that became his trademark.

Life in Tampa was improving for RC. It got better still when he became the featured vocalist and pianist with a new group called the Manzy Harris Quartet that specialized in the sophisticated blues and ballad style of Nat King Cole. Ray also purchased a wire recorder and made some informal home recordings on this primitive device. These lo-fidelity tracks (such as "Walking and Talking" and "I Found My Baby There") would surface years later on various cheaply packaged compilation albums. Despite the poor sound quality and uncertain backing of his accompanists, RC's piano playing cuts through the fog with sophisticated chords and explosive single-note runs.

RC's musician friend Gossie McKee had done some touring around the United States and returned to Tampa with exciting tales from the road—and of cities in the North and West that were free of Florida's segregationist codes. In the spring of 1948, Ray rode a Trailways bus from Tampa to Seattle, Washington, where Gossie already had settled into the black entertainment district centered on Jackson Street. There was plenty of work for a musician as talented as Ray Charles on a circuit of gigs that extended north to Vancouver and south to Portland, Oregon. RC formed the McSon Trio with Gossie on guitar and Milt Garred on bass. For professional purposes, he dropped his last name in deference to the established fame of welterweight boxing champion Sugar Ray Robinson.

West Coast Rhythm and Blues

When Ray Charles moved from Florida to Seattle in 1948, he joined a long-term mass migration that brought large numbers of African American musicians to the West Coast from the Deep South and Southwest. This movement gained momentum with the outbreak of World War II and the need for workers in factories and shipyards revitalized by the war effort. In Los Angeles, Central Avenue was the city's African American business district and home to such flourishing nightspots as Club Alabam, Little Harlem, and the Downbeat.

Many early pioneers of West Coast rhythm and blues had personal roots in the South and professional ones in the swing era of the 1930s including Rock and Roll Hall of Fame inductees Aaron "T-Bone" Walker, Nat King Cole, and Charles Brown.

Born 1910 in rural Texas, T-Bone Walker was the first to popularize the electric guitar in blues and swing music with the big bands of Les Hite and Freddie Slack. Walker's 1948 recording of "Call It Stormy Monday" "drove me crazy," B.B. King recalled years later. "I never believed a sound could be that pretty on an instrument."

Nat King Cole and Charles Brown (born in Alabama and Texas in 1917 and 1922, respectively) rose to prominence in the 1940s, singing and playing piano in a smooth small-group format sometimes known as "club blues." Nat Cole overcame barriers of institutional racism to become a beloved mainstream entertainer. He briefly hosted his own television show, headlined in Las Vegas, and placed twenty-seven songs in the Top Forty from 1954 until his death from cancer in 1965. Charles Brown recorded such West Coast standards as "Trouble Blues" (1949), "Black Night" (1951), and the holiday perennial "Please Come Home for Christmas" (1960). After many years in obscurity, this openly gay bluesman made a late 1980s comeback with the help of Bonnie Raitt (who took him on tour as her opening act) and several Grammy-nominated albums recorded in his classic style.

Johnny Otis was a key player on the Los Angeles R&B scene for decades, less important as a vocalist than as a bandleader, multi-instrumentalist, and talent scout. He was born John Veliotes in 1921—a white man of Greek heritage who lived his life entirely within the African American community. (Indeed, many of his fellow musicians believed that Otis *was* black.) His discoveries included future soul stars Esther Phillips and Etta James, and the great vocal group Hank Ballard and the Midnighters. Otis was the bandleader and *de facto* producer for two landmark number one R&B hits of the 1950s: "Pledging My Love" by Johnny Ace and Willie Mae "Big Mama" Thornton's original version of "Hound Dog," later a number one hit for Elvis Presley. Fifty years later, Johnny Otis was still active as a record producer, author, lecturer, painter, and radio personality.

Andy Schwartz

As a musician, RC had both growing technical command and deep Southern feeling; as a man, he was already supporting himself and his girlfriend, Louise Mitchell. Ray seemed older than his eighteen years and younger Seattle musicians like saxophonist Buddy Catlett and trumpeter Quincy Jones held him in high esteem for his abilities as an arranger. "He showed me how to voice the first brass section writing I ever did," Quincy told writer Nat Hentoff. "He really showed me the function of an arranger, what he was capable of doing."[3]

But in this same eventful year of 1948, Ray Charles discovered drugs. He became a heroin addict and remained one for the next seventeen years despite the personal and financial toll extracted by his habit.

"It was more curiosity than anything," Ray explained to David Ritz in his characteristically blunt manner. "The way I was around mechanical devices, the way I was around musical instruments, electronic playthings—well, that's how I was around drugs. Once I started, I saw no reason to stop. In those days, [heroin] didn't even cost that much."[4]

One night during an extended engagement at the Rocking Chair in Seattle, the members of the McSon Trio were introduced to Jack Lauderdale, the proprietor of a small independent label called Down Beat Records. The next day, Lauderdale brought the group into a local studio to cut two sides, "I Love You, I Love You" and "Confession Blues." In early 1949, Down Beat released the songs on the debut single by the Maxin Trio; authorship of both tunes was credited to Ray Charles.

To the surprise of all concerned, this disc made it into the Top Ten of *Billboard*'s Best Selling Retail Race Records chart (the industry term "race records" had not yet been supplanted to "rhythm and blues") and in June Jack Lauderdale returned to Seattle to record more songs with the trio. He brought along a recording contract that Gossie McKee quickly signed on behalf of the group even though its extravagant guarantees were pure fiction—for example, the promise that Down Beat would record at least 200 songs by the group during the six-year term of the agreement.

More sessions followed but internal tensions soon broke up the McSon Trio. RC's relationship with Louise Mitchell was also crumbling; when at last she returned to her family in Florida, neither of them even knew that Louise was pregnant with Ray's first child, a daughter who they named Evelyn. Jack Lauderdale was undeterred by these developments. Ray was clearly the star of the group, was still under contract to Lauderdale's label (now renamed Swingtime Records), and was now free to relocate to Los Angeles, where he arrived alone by train in the spring of 1950.

SOLO ARTIST

Black L.A. was jumping. Its central business district, along a six-mile-long stretch of Central Avenue, was filled with restaurants, bars, hotels, nightclubs, and movie theaters. Ray's new Swingtime release, "Late in the Evening" backed with "Th' Ego Song," gave him the brassy backing of an eight-piece band and extra pay as the session leader. But just weeks after his arrival in town, RC was on the road with blues singer and guitarist Lowell Fulson, then riding high on his career-making Swingtime hit "Every Day I Have the Blues." While playing piano for Fulson, Ray also received a featured spot of his own which earned him his first notices in the black press.

Jack Lauderdale reverted to the drum-less trio format for the next Swingtime session and came up with a winner in "Baby Let Me Hold Your Hand." Ray's closely miked vocal and delicate keyboard intro—played on a celeste rather than piano—imbued the track with a distinctive sound that was part Nat King Cole, part Charles Brown, and part pure RC. The song hit the stores and airwaves in January 1951 when the Lowell Fulson tour was still out on the road. Saxophonist Stanley Turrentine was not quite seventeen when he signed on with the Fulson show. It was the future jazz superstar's first national tour: "I got on that raggedy bus . . . we turned south and we *stayed* south."[5]

During an extended engagement in Cleveland in July, Ray met Eileen Williams, a beautician from Columbus, Ohio. The two had known each other for about three weeks when they were wed in Atlanta on July 31; Ray went back on the road while Eileen returned to Columbus. Within a year, the marriage was effectively over and the couple later divorced.

Peaking at number five on the *Billboard* R&B Jukebox chart, "Baby Let Me Hold Your Hand" was Ray's first hit under his own name. It became a national best-seller and led to his signing by the powerful Shaw Artists booking agency (he remained with the firm for the next fifteen years). But the sound was still too derivative to establish RC as a viable artist in his own right.

Out on the road, Ray's superior musicianship made him invaluable to Lowell Fulson and earned him multiple salary increases. Between those performance earnings and occasional record royalties, RC could afford to buy his first car and pay someone to drive it while making regular deposits to the savings account he maintained back in Greenville. But he chafed under the limitations of a supporting role, and the Shaw Agency began to book Ray under his own name on selected dates.

"Kissa Me Baby," the next Swingtime release by Ray Charles, fell short of the R&B Top Five and quickly faded from the chart. Jack Lauderdale found his cash flow squeezed by tight-fisted distributors who postponed payment as long as they possibly could. In January 1952, Lauderdale sold RC's recording contract for $2,500 to Ahmet Ertegun and Herb Abramson, the founding partners of New York–based Atlantic Records.

"I heard 'Baby, Let Me Hold Your Hand' once and I said this is the most fabulous singer alive today," Ertegun recalled in a 2005 interview. "A booking agent named Billy Shaw said to me, 'We have Ray Charles but we can't book him as a headliner. Do you think you can make hit records with him?' and I said, 'I *know* I can make hit records with him.' . . . I was the only one who thought so."[6]

THE ATLANTIC YEARS

In September 1952, Ray Charles arrived in New York City for his first Atlantic recording session. Jesse Stone, the company's main man in the studio, had booked some of his regular musicians for the date, which produced four finished masters in three hours. "Roll with My Baby" evoked Nat King Cole, just as "Midnight Hour" did Charles Brown. But "The Sun's Gonna Shine Again" pointed toward a more distinctively original sound with its somber mood, plaintive vocal, and Ray's repeated exclamations of "Lord."

The first single, "Roll with My Baby" backed with "Midnight Hour," received good notices in the trade publications though not much in the way of sales or airplay. It was the same story with "Jumping in the Morning" backed with "The Sun's Gonna Shine Again," released in early 1953. But Atlantic had scored several of the biggest Top Ten R&B hits of 1952 with other artists such as Ruth Brown ("Mama, He Treats Your Daughter Mean"), and these sales allowed the company to continue recording Ray until he came up with a hit.

When the army suddenly recalled Herb Abramson to active duty in Germany, Ahmet found a new partner in Jerry Wexler. A former song promoter, *Billboard* staff writer, and fellow black music buff, Wexler had coined the phrase "rhythm and blues" in an essay for *The Saturday Review of Literature.*

In his 1995 autobiography, Jerry recounted his first meeting with RC at the old Atlantic offices on West 56th Street in Manhattan.

"I was struck by his physical presence," he wrote, "strong, broad-shouldered, barrel-chested, his rhythms simultaneously quick and cautious. . . . His speaking voice, like his singing voice, was deep but ever-changing, sometimes sounding old beyond his years, sometimes filled with youthful ebullience, sometimes sullen and withdrawn. His dark glasses were a symbol of his mystery, an emblem of some secret pain."[7]

Years later, Ray reflected upon his solitary mode of existence: "Loud parties, large crowds, being out with the gang—none of these things interested me. . . . Of all the people I've met in my life, I'd have to struggle hard to find five I'd call my friends, people I can really count on. And that's my doing. I'm just not the type to have scores of long-lasting, intimate friendships."[8]

Wexler was present for Ray's second Atlantic session, in May 1953. This time, everyone played it by ear, without a pre-set repertoire. Ahmet called out song titles and stray lyrics from the history of jazz and blues; at the piano, Ray blithely ran off boogie-woogie motifs and swing era quotations. Ertegun sang a twelve-bar blues stomp he'd written called "Mess Around" and Ray cut it fast, loose, and hard-driving. "Losing Hand" was a ghostly minor-key blues with atmospheric guitar work by Mickey Baker. "It Should've Been Me" was a sly mid-tempo tale of ghetto street life as told by an envious also-ran watching "a real sharp cat, with a $300 suit and a $100 hat" and his "real fine chick, driving that Dynaflow!"

Released as a single, "It Should've Been Me" climbed to number five R&B and hung on the chart for nine weeks—a respectable showing if not a career breakthrough. But more important, on at least half the tracks from this session, Ray had moved away from his skillful emulations of Nat King Cole and Charles Brown toward his own style of phrasing and delivery. Ahmet Ertegun sensed the beginning of this transformation and knew it was only a matter of time and circumstance until he had the Ray Charles hit he craved.

In his travels with Lowell Fulson, RC had been particularly well received in New Orleans; he settled there temporarily in the summer of 1953. In August, Ahmet and Jerry flew down for sessions at J&M Recording, working with J&M owner/producer/engineer Cosimo (Cosmo) Matassa. With time left over from a date with local singer Tommy Ridgley, they let Ray cut a pair of slow blues numbers. Atlantic rush-released "Feelin' Sad" in late September but it too failed to catch on.

New Orleans Rhythm and Blues

It's not surprising that New Orleans should have been the place where Ray Charles found his true voice as a recording artist. From the end of World War II into the early 1960s, the Crescent City was a leading producer of rhythm and blues just as it had been the cradle of jazz in earlier decades. The history of New Orleans is marked by deep poverty, political corruption, and racial segregation. But its citizens take great pride in the city's centuries-old cultural traditions, showing a special affection for local musicians whether or not they ever find success beyond the city limits. A New Orleans artist who barely brushed the national charts with a single song could still be "a star in the ghetto" decades later in one or another of the city's close-knit neighborhoods.

Singer/pianist Antoine "Fats" Domino remains the most famous name in the history of New Orleans rhythm and blues, more than fifty years after making his *Billboard* R&B chart debut in 1950 with the rocking, self-mocking blues "The Fat Man." Between 1950 and 1963, Fats placed thirty-seven songs in the Pop Top Forty including "I'm Walkin'," "Whole Lotta Loving," and "I'm in Love Again." The tunes were infectiously simple but arranged for maximum danceability by Domino's co-writer and bandleader, Dave Bartholomew, and played by a stellar studio group that included saxophonist Lee Allen and drummer Earl Palmer. When recording activity in New Orleans declined in the mid-1960s, these and other musicians moved to Los Angeles. But until the floods of Hurricane Katrina destroyed his home in 2005, Fats Domino continued to live in the Lower Ninth Ward—the same New Orleans neighborhood where he was born in 1928. In 1986, Domino was among the first group of artists inducted into the Rock and Roll Hall of Fame.

Roy Brown (1925–81) sang the blues with gospel fervor and put New Orleans on the post-war musical map with his 1947 hit "Good Rockin" Tonight." Larry Williams (1935–80) was a favorite of the Beatles, who covered his late 1950s hits "Slow Down" and "Bad Boy." Eddie Jones aka Guitar Slim (1926–59) created an all-time blues standard with his only R&B chart hit, "The Things That I Used to Do." With his hundred-foot guitar cord and brightly colored suits, Slim was a flamboyant performer so much in demand that other Crescent City singer/guitarists like Earl King were sometimes booked to perform in his stead, using his name.

Rock and Roll Hall of Fame honoree Allen Toussaint began his career in 1958 and rose to become the city's best-known songwriter and producer. Artists ranging from Lee Dorsey ("Workin" in a Coal Mine") to the Pointer Sisters ("Yes We Can-Can") have reaped major hits from Toussaint's catalog of compositions. In August 2005, Allen Toussaint lost his home in the flooding after Hurricane Katrina. But in collaboration with English singer-songwriter Elvis Costello, he released a new album, *The River in Reverse*, that brought the New Orleans rock and roll tradition into the twenty-first century.

A. S.

On October 16, 1953, Ray participated in another session at J&M, this one starring Guitar Slim (Eddie Jones Jr.). The flamboyant blues singer/guitarist had passion and energy to burn but none of Ray's technical skill or organizational ability. RC quickly took command of the session: playing piano, humming improvised horn riffs to the band, and reining in the excitable Slim, who tended to rush the tempo and wander off the microphone. It was nearly dawn when they cut the master take of the last song of the date, "The Things That I Used to Do."

Released on Specialty Records in December, "The Things That I Used To Do" became the biggest-selling R&B disc of 1954 and topped the Billboard R&B chart for six straight weeks. The Guitar Slim date showed Ray that he had what it took to create a smash hit, albeit for another artist.

Jerry and Ahmet returned to New Orleans in December for an all-night session at a local radio studio. This time RC brought along several original blues-based tunes including the infectious "Don't You Know." "Now you can hear the real Ray emerging," Wexler noted. "It's Ray's tune, Ray's chart, Ray's irresistible spirit that sets the sexy agenda. From his opening falsetto scream . . . to the horn voicings to the super-hip medium-mellow groove, the production is brilliant."[9] In its very brief R&B chart appearance, "Don't You Know" struggled to number ten.

Ray would not return to the studio for nearly a year. But in the interim, he took a major step forward in his career when he formed his own seven-piece band. Any horn player auditioning for RC had to be able to read music, to improvise jazz solos, and to play the blues. One of RC's key early recruits was saxophonist David "Fathead" Newman, a Dallas native who would remain with Ray for the next ten years. As band director or "straw boss," New Orleans trumpeter Renald Richard was responsible for overseeing rehearsals and making sure the musicians took the stage on time, properly attired, and more or less sober. In addition to playing piano and singing his featured numbers, Ray also soloed on alto sax during a portion of the show.

The group was assembled initially to back Ruth Brown for two weeks of shows, the first of which necessitated a breakneck 750-mile drive from Houston to El Paso. The second date, the next night in Alexandria, Louisiana, required driving all the way *back* to Houston and then 200 miles further east. Such grueling trips were fairly typical of RC's early life on the "chitlin' circuit" along with shortchanged or non-existent performance fees, segregated accommodations, and frequent police harassment.

By November 1954, when he was due to appear at the Royal Peacock in Atlanta, RC had worked up several new originals in anticipation of his next studio session. One of them was "I Got a Woman," a fast-paced tune co-written with Renald Richard and based on the melody of a gospel song Ray had heard one night on the car radio. The response from live audiences had RC so excited that he called Ahmet Ertegun and Jerry Wexler to ask if they could fly to Atlanta for a recording date. A few days later, they sat in the empty club and listened intently as singer and band ran through "I Got a Woman," Renald's humorous "Greenbacks," the aching soul-blues ballad "Come Back Baby," and more.

The two Atlantic executives were overwhelmed by the range, power, and precision of the music; they hastened to book recording time at a local radio station. "I Got a Woman" was the obvious choice of a first single from the session, and test pressings were sent out to key disc jockeys and distributors in mid-December. A few days into the New Year of 1955, it was clear that Ray Charles and Atlantic Records had a smash hit on their hands.

By March, "I Got a Woman" was *Billboard*'s number one R&B song—and it hung on the chart for twenty weeks. More than a hit record, "I Got a Woman" was a defining musical statement that bridged the long-standing divide within the African American community between blues and gospel.

"The record blended elements like a hybrid flower," wrote Michael Lydon. "It had a dancing beat like a jump blues, but it was built on gospel's 'rise to glory' chords, and the cheerful lyric, infectiously delivered by Ray, gave that mix a pop music gloss."[10] Although he would never refer to or think of himself as a rock and roller, in the public's eyes Ray Charles now counted as one of the black rock and roll artists—including Chuck Berry, Bo Diddley, Little Richard, and Fats Domino—who were revolutionizing Western popular music.

RC was now based in Dallas, where on April 5, 1955, he married Della Bea Howard. A former gospel singer, modest and soft-spoken, Della seemed content to make a comfortable home for her husband to enjoy during his irregular interludes in residence even as Ray's inveterate womanizing and continued heroin use became open secrets between them.

The next recording session, convened in April in Miami, produced more gems written, arranged, conducted, and sung by Ray Charles. "This Little Girl of Mine" was Ray's rewrite of the gospel standard "This Little Light of Mine" with the addition of a jazzy horn chart and Latin-tinged syncopation. As for the confessional slow blues "A Fool for You," Ahmet Ertegun and Jerry Wexler thought it was simply the best record Atlantic had made to date—even if they'd done little more than book the studio time and make sure the engineer didn't erase the completed takes. By July, "A Fool for You" was RC's second *Billboard* number one record; his next two songs, "Greenbacks" and "Blackjack," also made the R&B Top Ten.

Ray's band now included fellow heroin addicts Fathead Newman, baritone saxophonist Jay Dennis, and bassist Roosevelt "Whiskey" Sheffield. On November 17, backstage at a gig in Philadelphia, all four musicians were arrested and charged with possession of drugs and drug paraphernalia. Road manager Jeff Brown bailed out RC but the others remained in jail for a week. Finally Jeff retained a New York attorney who succeeded in having all charges dropped, reportedly in exchange for payoffs totaling around $6,000.

The arrest didn't curb Ray's drug use simply because, as Jerry Wexler observed, "there wasn't an instance where his addiction interfered with his work . . . . As a bandleader and producer, he was more than conscientious; he was meticulous and demanding, ready to reject the least instance of faulty intonation or rhythm. His own singing and playing were beyond reproach, his writing a paragon of art and commerce combined. When it came to Ray's professionalism, there could be no grounds for complaint. He worked his ass off."[11]

Two weeks later, Ray was in Atlantic's New York studio for another session. This date produced "Mary Ann," a lightly lascivious tune dedicated to singer Mary Ann Fisher, a recent addition to the Ray Charles show. Two other highlights were the strutting, jubilant "Hallelujah I Love Her So," with its Count Basie–style horn chart, and "Drown in My Own Tears," a stately slow blues in the mode of "A Fool for You" that became Ray's third R&B number one in early 1956.

The latter song featured the first appearance on any of RC's records by a young female trio called the Cookies, who were Atlantic recording artists in their own right. Ray loved the blend of his rougher voice with their dulcet harmonies, and he found lead singer Margie Hendricks's churchy, growling solos irresistible. But it wasn't until 1958 that RC felt financially able to add the women (Hendricks, Ethel McRae, and Pat Lyles) to his touring organization. When he did, he gave them a new name: the Raeletts. Although the personnel would change frequently with the passing years, from this time on the group would always be a key element of the Ray Charles road show. The star carried on countless short- and long-term affairs with various female members of his troupe, in which it was often said that in order to become a Raelett, you had to "let Ray."

RISING STAR

In 1956, Elvis Presley's RCA debut album included a cover of "I Got a Woman" that earned Ray his first substantial royalty check as songwriter. The level of RC's income from live performances was such that he was able to loan money to the Shaw Agency when the company fell on hard times after founder Billy Shaw died suddenly from a heart attack. Ahmet Ertegun's older brother Nesuhi Ertegun had recently joined Atlantic to oversee its production of jazz and long-playing albums. In April, Nesuhi cut a few piano trio tracks with Ray; subsequently, he brought in the full road band to complete a pure jazz album titled *The Great Ray Charles*, released the following year. With arrangements by RC or Quincy Jones, the tunes included Tin Pan Alley standards ("I Surrender Dear," "My Melancholy Baby") and Horace Silver's hard-bop classic "Doodlin'."

In terms of record sales, 1957 was a comedown after the stunning success of the previous two years. Atlantic released several new Ray Charles singles that were moderate sellers at best. The rigors of the road inevitably precipitated further personnel changes in Ray's band. Edgar Willis replaced Whiskey Sheffield and remained RC's bassist for the next two decades. Baritone saxophonist Leroy "Hog" Cooper initially signed on for just a few months' roadwork but wound up staying with Ray into the 1970s. Hank Crawford possessed a singing, soulful tone on alto saxophone that eventually made him a jazz star in his own right while Don Wilkerson and Fathead Newman played tenor sax in contrasting but equally compelling styles.

In June 1957, Atlantic compiled various singles and B-sides to create the eponymous debut album, *Ray Charles*. That it failed to chart was not surprising: The seven-inch single still dominated R&B and Ray's album (later retitled *Hallelujah I Love Her So*) was one of Atlantic's early entries in the burgeoning LP field. Had Ertegun and Wexler waited a few more months, they would have had a brand-new Ray Charles hit to include on the album.

In November 1957, RC made an unexpected breakthrough with his recording of "Swanee River Rock"—a gospelized, up-tempo transformation of Stephen Foster's sentimental nineteenth-century ballad "Old Folks at Home," with Mongo Santamaria on conga drum and a hot tenor solo by Fathead Newman. For Michael Lydon, this track revealed "Ray's emerging grand ambition: to absorb all American music . . . . For pop singers, Stephen Foster belonged to the square and distant past; jazzmen looking for songs to jam on seldom reached further back than Irving Berlin and Jerome Kern. In recording rock 'n' roll Foster, Ray declared American music of any era fair game for his devices."[12] The Atlantic single not only made it to number fourteen R&B but to number thirty-four on the *Billboard* Hot 100—Ray Charles's first entry on the pop chart.

R&B, pop, jazz—Ray was determined to do it all and do it as well or better than anybody. For another 1957 session, Nesuhi Ertegun put him together with vibraphonist Milt Jackson of the Modern Jazz Quartet, Atlantic's best-selling jazz act, for a languid session of extended jazz instrumentals (some reaching the nine-minute mark) that featured RC on both piano and alto sax. The resulting tracks were issued on the albums *Soul Brothers* and *Soul Meeting*—titles that incorporated the word "soul" several years before the term was applied to the music of Sam Cooke, Otis Redding, and Aretha Franklin.

When Ray bought his first home in Los Angeles in March 1958, it was a clear sign of his increasing wealth. His rising stature within the music industry was certified on July 5 by his first appearance at the prestigious Newport Jazz Festival. On a festival bill that included Duke Ellington, Miles Davis, and John Coltrane, RC and his fiery band held their own with a set that ranged from jazz instrumentals to R&B hits, closing with a long, ecstatic version of "I Got a Woman." Nesuhi Ertegun edited the tapes to make a live LP, *Ray Charles at Newport*, that Atlantic issued in the fall of the year. For many jazz listeners and others of the American intelligentsia, this album was their first introduction to RC—one that set him apart from the black rock and rollers and urban blues singers.

WHAT'D I SAY

One night in December 1958, headlining at a dancehall outside of Pittsburgh, Ray and the band found they'd played through their entire "book" of sheet music arrangements but still had fifteen minutes left to fill. Ray told the musicians to follow his lead and the Raeletts to simply repeat whatever he sang. As he bore down on an up-tempo Latin-tinged piano riff, "I could feel the whole room bouncing and shaking and carrying on something fierce. . . . When I got through, folk came up and asked where they could buy the record. 'Ain't no record,' I said, 'just something I made up to kill a little time.' "[13]

The February 1959 session that brought forth the recording of this new song—now titled "What'd I Say"—was dispatched in Ray's usual all-for-business manner. It didn't feel especially momentous at the time yet the master take was over six minutes long, the stop-time verses divided by RC's fluid solos on electric piano (an instrument rarely heard in late 1950s R&B). The whole performance built through wave upon wave of barely disguised sexual tension and release as Ray's voice rose to a wail and the Raeletts moaned in unison behind him.

Ahmet Ertegun and Jerry Wexler held back the release of "What'd I Say" until April, when Atlantic issued the track as a two-part single. This first, frankly adult version met stiff resistance from radio programmers—which translated into scant orders from the label's distributors—so Atlantic's chief engineer Tom Dowd re-edited the track to give it a slightly more playful teenage atmosphere. In July, "What'd I Say" entered the *Billboard* Hot 100 at number eighty-two and then jumped to number forty-three the next week. By August, Ray Charles had his first Top Ten pop hit (peaking at number six) and his fourth R&B number one; the disc became the best-selling single in Atlantic's history and gave the company its first monthly sales gross of more than $1 million.

"What'd I Say" was the song that "brought Ray Charles to everybody. In faraway Liverpool, Paul McCartney heard 'What'd I Say' and chills went up and down his spine: 'I knew right then and there I wanted to be involved in that kind of music.' "[14]

Not content with having one of the biggest rock and roll/R&B hits of the year, in 1959 Ray went into the studio to record an album of standards from the Great American Songbook. On half the tracks, he was backed by a brassy big band, arranged by Quincy Jones; on the rest, by a full orchestra with arrangements by Ralph Burns. The rough edge of RC's voice and the "blue" quality of his phrasing turned oft-recorded songs like "Just for a Thrill" and "When Your Lover Has Gone" into modern masterpieces. After the tracks were issued on a 1960 LP titled *The Genius of Ray Charles*, the appellation "genius" stuck to the singer for the rest of his life.

The other side of Ray Charles—the raw rhythm and blues shouter who could drive his audiences into a frenzy—was captured on a tape made by disc jockey Zenas Sears during a May 1959 performance at Herndon Stadium in Atlanta. The sound of this single-microphone recording is startlingly clear and RC's performance raises the roof, especially his call-and-response with Margie Hendrix on "(Night Time Is) The Right Time" and an epic six-minute version of "Drown in My Own Tears." A joyful Jerry Wexler worked with Tom Dowd to edit the tape into Ray's second live album, *Ray Charles in Person*.

Both *The Genius of Ray Charles* and *Ray Charles in Person* made the *Billboard* Top Twenty—a rare feat for a black artist in 1959. Along with Bobby Darin, Ray Charles was one of the two best-selling artists on Atlantic Records. But his contract was about to expire and Ray would soon be moving on.

THE ABC YEARS

When Ray Charles left Atlantic for ABC-Paramount at the end of 1959, Ahmet and Jerry were hurt and angry but not really surprised. The backing of two major entertainment corporations, the American Broadcasting Company and Paramount Theaters, allowed the label—founded in 1955 and headed by Sam Clark—to make RC an offer that Atlantic simply couldn't match.

The new three-year contract gave Ray an advance of $50,000 per year and 75 percent of net sales after the label recouped its manufacturing and promotion costs. Most important, Ray was granted both creative control and 100 percent *ownership* of his master recordings, which ABC-Paramount would license for a period of just five years after delivery. This was an unprecedented achievement for a black artist—one never to be repeated even by future superstars like James Brown, Stevie Wonder, or Michael Jackson.

Ray's first ABC-Paramount album, *Genius Hits the Road*, released in the fall of 1960, became his first Top Ten LP. It was also the first in a series of RC concept albums—this one based on songs about places ("Moonlight in Vermont," "California, Here I Come," etc.)—and the singer's first full-length collaboration with Sid Feller, his new producer/A&R man. The album's indisputable high point was "Georgia on My Mind." Ray's beautifully orchestrated rendition made this song (written in 1930) into something much more than just a nostalgic paean to the state of his birth. Coming from one who'd traveled so far for so long, "Georgia" captured a profound sense of yearning for home; it also invoked the collective spirit of all the black women who'd nurtured and cared for the singer. "Georgia on My Mind" became Ray Charles's first number one pop single as well as a number three R&B hit and won two Grammy Awards. He would sing the song almost nightly for the rest of his life.

By the end of the year, Ray's performance fee was up to $1,500 per night thanks to the effort of promoter Hal Zeiger, who was determined to present RC as a "class act" who could play Carnegie Hall and the Hollywood Palladium as successfully as any ghetto dancehall. Previously, Ray's original songs were published by Atlantic's Progressive Music. But the creation of his own Tangerine Music allowed RC to keep every dime earned from airplay royalties, cover versions, and licensing fees. His touring band nearly doubled in size, with every man on a regular weekly salary. RC was earning as much as

$300,000 per year at a time when the annual per capita income for an African American male was just $2,260.

Dedicated to You, comprising songs named for women ("Nancy," "Margie," "Ruby," and the like), reached number eleven on the *Billboard* chart. *Genius + Soul = Jazz* (1961) was a snappy instrumental set with Ray on organ backed by the Count Basie band; it was followed that same year by *Ray Charles & Betty Carter*, a set of intimate duets. In July 1961, Ray and his road band cut Percy Mayfield's "Hit the Road Jack," a minor-key song set to an up-tempo groove. Mayfield's clever, down-home lyrics cast Ray as a no-account lover begging not to be cast out by his girl, a role sung with convincing fervor by Margie Hendrix. Tough and bluesy as any Atlantic track, "Hit the Road Jack" epitomized the vocal interplay between RC and the Raeletts. It shot to number one on the Hot 100 and topped the R&B Singles chart for five weeks.

In the spring of 1962, Ray released *Modern Sounds in Country & Western Music*. This unprecedented collection comprised songs originally made famous by (among others) Hank Williams, Eddie Arnold, and the Everly Brothers, arranged either as lush ballads with orchestra and chorus or as bluesy big-band numbers. Despite the initial misgivings of ABC executives, *Modern Sounds* became the label's first million-selling album—a massive across-the-board hit that held the number one position for fourteen weeks and stayed on the chart for two years. RC's version of Don Gibson's "I Can't Stop Loving You" topped the Hot 100 for five weeks; it became a number one R&B hit and won the Grammy Award for Best Rhythm & Blues Recording. Country radio programmers, however, simply ignored Ray's landmark achievement.

A true pop music event, "I Can't Stop Loving You" inaugurated a year in which Ray Charles scored four Top Ten pop singles and four Top Five albums including the inevitable *Modern Sounds in Country & Western Music (Volume II)* and the number two album *Ingredients in a Recipe for Soul*. Although a consistent presence on both the Pop and R&B charts into the early 1970s, Ray reached the pinnacle of his commercial success as a recording artist in the period 1960–64. He founded the ABC-distributed Tangerine label to release the recordings he produced for the Raeletts, the blues singer/songwriter Percy Mayfield, and the brilliant jazz balladeer Jimmy Scott. To ensure a steady supply of new material and publishing royalties, he signed talented writers such as Jimmy Lewis to his own Tangerine Music.

Ray was still a heroin addict—albeit one protected by wealth, prestige, and a personal retinue headed by his hawk-eyed new manager Joe Adams. He endured police harassment and several minor busts but always managed to avoid a jail term. On October 31, 1964, in Boston, Ray Charles was arrested at Logan Airport. This time, there would be no easy way out.

RC's private jet had landed before dawn and he'd been driven to his hotel, where he realized that he'd left his drugs behind. The singer, who never entrusted anyone else with his stash, had his chauffeur return him to the air-field to retrieve some of the marijuana and heroin he'd left on board. When suspicious U.S. Customs agents stopped the two men on the tarmac, they found pot and a small amount of white powder in Ray's overcoat. A subsequent search of the aircraft uncovered three ounces of heroin.

RC was released on his own recognizance, but the impact of the bust was severe and immediate. The story made the front page of the Boston papers and quickly spread throughout the international media. When Customs impounded his plane, Ray's agent was forced to cancel a string of cross-country dates and the band members were laid off.

Between November 1964 and March 1966, Ray Charles took his longest-ever hiatus from live performance. In the interim, Ray returned to Los Angeles where he focused on moving Della Bea and their three sons (Robert, David, and Ray Jr.) into a new home and his businesses into a new headquarters. One of his only public appearances during this period came in December 1964, when soul singer Sam Cooke was shot and killed by a motel manager in Los Angeles. When Ray arrived at the funeral and heard the huge crowd call out to him, he sat down at the piano and sang a heartbreaking impromptu version of the gospel hymn "The Angels Keep Watching Over Me."

Facing four narcotics charges handed down by a federal grand jury, RC made the decision to quit heroin. On July 26, 1965, he entered St. Francis Hospital in L.A. and endured four days of "cold turkey" withdrawal with its attendant waves of nausea, chills, and diarrhea. As part of his therapy Ray met three times per week with a psychiatrist, Dr. Friedrich Hacker, who taught his patient the basics of chess—a game that RC loved and quickly mastered. When the singer returned to the recording studio in October, the result was *Crying Time*—"one of Ray's true masterpieces, the self-portrait of an artist in a season of despair. . . . Every track, every note, bears the scars of experience."[15] The title song, previously a country hit for Buck Owens, reached number six Pop and won the Grammy Awards for Best Rhythm & Blues Solo Vocal Performance and for Best Rhythm & Blues Recording. Another track, the wry, witty soul-blues "Let's Go Get Stoned," became RC's tenth R&B number one.

On November 22 in federal court in Boston, Ray Charles pleaded guilty to all charges. Prosecutors called for two years in prison and a hefty fine, but Judge George Sweeney listened carefully to Dr. Hacker's account of RC's determination to get off drugs and his thus-far-successful program of treatment and rehabilitation. The judge offered to postpone the verdict for a year if the defendant would agree to undergo regular examinations by government-appointed physicians. For Ray, the offer was a no-brainer. He knew he was done with heroin for good. When the singer returned to court in November 1967, he received a five-year suspended sentence, four years' probation, and a fine of $10,000. Ray never spent a day in prison and never touched heroin again, although he continued to smoke marijuana on occasion. Later he favored a mixture of heavily sugared black coffee and Bols gin, which he would sip throughout the day from a ceramic mug.

Throughout the latter half of the 1960s, Ray Charles maintained a rigorous international touring schedule booked by the prestigious William Morris Agency. He appeared on national television and recorded the title theme song for the Academy Award–winning film *In the Heat of the Night*. He amassed a large personal fortune.

But the big hits tapered off after 1967. The interracial and cross-generational audience Ray had brought together from the time of "I Got a Woman" and "Swanee River Rock" through "I Can't Stop Loving You" and "Crying Time" had begun to fragment. Young black listeners had turned steadily toward the sounds of Motown, James Brown, and Sly Stone; young whites, toward the Beatles, Bob Dylan, and a host of new pop and rock performers from both sides of the Atlantic. At the end of 1969, ABC declined to renew Ray Charles's recording contract although the company continued to distribute his albums on the Tangerine label. (*Volcanic Action of My Soul* and *A Message from the People*, from 1971 and 1972 respectively, were two of RC's most successful post-ABC efforts both artistically and commercially.)

Unlike Sam Cooke, James Brown, or Nina Simone, Ray was not perceived as an ardent supporter or a musical voice of the 1960s civil rights movement. Although he bitterly condemned American racism in interviews, Ray's involvement in the freedom struggle didn't go much beyond writing the occasional check. As a self-made man, RC believed in the power of his music to gradually break down society's walls and to overcome fear and hatred among people.

LATER YEARS

Over the course of the next decade, this singularly gifted artist came to be taken largely for granted by American audiences. Ray Charles was like a president's face carved on Mount Rushmore: a revered but remote figure whose legacy lay in the past. Ray himself was partly to blame. Too often, his live show was a rote run-through of an over-familiar repertoire. His albums were of uneven quality; he refused either to accept outside musical direction or to curry favor with the press and the music industry.

Occasionally a special event or guest appearance would create a small stir in the media and reintroduce RC to a new subset of listeners. One such moment was his high-spirited stage jam with Aretha Franklin on "Spirit in the Dark," from her 1971 album *Live at Fillmore West*; another was his brief but lively screen performance in the 1980 box office hit *The Blues Brothers*.

Off stage, Ray's marriage was crumbling under the strain of his mood swings, career pressures, and numerous affairs; he and Della Bea finally divorced in 1978. In total, the singer fathered nine children outside his marriage.

They included Charles Wayne Robinson, Ray's son by Margie Hendricks (she died in 1973); and his youngest son, Corey Robinson den Bok, born in 1988.

A new deal with Ahmet Ertegun resulted in four albums on Atlantic Records. But only the first, *True to Life*, made the chart, peaking at number seventy-eight in 1977. The following year, Dial Press published *Brother Ray: Ray Charles' Own Story*, a frank if sketchy autobiography co-written with David Ritz, and in 1979 Ray's version of "Georgia on My Mind" was declared the state's official song. Another positive note was struck in the spring of 1980 when PBS broadcast Ray Charles in concert with the Boston Pops Orchestra conducted by John Williams. This well-received program led to many more orchestral bookings, in which RC's soul-stirring interpretation of "America the Beautiful" was always an emotional high point.

Ray Charles was about to enjoy his last sustained run of radio hits—this time, on the country airwaves. In 1982, he was signed to the Nashville division of Columbia Records and released *Wish You Were Here Tonight*, self-produced mostly at the singer's own RPM Studio in L.A. Although musically bland and formulaic, the set received decent sales and engendered a Top 20 Country single in "Born to Love Me." In 1984, Ray handed the reins to top Nashville producer Billy Sherrill for *Friendship*, a collection of duets with country stars like George Jones, Merle Haggard, and Ricky Skaggs. The result was the most fully realized Ray Charles album in years and the number one Country single "Seven Spanish Angels," a mythic cowboy ballad sung with Willie Nelson.

Ray's country crossover reaffirmed the transcendent appeal of his voice—an instrument now readily available for hire in exchange for a substantial payday or some valuable exposure. His fervent delivery stood out among the all-star cast (including Michael Jackson, Bob Dylan, and Bruce Springsteen) that recorded the chart-topping charity anthem "We Are the World" in 1985. Ray performed "America the Beautiful" at Ronald Reagan's second inauguration and sang with Billy Joel on "Baby Grand," an homage to RC included on Joel's 1986 Top Ten album *The Bridge*.

The awards and honors came in a steady stream. In 1986, Ray Charles was named a Kennedy Center honoree and one of the inaugural inductees into the Rock and Roll Hall of Fame. In 1987, he was given a Grammy Lifetime Achievement Award by the National Academy of Recording Arts and Sciences (NARAS). In 1989, an RC duet with jazz singer Dee Dee Bridgewater titled "'Til The Next Somewhere" became a number one hit all across Europe.

These events seemed to set the stage for Ray to take one more shot at American pop radio, and in late 1989 he got his chance with "I'll Be Good to You." A high-tech, hip-hop flavored duet with Chaka Khan, it was the first single released from Quincy Jones's glossy all-star album *Back on the Block*. The song topped the *Billboard* R&B/Hip-Hop Singles chart and reached number eighteen on the Hot 100. "I'll Be Good to You" propelled *Back on the*

Block to platinum status and later won the Grammy Award for Best R&B Performance by a Duo or Group with Vocal.

Vast numbers of television viewers came to recognize Ray Charles from his appearances in an ad campaign for Diet Pepsi that kicked off with the Super Bowl XXIV telecast on January 28, 1990. The ad proved so popular that Pepsi extended the campaign for almost two years, with RC starring in every installment. Ray's key line was *"You got the right one, baby—uh-huh!"* and in this case he most certainly did: Pepsi paid the singer in seven figures and the catch phrase briefly entered the pop culture lexicon. Small children now recognized Ray in airports, and he had to explain to reporters that a Diet Pepsi commercial was not, in fact, the biggest or most significant event of his long career.

Ray's renewed visibility attracted the interest of Mo Ostin, the chairman of Warner Bros. Records, who signed him to the label in 1990. Ostin was soon disappointed by the two discs that resulted, *Would You Believe?* and *My World*. Despite a costly and concerted media push by Warners and a Grammy Award for "A Song for You" from *My World*, the albums received little exposure on radio and only a half-hearted response from record buyers. Old friend Quincy Jones released Ray's *Strong Love Affair* on his own Warner-distributed Qwest label in 1995, but the album was virtually ignored by audiences and critics alike.

In 1997, a lavish five-CD box set on Rhino Records titled *Ray Charles: Genius and Soul* brought together the best and most popular recordings from every phase of his career. Ray demanded and received an advance in excess of $1 million for granting Rhino the right to reissue his post-1959 master recordings. Two tracks culled from a Japan-only live album, "Till There Was You" and "Am I Blue," served to remind listeners that on any given night, RC was still capable of a masterful and profoundly moving performance. *Genius and Soul* earned overwhelmingly favorable media coverage and sold well considering its high retail price.

In November 2004, *Jet* magazine published excerpts from an interview with Reverend Robert Robinson—Ray's second eldest son, now an ordained minister. Robinson told the reporter that in December 2002, his father had organized a luncheon in Los Angeles attended by all twelve of his children (some had never met each other before) and that, at the conclusion of the meal, Ray had presented each of his offspring with a check for $1 million.

In the summer of 2003, Ray Charles was diagnosed with hepatocellular carcinoma, a form of liver cancer, and abruptly canceled all further live performances. The singer underwent chemotherapy while he continued to work on *Genius Loves Company*, a new album jointly backed by Concord Records and HEAR Music, an offshoot of the Starbucks coffee chain. Veteran producers John Burk and Phil Ramone were at the controls for this duets collection that paired Ray with longtime admirers like Van Morrison, James Taylor, Johnny Mathis, Natalie Cole, Elton John, and Bonnie Raitt. The songs were all standards of one sort or another, including the Lowell Fulson blues classic

"Sinner's Prayer" (with B.B. King) and the Frank Sinatra anthem "It Was a Very Good Year" (with Willie Nelson). RC revisited his own catalog of 1960s hits to cut new versions of "Here We Go Again" with Norah Jones and "You Don't Know Me" with Diana Krall.

Ray's indefatigable energy and iron constitution had borne him through countless trials and triumphs, and he'd kept his illness hidden from all but his inner circle. Thus, many friends and fans were shocked to see him in a wheelchair when the singer made his final public appearance on April 30, 2004, for the dedication of his RPM Studios building at 2107 West Washington Boulevard as a Los Angeles historic landmark.

In one of his last conversations with David Ritz, Ray spoke admiringly of some of the great musicians he'd worked with over the years—not only Fathead Newman and Hank Crawford but lesser-known and equally gifted players like the saxophonists James Clay and Don Wilkerson and the trumpeters Marcus Belgrave and Johnny Coles.

With the locomotive rush of his career and the intensity of his demands, RC admitted that "I feel like I hurt people. I *know* I hurt people. Well, tell them I'm not an asshole. Tell them I have feelings too. I can feel their feelings, man. Tell them I appreciate them. Tell them . . . just tell them Brother Ray loves them."[16] Then he began to cry.

Ray Charles died at his home in Beverly Hills, California, on June 10, 2004, at the age of seventy-three. The Reverend Robert Robinson presided over the funeral on June 18 at the First African Methodist Episcopal Church. The more than 1,200 mourners in attendance included actor/director Clint Eastwood, singer Glen Campbell, and the Reverend Jesse Jackson; there were musical tributes from Stevie Wonder, Willie Nelson, and B.B. King. Later, Ray's body lay in state at the Los Angeles Convention Center, where thousands of fans slowly filed past to pay their last respects.

Genius Loves Company was released on August 31 and entered the *Billboard* chart at number two—the first Ray Charles album to reach the Top Ten since *Sweet and Sour Tears* in 1964. On February 13, 2005, *Genius Loves Company* swept the Forty-Seventh Annual Grammy Awards, winning eight categories including Album of the Year and Best Gospel Performance (for "Heaven Help Us All," featuring Gladys Knight) as well as Record of the Year and Best Pop Collaboration with Vocals (both for "Here We Go Again"). The album sold over three million copies in the United States alone.

On October 29, the biographical motion picture *Ray* was released in U.S. theaters. Director Taylor Hackford and screenwriter James L. White didn't shy away from depicting RC's womanizing and drug addiction, but the film emphasized Ray's monumental artistic achievements and the struggle to overcome his physical and social handicaps. Jamie Foxx won the Academy Award for Best Actor for his uncanny performance in the title role; a talented singer and pianist, Foxx mostly lip-synched to RC's original recordings on the soundtrack.

As *Ray* was filling the theaters, rap star Kanye West's "Gold Digger" (from his album *Late Registration*) was en route to becoming the nation's best-selling single. The song was built upon a vocal sample from "I Got a Woman," RC's breakthrough hit of 1955, along with an *a cappella* introduction by Jamie Foxx. "Gold Digger" was the second-longest-running number one of 2005, spending ten weeks at the top, and won the Grammy Award for Best Rap Solo Performance.

LEGACY

Ray Charles changed the sound of popular music by combining the melodies and emotional fervor of African American gospel music with the secular lyrics and earthy sensibility of the blues. He added elements of traditional pop, jazz, and country music in the course of becoming the single most important figure in the transition from the rhythm and blues of the 1950s to the soul music of the 1960s. Charles was a gifted singer, pianist, arranger, and bandleader who truly deserved his oft-bestowed appellation of "The Genius." He became an international star who put his unmistakable vocal imprint on everything he sang, from low-down blues to Broadway show tunes to country ballads.

Beyond his skills as a live performer and recording artist, Ray Charles was a canny entrepreneur. He presided over a large touring organization; produced and engineered recordings for himself and others in a custom-built studio; and founded his own recording, publishing, and management companies. Between 1957 and 1989, Ray placed more than thirty songs in the Top Forty of the *Billboard* Hot 100 and more than seventy on the R&B singles chart. He earned a career total of seventeen Grammy Awards.

Elton John, Billy Joel, Van Morrison, Michael McDonald (Doobie Brothers), Richard Manuel (The Band), and Stevie Wonder all have acknowledged Ray's influence, either through their public statements or their recording of songs long associated with him. (Wonder's second album, issued in 1962, was titled *A Tribute to Uncle Ray*.) Joe Cocker, Michael Bolton, and Gregg Allman are among the many post-Beatles rock and pop vocalists who owe a clear stylistic debt to RC's sound and style. Singer Taylor Hicks's victory in the 2006 season of "American Idol" was due in part to his convincing take on Ray's eternal "Georgia on My Mind."

"The variety and vitality" of Ray Charles's lifetime output "have been staggering and [have] permanently affected the course of popular music," wrote author and musicologist Lee Hildebrand. "While he charted little new musical territory after the mid-1960s, he had clearly demonstrated that the diverse strains of American music, though divided by ethnic, regional, and class distinctions, were all parts of a common cultural heritage."[17]

TIMELINE

September 23, 1930
Ray Charles Robinson is born in Albany, Georgia.

October 23, 1937
He enrolls at the Florida School for the Deaf and Blind in St. Augustine, Florida. Schoolmates give him the nickname RC.

October 1945
Ray Charles Robinson moves Jacksonville, Florida, to find work as a professional musician.

March 1948
RC moves to Seattle, Washington, to join guitarist Gossie McKee in the McSon Trio.

April 9, 1949
Released on Down Beat Records of Los Angeles, "Confession Blues" by the Maxin Trio enters the *Billboard* R&B Singles chart, featuring Ray Charles Robinson on lead vocal and piano. The song peaks at number two and remains on the chart for eleven weeks.

May 1950
RC relocates to Los Angeles. For professional purposes, he drops his last name and is known hereafter as Ray Charles.

February 10, 1951
"Baby Let Me Hold Your Hand" on Swingtime Records is the first song credited to Ray Charles to enter the *Billboard* R&B Singles chart. It reaches number five and remains on the chart for six weeks.

June 1952
Ahmet Ertegun of Atlantic Records buys out RC's contract from Swingtime for $2,500.

September 8, 1952
Ray Charles's first Atlantic recording session in New York.

April 3, 1954
"It Should've Been Me" is the first Ray Charles single on Atlantic to enter the R&B chart. It reaches number five and remains on the chart for nine weeks.

January 22, 1955
"I've Got a Woman" enters the chart and soon becomes RC's first number one R&B single. The song combines gospel with rhythm and blues and is a prototype of a new style called "soul music."

April 5, 1955
Ray Charles marries Della Bea Howard in Dallas, Texas. She is the mother of his sons Robert, David, and Ray Jr.

November 11, 1957
"Swanee River Rock (Talkin' 'Bout That River)" enters the R&B chart and later becomes the first Ray Charles single to enter the *Billboard* Hot 100 (Pop chart), reaching number thirty-four.

July 5, 1958
RC makes his first appearance at the Newport Jazz Festival in Newport, Rhode Island. The show is recorded and later issued as the Atlantic LP *Ray Charles at Newport*.

February 18, 1959
RC records "What'd I Say" in New York. Released in July, it becomes his first million-seller and the biggest-selling single in the twelve-year history of Atlantic Records, reaching number one R&B and number six Pop.

November 1, 1959
Ray Charles signs a new long-term recording contract with ABC-Paramount that, among other favorable terms, grants him ultimate ownership of his master recordings.

February 1960
The Genius of Ray Charles (Atlantic) is the artist's first LP to enter the *Billboard* chart. It peaks at number seventeen and remains on the chart for eighty-two weeks.

November 14, 1960
"Georgia on My Mind" becomes RC's second million-seller and the first of three Ray Charles singles to reach number one on the Hot 100. The song spends eighteen weeks on the chart including five weeks at number one.

December 3, 1960
RC's first album for ABC, *The Genius Hits the Road*, reaches number nine on the *Billboard* chart. His first Top Ten LP, it stays on the chart for fifty weeks.

April 12, 1961
At the third annual Grammy Awards, "Georgia on My Mind" by Ray Charles wins Best Vocal Performance, Single Record or Track—Male and Best Performance by a Pop Single Artist. *The Genius Hits the Road* wins for Best Vocal Performance, Male, and RC's recording of "Let the Good Times Roll" wins for Best R&B Performance.

May 1961
Ray Charles headlines at Carnegie Hall in New York for the first time in his career.

October 9, 1961
"Hit the Road Jack," written by Percy Mayfield, becomes the second Ray Charles single to top the Hot 100 (for two weeks) and the number one R&B song for five weeks.

April 21, 1962
Modern Sounds in Country and Western Music by Ray Charles enters the *Billboard* chart. By July, it is the number one album in the country and remains on the chart for 101 weeks including 14 weeks at Number One.

June 2, 1962
"I Can't Stop Loving You," the first single from *Modern Sounds in Country and Western Music*, becomes RC's third number one Pop hit. It tops the Hot 100 for five weeks and the R&B chart for ten weeks.

November 17, 1962
Ray Charles's recording of "You Are My Sunshine" enters the Hot 100, where it reaches number seven and also tops the R&B chart for three weeks.

October 31, 1964
RC is arrested at Logan Airport in Boston, and later indicted by a federal grand jury on four charges related to possession of heroin and marijuana.

July 26, 1965
The singer enters a heroin withdrawal program at St. Francis Hospital in Los Angeles.

November 1967
Having pleaded guilty to all charges, RC receives a five-year suspended sentence, four years on probation, and a $10,000 fine.

March 2, 1967
In the ninth annual Grammy Awards, Ray Charles's hit single "Crying Time" (number six Pop/number five R&B) is named Best R&B Recording and Best R&B Solo Vocal Performance, Male.

December 1972
RC's final album through ABC Records, *Through The Eyes of Love*, peaks at number 186 on the *Billboard* chart.

April 24, 1979
Ray Charles's version of "Georgia on My Mind" is declared "the official song of the State of Georgia."

June 20, 1980
The Blues Brothers, directed by Jon Landis, opens in U.S. theaters. Ray Charles plays "Ray," a streetwise storeowner, and performs "Shake a Tail Feather."

January 21, 1985
RC performs during festivities for the second inauguration of President Ronald Reagan.

April 23, 1985
"Seven Spanish Angels," a duet by Ray Charles and Willie Nelson, reaches number one on the *Billboard* Hot Country Singles chart.

January 23, 1986
Quincy Jones inducts Ray Charles into the Rock and Roll Hall of Fame at the organization's first induction dinner, held in New York City.

March 2, 1988
The National Academy of Recording Arts and Sciences (NARAS) presents RC with a Lifetime Achievement Award at the Thirtieth Annual Grammy Awards.

January 27, 1990
"I'll Be Good to You," a Quincy Jones–produced duet by Ray Charles and Chaka Khan, reaches number eighteen on the Hot 100—RC's first Top 30 Pop hit since 1967.

February 21, 1991
The Rhythm and Blues Foundation presents RC with its Legend Award at a ceremony in New York.

March 1, 1994
Ray Charles wins his twelfth career Grammy Award, for "A Song for You" as Best Male R&B Performance, in the Thirty-Sixth Annual Grammy Awards.

March 2, 1995
Ray Charles is given the Lifetime Achievement Award at the Rhythm and Blues Foundation's annual Pioneer Awards.

April 30, 2004
Ray Charles makes his final public appearance when his RPM Studios building at 2107 West Washington Boulevard is declared a Los Angeles historic landmark.

June 10, 2004

At the age of seventy-three, Ray Charles dies of hepatocellular carcinoma, a form of liver cancer, at his home in Beverly Hills, California.

August 31, 2004

Genius Loves Company enters the *Billboard* Top 200 at number two—the first Ray Charles album to reach the Top 10 since *Sweet and Sour Tears* in 1964. The twelve tracks feature Ray in duet performances with Natalie Cole, Elton John, Norah Jones, Gladys Knight, B.B. King, Johnny Mathis, Van Morrison, Bonnie Raitt, and James Taylor, among others.

February 13, 2005

In the Forty-Seventh Annual Grammy Awards, *Genius Loves Company* wins in eight categories including Album of the Year and Best Gospel Performance (for "Heaven Help Us All," featuring Gladys Knight) as well as Record of the Year and Best Pop Collaboration with Vocals (both for "Here We Go Again," featuring Norah Jones).

SELECTED DISCOGRAPHY

Genius and Soul: The 50th Anniversary Collection

Pure Genius: The Complete Atlantic Recordings (1952–1959)

The Complete Country & Western Recordings (1959–1986)

Ray Charles in Concert

Genius Loves Company

NOTES

1. Ray Charles and David Ritz, *Brother Ray: Ray Charles' Own Story* (New York: Da Capo Press, 2004), p. 31.

2. Ibid., p. 72.

3. Quincy Jones quote from Nat Hentoff's liner notes to *The Genius of Ray Charles* (Atlantic LP 1312, 1961).

4. Charles and Ritz, p. 111.

5. Michael Lydon, *Ray Charles: Man and Music* (New York: Riverhead Books, 1998), p. 72.

6. A.L. Bardach, "Interrogating Ahmet Ertegun," Slate.com (February 25, 2005), www.slate.com/id/2114074.

7. Jerry Wexler and David Ritz, *Rhythm and the Blues* (New York: Alfred A. Knopf, 1993), p. 104.

8. Charles and Ritz, p. 138.

9. Wexler, from the book accompanying *Pure Genius: The Complete Atlantic Recordings (1952–1959)*, Rhino R2 74731 (2005), p. 27.

10. Lydon, p. 114.

11. Wexler and Ritz, p. 108.
12. Lydon, p. 139.
13. Charles and Ritz, p. 191.
14. Lydon, pp. 164–65.
15. Ibid., p. 256.
16. Charles and Ritz, p. 331.
17. Lee Hildebrand, *Stars of Soul and Rhythm & Blues* (New York: Billboard Books, 1994), p. 40.

FURTHER READING

Charles, Ray and David Ritz, *Brother Ray: Ray Charles' Own Story*. New York: Da Capo Press, 2004.

Ertegun, Ahmet, *What'd I Say: The Atlantic Story*. New York: Welcome Rain, 2001.

Gillett, Charlie, *The Sound of the City: The Rise of Rock and Roll*. New York: Da Capo, 1996.

Lydon, Michael, *Ray Charles: Man and Music*. New York: Riverhead Books, 1998.

Wexler, Jerry and David Ritz, *Rhythm and the Blues*. New York: Alfred A. Knopf, 1993.

Courtesy of Photofest.

Chuck Berry

Scott Schinder

BROWN-EYED HANDSOME GENIUS

Attempting to credit one person with the invention of rock and roll is a mis-guided and pointless pursuit. But no early rocker played a bigger role in creating the basic template for guitar-driven electric rock and roll than Chuck Berry, and no artist of his era did a more effective job of merging an original musical vision with a cohesive and distinctive songwriting persona.

The St. Louis–bred singer/guitarist was rock's first great songwriter/performer. In his first decade as a recording artist, Berry released a remarkable run of singles that became so deeply woven into rock and roll's foundation that it's difficult to imagine the genre existing without them. Long before Bob Dylan and the Beatles officially established it as a legitimate art form in the 1960s, Chuck Berry emerged as rock's first great poet.

Berry made his name writing infectious, exuberant songs that used evocative wordplay and whimsical humor to document 1950s American teenage life. His compositions played a crucial role in chronicling and defining the youth culture that spawned rock and roll, and in introducing much of the cars-and-girls iconography of early rock and roll. Berry's uncanny ability to tap into teen psychology and youthful slang was doubly impressive, given the fact that he didn't begin his recording career until he was nearly thirty years old.

On such enduring anthems as "Roll Over Beethoven," "Rock and Roll Music" and "Johnny B. Goode," Berry celebrated the music's liberating spirit. On "School Day," "Sweet Little Sixteen," and "Reelin' and Rockin'," he vividly documented teen social, recreational, and romantic rituals. His skill for shaggy-dog storytelling on "Nadine," "You Can't Catch Me," and "No Particular Place to Go" was balanced by his knack for spinning such poignant vignettes as "Memphis" and "Havana Moon." And with such numbers as "Brown-Eyed Handsome Man," "Promised Land," and "Back in the U.S.A.," he conjured a colorful American landscape fraught with pitfalls but brimming with hope and promise.

Berry's 1955 debut single "Maybellene" is considered by some to be the first fully realized rock and roll record, the first to fully synthesize the music's blues and country influences into a cohesive and compelling style. Berry was also the first prominent rocker to write most of his own material, and the first to double on vocals and electric guitar.

While much of rock and roll's foundation was laid by white musicians emulating and adapting African American musical forms, Berry demonstrated that the music's influence was a two-way street. He forged his style by mixing country guitar licks and country-inspired narrative songwriting with a rhythm and blues beat and the rudiments of Chicago-style electric blues. He enunciated his lyrics with clear, careful phrasing that contrasted the raw conventions of blues singing. Berry's synthesis of black and white influences, and his energetic performing style, made him the first black rocker to cross over from the R&B charts to achieve consistent success with white teenagers, without alienating his black audience.

Berry's distinctive guitar style—drawn from elements of blues, country, and jazz—is generally considered to be the wellspring for modern rock and roll guitar. His playing was an essential cornerstone of rock and roll, and was emulated, to one degree or another, by virtually every significant guitar band of the 1960s. Most of those bands included Berry material in their repertoire.

Indeed, Berry remains one of the most-covered composers in pop history; his songs have remained essential staples of jukeboxes, oldies radio stations, and garage band set lists ever since.

But Berry's playful musical persona, and his energetic performing style, belie a complex, thorny personality embittered by years of racism, rip-offs, and government harassment. Obstinate, obsessively private, distrustful of outsiders, and mercenary to a fault, Berry has long squandered his legendary status and severely tested his fans' goodwill. Once renowned as one rock's most electrifying stage performers, for decades he's been notorious for delivering spotty, sloppy live shows. Berry's inelegant approach to live gigs long ago attained mythic status, with the artist typically turning up at the venue minutes before set time, receiving payment in cash prior to taking the stage, and playing with under-rehearsed (or unrehearsed) local pickup bands.

ST. LOUIS BLUES

Charles Edward Anderson Berry was born on October 18, 1926, in St. Louis, Missouri, the fourth of Martha and Henry Berry's six children. He grew up in the Ville, a six-by-nine-block neighborhood north of downtown St. Louis that was one of the few sections of the heavily segregated city where blacks were allowed to own property. Because the city's white institutions were so inhospitable, the Ville became a self-contained community within the racially divided city, an oasis of African American–owned businesses and cultural institutions.

Martha and Henry Berry were the grandchildren of Southern slaves, and were among the many rural blacks that had migrated to St. Louis in search of employment. Unlike most African American women of the era, Martha possessed a college education. Henry was a contractor and carpenter, as well as a deacon of the local Antioch Baptist Church. The middle-class Berry family maintained a strong grounding in the church, and stressed discipline, enterprise, and educational achievement as a means to prosper within the societal barriers of the time.

In his youth, Chuck did carpentry work for his father, and developed an interest in photography through his uncle Harry Davis (who would later shoot many enduring images of his nephew). Unlike his siblings, though, Chuck gravitated toward trouble in his teen years. He attended the prestigious Sumner High School, the first black high school west of the Mississippi, but bristled against its stringent educational and disciplinary standards.

Although he'd begun singing in his church's choir at the age of six, Chuck didn't take up the electric guitar until his teens. He was inspired to learn to play after singing Jay McShann's "Confessin' the Blues" (a song he would later record on his 1960 LP *Rockin' at the Hops*) at a school talent show, accompanied by a guitar-playing friend. While some faculty members strongly disapproved of such down-and-dirty material, the positive crowd response drove Berry to pick up the instrument, developing his skills with some help from local jazz player Ira Harris.

In the fall of 1944, Berry dropped out of high school, and decided to head for California with two friends. They only got as far as Kansas City, where they were arrested and convicted for armed robbery. All three were sentenced to ten years in the Intermediate Reformatory for Young Men at Algoa, near Jefferson, Missouri.

Berry was released from the reformatory after three years, on his twenty-first birthday on October 18, 1947. A year and ten days later, he married Themetta "Toddy" Suggs, with whom he would eventually have four children. In addition to doing work for his father's construction business, he worked as a photographer and as a janitor in an auto assembly plant, and trained to be a hairdresser and cosmetologist. He also continued to hone his guitar skills, drawing upon such influences as electric-blues pioneer T-Bone Walker, jazz innovator Charlie Christian and Carl Hogan of Louis Jordan's Tympani Five. One of Berry's favorite vocalists was Nat "King" Cole, whose combination of jazz/blues grit and cultured sophistication would influence Berry's own musical sensibility, as well as his careful vocal enunciation.

By 1951, Berry had become a skillful enough guitarist that his high school classmate Tommy Stevens invited him to join his trio. The Tommy Stevens Combo worked the rough, sometimes violent clubs of East St. Louis, Illinois, just across the Mississippi River, and specialized in black blues and pop standards. Berry's addition to the group brought out his natural sense of showmanship, and he expanded the group's repertoire by adding country and novelty tunes.

At around this time, Charles Berry began adding an "n" to his last name and billing himself as Chuck Berryn, apparently in deference to the church ties of his father, who couldn't have looked kindly on his son's decision to play the devil's music.

At the end of 1952, Johnnie Johnson (1924–2005), a local jazz/boogie-woogie piano player who'd recently arrived from Chicago, hired Berry to play a New Year's Eve gig with his group, Sir John's Trio, at the Cosmopolitan Club in East St. Louis, where they were a frequent attraction. He'd initially been hired to substitute for an unavailable musician, but Johnson was impressed enough with Berry's abilities that he invited the guitarist to become a permanent member of the act. Before long, the newcomer would come to dominate the group.

As he had with his previous band, Berry energized Johnson's sets, augmenting the pianist's repertoire of 1930s and 1940s pop standards with his own up-tempo country-style numbers. Berry's urban hillbilly act enhanced the group's local reputation, drawing white patrons to the black club and establishing Chuck as a competitor to such local guitarists as Ike Turner, Albert King, and Little Milton. Although Berry's humorous narrative songs had little precedent in the blues at the time, black jump-blues bandleader Louis Jordan—an early Berry hero—had been doing something comparable, with considerable commercial success, since the early 1940s.

PLAYING CHESS

In the spring of 1955, Berry began making trips to the black musical mecca of Chicago, looking for contacts and recording possibilities. He met legendary electric bluesman Muddy Waters, who suggested that Berry contact Leonard Chess, who ran Chess Records, the influential independent label for which Waters recorded.

Chess Records, run by Polish-born immigrant brothers Leonard and Phil Chess, was already one of America's most successful specialists in recording and selling black music. The company's artist roster included such popular bluesmen as Waters, Howlin' Wolf, John Lee Hooker, Little Walter, and Sonny Boy Williamson, as well as the influential vocal groups the Flamingos and the Moonglows.

Doo-Wop at the Dawn of Rock and Roll

The vocal group harmony style, with roots in black gospel quartet singing, was an important part of the original rock and roll explosion of the 1950s. Years later, this sound became known as doo-wop, so called because the background singers often intoned such nonsense syllables to accompany the lyrics sung by the lead vocalist.

In some respects, the vocal groups were at a disadvantage in the intensely competitive and exploitive music industry of the period. Most did not write their own material or play instruments on their own recordings, so they were dependent on others for their material and backing. The reinforcement of the group image tended to obscure the individual members' identities, and often the group's name was owned by a manager or record company entrepreneur.

The person holding legal title to the name could hire and fire the group members almost at will. An entire group such as the Drifters could be reconstituted and then sent into the recording studio or out on tour. Meanwhile, former members continued to appear as (for example) Charlie Thomas of the Drifters. These practices created confusion and resentment among performers and fans alike—along with a tide of lawsuits, some extending to the present day.

Two of the most important black vocal groups at the birth of rhythm & blues were the Ravens and the Orioles. The Ravens' recordings of "Ol' Man River" and "Send for Me If You Need Me" (both 1948) contrasted the soaring tenor of Maithe Marshall (sometimes singing in falsetto) with the deep bass of Jimmy Ricks. It was a combination that other groups would emulate for decades to come. The Orioles' overall vocal tone was less polished and slightly more soulful than that of the Ravens. On their number one R&B hit of 1949, "Tell Me So," a wordless falsetto entwined around Sonny Til's angelic tenor lead—another device that later would be appropriated on countless vocal group recordings.

The Orioles' success with R&B renditions of Tin Pan Alley standards ("What Are You Doing New Year's Eve?") gave rise to a host of so-called bird groups: the Penguins ("Earth Angel"), the Flamingos ("I Only Have Eyes for You"), and so on. In 1954, the Crows created one of rock and roll's greatest one-shot hits with "Gee." This song, wrote vocal group authority Philip Groia, "became the first recording of black street-corner singing to transcend the realm of R&B into the white pop market. It was a million-seller and the first doo-wop record to be recognized by the white media. In hindsight, it has often been referred to as the first rock and roll group record."

Andy Schwartz

"You could tell right away," Phil Chess recalled in Peter Guralnick's book *Feel Like Going Home*. "He had that something special, that—I don't know what you'd call it. But he had it."[1]

Chess told the young hopeful to bring him a demo tape, so Berry went home and cut some songs on a borrowed wire recorder with Johnson's band. The resulting demo included the slow blues original "Wee Wee Hours" and an up-tempo reworking of a much-recorded country standard titled "Ida Red," which Berry knew from a popular 1938 version by western swing pioneers Bob Wills and His Texas Playboys.

Berry felt that "Wee Wee Hours" would be a natural for the blues-oriented Chess Records. But Leonard Chess, eager to tap into the emerging rock and roll market that had begun to eat into the sales of his label's blues releases, saw more potential in "Ida Red." Chess's preference was understandable. At the time, a successful blues single was unlikely to sell more than 10,000 copies, while a rhythm and blues hit could sell hundreds of thousands, and a rock and roll crossover might shift as many as a million.

"The big beat, cars, and young love," said Leonard Chess. "It was a trend and we jumped on it."[2]

At Chess's suggestion, "Ida Red" was renamed "Maybellene." The new title was inspired by the Maybelline cosmetics company, although Chess was careful to change the spelling to avoid potential legal problems. The retitled number was recorded at the Chess studio on May 21, with Johnnie Johnson on piano and Johnson's drummer Ebby Hardy, plus legendary Chess musician/songwriter Willie Dixon on bass.

Most of the elements of Berry's signature sound were already in place on "Maybellene," including his inventive blues/country picking style, his sly singing and the rhythm section's propulsive backbeat. Meanwhile, Johnson's rolling boogie rhythms and distinctive right-hand technique were already firmly in place, underlining the importance of the pianist's contribution to Berry's sound.

Beyond its snappy sound, "Maybellene" showcase Berry's already impressive lyrical gifts. He invests the song's simple story—an auto chase in pursuit of a wayward lover—with such a wealth of crafty wordplay and evocative detail that the narrative takes on the quality of an epic quest.

"Maybellene," with the more pedestrian "Wee Wee Hours" as its B-side, was released by Chess as Chuck Berry's first single in July 1955. By then, "Maybellene" had mysteriously acquired a pair of co-authors. The first was influential rock and roll disc jockey Alan Freed, with whom Chess Records had a close working relationship, and whose airplay could make a song a hit. The other was Russ Fratto, the landlord of the building where Chess's headquarters were located as well as the Chess brothers' partner in the pressing plant that manufactured the company's product. Credited as co-writers alongside Berry, Freed and Fratto were entitled to equal shares of the song's publishing royalties. Such exploitive arrangements were common in rock and roll's early days, and Berry was unaware of the chicanery until the song was released.

Great Groups and Solo Stars of the 1950s

Billy Ward was a Juilliard-trained musician and entrepreneur with an ear for talent. In 1950, he formed the Dominoes and recruited a series of exceptional singers to front the group. The first was Clyde McPhatter (1932–72), who injected the Dominoes' 1952 smash "Have Mercy Baby" with a blend of youthful abandon and adult sensuality, then later wept convincingly on their sentimental ballad "The Bells" (1953).

McPhatter left the group shortly thereafter to make an even bigger impact as lead singer for the Drifters on their number one R&B hits "Honey Love" and "Adorable." His successor in the Dominoes was a former Golden Gloves boxer from Detroit named Jackie Wilson (1934–84), who announced his arrival on the group's version of "St. Therese of the Roses" in 1956. It was not a chart hit, but Wilson's bravura performance attracted enough attention to propel him into a solo career soon after the record was released.

Frankie Lymon was a preternaturally gifted singer who became the first black teenage pop star at age thirteen when his group, the Teenagers, shot to number one R&B and number six Pop in 1956 with their first single, "Why Do Fools Fall In Love." Lymon's rich vibrato and jazz-tinged phrasing would exert a profound influence on artists ranging from Ronnie Spector to Michael Jackson, and great things were expected from his solo career when he left the group after just eighteen months. But neither he nor the other Teenagers ever repeated (or even came close to) their first astounding success, and Frankie Lymon was only twenty-six when he died from a drug overdose in 1968.

Amid the turbulent atmosphere of 1950s rhythm and blues, the Platters were one of the few black vocal groups to establish a stable career in the mainstream of show business. Under the careful guidance of manager and songwriter Buck Ram, the group scored twelve Top Ten R&B hits from 1955 to 1959, four of which reached number one on the Pop chart. The Platters' classic ballads "Only You," "The Great Pretender," and "Twilight Time" all featured the polished lead of Tony Williams within sumptuous male/female vocal blends and lush orchestrations.

Another black vocal group to enjoy great popularity with young white audiences was the Coasters, whose raucous, comedic musical mini-dramas were the virtual opposite of the Platters' staid elegance. In 1953, the L.A.-based quartet then known as the Robins joined forces with two young white songwriter/producers, Jerry Leiber and Mike Stoller, in 1953 to create the groundbreaking R&B protest number, "Riot in Cell Block #9."

When the Robins split up, lead singer Carl Gardner and bass man Bobby Nunn formed the Coasters, who continued to work with Leiber and Stoller. In 1957, the team struck gold with the two-sided hit single, "Searchin'" backed with "Young Blood," the former title topping the R&B chart for twelve straight weeks and reaching number three Pop. The following year, the Coasters scored a number one Pop hit with "Yakety Yak," then extended their hot streak with "Charlie Brown," "Along Came Jones," and "Poison Ivy." These songs, as carefully and imaginatively produced as any Madison Avenue television commercial, represented the final flowering of the original black vocal group sound.

A. S.

Not surprisingly, Freed played "Maybellene" enthusiastically on his popular show on New York's WINS. The exposure helped "Maybellene" to become one of the first national rock and roll hits, rising to the number one slot on *Billboard*'s R&B chart and number five on the pop chart.

The crossover success of "Maybellene" demonstrated Berry's ability to transcend the racial barriers that ruled the music industry in the 1950s. At a time when it was common for discs by black performers to be outsold by watered-down cover versions by white acts, it was Berry's original that white teenagers bought, beating out cover attempts by Jim Lowe and Johnny Long, as well as one by future country star Marty Robbins.

Beyond the issue of writing credits, Berry would maintain an ongoing association with Alan Freed. After making his New York stage debut at Freed's all-star show at the Brooklyn Paramount theater during Labor Day weekend 1955, he would perform on several of Freed's multi-artist tours and appear with him in the quickie movie musicals *Rock Rock Rock, Mister Rock and*

Roll, and *Go Johnny Go.* Berry had a substantial speaking role in the latter film.

Thanks to the stage chops he'd honed in the clubs of East St. Louis, Berry quickly established himself as a magnetic, high-energy live performer, with such memorable trademark stage moves as his famed duckwalk. On some occasions, Berry would claim to have introduced the duckwalk during his Brooklyn Paramount debut. But he would also claim to have originated it as a child to entertain his mother and her friends.

Berry initially had trouble following up the crossover success of "Maybellene." "Roll Over Beethoven," a highly original ode to rock and roll's appeal invoking the names of classical composers, reached number twenty-nine on *Billboard*'s pop chart in May 1956. But otherwise, the string of singles that Berry released in 1955 and 1956—songs like "Too Much Monkey Business," "You Can't Catch Me," "Thirty Days," and "No Money Down," all now acknowledged as classic examples of Berry's genius—performed well on the R&B charts, but failed to catch on in the more lucrative rock and roll market.

If those songs were less commercially successful than their predecessors, they were every bit as inventive and compelling, demonstrating Berry's eye for detail and knack for singular turns of phrase. "Too Much Monkey Business," for instance, cataloged an array of everyday irritations and injustices. If it wasn't exactly a protest song, it was certainly a masterful example of Berry's ability to use of humor to transcend life's indignities.

The B-side of "Too Much Monkey Busines," "Brown Eyed Handsome Man," was equally noteworthy. The song is often cited as rock's first black-pride anthem, subtly acknowledging institutionalized racism while maintaining a sunny sense of optimism.

In the fall of 1956, Berry split with his original touring band of Johnnie Johnson and Ebby Hardy. Johnson and Hardy returned to the East St. Louis club scene, although both would work with Berry in the studio and on stage at various points in the future. Johnson's piano work would remain prominent on many of Berry's future Chess releases, although pianists Lafayette Leake and Otis Spann would also play on some Berry sessions. For rest of his career, Berry would usually travel alone and use local pickup bands as backup—an approach that would frustrate fans and critics to no end.

Berry's chart fortunes turned around decisively in early 1957, when "School Day"—an irresistible evocation of adolescent frustration and the transcendent uplift of rock and roll—reached number five on the *Billboard* pop chart. The song's success established Berry as a top draw on the live circuit, leading to him playing no fewer than 240 one-nighters that year.

Over the next two and a half years, Chuck Berry scored an impressive run of Top Ten hits—"Rock and Roll Music," "Sweet Little Sixteen," "Carol," and the seemingly autobiographical "Johnny B. Goode"—that neatly encapsulated the teenage experience and rock and roll's mythic pull. His minor hits during this period—for example, "Sweet Little Rock and Roller," "Almost Grown," and "Back in the U.S.A."—were no less memorable.

"Back in the U.S.A." was one of Berry's most impressive achievements. A vibrant ode to the artist's homeland, written upon his return from his first tour of Australia, the song painted America as a day-glo wonderland of blaring jukeboxes, flashing neon signs and twenty-four-hour burger joints. Its original B-side, the slyly sentimental "Memphis," was one of Berry's most poignant efforts, and became a Top Ten hit after disc jockeys began flipping the single.

Berry also revealed an inclination for playful experimentalism that manifested itself both in offbeat lyrical subject matter, such as the Italian American themes of "Anthony Boy," and the exotic musical elements heard in the Latin excursions "Havana Moon" and "La Juanda." But he wasn't above padding such early LPs as *One Dozen Berrys* (1958), *After School Session* (1958), and *Chuck Berry Is on Top* (1959) with silly novelties and throwaway blues numbers.

Berry toured extensively through the late 1950s, often performing on multi-act road shows alongside such fellow rock and roll pioneers as Buddy Holly, the Everly Brothers, Bill Haley and the Comets, Little Richard, and Carl Perkins. On one such package tour, a seventy-five-day trek hosted by Alan Freed, Berry was drawn into a rivalry with volatile piano pounder Jerry Lee Lewis, which gave rise to some memorable but largely apocryphal anecdotes. On a Boston date during that tour, fights broke out in the audience during Berry's set. When the police turned on the theater's house lights, Freed made some unflattering comments about the cops, which led to him being arrested for inciting a riot.

Berry's 1958 appearance at the prestigious Newport Jazz Festival—an early example of rock and roll being accorded respect from the high-brow jazz world—was much calmer. The set, on which Berry was backed, somewhat awkwardly, by Jack Teagarden's ten-piece jazz band, was captured for posterity in the acclaimed documentary film *Jazz on a Summer's Day*.

With nearly twenty chart hits between 1957 and 1960, Berry became Chess Records' best-selling artist, and the first Chess act to cross over to sell large quantities of records to white teenagers. Despite his success, Berry was still subject to the financial ripoffs and personal humiliations that routinely confronted rock and roll performers at the time.

When Berry discovered that his first road manager, Teddy Reig, was skimming money from his live appearances, he immediately fired Reig along with manager Jack Hooke, and took control of his own business affairs. Such experiences made a permanent imprint on Berry's personality, making him suspicious of outsiders and causing him to maintain an obsessive level of control in financial matters.

"Let me say that any man who can't take care of his own money deserves what he gets," Berry later declared in a *Rolling Stone* interview.[3]

Berry's frugal on-the-road habits—sometimes sleeping in his car rather than hotels, and cooking meals on his own hotplate rather than dining in restaurants—would soon become legendary. But they likely had as much to do with a desire to avoid the indignities that faced an African American man traveling alone in 1950s America as they did with saving money.

HAVE MERCY, JUDGE

Berry's success allowed him the financial independence that his parents had always aspired to. In April 1957, he purchased thirty acres of land in rural Wentzville, Missouri, about thirty miles west of St. Louis. There, he built Berry Park, an amusement park complex that would open to the public in the summer of 1961, encompassing a hotel, a nightclub, a golf course, an outdoor bandstand, a recording studio, a guitar-shaped swimming pool, and Berry's fleet of Cadillacs.

In 1958, Berry opened Club Bandstand in a largely white business district of St. Louis. Not surprisingly, the presence of a racially integrated nightclub owned by a successful black entertainer in a city with St. Louis's troubled racial history didn't sit well with the local power brokers, and it didn't take long for Berry to come under the scrutiny of the authorities.

On December 1, 1959, following an engagement in El Paso, Texas, Berry visited nearby Juarez, Mexico. There, he met Janice Escalanti, a fourteen-year-old Native American waitress and sometime prostitute from Yuma, Arizona, and hired her to work as a hat-check girl at Club Bandstand. Berry brought her back to St. Louis, but fired her after two weeks. On December 21, Escalanti was arrested on a prostitution charge at a St. Louis hotel, leading to charges being filed against Berry for violating the Mann Act, which forbade interstate transport of women for "immoral purposes."

When the case first came to trial, Berry was found guilty, but some overtly racist courtroom remarks by the judge led to the verdict being overturned. A second trial in October 1961 arrived at the same verdict, and Berry was sentenced to three years in prison and a $10,000 fine.

Berry began serving his sentence on February 19, 1962. While in prison, he took courses to earn his high school degree and continued to write songs. In his absence, his influence continued to be felt in the rock and roll world. In early 1963, for instance, the Beach Boys scored a hit with "Surfin' U.S.A.," a fairly blatant rewrite of "Sweet Little Sixteen." When Chess Records threatened legal action, Berry was granted writing credit for the song.

Meanwhile, across the Atlantic, a new generation of British guitar bands was making the most of Berry's influence, as well as covering his compositions on a regular basis. In June 1963, for example, the Rolling Stones released their first single, an earnest cover of Berry's "Come On," which they would follow with versions of nearly a dozen more Berry tunes. The Beatles also cut popular versions of "Rock and Roll Music" and "Roll Over Beethoven," while the Animals would dip into the Berry songbook more than half a dozen times. Indeed, of the countless U.K. rock and roll combos who sprang to life in the first half of the 1960s—not to mention the legion of American garage bands who would emulate them—it would be hard to find many whose set list didn't include at least one Berry number.

After serving twenty months of his sentence at the Indiana Federal Prison, Leavenworth Federal Prison in Kansas, and the Federal Medical Center in Springfield, Missouri, Berry was released on his thirty-seventh birthday, October 18, 1963.

Although he would successfully resume his musical career following his release, most observers agreed that Chuck Berry's experiences with the law left him bitter, distrustful, and suspicious of all but his closest friends. He felt, with some justification, that he had been unfairly targeted and persecuted by a bigoted legal system, and hounded by the press.

"Never saw a man so changed," observed rockabilly pioneer Carl Perkins, who'd shared bills with Berry in the past and worked with him again on his British comeback tour in 1964. "He had been an easygoing guy before, the kinda guy who'd jam in dressing rooms, sit and swap licks and jokes. In England he was cold, real distant and bitter. It wasn't just jail, it was those years of one nighters, grinding it out like that can kill a man, but I figure it was mostly jail."[4]

However much his experiences had affected his personality, they didn't diminish the quality of Berry's songwriting. Between February 1964 and March 1965, he placed six singles in the *Billboard* Top 100, including the shaggy-dog tour de force "Nadine," the rollicking "No Particular Place To Go," the witty, French-themed "You Never Can Tell," and the poignantly autobiographical "Promised Land," which chronicles a cross-country journey from Norfolk, Virginia, to California.

The latter song was one of Berry's most impressive achievements, a richly detailed, partially autobiographical account of a rock and roll pilgrim's progress. The song's sense of aspiration and optimism was all the more impressive in light of its author's harsh experiences with his homeland's darker side.

For a while, Berry was one of a small handful of American rock and rollers to maintain chart success during the British Invasion. But 1965's "Dear Dad" would be his last chart entry for seven years.

In 1966, Berry left Chess to sign with Mercury Records. Although the deal was a lucrative one for Berry, the move proved disastrous in nearly every other respect. Where the small, family-owned Chess could accommodate the artist's idiosyncratic personality and contrary streak, Mercury's more formal corporate structure was a much less comfortable fit. And without the sympathetic studio treatment he received from the Chess brothers, Berry foundered musically.

Berry's four-year stint with Mercury began unpromisingly with *Chuck Berry's Golden Hits,* a pointless collection of lackluster remakes of his Chess classics, and continued with such underwhelming LPs as *Chuck Berry in Memphis, From St. Louie to Frisco,* and the bloated, jam-dominated *Concerto in B. Goode.* Far better was 1967's *Live at the Fillmore,* on which Berry received backup from the Steve Miller Band and demonstrated that he was still capable of turning in solid performances in the right circumstances. Otherwise, his Mercury output mainly served to make Berry sound like a disengaged relic of a bygone era.

It's unfortunate that Berry's recordings during this period were so shoddy, since his series of well-received appearances at San Francisco's Fillmore—a revered bastion of the new hippie musical culture—demonstrated that he could still appeal to the new underground rock audience. But Berry, still making good money performing one-nighters, seemed largely unconcerned with reinventing himself creatively or maintaining momentum as a contemporary artist.

Berry re-signed with Chess Records in 1970, and the change made for an upswing in the quality of his output. The three studio LPs he released after his return—*Back Home, San Francisco Dues,* and *Bio*—were something of a return to form, adapting Berry's sound somewhat to fit changing times without sacrificing his personality or songwriting style.

Berry's reignited inspiration was evident on *Back Home*'s hippie-themed "Tulane," whose tale of a pot-dealing couple adapted his storytelling approach to the Woodstock era. Tulane's boyfriend Johnny is busted, and finds himself in court on the song's sequel, "Have Mercy Judge." That song, also included on *Back Home,* was one of Berry's more successful attempts to write in a blues vein.

But Chess Records was no longer the small family operation that Berry had originally known. The company had recently been sold to tape-manufacturing giant GRT, and Chuck's main mentor Leonard Chess had died of a heart attack a few months prior to his return. Leonard's brother Phil and son Marshall would leave the company by 1972, and Berry would soon follow.

By then, a widespread resurgence of interest in 1950s rock and roll had revitalized the careers of many vintage performers, and Berry found himself in increased demand as a live act. The revival actually had actually begun to gather steam in late 1969, when New York promoter Richard Nader staged a pair of all-star concerts at Madison Square Garden, with a bill that included Berry, Bill Haley, the Coasters, the Platters, and the Shirelles. Although Berry's sets were marred by business disputes with Nader, the shows were a smash, and Nader continued to stage similar events around the country, often with Berry on the bill.

Although Chess Records was on its last legs, Berry would score the biggest hit of his career in 1972. That year, he released *The London Chuck Berry Sessions,* which combined tracks recorded at a concert in Coventry,

England, with studio recordings made with British players including Faces members Ian McLagan and Kenney Jones. Although the album was patchy and unmemorable, it spawned an unlikely smash single in an edited version of the live "My Ding-A-Ling," a sophomoric, double entendre–laden ode to masturbation.

While "My Ding-A-Ling" (which Berry had first recorded as "My Tambourine" on his 1968 Mercury LP *From St. Louie to Frisco*) credited Berry as writer, the song was actually written and recorded by noted New Orleans R&B bandleader Dave Bartholomew in 1952 and covered by the Bees as "Toy Bell" the following year.

Whatever its pedigree, the lightweight novelty tune became the best-selling single of Berry's career in the summer of 1972, topping the pop charts on both sides of the Atlantic. Adding to the irony was the fact that it kept "Burning Love" by fellow 1950s icon Elvis Presley—who was then also in the midst of a chart resurgence—out of the number one slot in the United States. In England, the song's risqué lyrics made it the first number one song not to be performed on the venerable TV pop institution *Top of the Pops*.

Veteran rock critic Robert Christgau noted the discomfort that the left-field hit had caused to many longtime Berry fans. "A lot of his raving fanatics are mortified," Christgau wrote at the time. "We've always dreamed of another big single for our hero—his last was 'You Never Can Tell' in the Beatle summer of 1964—but 'My Ding-a-Ling' has been embarrassing us at concerts for years, and not because we wouldn't sing along. It was just dumb, inappropriate to the sophistication of his new, collegiate audience. Anyway, that's how the rationalization went."

"Obviously," Christgau reasoned,

> what we meant was that it wasn't sophisticated enough for us—his other stuff was so much better. But popularity has changed the song. I feel sure that it's delighting all the twelve-year-olds who get to figure out that they've snuck something dirty onto the AM radio—a rock 'n' roll tradition that has been neglected since the concept of dirty became so passé—because I'm fairly delighted myself. Believe me, twenty-one thousand rock 'n' roll revivalists filling Madison Square Garden to shout along with a fourth-grade wee-wee joke constitutes a cultural event as impressive as it is odd, a magnificent and entirely apposite triumph in Chuck Berry's very own tradition. . . . Unless we somehow recycle the concept of the great artist so that it supports Chuck Berry as well as it does Marcel Proust, we might as well trash it altogether.[5]

The London Chuck Berry Sessions produced another minor hit, a live version of "Reelin' and Rockin'" that reached the U.S. Top Thirty. But it and "My Ding-A-Ling" marked Berry's farewell to the charts. Thereafter, he would focus the bulk of his musical energies on live performing. Through the 1970s, he was a regular presence on the rock and roll revival circuit, playing numerous multi-act nostalgia concerts, including the Richard Nader concerts that were filmed for the popular 1973 theatrical documentary *Let the Good*

Times Roll. He also appeared as himself in *American Hot Wax*, a fictionalized 1978 Alan Freed biopic whose narrative climaxed with the Brooklyn Paramount shows that had helped to make Berry a star.

ALL ALONE

By now, Berry had developed a reputation for delivering sloppy, indifferent live performances, usually backed by local pickup bands whom he'd rarely met (let alone rehearsed with) before taking the stage. His standard touring method involved traveling alone with his guitar to gigs, where his standard performance contract called for promoters to provide two Fender Dual Showman amplifiers, a backup band, and payment in cash prior to the show. Promoters who violated the terms of the contract, even inadvertently, found themselves forced to pay additional fines before Berry would agree to perform.

Berry's cut-rate touring methods provided amusing and harrowing anecdotes for multiple generations of musicians who'd found themselves playing behind the prickly legend. One of those was Bruce Springsteen, who in the 1986 Berry documentary *Hail! Hail! Rock 'n' Roll* related his early experience of being hired to play guitar behind Berry, who showed up alone five minutes before show time, collected his cash, unpacked his guitar on stage, and barely acknowledged the musicians, who, in lieu of a set list, were left to pick up their cues from Berry's inscrutable onstage signals.

While some artists might find that story unflattering, Berry was proud enough to quote Springsteen's anecdote as the introduction to his autobiography. Springsteen, by the way, would back Berry once more, at a 1995 concert inaugurating the new Rock and Roll Hall of Fame.

Chuck Berry would release only more album of new material in the twentieth century. 1979's *Rockit* was recorded in two days in Berry Park's in-house studio with several longtime cohorts including Johnnie Johnson. Berry delivered the finished album to Atco Records, accepting no A&R input from the label. *Rockit* was solid and workmanlike if not particularly inspired, and featured some scattered flashes of Berry's original wit and energy, including, the sly "Oh What a Thrill."

Not long after *Rockit*'s release, Berry pleaded guilty to charges of tax evasion and filing false tax returns. The charges stemmed from his habit of taking undocumented cash payments for his live performances. The judge suspended his original three-year sentence, and instead sentenced Berry to serve four months in prison and perform 1,000 hours of community service. Berry would end up spending just over three months at Lompoc Prison Camp in California. Just three days before his sentencing, Berry had performed at the White House, as part of an event staged by the Black Music Association.

While serving his sentence at Lompoc, Berry began writing his version of his life story, which would be published in 1987 as *Chuck Berry: The Autobiography*. The book presented a colorful account of the author's musical, legal, and sexual exploits, but glossed over many of his life's more troublesome issues, and ultimately did little to reveal what really made him tick.

In 1986—the same year that he became one of the new Rock and Roll Hall of Fame's first set of inductees—Berry was honored with a pair of star-studded sixtieth-birthday concerts that became the jumping-off point for *Hail! Hail! Rock 'n' Roll*, a high-profile feature film documentary that chronicled the shows and delineated Berry's musical legacy. The shows took place at St. Louis's Fox Theater, a venue that had once refused entrance to a young Berry and his father due to their skin color.

Rolling Stone Keith Richards, perhaps the most prominent acolyte of Berry's guitar style, signed on as the event's musical director. Richards assembled a first-rate band, with Johnnie Johnson on piano, determined to present his idol's songs with the respect they deserved.

But Berry, uncomfortable ceding control to others, had other ideas. He clashed constantly with Richards, with whom he'd tangled in the past (he'd punched Richards in the face at a New York show in 1981). Further tensions erupted between Berry and the film crew that director Taylor Hackford had assembled to document the shows.

"I signed on to this as a celebration of somebody who had had a major impact on our lives," Hackford said twenty years later, on the occasion of the film's DVD release. "So we went there to celebrate him, and we had every expectation to expect a lot of cooperation. . . . We found quite a different situation."[6]

Berry reportedly ate up a substantial percentage of the film's $3 million budget by demanding daily cash payments just to show up for filming, despite being one of the film's producers. When the filmmakers and Berry visited a prison where he'd served time on his armed robbery conviction, the presence of Berry's provocatively attired girlfriend nearly drove the prisoners to riot, until Berry calmed the captives by playing for them. Although Hackford captured the dramatic incident on film, Berry refused to allow the director to use the footage in the film.

When it came time for the concerts, Berry—who'd lost much of his voice arguing with Richards during rehearsals—played out of tune, as well as changing arrangements and keys in mid-song, throwing the carefully rehearsed all-star backup band into chaos.

Most who witnessed the shows described them as disasters. But some substantial post-production retooling—including Berry rerecording his vocals in the studio, for which he charged the producers once again—made the performances presentable enough for the film and its soundtrack album.

Despite being put through the wringer by his subject, Hackford couldn't bring himself to speak ill of Berry. The director also suggested that no film could ever really do justice to Berry's essence.

"Nobody is ever gonna know what really goes on inside that head," Hackford stated. "No one's ever gonna do the entire picture of Chuck Berry because it's just too deep and dark."[7]

In the film, Richards expressed a similar mixture of irritation and fondness. Despite his frustrations working with Berry, Richards was thrilled to have the opportunity to work with Johnson, who had retired from music and was driving a van for the elderly at the time.

"I knew Johnnie and Chuck hadn't been together for years and years, and I didn't honestly know if Johnnie was still playing," Richards recalled. "The most surprising thing was Chuck said, 'Yeah, he's in town, I'll give him a call.' "[8]

"Johnnie had amazing simpatico. He had a way of slipping into a song, an innate feel for complementing the guitar," Richards said. "I was fascinated by those huge hands, doing such incredibly precise, delicate work. I always compared (his fingers) to a bunch of overripe bananas. But he could do amazing things with those bananas."

Beyond its troubled production process and flawed concert performances, *Hail! Hail! Rock 'n' Roll!*'s blend of live footage, interviews, and candid footage of Berry's contentious interactions with Richards proved to be both a heartfelt tribute to, and a revealing portrait of, its prickly subject. Its highlights included some new performances filmed at the long-shuttered Cosmopolitan Club, interview footage shot at the now-crumbling Berry Park and enthusiastic testimonials from the likes of Little Richard, Bo Diddley, Bruce Springsteen, and even old rival Jerry Lee Lewis, who revealed that his own mother preferred Berry's music to her son's.

The Diva and the Dynamos: Little Richard, Ruth Brown, and Bo Diddley

Rhythm and blues and rock and roll brought forth a host of singular talents throughout the 1950s. Some, like Little Richard and Bo Diddley, were daring iconoclasts who broke or bent musical conventions to shape their own unique styles. Others, like Ruth Brown, were more conservative but still significant transitional figures bridging the gap between pre-rock popular music and the new big-beat sound.

Little Richard was born Richard Wayne Penniman in Macon, Georgia, in 1932. His early recordings (1951–54) were unexceptional blues numbers, but in 1955 Little Richard made an unexpected leap into flat-out rock and roll with "Tutti Frutti." Much influenced by female gospel shouters like Sister Rosetta Tharpe, Richard seemed to be singing himself hoarse on this raving, almost nonsensical rocker that not only reached number two R&B but crashed into the Pop Top Twenty.

"Tutti Frutti" spawned a series of similar-sounding but no less potent follow-ups: "Long Tall Sally," "Rip It Up," and "Lucille" were all number one R&B hits.

A cross-over sensation, Little Richard performed the title song in the 1956 film *The Girl Can't Help It* and thrilled audiences with his campy, high-energy stage shows. Suddenly, in late 1957, he left the music business to enter an Alabama Bible college; his subsequent gospel recordings passed unnoticed.

But in 1962 he returned to rock and roll for a rapturously received U.K. tour, and two years later the Beatles' cover of "Long Tall Sally" reintroduced his classic sound to a new generation. Although he never had another major hit record, his original seismic impact was enough to earn Little Richard a place among the first group of artists inducted into the Rock and Roll Hall of Fame in 1986.

There was nothing especially wild or unpredictable in the blues and ballad singing of Ruth Brown. But she projected a sassy, proto-feminist energy on infectiously danceable songs like her number one R&B classic "Mama, He Treats Your Daughter Mean." In the decade from 1949 to 1959, Brown accumulated twenty Top Ten R&B hits including the chart-toppers "Teardrops from My Eyes," "5-10-15 Hours," and "Oh What a Dream." Her label, Atlantic Records, became known in the music industry as "The House That Ruth Built."

None of these Ruth Brown recordings reached the Pop Top Forty, however, due in part to the release of competing cover versions on bigger labels. In her autobiography, Brown recalled that throughout her hit-making period she was forced to stand by as white singers copied her note for note and were featured on top television shows from which she was excluded.

Brown's career declined after 1960, and eventually one of the leading female stars of 1950s R&B was forced to seek work as a home health care aide. But beginning in the late 1970s Ruth Brown embarked on a new career in musical theater, including roles in the Broadway revue *Black and Blue* (for which she won a Tony Award) and in the John Waters film *Hairspray*. This exposure led to a new recording contract with Fantasy Records and in 1989 her album *Blues on Broadway* won the Grammy Award for Best Female Jazz Vocal Performance. The singer also waged a protracted struggle on behalf of royalty rights for veteran rhythm and blues artists, embodied by her own personal legal battle with Atlantic Records. Ruth's determined efforts led to the creation of the Rhythm and Blues Foundation, with funding from Atlantic and other major labels. She was inducted into the Rock and Roll Hall of Fame in 1993. Following surgery in October 2006, Ruth Brown suffered a heart attack and a stroke; she died a few weeks later, on November 17, at age seventy-eight.

On Bo Diddley's first self-titled hit "Bo Diddley" (which reached number two R&B in 1955), the singer/guitarist popularized an African-based rhythm pattern soon known as "the Bo Diddley beat." This beat became the basis for rock and roll classics ranging from "Not Fade Away" by Buddy Holly and "Willie and the Hand Jive" by Johnny Otis to the Who's "Magic Bus" and Bruce Springsteen's "She's the One." On "Say Man" and "Who Do You Love," Bo Diddley combined rock and roll music with a type of African American street slang known as "the dozens." His ritualized bragging and playful insults on these songs made him an early progenitor of rap.

He also designed and built his own rectangular-shaped guitars, constructed his own home recording studio, and was an early experimenter with futuristic guitar effects like sustain and feedback. In an essay written a few years after the artist's 1987 induction into the Rock & Roll Hall of Fame, Robert Palmer called Bo Diddley "a singularly important catalyst in one of the most far-reaching transformations of post-World War II American music" and "one of the most versatile, innovative, and *complete* musical talents of our time."*

A. S.

* Robert Palmer, liner notes for the box set Bo Diddley (Chess/MCA CHD2-19502, MCA Records, 1990).

Some of the film's most compelling moments were provided by Berry's onscreen refusal to address such topics as his prison terms and his extramarital affairs. At one point, he angrily cuts his wife off in mid-interview.

In one memorable scene shot during the concert rehearsals, Berry and Richards clash over the chords for "Carol," which the Rolling Stones covered early in their career. In another segment, Richards accompanies Berry on a casual rendition of the pop standard "I'm Through with Love," and Berry graciously compliments Richards on his guitar work. That brief, unguarded moment provides a rare glimpse into a more gentle, generous side that's sometimes been described by Berry's close friends but rarely displayed in public.

Berry was in more legal jeopardy in 1990, when several women alleged that he had videotaped them in the bathrooms at Berry Park and the Berry-owned Southern Air restaurant in Wentzville. When a former employee alleged that Berry had been trafficking in cocaine, Berry's estate was raided by DEA agents who confiscated marijuana, hashish, and various pornographic films and videotapes. But Berry denied the cocaine charge, and no evidence was ever presented to suggest that it had any merit.

In November 2000, just a few days before Berry was awarded a prestigious Kennedy Center Honor in Washington, D.C., Johnnie Johnson sued Berry, claiming co-authorship of fifty-seven vintage Berry songs. According to many reports, the lawsuit was initially inspired by observations that Keith Richards had made in *Hail! Hail! Rock 'n' Roll*, regarding Johnson's neglected contributions to Berry's music. But a judge ruled that too much time had passed since the songs were written, and the matter never came to trial.

While Johnson wasn't able to collect on his claims of co-writing Berry's songs, his appearance in *Hail! Hail! Rock 'n' Roll* helped to spark a late-blooming career resurgence for the veteran musician. The resulting attention led to him releasing a series of solo albums—including 1992's *Johnnie B. Bad*, on which Richards produced two tracks—and performing as a sideman on high-profile projects with a variety of artists.

In addition to playing on Richards's 1988 solo debut *Talk Is Cheap*, Johnson was featured on subsequent albums by Eric Clapton, Aerosmith, Bo Diddley, Buddy Guy, John Lee Hooker, Al Kooper, Styx, Susan Tedeschi, and George Thorogood. Johnson also played live shows fronting his own band, up until his death on April 13, 2005. One of his last live appearances was sitting in with the Rolling Stones to play "Honky Tonk Women" on a Houston gig during their 2003 tour.

Regardless of the controversies that continue to surround him, Berry's musical contributions continued to be widely honored, and his classic work continued to inspire new generations of listeners. MCA's acquisition of the Chess catalog in the 1980s allowed Berry's greatest recordings to gain new exposure in the CD format, thanks to a lengthy series of digital reissues, including an acclaimed 1989 box set.

But Berry's ongoing prestige as one of rock and roll's living legends and elder statesmen didn't alter his approach to his musical career. He's maintained his working routine, continuing to play an endless stream of half-hearted one-nighters with an equally endless series of subpar pickup bands. Other than the *Hail! Hail! Rock 'n' Roll* soundtrack album, he released no new music in the quarter-century that followed *Rockit*; sporadic talk of new material has yielded no tangible results as of this writing, although new songs have occasionally found their way into Berry's live sets.

St. Louis residents have had regular opportunities to see Berry perform low-key club gigs in his hometown, where he still plays regularly at a club called Blueberry Hill, performing in the club's Duck Room (named after his famous stage walk) backed by a regular group of musicians familiar with his material as well as his moods.

Otherwise, Berry, in his sixth decade in music and his eighth decade of life, continues to operate, for better or worse, on his own terms, continuing to exasperate club owners and sidemen as well as his own fans, who continue to hold out hope of catching him on a good night. Considering the magnitude of his influence and the life-affirming brilliance of his greatest music, one can hardly fault them for keeping the faith.

Regardless of what Chuck Berry does in the rest of his time on Earth, his music has already transcended the bounds of his home planet. When NASA scientists assembled a record of music to travel on its *Voyager* I spacecraft to deliver the sounds of the human race to alien civilizations, the space agency chose Berry's original Chess version "Johnny B. Goode" to represent rock and roll alongside pieces by Bach, Mozart, and Stravinsky and ethnic recordings from around the world. As if his earthly achievements weren't impressive enough, Berry is now also the first rocker in outer space.

TIMELINE

December 31, 1952
Pianist Johnnie Johnson hires Chuck Berry to fill in with his band, Sir John's Trio, for a New Year's Eve gig at the Cosmopolitan Club in East St. Louis.

May 1, 1955
Chuck Berry signs with Chess Records.

May 21, 1955
Chuck Berry records "Maybellene" as his first Chess single.

August 1, 1955
"Maybellene" reaches number five on *Billboard*'s pop chart.

September 1955
Berry makes his New York stage debut at disc jockey Alan Freed's all-star show at the Brooklyn Paramount theater.

May 1, 1957
Chuck Berry's first album, *After School Session*, is released.

June 14, 1958
"Johnny B. Goode" enters the Top Ten.

May 31, 1961
Chuck Berry's entertainment complex Berry Park opens in the St. Louis suburb of Wentzville, Missouri.

February 19, 1962
Berry begins serving a prison sentence for violating the Mann Act.

October 18, 1963
Berry is released from prison.

May 25, 1963
The Beach Boys score their first Top Ten hit with "Surfin' USA," Brian Wilson's re-working of Chuck Berry's "Sweet Little Sixteen."

June 1, 1966
Chuck Berry leaves Chess to sign with Mercury Records.

October 21, 1972
Chuck Berry achieves the biggest-selling single of Berry's career with the risqué novelty song "My Ding-A-Ling."

March 1, 1978
American Hot Wax, a film biography of seminal rock and roll disc jockey Alan Freed, with Berry playing himself, premiers.

June 1, 1979
Chuck Berry performs at the White House at the request of President Jimmy Carter, a month before he begins serving a four-month sentence for income tax evasion. While in prison, Berry begins writing his autobiography.

February 26, 1985
Chuck Berry receives a Lifetime Achievement Award at the Twenty-Seventh Annual Grammy Awards. He is cited as "one of the most influential and creative innovators in the history of American popular music."

January 23, 1986
Chuck Berry becomes one of the new Rock and Roll Hall of Fame's first set of induct-ees. He's inducted by Keith Richards, who in his induction speech confesses to bor-rowing every guitar lick Berry's ever played.

October 8, 1987
Hail! Hail! Rock 'n' Roll, director Taylor Hackford's documentary tribute to Berry, with Keith Richards as musical director, makes its theatrical debut.

November 2000
Chuck Berry receives a prestigious Kennedy Center Honor in Washington, DC.

SELECTED DISCOGRAPHY

The Great Twenty-Eight, 1982
His Best, Vol. 1, 1997
His Best, Vol. 2, 1997
Anthology, 2000
Gold, 2002
The Definitive Collection, 2006

NOTES

1. Peter Guralnick, *Feel Like Going Home: Portraits in Blues and Rock 'n' Roll* (New York: Vintage, 1981), p. 234.
2. Ibid.
3. The Editors of Rolling Stone, *The Rolling Stone Interviews 1967–1980* (New York: St. Martin's Press/Rolling Stone Press, 1989), p. 229.
4. Bruce Pegg, *Brown Eyed Handsome Man: The Life and Hard Times of Chuck Berry* (New York: Routledge, 2002), p. 171.
5. www.robertchristgau.com/xg/bk-aow/berry.php.
6. "The Dark Side of Chuck Berry." Available online at www.cnn.com/2006/SHOWBIZ/Movies/06/22/leisure.berry.reut/index.html.
7. Ibid.
8. "Keith Remembers Johnnie." Available online at www.rollingstone.com/news/story/7250961/keith_remembers_johnnie.

FURTHER READING

Berry, Chuck. *The Autobiography*. New York: Fireside, 1988.
The Editors of Rolling Stone, *The Rolling Stone Interviews 1967–1980*. New York: St. Martin's Press/Rolling Stone Press, 1989.
Groia, Philip. *They All Sang on the Corner: A Second Look at New York City's Rhythm and Blues Vocal Groups*. West Hempstead, NY: Philly Dee Enterprises, 1983.
Guralnick, Peter. *Feel Like Going Home: Portraits in Blues and Rock 'n' Roll*. New York: Vintage, 1981.
Pegg, Bruce. *Brown Eyed Handsome Man: The Life and Hard Times of Chuck Berry*. New York: Routledge, 2002.

Courtesy of Photofest.

Buddy Holly

Scott Schinder

THE ROCK AND ROLL STAR NEXT DOOR

Buddy Holly was one of the key innovators of rock and roll's early years, and a crucial link between the music's 1950s roots and the more electric direction that it would take in the Beatles era. In his brief but incredibly productive career, the Texas-bred singer/songwriter/guitarist/producer created a remarkable body of work that permanently altered the face of contemporary music, leaving behind the tantalizing potential of what else he might have achieved if he had not died in at the age of twenty-two.

Although he attained international stardom and scored a string of memorable hits, Holly's impact far outweighs his record sales. What makes his achievements all the more remarkable is that they took place during a mere eighteen months, between his first hit "That'll Be the Day" in the summer of 1957 and his death in a plane crash on February 3, 1959.

A distinctive songwriter, compelling performer, inventive stylist, and innovative sonic architect, Holly was instrumental in elevating rock and roll into an art form and a vehicle for personal expression, broadening rock's stylistic range and compositional sophistication without diluting its raw energy. A versatile craftsman who was equally adept at raucous rockers and gentle ballads, Holly's output balanced youthful exuberance, yearning romanticism, and playful humor. His sound provided a bridge between the raw rockabilly of Elvis's Sun Records sides and the more sophisticated styles that would follow.

Holly was also a strong-willed self-starter who possessed a clear musical vision, as well as the technical skills to create his music on his own terms. In his short life, he conquered the recording medium and achieved a remarkably swift musical evolution. He was also the first rocker to use his commercial clout to gain artistic control over his musical output—and the first with the talent to take advantage of that freedom.

If Elvis Presley personified rock and roll's sexuality, Little Richard embodied the music's unpredictable edge, and Chuck Berry was the bard who chronicled the rituals of teen culture, Holly's innovations were more musical in nature. With his band the Crickets, he pioneered the self-contained electric guitar/bass/drums format that was adopted by avowed Holly acolytes the Beatles and continued by the countless British and American combos who followed in their wake, and which remains rock's standard instrumental lineup to this day. Holly's guitar style, meanwhile, would provide the blueprint for the guitarists of the British Invasion and subsequent generations of pop rockers.

While Berry beat him to the honor of being the first major rock artist to write most of his own material and double as his own lead guitarist, Holly was the first to take charge of every stage of the creative process. In addition to his singing, songwriting, and guitar work, Holly's trailblazing experiments with such innovations as echo, overdubbing, and vocal double-tracking introduced enticing new sounds to the genre's limited early palette. He was also the first major rock and roll performer to move behind the scenes to produce and promote other artists, activities that he was actively pursuing prior to his death.

Where Elvis and most of his acolytes carried an enticing aura of danger, the lanky, bespectacled Holly wasn't a delinquent, an outlaw, or a sex symbol. His persona was as earthy and accessible as Elvis's was exotic and untouchable, giving Holly an unpretentious everyman quality that was rare among 1950s rockers.

Those who knew Buddy describe him as polite, unassuming, and down-to-earth, yet incredibly focused and driven to succeed, motivated to embrace new musical challenges and pursue his abiding fascination with the recording process.

Holly's rise to prominence coincided with several of rock's original stars temporarily exiting the spotlight. In late 1957, Little Richard abandoned popular music for the ministry, and the early months of 1958 saw Elvis enter the army and Jerry Lee Lewis all but blacklisted after marrying his thirteen-year-old second cousin. The resulting void offered opportunities for new artists, and Holly was in the vanguard of a second wave of rock and rollers that kept the music vital in the late 1950s.

Buddy was born Charles Hardin Holley (he would drop the "e" after it was misspelled that way on an early contract) on September 7, 1936, in Lubbock, Texas, the youngest of Ella and Lawrence Odell Holley's four children. L.O., as Buddy's dad was known, had worked as a carpenter, cook, tailor, and boxing-ring timekeeper to support his family amid the privations of the Great Depression, and had moved with Ella to Lubbock from Vernon, Texas, in 1925, in search of the work which the town's cotton economy and its new Texas Technological College might provide.

Lubbock was a conservative city in the vast expanses of west Texas flatlands, whose preponderance of devout Christian sects had earned the town its nickname of the "City of Churches." At the time, it was illegal to serve liquor in Lubbock's public places (it would remain so until 1972), although a string of liquor stores and honky-tonks awaited just outside of town. When Buddy was born, Lubbock had only been a city for forty-five years. Its population numbered just 21,000, but was rapidly growing with the influx of new additions who, like Buddy's parents, had migrated from smaller towns and farming communities.

By all accounts, Buddy (who received his nickname from his parents during early childhood) was raised in a stable, loving household, and a musical one. Even when times were hard, Ella and L.O. managed to pay for music lessons for their children. Buddy's big brothers Larry and Travis each played multiple instruments, and often teamed up to play country-and-western songs at social functions and talent contests. Sister Pat often sang duets with her mother at the living room piano. And the entire Holley family sang hymns when attending Sunday services at the local Baptist church.

At the age of five, Buddy, and his brothers, had won a $5 prize singing "Down the River of Memories," a song his mother had taught him, at a local talent show. Although he wouldn't take an active interest in music until his teens, he began taking piano lessons, at his mother's urging, at the age of eleven. He quickly showed a natural musical aptitude, but quit after nine months. He then took a few lessons in steel guitar before switching to acoustic guitar.

He learned his first guitar chords from his brother Travis, and took to the instrument immediately. He quickly mastered the guitar and was soon the best musician in the Holley family.

BUDDY AND BOB

By the time Buddy entered J.T. Hutchinson Junior High School in 1949, he was already proficient on guitar, banjo, and mandolin. He soon found a kindred spirit in fellow seventh-grader Bob Montgomery, an avid country-and-western music fan who sang and played guitar. The two became fast friends and musical partners, absorbing the repertoires of such country stars as Hank Williams, Bill Monroe, and Flatt and Scruggs, and studying the live performances they would hear on such regional radio broadcasts as Nashville's *Grand Ole Opry*, Shreveport's *Louisiana Hayride,* and Dallas's *Big D Jamboree.*

Montgomery would be a strong influence on Buddy's musical development, and his budding songwriting efforts would encourage Holly to develop his own writing skills. The pair's tastes would soon expand to encompass blues and R&B, thanks to the sounds they heard on the faraway radio stations whose powerful signals would drift in at night. Lubbock, like most of the South, was racially segregated, but Buddy, like many other white teenagers of the era, was drawn to the energy and passion of black music, and soon began to integrate it into his own work.

In addition to Montgomery, Holly played informally with various friends during junior high and high school, including guitarist Sonny Curtis, drummer Jerry "J.I." Allison, and bassists Larry Welborn and Don Guess. While many parents disapproved of the strange new music that their kids were listening to, Ella and L.O. appreciated black music and recognized its connection to their own favorite styles. They enthusiastically encouraged Buddy's musical pursuits, allowing him and his pals to conduct informal jam sessions at their home.

Billed as Buddy and Bob and advertising themselves as a "western and bop" combo, Holly and Montgomery initially patterned their act after such country duos as the Louvin Brothers and Flatt and Scruggs. They became a popular local attraction, playing country and bluegrass material at school and church events, teen parties, and local business events. They became a trio with the addition of Larry Welborn on standup bass, although they continued to be billed as Buddy and Bob. In September 1953, they won a half-hour weekly Sunday-afternoon slot on Lubbock's KDAV, which had just become the nation's first radio station to adopt a full-time country music format.

With KDAV disc jockey Hipockets Duncan serving as their manager, Buddy and Bob eventually graduated to more formal gigs at such venues as Lubbock's Cotton Club, as well as playing live remote broadcasts for KDAV advertisers.

Initially, Montgomery handled most of the lead vocals, with Buddy singing harmony, but the act's sound and repertoire expanded as Buddy began singing lead on more blues, R&B, and rockabilly numbers.

After graduating from high school in 1954, Holly and Montgomery took steps to pursue their musical careers more seriously. They undertook their first formal studio sessions, cutting a series of demo recordings of their compositions, and using their contacts with fellow musicians to try and get their demos into the hands of anyone who might be able to steer them toward a record deal.

The gradual cross-pollination of black and white musical styles that would form rock and roll's foundation was about to explode full-blown in the person of Elvis Presley, who would serve as a key inspiration in Holly's evolution from aspiring country musician to pioneering rocker. In early 1955, Buddy witnessed the young Presley's first Lubbock performance at a KDAV-sponsored show at the Cotton Club. The following day, Elvis played at the grand opening of a local Pontiac dealership, an event at which Buddy and Bob also appeared.

By all accounts, the experience of seeing Elvis on stage had a profound effect on Holly. "Presley just blew Buddy away," Sonny Curtis later recalled. "None of us had ever seen anything like Elvis, the way he could get the girls jumping up and down, and that definitely impressed Holly. But it was the music that really turned Buddy around. He loved Presley's rhythm. It wasn't country and it wasn't blues; it was somewhere in the middle and it suited just fine. After seeing Elvis, Buddy had only one way to go."[1]

At one point, Presley offered to get Buddy and Bob a spot on the popular Louisiana Hayride radio show, on which he was a regular. Holly, Montgomery, and Welborn impulsively drove all the way to Shreveport to take Elvis up on his offer, but Presley was out on tour that week and the young hopefuls were shown the door.

Buddy and Bob often served as opening act on local KDAV-sponsored shows by touring country acts, and they had the opportunity to appear on the bill the next time when Elvis performed in Lubbock in October 1955. By then, the group had expanded to a quartet with the addition of Jerry Allison on drums (Buddy had decided to add a drummer when Elvis did), and had begun moving toward the rocking style that Holly would later perfect.

The day before they opened for Elvis, the Holly/Montgomery combo performed at Lubbock's Fair Park Coliseum on a KDAV bill that included early rock and roll pioneers Bill Haley and the Comets. That night, Holly impressed Nashville agent Eddie Crandall, who also managed country star Marty Robbins. When Buddy and Bob opened a show for Robbins two weeks later, Crandall offered to shop their demos around Nashville for a recording contract.

In early 1956, Crandall secured a deal with the Nashville division of the prestigious Decca Records. But the company was interested in Holly as a solo act, rather than Buddy and Bob as a team. Despite Holly's initial misgivings,

Montgomery (who would subsequently have a long and successful career as a Nashville songwriter and record producer) urged his friend to take advantage of the opportunity. The contract for Buddy's concurrent publishing arrangement with Cedarwood Publishing mistakenly omitted the "e" from his surname, and the artist adopted that spelling thereafter.

Buddy would make a smooth transition to his new solo status, but his stint with Decca would be a frustrating one. Rock and roll had already exploded as a commercial and social force, and Paul Cohen, A&R director of Decca's Nashville division, had signed Holly with the hope that he could appeal to traditional country audiences as well as rock and roll–loving teens. But Cohen, and Decca's Nashville arm, had no practical experience with the new music, and little experience making rock and roll records.

The conflicting agendas of artist and label became apparent at Holly's first Decca session on January 26, 1956. While producer Owen Bradley was one of Nashville's foremost hit-makers, Buddy clashed with the respected studio veteran, who wouldn't him play guitar on the sessions and insisted on augmenting his new band—Sonny Curtis, Don Guess, and Jerry Allison, who was replaced by a session drummer—with country-oriented studio players.

The January Nashville session produced four songs. Two of those—"Blue Days, Black Nights," written for the occasion by KDAV announcer Ben Hall, and the Holly original "Love Me"—appeared as Buddy's first Decca single, released in April. The disc was an engaging enough effort, offering a promising glimpse of the artist's rockabilly-inflected style as well as his trademark vocal hiccup. But the collision between Holly's rock and roll vision and Bradley's relatively staid approach kept the tracks from realizing the transcendent exuberance that Buddy would subsequently achieve.

"Buddy couldn't fit into our formula any more than we could fit into his—he was unique, and he wasn't in a pattern. It was like two people speaking different languages," Bradley later reflected. "I think we gave him the best shot we knew how to give him, but it just wasn't the right combination, the chemistry wasn't right. It just wasn't meant to be. We didn't understand, and he didn't know how to tell us."[2]

Buddy's new status as a major-label recording artist was big news in his hometown, as an October 23 story in the *Lubbock Avalanche-Journal* noted. But the local hero would not achieve national prominence during his short stint with Decca. A second Nashville visit in July spawned another underwhelming single, "Modern Don Juan" and "You Are My One Desire," which Decca didn't issue until December. Like its predecessor, it didn't find much of an audience.

Although his recording career seemed stalled for much of 1956, Holly and his sidekicks spent a large part of the year gaining valuable stage experience, with touring slots on a couple of country package tours that traveled the Southwest, playing their own set as well as backing up such country stars as George Jones, Sonny James, Hank Thompson, and Faron Young.

In addition to polishing and sharpening his live act during this period, Holly also wrestled with the question of whether to wear his eyeglasses on stage. He'd briefly tried contact lenses, but gave up on that idea after losing a lens in mid-set. An attempt to perform sans eyewear proved impractical when he dropped a guitar pick and couldn't see well enough to find it. He also had his teeth capped, to disguise the hard-water stains that were common to those who'd grown up in the Southwest at the time.

No one was particularly surprised when Decca dropped Buddy Holly from its artist roster in January 1957. By then, Sonny Curtis and Don Guess had moved on to other pursuits, and Buddy and Jerry Allison spent a period playing locally as a drums-and-guitar duo. The two-man lineup allowed the pair to refine their rhythmic chemistry, as well as giving Buddy a chance to develop a distinctive, powerful lead/rhythm guitar style that would remain a touchstone for rock guitarists for generations to come.

ROCKIN' IN CLOVIS

Although his Decca tenure had been a disappointment, Holly's drive and determination were undiminished, and he soon devised a new route to revive his profile as a recording artist. The key to his future would be his discovery of independent producer Norman Petty's studio in Clovis, New Mexico. The studio was close to the Texas border, but light years away from the conservatism of the Nashville establishment.

Although he was only eight years older than Buddy, Norman Petty possessed a wealth of recording experience that would, for a while anyway, make him a useful mentor and father figure to the fledgling artist. Petty was no rock and roller, but he was an adept technician with an ear for what sounded good on the radio. His own musical tastes were reflected in the middle-of-the-road cocktail jazz that he and his wife Vi played as members of the Norman Petty Trio. The group had scored a minor 1954 hit with a version of Duke Ellington's "Mood Indigo," and Norman had used the proceeds to finance his studio.

As a musician, Petty had long been frustrated by the hourly rates routinely charged by studios. So when he opened his own facility, he adopted the artist-friendly policy of charging by the song rather than by the hour, an approach that was far more conducive to creativity and experimentation than the time constraints imposed on conventional sessions.

On February 25, 1957, Holly went to Petty's studio to record a pair of tracks, the new original "I'm Looking for Someone to Love" and an energetic reworking of "That'll Be the Day," an unreleased Holly/Allison collaboration that had been cut during the Nashville sessions. Buddy had borrowed the title from a catchphrase used by John Wayne in the Western classic *The Searchers.*

For the occasion, Holly assembled a new lineup of Lubbock chums, with old cohorts Larry Welborn and Jerry Allison returning on bass and drums.

Sonny Curtis had moved on to gigs backing Slim Whitman and playing with the Philip Morris tobacco company's touring country show, so Buddy brought in rhythm guitarist Niki Sullivan. Sullivan's lanky, bespectacled looks would have allowed him to pass for Buddy's brother; in fact, the two subsequently learned that they were distant cousins. Joe B. Mauldin, at the time still attending high school in Lubbock, would soon replace Welborn on standup bass, and the new lineup would come to be known as the Crickets.

Petty signed on as the group's manager and took control of the publishing rights to Holly's songs. Buddy would soon come to regret surrendering control of his business affairs, and Petty's questionable business practices would become a source of considerable consternation for him. But at the time, Petty's involvement was a godsend. The producer's open-ended studio policy and willingness to let Holly make music on his own terms offered an invaluable opportunity for him to develop his sound and master the mechanics of the recording process. And Petty's New York music industry connections enabled him to find his client a new record deal.

Petty used his relationship with Murray Deutch, executive vice president of the powerful music publisher Peer-Southern, to bring "That'll Be the Day" and "I'm Looking for Someone to Love" to the attention of Bob Thiele, head of Coral Records. Ironically, Coral was a subsidiary of Decca, the company that had recently given Holly the boot. Thiele, whose varied background encompassed jazz, R&B, and big-band pop, recognized Holly's commercial potential, and persuaded his skeptical superiors at Decca to release the tracks as a single on the company's R&B/jazz imprint Brunswick.

Recognizing Holly's capacity for delivering hits in multiple styles, Thiele cannily signed him to two contracts, enabling him to record under his own name for Coral and under the Crickets banner for Brunswick. Although the Crickets would back Holly on both group and solo releases, ballads were more likely to be credited to Holly while songs released under the Crickets' name tended toward harder-edged rock and roll material.

The Crickets' group moniker may also have initially been an attempt to disguise Holly's involvement in the new version of "That'll Be the Day," since his old Decca deal prohibited him from rerecording songs he'd already cut for the label. But the dual identities would prove useful in multiple ways. For one thing, the situation allowed the prolific Holly to release a wealth of varied material in a short period of time. It also allowed him to advance his musical evolution at an accelerated pace, while giving him more stylistic leeway than he might be granted otherwise.

The "That'll Be the Day"/"I'm Looking for Someone to Love" single, credited to the Crickets, initially stirred up little attention when it was released in June 1957. But a DJ in Buffalo, New York picked up on "That'll Be the Day" and began playing it with unusual frequency (although he didn't lock himself in his studio and play the track nonstop, as the spirited but highly inaccurate 1978 biopic *The Buddy Holly Story* would claim). The song continued to break out in various regional markets, including Boston, Cleveland, and Philadelphia, even winning substantial airplay on several black R&B stations. By the end of September, it had hit number one on the *Billboard* sales chart. It also reached the Top Ten on the rhythm and blues charts, demonstrating how effectively Buddy had absorbed the influence of African American music.

"That'll Be the Day" had yet to take off in June, when Coral released "Words of Love" under Buddy's name. With a buoyant melody, swoony romantic lyrics, and Holly's distinctive double-tracked guitar and vocals, the song demonstrated that Buddy's skills were evolving at a rapid pace. It marked Holly's first use of overdubbing which, in the days before multi-track recording, was still an uncommon practice that had to be achieved through painstaking trial and error. Despite the sonic uniqueness of "Words of Love," a cover version by vocal quartet the Diamonds beat the Holly disc to the marketplace, stealing its chart thunder in the process.

One important factor in Holly's musical development was the fact that Thiele allowed him to continue to record at Petty's studio, far from the prying eyes and undue influence of record company personnel. This was highly unusual at a time when it was standard practice for artists to cut their records in their label's own studios, overseen by the company's A&R men, who usually chose the songs and musicians. Those formal sessions typically operated within the strict time restrictions imposed by record company policy and musicians union rules. The looser atmosphere in Clovis gave Holly the freedom to try new sounds and arrangement ideas, resulting in records that sounded like no one else's.

As he continued to experiment in the studio, Holly's songwriting gained in confidence and variety. Where in the past he had often relied on friends and bandmates to provide material, by now he was writing most of his own. That issue was blurred somewhat by Petty's tendency to add his name to the writing credits of Buddy's songs—including several that Holly is known to have recorded and/or performed before he'd even met Petty.

While Holly's dual recording deals allowed him to release a prodigious quantity of material within a short period, his chart successes made he and his band—billed for live dates as Buddy Holly and the Crickets—an in-demand live act. For most of its existence, the group maintained a punishing touring regimen that allowed them to hone an exciting live show that maintained the raw energy of their recordings.

The quartet's mettle was tested in August 1957, when they were booked for a package tour of East Coast theaters in African American neighborhoods, alongside such prominent R&B acts as Clyde McPhatter, the Cadillacs, and Lee Andrews and the Hearts. According to popular legend, they'd been hired by an unsuspecting agent who'd assumed "That'll Be the Day" to be the work of a black act. The tour culminated in a well-received week-long run at New York's Apollo Theater.

"That'll Be the Day" was still a hit in September when Coral released a second Buddy Holly "solo" effort, "Peggy Sue." The song was an exuberant embodiment of Holly's rock and roll vision, driven by his hiccupy vocal and infectious guitar line, Allison's rolling, echo-laden drumbeat, and a minimalist lyric that was as insistent as the music. It had originally been titled "Cindy Lou" after a former girlfriend, until Allison prevailed upon Buddy to retitle it in honor of his fiancée, Peggy Sue Gerron. The irresistible rocker became Holly's second smash single, climbing to the number three slot on the Billboard chart. Meanwhile, "Peggy Sue"'s B-side, "Everyday," revealed a knack for gentle, heart-tugging balladry that Holly would continue to refine.

Following their run at the Apollo, Buddy and the Crickets appeared on Dick Clark's American Bandstand in Philadelphia and spent a week and a half performing in Alan Freed's all-star show at New York's Paramount Theater, alongside Little Richard, the Del-Vikings, the Diamonds, Mickey and Sylvia, the Moonglows and Larry Williams. They then hit the road as part of the Biggest Show of Stars for 1957, spending much of the next three months touring the United States and Canada with a racially mixed all-star bill that included Paul Anka, Lavern Baker, Chuck Berry, Fats Domino, the Drifters, the Everly Brothers, and Frankie Lymon and the Teenagers.

The package tour allowed Buddy and the Crickets to interact with many of their musical heroes, but it also forced them to confront the viciousness of racism once the tour hit the deep South. Although they'd grown up in segregated Lubbock, they were unprepared for such indignities as the tour's black and white acts being prohibited from staying in the same hotels or eating in the same restaurants. At shows in Memphis, New Orleans, Birmingham, Chattanooga, and Columbus, Georgia, the Crickets and the tour's other white acts did not perform because local laws forbade black and white entertainers from appearing on the same stage.

One positive aspect of the Biggest Show of Stars tour was that it gave Holly the chance to bond with the Everly Brothers, who shared his country-and-western roots but were considerably more worldly. The impeccably groomed duo had a significant impact on Buddy's sense of style, instilling a taste for tailored suits. Phil Everly is also often credited for suggesting that he trade his half-frame glasses for the black horn-rim frames that would soon become his trademark. Holly and Bob Montgomery would later write and demo a pair of songs, "Wishing" and "Love's Made a Fool of You," for the Everlys, but the siblings' commitment to only record songs controlled by the powerful publisher Acuff-Rose prevented them from cutting those tailor-made tunes.

A second Crickets single on Brunswick appeared in October 1957, the playful, urgent "Oh Boy," by Petty-associated Texas rockabilly singer Sonny West and his songwriting partner Bill Tilghman. The B-side was the equally impressive Holly original "Not Fade Away," which infused a blunt Bo Diddley–style beat with an unmistakable Texas twang. "Oh Boy" occupied the Top Ten simultaneously with "Peggy Sue," giving Buddy and company their third Top Ten hit in January 1958.

CHIRPING UP THE CHARTS

November 1957 saw the release of the Crickets' first LP, *The "Chirping" Crickets*, consisting of the four Brunswick singles sides plus eight new tracks. At a time when rock and roll LPs routinely comprised one or two hits padded with inferior filler, it was a consistently dynamic set that ranks as one of rock's most compelling debut albums.

The "Chirping" Crickets is divided between Holly compositions and Petty-controlled outside material. Not surprisingly, the originals—including "Maybe Baby," which Brunswick would release as a single the following February—are the strongest, but Holly's performances and the Crickets' solid, subtly inventive rhythmic support assured that even the least impressive material was delivered with bracing conviction.

Buddy and the Crickets closed out 1957 with an appearance on Ed Sullivan's hugely influential TV variety show, at the time one of the few national prime-time outlets for rock and roll acts. The quartet played two songs, and Sullivan gave his official thumbs-up by informing his mom-and-pop audience that the visiting Texans were "nice boys."

Show Biz Kids: Rock in the Mainstream

By the time Buddy Holly died, rock and roll had been integrated into the mainstream of American show business. The changes that had occurred during the previous five years are evident from a look at the Top Five on the *Billboard* Pop chart for a single week in February 1959—the month of Holly's fatal plane crash.

The number one song was "Stagger Lee" by the black rhythm and blues singer Lloyd Price. He had recorded steadily since 1952, but this was his first release to reach the Pop chart. Price's early hits, beginning with the R&B number one "Lawdy Miss Clawdy," appeared on the independent Specialty label. Now he was signed to ABC-Paramount, the first major label created after the start of the rock and roll era.

Other songs and artists in the Top Five during this particular week included "Sixteen Candles" (number two) by a white doo-wop group, the Crests, and "Donna" (number three), by the Chicano rock and roller Ritchie Valens, who died in the same crash that killed Buddy Holly. "Smoke Gets in Your Eyes" (number four) was a new version of an old standard (written in 1933) by the Platters, the top-selling black vocal group of the 1950s. "All American Boy" by Bill Parsons (number five) was a drawling, guitar-driven story-song that parodied Elvis Presley's rise to stardom and subsequent induction into the army.

None of these songs had the raw excitement and untamed energy of "Lucille" by Little Richard or "Blue Suede Shoes" by Carl Perkins. But for teenage music fans, this Top Five was a marked improvement over that of February 1956. During that year, three out of five slots were held by non-rock artists: Italian American crooner Dean Martin ("Memories Are Made of This"), pop singer Kay Starr ("Rock and Roll Waltz," which didn't "rock" at all), and composer/arranger Nelson Riddle ("Lisbon Antigua").

Chart positions and record sales were not the only indicators of rock and roll's increasing (if often begrudging) acceptance by American show business and society at large. In addition to American Bandstand, the music was represented on television by various regional "dance party" shows hosted by local disc jockeys. Ed Sullivan's hugely popular CBS network variety show featured rock and roll artists as early as 1955, beginning with an appearance that year by Bo Diddley.

Andy Schwartz

Four days after the Ed Sullivan appearance, Niki Sullivan left the Crickets. Although the official reason was exhaustion from the intense pace of the band's roadwork, many believe that the guitarist's departure was precipitated by Sullivan's contentious relationship with Jerry Allison. The two musicians' animosity had reportedly erupted into fisticuffs while they were in New York during the Apollo Theater engagement, resulting in Allison getting a black eye that had to be airbrushed from the cover photo of *The "Chirping" Crickets*. The fact that the group was able to continue as a trio—a format that was unprecedented in rock and roll at the time—was a testament to Buddy's guitar skills.

Early 1958 saw Holly, Allison, and Mauldin embark on their first overseas excursion. In January, following a pair of shows in Honolulu, they undertook a week-long tour of Australia, on a bill that also included Jerry Lee Lewis and Paul Anka, along with Australian acts Johnny O'Keefe and Jodie Sands.

Buddy and the Crickets then spent most of March touring in England, where they played fifty shows in twenty-five days. Since the British touring circuit was not yet geared toward rock acts, the band found itself touring with a bill comprised of clean-cut mainstream pop performers.

Despite the inappropriate bill, the Crickets' visit was greeted as a major event by English fans. Buddy was even more popular in Britain than in the United States; indeed, his impact there rivaled that of Elvis Presley, who never performed in Britain. Additionally, Buddy and the Crickets were only the second major American rock act (after Bill Haley and the Comets) to tour Britain. The shows were greeted by unprecedented fan pandemonium, and would continue to resonate in the consciousness of the young fans that would soon mount the next decade's British Invasion. That impressionable audience included the future Beatles, who would choose their combo's entomological moniker in honor of the Crickets.

It was easy for U.K. listeners to relate the Crickets' country-rooted sound to that of skiffle, the do-it-yourself folk-country style that had seized the imagination of young Brits who'd yet to gain access to electric instruments. Unlike such bigger-than-life figures as Elvis, Eddie Cochran, and Gene Vincent, Buddy struck young British teens as a regular guy who'd succeeded on the strength of his musical abilities rather than looks or mystique. His relatively low-key image resonated strongly with British kids, who saw in Holly an idol whom they could actually emulate. His U.K. tour was also the first chance that British audiences had to see an electric guitar—specifically Fender Stratocaster, reputedly the first Strat to arrive in England—in action.

Pioneers of Rock and Roll Guitar

The electric guitar was not the predominant solo instrument of 1950s rock and roll. The tenor saxophone held that position into the early 1960s, with guitar and piano vying for second place. But with the decline of the big bands and their multiple soloists, the role of the guitar expanded within the new small group format.

T-Bone Walker, B.B. King, and Muddy Waters all used a call-and-response pattern between voice and electric guitar that became a cornerstone of urban blues. In country music, skilled Nashville pickers like Hank Garland and Grady Martin enlivened countless sessions with their fluid, jazzy fills and solos. The guitar work of Scotty Moore was crucial to the sound and success of Elvis Presley's early hits: "Mystery Train," "Heartbreak Hotel," "Jailhouse Rock," and many more.

Only a few of the lead 1950s rock and roll singers were accomplished instrumentalists. Buddy Holly and Eddie Cochran were two notable exceptions, while Link Wray, and Roy Buchanan were known for their singular six-string skills.

On "C'mon Everybody" and "Summertime Blues" (both 1958), Eddie Cochran (1938–60) overdubbed multiple acoustic and electric guitar parts to create a primitive but powerful "wall of sound" that was highly advanced for its time. He unleashed some intense guitar choruses on the instrumental "Eddie's Blues," and played inventive Chuck Berry–style solos on up-tempo rockers like "Pink Pegged Slacks." Singer, songwriter, producer, engineer, and guitarist: Eddie Cochran seemed to have it all together when he was killed in a one-car accident while on tour in England. Nearly twenty years later, former Sex Pistols bassist Sid Vicious paid tribute to his legend with a punk rock version of the Cochran classic "Somethin' Else."

Link Wray (1929–2005) couldn't match Eddie Cochran for versatility, popularity, or good looks. But his signature 1958 instrumental hit "Rumble" was a seminal influence on successive generations of rock and roll guitarists.

The North Carolina native (who was part Shawnee Indian) created the power chord—the essential building block of hard rock and heavy metal. He expanded rock's sonic palette with his pioneering use of fuzz, feedback, and distortion, achieving some of these effects simply by puncturing the speaker cone of his amplifier. Link Wray's raw, rocking style was exposed to a new generation of fans when his 1950s songs were used in such films as *Pulp Fiction* ("Ace of Spades") and *Twelve Monkeys* ("Comanche"). Wray was seventy-four years old, still touring, and still capable of igniting a firestorm of high-volume rock and roll when he was named one of the 100 Greatest Guitarists of All Time by *Rolling Stone* magazine in 2003.

Roy Buchanan (1939–88) was a "musician's musician." Long before the invention of the wah-wah pedal and the distortion booster, he was coaxing such effects from his Fender Telecaster with nothing more than six strings, ten fingers, and a medium-sized amplifier turned up to maximum volume. Buchanan could make his instrument sustain like a pedal steel guitar, or sound like two instruments (guitar *and* bass) played simultaneously. Throughout the 1960s, this dazzling innovator toiled for workman's wages in a series of anonymous, unrecorded groups on the bar circuit of suburban Washington, DC. In 1971, "The Best Unknown Guitarist in the World" (as he was billed) starred in a public television special that included scenes of Roy expertly playing both country music with Merle Haggard and rhythm and blues with Johnny Otis. This national exposure led to the release of Buchanan's self-titled major label debut album in the following year and launched a solo career that continued until his untimely death.

A. S.

Buddy Holly, the artist's first official solo LP, was released in the United States in February 1958. Beyond its dreamy cover photo (atypically depicting Buddy without his glasses), the disc featured such soon-to-be-classic rockers as "Peggy Sue," "Rave On," and "I'm Gonna Love You Too" along with an assortment of ballads, most notably the lilting "Listen to Me." The album also found Holly paying tribute to Elvis and Little Richard, respectively, with high-energy covers of "(You're So Square) Baby I Don't Care" and "Ready Teddy."

Upon their return from Britain, Holly and the Crickets continued their grueling tour schedule with a forty-four-day run on Alan Freed's Big Beat Show, kicking off with a show at the Brooklyn Paramount. Other artists on the tour included Chuck Berry, Screamin' Jay Hawkins, Jerry Lee Lewis, Frankie Lymon and the Teenagers, the Shirelles, and Larry Williams.

The fact that Coral and Brunswick were subsidiaries of Decca didn't keep the parent company from competing with Holly's new releases, exploiting its cache of Holly recordings cut the previous year. In April, the company released *That'll Be the Day,* an LP comprising the tracks Buddy had cut in Nashville with Owen Bradley. The collection's title confused purchasers, who expected to hear the familiar hit but got the inferior original instead.

On their way home from the Alan Freed tour, Buddy, J.I., and Joe B. stopped off in Dallas and purchased a trio of new motorcycles, riding them home to make a splashy return to Lubbock. The fact that they now felt comfortable making such an impulsive purchase hinted that their commercial successes and overseas adventures had enhanced their sense of independence—and that they might be outgrowing the paternalistic influence of Norman Petty, who still tightly controlled the group's finances.

For the band's session in Clovis in May, Buddy relinquished lead guitar duties to Tommy Allsup, a talented twenty-six-year-old from Oklahoma with a background in western swing. Allsup contributed a distinctive lead on the fluid rocker "It's So Easy" and added a Latin flourish to the sweet ballad "Heartbeat," impressing Holly enough to invite Allsup to join up and make the Crickets a quartet once again.

In June, Holly visited Manhattan and—without Norman Petty or the Crickets—recorded a pair of Bobby Darin numbers, the splashy, gospel-flavored "Early in the Morning" and the upbeat pop tune "Now We're One." The session, on which Holly was backed by an assortment of New York jazz/R&B players, was done at the behest of Coral Records, which wanted the tracks out as a single after Darin's version had to be withdrawn from release for contractual reasons. Although "Early in the Morning" rose no higher than number thirty-one on the *Billboard* singles chart, the session provided Holly with valuable experience working in a different musical mode—and confirmation that he could make compelling music outside of the creative comfort zone provided by his usual producer and band.

While visiting Peer-Southern's Manhattan office, Holly met Maria Elena Santiago, Murray Deutch's receptionist. He fell in love with the Puerto Rico–born beauty immediately, asking her out within thirty seconds of their first meeting and proposing marriage on their first date. Buddy and Maria (whose aunt, Provi Garcia, ran Peer's Latin division) were married on August 15, 1958, less than two months after their first meeting. Following a quiet wedding ceremony at Buddy's parents' house, they honeymooned in Acapulco with fellow newlyweds Jerry and Peggy Sue Allison.

A disapproving Norman Petty reportedly advised that the nuptials be kept quiet, to keep Buddy's female fans from being alienated by his new status—and, perhaps, to keep less enlightened observers from taking offense at his "mixed" marriage. It has also been theorized that Petty may have been threatened by Maria's knowledge of the music business, or by her access to Peer-Southern files that might reveal irregularities in Petty's handling of her husband's affairs.

Whatever his reasons, Petty's attitude toward Buddy's marriage—and his condescending attitude toward the new bride—couldn't have done much to bolster Holly's diminishing regard for his mentor. The father figure who'd once seemed so knowledgeable and well connected had begun to seem unimaginative and provincial, and his vague accounting practices caused Holly to question the trust he'd placed in Petty when he'd handed over control of his career. Holly, Allison, and Mauldin also resented the fact that, despite their status as international rock and roll stars, they still had to go to Petty any time they needed cash.

Despite his growing reservations, Holly continued to record at Petty's studio. In September, he brought renowned R&B saxophonist King Curtis in from New York to play on a pair of tracks, "Reminiscing" and "Come Back Baby." At the same session, Buddy produced a debut single, the classic Cajun tune "Jole Blon," for his old Lubbock friend Waylon Jennings. Jennings, a promising singer and sometime DJ on Lubbock's KLLL, would emerge more than a decade later as one of country music's most influential stars.

While he continued to make first-rate music, Holly's record sales had begun to slip somewhat. "It's So Easy" is now considered a classic, but it failed to make Billboard's Top 100 when it was released in September 1958. The breathy ballad "Heartbeat," co-written with old pal Bob Montgomery, stalled at number eighty-two when it was released under Buddy's name two months later.

In October 1958, Buddy and the Crickets embarked on another edition of the Biggest Show of Stars, this time sharing the bill with the Coasters, Bobby Darin, Dion and the Belmonts, and Clyde McPhatter.

If Holly was demoralized by his recent disappointing sales, he didn't show it, continuing to forge ahead with new challenges. He relocated to Manhattan, where he and Maria bought an apartment in Greenwich Village. Buddy enthusiastically embraced life in New York, enjoying being at the center of the entertainment business and the creative community—and relishing the opportunity to absorb new styles of music. He went to coffeehouses and enjoyed jazz gigs at the Village Vanguard, and developed an affinity for Latin music and flamenco guitar. He formulated plans to establish his own record label and build a recording studio in Lubbock, discussed the possibility of cutting gospel and Latin-style albums, and took steps to pursue his interest in writing and producing for other artists.

Rock and Roll in the Movies

Rock and roll also found a place in Hollywood movies. Most were of the "teen exploitation" variety, with flimsy plots, awkward acting, and low-budget production values. One of the first and best of the genre, *The Girl Can't Help It* (1956), was a funny, fast-paced film with memorable appearances by Fats Domino, Little Richard, Gene Vincent, and Eddie Cochran. *Don't Knock the Rock* (1957), on the other hand, was an excruciating hour of ersatz rock and roll according to a review in *Hollywood Rock: A Guide to Rock 'n' Roll in the Movies*.

In New York, Holly recorded a quartet of ballads—"True Love Ways," "Raining in My Heart," the Norman Petty composition "Moondreams," and the Paul Anka–penned "It Doesn't Matter Anymore"—featuring lush string arrangements. The direction of those songs—his last formal recordings—have led some fans to speculate that Buddy was abandoning rock and roll in favor of a sophisticated adult pop style. But it seems more reasonable to assume that this was a one-off experiment by an adventurous artist exploring his options.

In early November, Holly informed Norman Petty that he was severing their business and creative relationship. He had initially convinced Allison and Mauldin to join him in breaking away from Petty and joining him in New York. But Petty managed to persuade the drummer and bassist that their prospects would be brighter if they'd stay with him and continue to record as the Crickets.

Although he was hurt and disappointed by his bandmates' decision to stick with Petty, he gave them his blessing, granting them the rights to the Crickets name. More troubling was Petty's announcement that he would be withholding Buddy's record and publishing royalties until their disputes were resolved.

COLD WINTER

Although Holly was exhilarated by his new prospects and relieved to be free of the grind of touring, Petty's refusal to pay his royalties put him in a financial bind. With Maria pregnant, his immediate priority in late 1958 was providing support for his growing family. So when he was offered the chance to headline the Winter Dance Party, a three-week tour of Midwestern one-nighters, he reluctantly accepted.

With Allison and Mauldin back in Texas attempting to relaunch the Crickets, Holly assembled a new set of musicians to accompany him and double as backup for the Winter Dance Party's other acts. In addition to tapping latter-day Cricket Tommy Allsup to play guitar, he hired his protégé Waylon Jennings to play bass, despite Jennings's unfamiliarity with the instrument; Buddy bought his friend an electric bass and gave him two weeks to learn to play it.

The lineup was completed by another Texan, drummer Carl Bunch. Despite his agreement to allow Allison and Mauldin to keep the Crickets name, Buddy's new touring band was billed as the Crickets.

Unlike some of the epic, star-studded package tours he'd done previously, the Winter Dance Party was a rather modest affair. Aside from Buddy, the bill featured three up-and-coming acts. Along with soulful Bronx doo-wop foursome Dion and the Belmonts, the show featured Ritchie Valens (née Valenzuela), a seventeen-year-old singer/guitarist from Pacoima, California, who'd become the first Hispanic rocker to hit the charts with his then-current Top Ten single "Donna," and the Big Bopper, aka J.P. Richardson, a garrulous songwriter and disc jockey from Beaumont, Texas, who'd recently scored a million-selling novelty smash with "Chantilly Lace." Rounding out the bill was now-forgotten crooner Frankie Sardo, who opened the shows with renditions of other artists' hits.

Even by the primitive standards of late 1950s touring, conditions on the Winter Dance Party were spartan. Rather than the big-city theaters that were the destinations of larger tours, most of the shows were booked into ballrooms in smaller, out-of-the-way markets, where the crowds consisted of music-starved teens—who rarely got the chance to see big-name rockers on stage. The performers traversed the frozen expanses of the upper Midwest in a series of cramped, worn-down, poorly heated school buses, which regularly broke down and had to be replaced by equally rickety vehicles.

To make matters worse, that winter was one of the most brutal in recent memory, with bitterly cold temperatures that sometimes dipped to −30°F, causing dangerously icy road conditions. It didn't help that the itinerary's convoluted routing forced the tour party to travel as far as 500 miles between shows. The schedule was so tight that the performers usually had to sleep on the bus as it traveled to the next night's venue, with little time for such niceties as laundry or showers.

By February 2, when the bedraggled troupe arrived at the Surf Ballroom in Clear Lake, Iowa, to perform their eleventh show in as many days, the tour had already been through six different buses. By then, drummer Carl Bunch had had to leave the tour after being hospitalized for frostbite, forcing Holly and Belmonts member Carlo Mastrangelo to take over drumming duties.

Following the Surf Ballroom performance, Buddy sought a respite from the miserable traveling conditions by chartering a private plane to carry himself and his sidemen to Fargo, North Dakota, the closest airport to the next tour date in Moorhead, Minnesota. The post-show flight would give them enough time to do their laundry and get a decent night's sleep in actual hotel room beds. At the last minute, the Big Bopper, who'd been suffering from the flu, talked Jennings into giving up his seat, while Allsup surrendered his seat to Valens after losing a coin toss.

In the snowy early morning hours of February 3, 1959, shortly after taking off from the airport in nearby Mason City, the four-seat Beechcraft Bonanza aircraft carrying Holly, Valens, and Richardson crashed into a soybean field. All three passengers were killed instantly, as was twenty-one-year-old pilot Roger Peterson.

In the day's news coverage, the event was overshadowed by another, deadlier plane crash, which took sixty-five lives at New York's LaGuardia Airport. But the emotional impact of the Clear Lake crash registered immediately with young people on both sides of the Atlantic. Not only was it many teenagers' first exposure to fatal tragedy, it was also the first time that the young rock and roll genre had been forced to confront the specter of mortality. No major rocker had ever died before, so for three of them to perish in such an abrupt and random manner was particularly shocking. In the ensuing decades, the crash would retain a potent mythological resonance, symbolizing the music's loss of innocence and offering a premonition of the turbulence and loss that would dominate the next decade.

Buddy Holly's funeral took place in Lubbock on the following Saturday. His pallbearers were six of his closest musical associates: Jerry Allison, Joe B. Mauldin, Niki Sullivan, Sonny Curtis, Bob Montgomery, and Phil Everly. An estimated 1,800 mourners packed the Tabernacle Baptist Church for the memorial service, which was performed by the same pastor who'd presided over Buddy and Maria Elena's wedding ceremony just five months earlier. Although the pregnant widow flew in for the funeral, she couldn't bring herself to attend the service or visit her late husband's grave; she had a miscarriage soon after.

The deaths of Holly, Valens, and Richardson cast a veil of darkness over the rock and roll world, and the pall wouldn't completely lift until the Beatles' arrival on the scene a few years later. The three fallen heroes were widely eulogized in song; perhaps the most poignant tribute was "Three Stars," written by Bakersfield, California, disc jockey Tommy Dee and recorded by Eddie Cochran, among others.

Two years after the crash, eccentric but innovative English producer Joe Meek and singer Mike Berry delivered one of the better tribute discs with "Tribute to Buddy Holly" which borrowed its subject's musical style to offer a melancholy musical epitaph. Meek would later claim to be in contact with Buddy, and that the deceased icon was giving him songwriting help from the spirit world; in 1967, Meek committed a violent murder/suicide on the anniversary of Holly's death. Somewhat less obsessive were Manchester-based admirers Allan Clarke, Tony Hicks, and Graham Nash, who were so affected by Buddy's work that they named their popular British Invasion combo the Hollies.

Meanwhile, Holly's record company, with Norman Petty's help, would continue exploiting the departed star's recorded legacy for years to come. Petty cobbled together a motley series of "new" Holly LPs from an assortment of outtakes, demos, and early tapes of varying quality, often with awkward new instrumental overdubs provided by New Mexico combo the Fireballs, who made several notable Petty-produced records of their own.

Many of the posthumous Holly releases were top sellers in Britain, where Buddy's profile remained high. It was a different story in America, though. By the end of the 1960s, Holly had been largely forgotten in his home country, where none of his essential releases remained in print. But his Stateside reputation would undergo a major resurgence in the 1970s. By the end of that decade, Holly had become the first rock and roll artist to be honored with a major U.S. box set retrospective.

One early factor in the revival of interest in Holly was Don McLean's 1971 hit "American Pie," which used "the day the music died" as the departure point for a metaphorical journey through the musical, social, and political changes of the 1960s.

In 1975, longtime Holly fanatic Paul McCartney's company MPL Communications purchased Buddy's publishing catalog from a nearly bankrupt Norman Petty. The deal initially did little to benefit Holly's survivors and collaborators, who had long ago accepted meager cash settlements from Petty rather than attempt to sort out his tangled financial records. But McCartney's patronage proved to be a boon, for Buddy's posthumous prestige as well as the income of his heirs, bandmates, and co-writers, since McCartney's savvy exploitation of the Holly songbook (including an annual week of Holly tributes in London) did much to restore the artist and his songs to prominence.

Also helping to make Holly a household name in America again was 1978's *The Buddy Holly Story*. The film was wildly inaccurate, romanticizing and simplifying Holly's life to the point where Buddy's ultra-supportive parents were reduced to disapproving caricatures, as well as replacing the real Crickets with fictional characters, and leaving Norman Petty out entirely. Despite the movie's blatant disregard for historical accuracy, Gary Busey's impassioned, Academy Award–nominated performance captured Holly's vibrant essence, establishing the movie's subject as a living, breathing, rocking presence rather than an arcane oldies act.

The city fathers of Lubbock eventually awakened to the commercial benefits of promoting its status as Holly's hometown. In the 1980s, Lubbock unveiled a bronze statue of Buddy, followed by a park bearing his name, a memorial concert celebrating the fiftieth anniversary of his birth, and a Walk of Fame honoring notable Lubbock-born musicians. Lubbock's Texas Tech University now houses one of the world's largest collections of Holly memorabilia.

When the Rock and Roll Hall of Fame was established in 1986, Buddy Holly was among the first group of inductees. A 1990 auction of Holly memorabilia in New York raised over $703,000, with Gary Busey paying $242,000 for one of his guitars and the Hard Rock Café purchasing a pair of his eyeglasses for $45,100. The 1990s saw the debut of Buddy, a successful stage musical documenting his career; the show ran for seven years in London's West End. And alt rockers Weezer invoked Holly's name as the title of their 1994 debut hit.

In Buddy's absence, the Crickets, in various configurations, have maintained a remarkably durable recording and performing career. As of 2007, the band continues to keep the Holly songbook alive on stage, with Allison, Mauldin, and Sonny Curtis still anchoring the lineup.

The crash in Clear Lake ended the life and career of an artist whose musical potential, perhaps more than any other rock and roll performer of his era, seemed limitless. There's no telling what Buddy Holly might have achieved if he'd lived. Whatever direction he would have taken, it's hard to imagine that the clear-eyed, level-headed Holly wouldn't have had a long and productive career.

Buddy Holly's musical legacy retains the same youthful freshness and unpretentious energy that first engaged listeners in the late 1950s. His songs continue to be covered by a wide variety of artists, while his musical and technical innovations have become deeply woven into the fabric of contemporary music.

TIMELINE

September 1, 1953
Buddy Holly and Bob Montgomery audition for Lubbock radio station KDAV, and are given a half-hour Sunday afternoon show, on which they perform country and bluegrass material.

October 14, 1955
Buddy and Bob, with Larry Welborn on bass, open for Bill Haley and the Comets in Lubbock and are seen by Nashville agent Eddie Crandall.

October 15, 1955
Buddy, Bob, and Larry open for Elvis Presley in Lubbock.

January 26, 1956
Buddy Holly's first official recording session, with veteran country producer Owen Bradley at Decca Records' Nashville studios. The session yields four tracks, including "Blue Days, Black Nights" and "Love Me," which will be released by Decca as Holly's Decca debut single.

February 25, 1957
Buddy Holly and the Crickets record "That'll Be the Day" at Norman Petty's studio in Clovis, New Mexico. The single, credited to the Crickets, will become the Holly's first single on the Brunswick label.

September 1, 1957
The band begins its first major tour with a four-night run at the Brooklyn Paramount Theater, launching the three-month Biggest Show of Stars tour.

September 23, 1957
"That'll Be the Day" becomes the number one single on *Billboard's* pop chart.

November 27, 1957
The Crickets' first LP, *The "Chirping" Crickets*, is released by Brunswick Records.

January 25, 1958
"Oh Boy!" becomes Buddy Holly's third Top Ten hit.

January 30, 1958
Buddy Holly and the Crickets begin a seven-date tour of Australia.

February 20, 1958
Buddy's first official solo album, *Buddy Holly*, is released by Coral Records.

March 1, 1958
Buddy Holly and the Crickets begin a month-long tour of England.

August 15, 1958
Buddy Holly marries Maria Elena Santiago in a quiet ceremony at Buddy's parents' house in Lubbock.

January 23, 1959
The Winter Dance Party, headlined by Buddy minus the Crickets, kicks off with a performance at the Million Dollar Ballroom in Milwaukee, Wisconsin.

February 3, 1959
After performing at the Surf Ballroom in Clear Lake, Iowa, Holly charters a small private plane to get him to the tour's next show in Fargo, North Dakota. The plane crashes shortly after takeoff, killing Holly and tourmates Ritchie Valens and the Big Bopper, as well as pilot Roger Peterson.

March 9, 1959
"It Doesn't Matter Anymore," recorded at Holly's last studio session, becomes a posthumous hit.

July 1, 1976
Paul McCartney purchases Buddy's entire publishing catalog from Norman Petty. Two months later, McCartney will stage the first annual Buddy Holly Week in London, celebrating the artist's music.

May 18, 1978
The Buddy Holly Story, a fictionalized film biography starring Gary Busey as Holly, is released. The film will become a hit, with Busey's performance getting an Academy Award nomination.

SELECTED DISCOGRAPHY

The "Chirping" Crickets, 1957
Buddy Holly, 1958
Buddy Holly: Gold, 2006

NOTES

1. http://www.buddyhollycenter.org/Buddy%20Holly%20Gallery/buddy_bio.html
2. Goldrosen, John and John Beecher. *Remembering Buddy*. New York: Penguin, 1986, p. 36.

FURTHER READING

Goldrosen, John. *Buddy Holly: His Life and Music*. Bowling Green, OH: Popular Press, 1975.

Goldrosen, John and John Beecher. *Remembering Buddy*. New York: Penguin, 1986.

Norman, Philip. *Rave On: The Biography of Buddy Holly*. New York: Fireside, 1996.

Tobler, John. *The Buddy Holly Story*. New York: Beaufort, 1979.

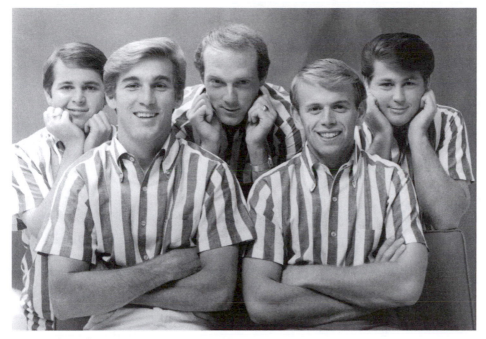

Courtesy of Photofest.

The Beach Boys

Scott Schinder

AN AMERICAN FAMILY

The Beach Boys' long and turbulent saga is a uniquely American epic, encompassing triumph and tragedy, innovation and excess, massive success and crushing disappointment, the highest highs of artistic transcendence and the lowest lows of showbiz mediocrity—as well as family dysfunction, financial chicanery, mental illness, drug abuse, unfulfilled potential, and unexpected redemption.

The Beach Boys' story also involves some of the most innovative and original pop music ever created, thanks largely to the prodigious talents of the band's troubled but brilliant leader Brian Wilson. Regarded by many as the greatest American composer of the rock era, Wilson was the Beach Boys' sonic architect and main creative force, using the group as the vibrant vehicle for his innovative songwriting and arrangements, as well as his intricate, groundbreaking approach to vocal harmony.

To the generation that came of age in the first half of the 1960s, the Beach Boys will forever be identified with a bucolic vision of an innocent, carefree pre-Beatles America. The quintet's lengthy string of early hits mythologized middle-class teenage life and the mythical ideal of California, extolling the virtues of hot rods, surfing, and youthful romance, with an undercurrent of melancholy romanticism that would assert itself more strongly in the group's later work.

For much of the early 1960s, the Beach Boys were America's best-selling rock and roll act. When the British Invasion took hold of the American teen consciousness in 1964, they posed the only serious threat to the Fab Four's chart supremacy. As the decade progressed and rock's creative vistas expanded, Brian Wilson's musical achievements advanced rapidly, sealing his position as one of the period's preeminent musical visionaries. His knack for creating unique sounds and his mastery of the recording studio yielded such groundbreaking classics as the 1966 album *Pet Sounds* and the epic single "Good Vibrations," which were as advanced—sonically, compositionally, and harmonically—as anything being made in popular music at the time.

But those musical highs soon gave way to darker times, as Wilson's refusal to stick with the group's tried-and-true formula led to his ambitious magnum opus, *Smile*, being shelved. While *Smile* became rock's most famous unreleased album, Brian Wilson became rock's best-known casualty. His descent into mental illness and substance abuse led him to withdraw from his band and from the world—a retreat from which many assumed he would never return.

The Beach Boys spent much of the 1970s and 1980s torn between its dual identities as contemporary recording group and pandering oldies act. Their story belatedly gained closure of a sort, when a resurgent Brian Wilson returned from decades in the shadows to launch an unprecedented return to live performance, and to revive his lost masterpiece *Smile* on record and on stage.

By that point, the music of Brian Wilson and the Beach Boys had been embraced by a new generation of listeners raised on alternative rock, for whom the music's originality and emotional resonance transcended mere nostalgia.

CATCH A WAVE

The Beach Boys' story began in the Los Angeles suburb of Hawthorne, California, in the home of Murry and Audree Wilson. Murry worked in the heavy machinery industry, but was also a part-time songwriter who'd had a brief brush with success when his novelty tune "Two-Step Side-Step" was performed by bandleader Lawrence Welk on his national radio show.

Murry could be stern, demanding, and, by most accounts, emotionally and physically abusive. But he also passed his musical interests on to his sons Brian, Dennis, and Carl, indulging them with lessons and instruments, and gathering the family to harmonize around the living-room piano.

The Wilson siblings were often joined in song by their cousin Mike Love, the son of Murry's sister Glee. The Love family was also musically inclined, and often joined the Wilsons for parties that included family musical performances.

Despite being deaf in his right ear (a disability that he would later attribute to a childhood beating by Murry), eldest brother Brian demonstrated a prodigious musical ability early on. He became proficient on multiple instruments, while revealing a beautiful, remarkably flexible singing voice and an uncanny ear for vocal harmony. He was particularly fascinated by the evocative orchestral pop of George Gershwin's "Rhapsody in Blue," and by the close harmonies of the Four Freshmen, who would provide the blueprint for the Beach Boys' intricate vocal blend.

Baby brother Carl also emerged as both a skillful guitarist and an excellent singer, with a beautiful tenor voice that would become an essential element of the Beach Boys' sound. He also developed a knack for acting as a peacemaker when Murry lashed out at his sons. These abilities would prove invaluable in the Beach Boys' more turbulent periods.

Although he would eventually develop into a musical talent in his own right, Dennis Wilson's teenage years were defined mainly by his rebellious behavior and his contentious relationship with his father. Although Dennis was too occupied with other pursuits to focus much on music, he was, largely at Audree's urging, included in his brothers' musical pursuits, channeling his natural aggression into his role as the group's drummer.

Although his rudimentary saxophone skills left something to be desired, Mike Love's cocky, extroverted personality made him a natural frontman. The group became a quintet with the addition of Brian's high-school football teammate Al Jardine, who was a capable rhythm guitarist and harmony singer.

Although the five teenagers had grown up near the ocean, the only actual surfer in the bunch was Dennis, who had embraced the popular sport and the culture that had sprung up around it in southern California. The surfing lifestyle had already inspired the beginnings of a musical genre, personified by guitarist Dick Dale, an avid surfer whose live performances at the Balboa Ballroom were popular among surfers. Dale's propulsive instrumental numbers replicated the physical sensations of the surfing experience, combing staccato picking with a reverb-heavy "wet" guitar sound.

It was Dennis who suggested that Brian try writing a song about surfing. With Dennis offering some helpful examples of surfer jargon, Brian and Mike came up with "Surfin'," a catchy, if primitive, ode to the sport.

Murry had put Brian in contact with Hite and Dorinda Morgan, who operated a small music publishing company that had handled some of Murry's compositions. The Morgans also ran a small studio in Hollywood, and Brian approached them about doing some recording there.

On Labor Day weekend 1961, Murry and Audree took a short vacation to Mexico City, leaving their sons with $200 in emergency cash. They used most of the fund to rent musical equipment from Wallichs' Music City in Hollywood, to allow the quintet to polish their performance of "Surfin'" for a prospective audition for the Morgans. Murry was furious when he found out, but softened after he heard the song.

On September 15, 1961—just a week after *Life* magazine had run a seven-page photo feature on the California surfing craze—the band cut an early take of "Surfin'" with the Morgans. On October 3, they recorded a more professional version at World Pacific Studios in Hollywood.

By then, the fledgling combo was calling itself the Pendletones, in honor of the plaid woolen Pendleton shirts that were popular among surfers. It wasn't until "Surfin'" was released as a single in December 1961, on the tiny local label Candix, that the group learned that Hite Morgan had rechristened them the Beach Boys. Another alteration was Murry's decision to speed up the master tape slightly, on the assumption that that would give the performance a more youthful sound. It wouldn't be the last time he'd use that gimmick—much to Brian's annoyance.

After making their public performing debut playing three songs at a Ritchie Valens tribute concert at the Long Beach Municipal Auditorium on December 31, the Beach Boys—with Mike as frontman, Brian on bass, Carl and Al on guitars, and Dennis on drums—embarked on a series of live appearances to promote "Surfin'." Authority figure Murry Wilson was often in tow, the better to put the kibosh on the sort of activities toward which five young men away from home might naturally gravitate.

Although it was primitive in comparison with the records that the group would soon be making, "Surfin'" became a regional hit on the West Coast, and sold well enough to reach number seventy-five on *Billboard*'s national singles chart. The single was such a success that it soon bankrupted Candix Records, which had shipped so many still-unpaid orders that they couldn't afford to meet the demand for more copies.

Murry Wilson immediately appointed himself the Beach Boys' manager. Although his abrasive personality would eventually alienate outsiders as well as his own clients, at this stage Murry was largely a positive influence, instilling focus and discipline in the inexperienced combo.

Murry's biggest early achievement was winning the band a deal with Capitol Records, home of Brian's beloved Four Freshmen. Capitol A&R executive Nik Venet wasn't charmed by Murry's blustery sales pitch. But he was excited by the band's demos of a pair of new tunes: Brian and Mike's "Surfin' Safari," the surfer slang–filled sequel to their first hit; and "409," an insistent hot-rod anthem which Brian had written with Gary Usher, the nephew of a neighbor of the Wilson family.

Usher was Brian's first collaborator outside of the Beach Boys family, but he would soon run afoul of Murry's jealous nature and find himself frozen out of the band's inner circle. Following his exile, Usher would become a key figure in the surf music scene. One of his early successes was as leader and producer of the studio group the Hondells, which scored a Top Ten hit in 1964 with Brian's "Little Honda."

"409" was the first in a long series of car-themed Beach Boys songs that reflected the prominence of automobiles in the identity of American male teenagers of the era. Usher would be one of many songwriting collaborators for Brian, who had already mastered composing and arranging but generally preferred to brainstorm lyrics with a co-writer.

By then, the Beach Boys had experienced their first personnel change. Al Jardine, who had been instrumental in the band's formation, exited in February, in order to study dentistry in Michigan. To take his place, the band drafted David Marks, a fifteen-year-old neighborhood pal who lived across the street from the Wilsons. Marks was a competent rhythm guitarist, but would not be permitted to sing on the band's recording dates.

"Surfin' Safari" and "409" were paired as the Beach Boys' first Capitol single in June 1962, and showed the band to be far more accomplished than the neophytes who'd cut "Surfin'" a few months earlier. Capitol initially focused on promoting "409," figuring that surf-themed material would have limited appeal outside of California. But "Surfin' Safari" broke out on radio stations in such unlikely locations as New York and landlocked Phoenix, launching the song's rise to number fourteen on the national charts, while its flipside stalled at seventy-six.

"Surfin'," "Surfin' Safari," and "409" all appeared on the first Beach Boys LP, *Surfin' Safari*, released by Capitol in October. Although still primitive in comparison to what the group would soon achieve on a regular basis, the album was spirited and energetic, and an impressive effort at a time when rock and roll LPs routinely consisted of one or two hits plus ten tracks of throwaway filler.

While *Surfin' Safari* contained little evidence of the compositional genius that Brian Wilson would soon reveal, the fact that it was comprised largely of originals (written by Brian with Gary Usher and/or Mike Love) instantly distinguished it from most rock albums of the period. Although Nik Venet was credited as producer, Brian was already largely calling the shots on the Beach Boys' recording sessions, and in charge of coaching his inexperienced bandmates through their performances. Although he lacked studio experience, Brian gained an able collaborator in recording engineer Chuck Britz, a seasoned studio pro whom he'd met while the band was cutting demos at Western Recorders in Hollywood.

Britz became the Beach Boys' in-house engineer, a position that he would hold through 1967. His technical expertise would be a major influence in Brian learning to translate the sounds that he heard in his head onto tape. In the

1960s, when record companies still routinely released albums in both stereo and mono versions, Britz would also be in charge of mixing the stereo versions of the band's recordings, while Brian—whose partial deafness contributed to his natural affinity for mono—handled the mono mixes.

Britz also served as a useful buffer between Brian and his father, who was often an overbearing, bullying presence in the studio. Later, the band would attempt to placate Murry by giving him a fake studio console that wasn't actually connected to anything, allowing him to turn the dials to his heart's content while Brian and Britz got on with the actual business of making Beach Boys records.

Brian and the Beach Boys made a remarkable amount of musical and commercial progress between 1963 and 1965. In addition to their prolific recording output—nine studio albums and one live LP in just three years—the band maintained a punishing touring schedule. They also cultivated a clean-cut image that was consistent with the innocent fun portrayed in Brian's songs, and the quintet's wholesome vibe was accentuated by their trademark outfit of striped button-down shirts and white pants, which would remain the band's stage uniform through 1966.

Although it was recorded just a few months after *Surfin' Safari*, the Beach Boys' second album *Surfin' USA* was a considerable progression from its predecessor. Although it followed the established pattern of surrounding a couple of hit singles with surf and drag novelties and cover versions, the quality of Brian's songwriting and the band's performances had taken a noticeable leap.

Surfin' USA's title track included a checklist of surfing hot spots provided by Jimmy Bowles, brother of Brian's girlfriend Judy. But it shamelessly borrowed its melody from Chuck Berry's "Sweet Little Sixteen," and the resulting legal threats led to the song's authorship being credited to Berry on subsequent pressings.

Although its success played a significant role in launching a nationwide surfing fad, *Surfin' USA* also showed Brian to be a truly accomplished melodist and arranger. Beyond its surf and car material—and no fewer than five forgettable instrumentals—the album included a pair of breakthrough ballads, the lilting "Farmer's Daughter" and the stark, melancholy "The Lonely Sea." Both featured evocative minor-key melodies and sensitive lead vocals by Brian, conjuring a haunting sense of yearning that offered a preview of the emotional depth that he would soon achieve on a regular basis.

Surfin' USA became the Beach Boys' first gold album, spending eighteen months on the U.S. album chart, where it just missed making the top slot. It was also their first to make the charts in Britain, where the group would remain reliably popular for decades to come.

Despite the continuing presence of the sort of filler that was probably unavoidable in light of Capitol's constant demand for new product, the September 1963 release *Surfer Girl* charted Brian's continuing growth as a composer and producer. The yearning title ballad carried a spiritual component that transcended its ostensible surf context, with the titular beach bunny a powerful metaphor for desire of a deeper nature. *Surfer Girl* also included Brian's most ambitious surf number to date in the majestic "Catch a Wave," on which Brian, Dennis, and Mike traded lead vocals. But the album's most arresting moment may have been "In My Room," a fragile evocation of solitude and vulnerability that was a startling demonstration of Brian's willingness to confront his fears in song.

Surfer Girl is also generally regarded as the first Beach Boys album to integrate substantial contributions from outside musicians, a practice that would become more prevalent in the band's recordings in the near future.

Del Shannon and Gene Pitney: Turning Heartaches into Hits

Tormented love stories and haunting minor-chord progressions set Del Shannon (1934–90) apart beginning with his 1961 number one hit, "Runaway." The Michigan-born singer/songwriter/guitarist remained a persistent chart presence for the next four years, thanks to such compelling originals as "Little Town Flirt," "Stranger in Town," and the Top Ten hit "Keep Searchin' (We'll Follow the Sun)." In 1963, Del released "From Me to You"—the first American cover of a John Lennon/Paul McCartney song to make the U.S. charts—and in 1965 the British duo of Peter and Gordon scored a Top Ten hit with Shannon's composition "I Go to Pieces." In 1982, Del Shannon reached the U.S. Top Forty for the last time with "Sea of Love," produced by Tom Petty. He committed suicide in 1990, after a long battle with depression.

Gene Pitney (1940–2006) began his career as a successful songwriter ("Hello Mary Lou" by Ricky Nelson). As a recording artist, the versatile Connecticut native specialized in dramatic orchestrated ballads like "I'm Gonna Be Strong," in which muffled drumbeats and swelling strings surged beneath his piercing, reedy voice. Pitney was only twenty-one when his first U.S. Top Twenty hit "Town Without Pity" was nominated for an Academy Award and he became the first rock and roller to perform on an Oscars telecast. His recording of "That Girl Belongs to Yesterday" was the first Mick Jagger/Keith Richards song to reach the American charts, and he played on the Rolling Stones' debut album. Along with Roy Orbison, Gene Pitney was one of the only American solo artists of the pre-Beatles era who continued to score major hits—"It Hurts to Be in Love" (1964), "Backstage" (1966), and more—on both sides of the Atlantic after the British Invasion. He remained a popular international concert attraction for decades until his death during a 2006 tour of Great Britain.

Andy Schwartz

The Beach Boys' punishing touring schedule took a particularly heavy toll on Brian, who had begun missing shows in 1963. That summer, the band brought in Al Jardine, who'd had second thoughts about his earlier decision to quit, to sub for Brian on bass on some live dates. The original intention had been to keep the band a sextet in order to ease Brian's workload. But that plan fell by the wayside when Murry fired David Marks a few weeks later, and Jardine returned to his original rhythm guitar slot.

Although Marks was pictured on the cover of the band's next album *Little Deuce Coupe*, released in October 1963, Jardine was actually back in the lineup in time to play on the album. *Little Deuce Coupe* was something of a concept album, comprising the car songs that had become a popular element of the Beach Boys' repertoire. It was also somewhat redundant, with four tracks recycled from previous LPs, along with several new tunes co-written by Brian with Roger Christian. Christian was a disc jockey on local Top Forty station KFWB, as well as an avid hot-rod enthusiast whose familiarity with the subculture's lingo added authority to Brian's auto-inspired tunes.

The only *Little Deuce Coupe* song not to mention cars is the student-spirit anthem "Be True to Your School." It would subsequently become a Top Ten single in a rerecorded version that added cheerleader-style backup vocals by the Honeys, a female vocal trio that included Brian's girlfriend Marilyn Rovell and her sister Diane.

The Honeys were one of several acts for which Brian wrote songs and produced records during the Beach Boys' rise. Also benefiting from Brian's extra-curricular pursuits was the popular surf duo Jan and Dean, to whom he gave "Surf City." It became a number one single for the pair in the summer of 1963. Murry Wilson was furious that his son had given away a smash hit, particularly since the Beach Boys had yet to top the charts themselves.

The next Beach Boys album *Shut Down Volume 2*—titled in recognition of a popular recent various-artists Capitol LP that reused "Shut Down" and "409"—contained such shameless throwaways as the contrived rank-out-fest "Cassius Love vs. Sonny Wilson" and the self-explanatory "Denny's Drums." But it also featured one of the band's best early rockers in the Chuck Berry–inspired Brian Wilson/Mike Love tune "Fun, Fun, Fun."

In later years, Love would, with considerable justification, be widely vilified by Wilson fans for his philistine tastes and his stubborn resistance to Brian's more experimental projects. But in the Beach Boys' early days, Love's contribution to the band was invaluable. As both a singer and lyricist, his assertive persona served as the self-assured counterpart to Brian's romanticism and sensitivity, embodying the youthful swagger of the band's car and surf songs.

Shut Down Volume 2 also introduced a pair of classic Wilson ballads, "Don't Worry Baby" and "The Warmth of the Sun." The former, co-written by Roger Christian, used a drag race as a vehicle to explore male insecurity, and featured production as advanced as anything being done in popular music at the time. Brian had initially offered "Don't Worry Baby" to the Ronettes, whose Phil Spector–produced "Be My Baby" was one of Brian's favorites. But the prickly Spector rejected it.

Princesses of Pop: The "Girl Group" Sound of the Shirelles, the Crystals, and the Ronettes

Women's voices have been part of rock and roll from the music's earliest days. In the 1950s, Ruth Brown, Lavern Baker, Etta James, and Esther Phillips represented the distaff side of rhythm and blues just as Wanda Jackson and Brenda Lee did for rockabilly and rock and roll.

But the "girl group" sound that flourished from 1960 to 1964 represented the fullest flowering of female rock and roll talent up to that time. Female groups and solo artists populated the charts in greater numbers than ever before, with songs and production that advanced the art of pop music. Behind the scenes, women achieved new heights of success as songwriters, producers, and record label entrepreneurs.

The Shirelles were the most successful black female group until the breakthrough of the Supremes. Beverly Lee, Doris Coley, Addie "Micki" Harris, and Shirley Owens were New Jersey high school students at the time of their first mid-chart hit, "I Met Him on a Sunday" (1958). Producer/songwriter Luther Dixon brought out the soulful innocence of their voices on "Mama Said" and "Baby, It's You"—one of two Shirelles songs, along with "Boys," later recorded by the Beatles.

In 1960, the Shirelles' "Will You Still Love Me Tomorrow" became the first girl group record to top the chart, and the first number one record written and produced by the team of Gerry Goffin and Carole King. Over the next three years, the Shirelles placed twelve songs in the Billboard Top Forty, including six in the Top Ten. All were released on Scepter Records, the independent label founded by Florence Greenberg, a New Jersey housewife.

As temperamental and controlling as he was passionate and talented, Phil Spector was the greatest and most influential producer of girl group recordings. The Crystals and the Ronettes were the most prolific groups to record for Spector's upstart Philles label, founded in 1961.

The Crystals gave the twenty-one-year-old producer his first Philles hit with "There's No Other Like My Baby" (number twenty). But like many of their black vocal group predecessors, the Crystals (Barbara Alston, Mary Thomas, Delores "Dee Dee" Kennibrew, and Dolores "LaLa" Brooks) had no control over their recording career. When the Brooklyn-based quintet couldn't make it to Los Angeles for one hastily scheduled session, Spector simply recorded "He's a Rebel" with the Blossoms—a trio of female session singers led by the great Darlene Love—and released it under the Crystals' name. In the fall of 1962, this socially conscious and infectiously danceable disc went all the way to number one.

The Ronettes' "Be My Baby" may be *the* archetypal girl group record. The song was written by Ellie Greenwich and Jeff Barry—one of the genre's top songwriting teams, along with Goffin and King—but the spotlight is on Ronettes lead singer Veronica "Ronnie" Bennett, who became Ronnie Spector after she and Phil were wed in 1968 (the couple divorced in 1974). Her vulnerable, soulful vibrato is framed by Spector's trademark "wall of sound," a dense instrumental mélange propelled by thunderous drumming and Jack Nitzsche's sweeping string arrangement. "Be My Baby" peaked at number two in the fall of 1963; it has since been heard in numerous films, television shows, and commercials. In 1986, Ronnie Spector made an unexpected return to the Top Five when she sang the "Be My Baby" refrain on Eddie Money's song "Take Me Home Tonight." In 2006, this ultimate girl group survivor released *The Last of the Rock Stars*, a solid album of contemporary rock and roll featuring such longtime admirers as Patti Smith and the Rolling Stones' Keith Richards.

A. S.

"The Warmth of the Sun," which Brian co-wrote with Love, is a haunting meditation on loss and acceptance, inverting the imagery of the band's beach-based hits to achieve a spiritual depth at which "Surfer Girl" had hinted. The song's narrator loses the love of his life, but takes solace in his memories of her. The lyrics are all the more poignant in light of Brian's revelation that he and Love wrote them as an expression of their grief in the wake of President John F. Kennedy's assassination in November 1963. Both "Don't Worry Baby" and "The Warmth of the Sun" were graced by lead vocals that demonstrated the technical and emotional range of Brian's soaring falsetto.

In contrast to the scattershot *Shut Down Volume 2*, 1964's *All Summer Long* was the most consistent and satisfying Beach Boys album to date. The title track utilized such exotic instrumental textures as piccolo and xylophone, and balanced an irresistibly uplifting melody with a wistful, nostalgic lyric. The song's bittersweet sense of parting would inspire filmmaker George Lucas to use it as the closing theme of his era-defining *American Graffiti* a decade later. "Wendy" similarly combined an upbeat tune with regretful lyrics, while the surf-themed "Don't Back Down" mixed a surging arrangement with an undercurrent of lyrical anxiety that contrasted the self-assurance of the Beach Boys' earlier surf numbers. *All Summer Long*'s strongest rocker was the infectious "I Get Around," which became the band's first number one single.

The demand for new Beach Boys product was reflected in the popularity of the band's other two 1964 LPs, the live *Beach Boys Concert* and the holiday release *The Beach Boys' Christmas Album*, which were released virtually simultaneously in October. The former demonstrated how tight a performing unit the band had become. The latter combined seasonally themed originals (including the hit "Little Saint Nick") with slickly orchestrated standards and harmony-heavy carols that allowed Brian to indulge his Four Freshmen fixation.

The stress of touring, combined with the pressure of carrying the Beach Boys' creative load, finally pushed Brian over the edge on December 23, 1964.

On that day, the bandleader, who had married Honeys member Marilyn Rovell just two weeks earlier, suffered an anxiety attack on a flight to Houston, where the Beach Boys were scheduled to begin a series of shows. Returning home immediately upon his arrival in Texas, Brian announced that he would no longer be a touring member of the band, instead staying at home to focus on writing and recording (he would, however, continue to make television appearances with the band).

Brian's first replacement in the touring Beach Boys, playing bass and singing high harmonies while Carl Wilson assumed the lion's share of his brother's lead vocals, was Glen Campbell. Already a busy L.A. studio guitarist and a participant in many Beach Boys recording sessions, Campbell toured with the band for three months, but declined an offer to join permanently. Instead, he opted to return to session work (he would continue to play on numerous Beach Boys recordings) and pursue his budding solo career.

Brian repaid Campbell's service by writing and producing a single, "Guess I'm Dumb," for him. Although the song wasn't a hit, it was one of Wilson's most memorable outside productions. Within two years, Campbell had settled into a smooth country-pop style that would make him one of Capitol Records' biggest-selling artists.

A long-term replacement arrived in April 1965 in the form of Bruce Johnston. Already a key figure in the West Coast surf music scene, Johnston was a multi-talented singer, instrumentalist, and producer who began playing sessions while still in high school. Johnston had worked extensively with Terry Melcher, his fellow staff producer at Columbia Records. Johnston and Melcher had had a fair amount of success recording surf and drag material under various guises, scoring hits as Bruce and Terry as well as the Rip Chords, whose Beach Boys sound-alike "Hey Little Cobra" had been a hit in 1964.

Brian's decision to quit the road proved to be a major jolt to his creative evolution. Freed from the demands of touring, he flourished musically, creating multi-layered backing tracks using the cadre of top-flight L.A. session musicians known as the Wrecking Crew, many of whom had already worked on prior Beach Boys sessions. The Wrecking Crew included such noted players as Glen Campbell and fellow guitarists Barney Kessel, Billy Strange, and Tommy Tedesco; bassists Carol Kaye, Ray Pohlman, and Lyle Ritz; keyboardists Larry Knechtel, Don Randi, and Leon Russell; saxophonists Steve Douglas and Jay Migliori; and drummer Hal Blaine, who'd supplanted Dennis Wilson on many Beach Boys tracks since 1964. These were many of the same musicians that Brian's idol Phil Spector used on his legendary "Wall of Sound" productions.

The first fruit of Brian's new status as full-time studio artist was the March 1965 release *The Beach Boys Today!*, on which Brian's production and songwriting took a substantial leap forward. *Today!*'s suite-like structure, with the album divided into a side of fast songs and a side of ballads, presented an early manifestation of the rock album format being used to make a cohesive artistic statement—an idea that Brian would soon explore more fully.

Beyond its absence of surf or car songs, *The Beach Boys Today!* largely abandoned teenage concerns in favor of a slightly more mature view of love. Such up-tempo numbers as "Good to My Baby," "Dance, Dance, Dance," and "When I Grow Up (To Be a Man)" featured Brian's most adventurous arrangements to date. On the ballad side, such introspective numbers as "Please Let Me Wonder," "Kiss Me Baby," She Knows Me Too Well" and the Dennis-sung "In the Back of My Mind" were startling, both in their lyrical vulnerability and their distinctive arrangements.

Indeed, *The Beach Boys Today!* would have been the first Beach Boys LP to be sublime from beginning to end, were it not for the closing track "Bull Session with 'Big Daddys,'" a silly bit of faux-spontaneous spoken-word tomfoolery whose status as obvious filler was all the more obvious in this context.

By comparison, the Beach Boys' next LP *Summer Days (And Summer Nights!!)* was something of a step backward, with such energetic but lightweight fare as "The Girl from New York City" and "Amusement Parks U.S.A." recalling the group's carefree early days. But *Summer Days* also featured the musically and emotionally complex "Let Him Run Wild," as well as the band's most sonically sophisticated single yet in "California Girls," which marked Bruce Johnston's recording debut as a Beach Boy. *Summer Days* also contained the band's second number one single, the Jardine-sung "Help Me, Rhonda," an upgraded remake of a song that they'd first tackled on *Today!*

Another milestone on *Summer Days (And Summer Nights!!)* was the Beatlesesque pop tune "Girl Don't Tell Me." The fact that it marked Carl Wilson's first lead vocal on a Beach Boys studio album is remarkable, considering the prominent role he had already began to assume within the band.

One of the most revealing tracks on *Summer Days (And Summer Nights!!)* was one that must have seemed frivolous at the time. The seemingly lightweight "I'm Bugged at My Ol' Man" found Brian bemoaning his unjust treatment at the hands of his cruel dad. Although it's delivered with tongue in cheek, the track takes on added gravity in light of the fact that Brian had recently fired Murry as the Beach Boys' manager, following a bitter confrontation during a recording session.

(Although Murry would retain a hand in the Beach Boys' business affairs due to his control of Brian's publishing catalog, he and Brian would maintain a strained relationship. In 1969, against Brian's will, Murry sold Brian's publishing company Sea of Tunes, a blunder that ultimately cost millions. When Murry died in 1973, neither Brian nor Dennis attended his funeral.)

The Beach Boys released a third album in 1965, the informal studio jam *Beach Boys Party!*, as well as the non-LP single "The Little Girl Once Knew." The latter boasted Brian's most idiosyncratic production yet, which may have explained why it was only the fourth Capitol Beach Boys single not to reach the Top Ten.

Recorded in a mere four days, *Beach Boys Party!* was a stripped-down, no-frills respite from Brian's increasingly elaborate studio work, as well as an early precursor of the "unplugged" trend, with the instrumentation limited to the band's own acoustic guitars, bass, and bongos, augmented by party sound effects taped later at Mike Love's house. Beyond a pair of reworked Beach Boys hits, the album comprised covers of some of the band members' favorite tunes, including R&B hits by the Olympics and the Rivingtons, an Everly Brothers ballad, a trio of Beatles numbers, and even Bob Dylan's protest anthem "The Times They Are A-Changin'." *Beach Boys Party!* produced a surprise smash single in a spirited reading of the Regents' 1961 doo-wop hit "Barbara Ann," on which Brian shared lead vocals with studio visitor Dean Torrance of Jan and Dean. It became the band's fourteenth Top Twenty single, climbing to number two in December 1965.

Dion: Blues from Belmont Avenue

Dion was born Dion DiMucci in 1939 in the Bronx, New York. His musical influences included country music legend Hank Williams and Mississippi Delta blues singer Robert Johnson: "I don't sing black, I don't sing white, I sing Bronx," he told the *New York Times* in 2006. In the late 1950s, as lead singer for the Belmonts, Dion scored with "A Teenager in Love" and a doo-wop arrangement of the Rodgers and Hart standard "Where or When." After going solo in 1960, he brought a street-smart swagger to such hits as "Runaround Sue" and "The Wanderer." Heroin addiction derailed Dion's career for a time, but in 1968 he quit drugs and earned (at number four) the highest-charting single of his career with the inspired folk-rock ballad "Abraham, Martin and John," commemorating the lives of Dr. Martin Luther King Jr. and U.S. presidents Lincoln and Kennedy. The singer/songwriter went on to release many more albums, including several sets of Christian material and (in 2005) the country-blues collection *Bronx in Blue*.

A. S.

But *Party!*'s real purpose was to give Capitol some new Beach Boys product to sell during 1965's Christmas season, buying Brian time to work on the new album that he was planning, which was to be his bravest and most cohesive musical statement yet.

PET VIBRATIONS

The Beach Boys' 1966 album 1966's *Pet Sounds* is regarded by many as Brian Wilson's creative apex. Although it divided opinion within the band and was considered a commercial disappointment at the time of its release, it's now embraced as one of rock's most beloved and influential albums, cited as a touchstone by multiple generations of fans, critics, and musicians.

Pet Sounds had its genesis when Brian heard the Beatles' *Rubber Soul*. Impressed by the album's cohesiveness, Wilson, who had always regarded his British labelmates with a combination of admiration and competitiveness, felt challenged to come up with something equally good.

Wanting to break away from the Beach Boys' history and his own established methods, Brian decided not to work with any of his prior co-writers. Instead, he chose Tony Asher, a recent acquaintance who'd been working writing advertising jingles, to help craft his thoughts into finished lyrics. The two began writing together in early 1966, and came up with an emotion-charged song cycle that surveyed the emotional challenges accompanying the transition from youth to young adulthood.

Pet Sounds' lyrics were matched by music that marked a quantum leap in Brian's achievements as a composer, arranger, and producer. He cut the instrumental tracks for *Pet Sounds* during a four-month period in late 1965 and early 1966, working at his favorite Hollywood studios: Gold Star, Western Recorders, and Sunset Sound.

While the Beach Boys were out on tour, Brian toiled in the studio, putting the Wrecking Crew through their paces to produce the sounds that he envisioned. Although the self-taught perfectionist couldn't write or read musical notation, he often had the complex, elaborate arrangements worked out in his head, and found other ways to communicate his ideas to the musicians. The veteran players came to enjoy the creative interaction of Beach Boys tracking sessions, and to appreciate Brian's openness to the players' own suggestions, as well as his willingness to incorporate accidents and apparent mistakes into the final product.

Brian achieved *Pet Sounds'* richly textured, almost symphonic arrangements by employing unconventional combinations of instruments to produce new and exotic sounds. In addition to having multiple musicians playing guitar, bass, and keyboard parts simultaneously (a technique he'd borrowed from Phil Spector), he mixed conventional rock instrumentation with various exotic stringed instruments, theremin, flutes, harpsichord, bicycle bells, beverage bottles, and even the barking of his dogs Banana and Louie.

When the other Beach Boys returned from touring to record their meticulously layered vocal tracks, some of Brian's bandmates expressed reservations about *Pet Sounds'* radical shift in direction. Most vocal in his objections was Mike Love, who couldn't have been pleased at having been turfed out of his position as lyricist by Brian's decision to write with Tony Asher. Love was particularly critical of the lyrics of "Hang On to Your Ego," which he insisted upon rewriting as "I Know There's an Answer."

Lyrically, *Pet Sounds* encompassed the loss of innocent idealism ("Caroline No"), the transient nature of love ("Here Today"), faith in the face of heartbreak ("I'm Waiting for the Day"), the demands and disappointments of independence ("That's Not Me"), the feeling of being out of step with the modern world ("I Just Wasn't Made for These Times"), and the longing for a happy, loving future ("Wouldn't It Be Nice"). The album also featured a series of intimate, hymnlike love songs, "You Still Believe in Me," "Don't Talk (Put Your Head on My Shoulder)," and "God Only Knows." The latter, with a gentle yet passionate lead vocal by Carl Wilson, would become one of Brian's best loved—and most covered—songs.

Also on *Pet Sounds* was "Sloop John B.," a rousing adaptation of a traditional Caribbean folk song that had been suggested by Al Jardine. It had been cut a few months before the main album sessions and had been a Top Five hit when released as a single in March 1966.

Pet Sounds also included a pair of richly atmospheric instrumentals, "Let's Go Away for Awhile" and "Pet Sounds." Both had been recorded with the intention of adding lyrics, but Brian decided that he preferred the tracks without them. "Pet Sounds" had originally been titled "Run, James, Run," reflecting Wilson's original intention of submitting it for use in a James Bond movie.

Beyond its alterations to the Beach Boys' established sound, *Pet Sounds* felt more like a Brian Wilson solo effort than any prior album. Although Carl did standout work on "God Only Knows," Love sang lead or co-lead on three songs and Jardine stepped up front for a few a lines on "I Know There's an Answer," Brian sang the remainder of the album's leads himself, driving home the songs' melancholy beauty with some of the most expressive vocals of his career.

Whatever problems they may have had with the album's divergence from the band's hitmaking formula, the other Beach Boys graced *Pet Sounds* with some of the finest harmonies of their career (although Brian overdubbed all of the vocal parts himself on a few songs).

Upon its release in May 1966, *Pet Sounds'* sales failed to match its artistic stature. Although it reached the Top Ten and produced an Top Ten single in "Wouldn't It Be Nice," sales were disappointing in comparison with the band's prior LPs. It didn't help that *Pet Sounds* received half-hearted promotion from Capitol, which signaled its lack of confidence in the album's potential by issuing a slapdash greatest-hits set, *The Best of the Beach Boys*, two months after its release.

Pet Sounds fared considerably better in Britain, where it was widely recognized as a major work and celebrated by many of the music scene's movers and shakers. It reached number two in England, where the Beach Boys beat out the Beatles as Group of the Year in *New Musical Express*'s influential year-end poll. Paul McCartney, who has long cited *Pet Sounds* as his all-time favorite album, acknowledged its influence on the Beatles' psychedelic landmark *Sgt. Pepper's Lonely Hearts Club Band*.

In the years since its release, *Pet Sounds* has steadily gained in reputation and prestige. In 1995, a panel of top musicians, songwriters, and producers assembled by *Mojo* magazine voted it the Greatest Album Ever Made. In 2004, it was one of fifty recordings chosen by the Library of Congress to be added to the National Recording Registry. In 2006, the German magazine *Spex* voted it the best album of the twentieth century. It also placed in the number two slot on *Rolling Stone*'s list of the 500 greatest albums of all time, right behind *Sgt. Pepper's Lonely Hearts Club Band*.

Pet Sounds' enduring appeal was confirmed by the 1997 release of *The Pet Sounds Sessions*, a four-CD box set encompassing a new stereo mix of the album (which was originally only mixed in mono), plus three discs' worth of outtakes, rehearsals, and instrumental tracks. Five years later, after Brian's return to touring, he staged a well-received tour performing *Pet Sounds* as a complete work, backed by a full orchestra.

Brian was not used to having his creative autonomy challenged, and was accustomed to seeing his experiments achieve commercial success. He was hurt by his bandmates' resistance to *Pet Sounds*, and disappointed by the album's failure to gain a wider audience. But the lack of support didn't stop him from forging ahead with his plans for the next Beach Boys single, "Good Vibrations."

Originally intended for *Pet Sounds* but pulled from the album so he could devote more time to its production, "Good Vibrations"—with Tony Asher's original lyrics rewritten by Mike Love—introduced Brian's new technique of modular recording. Rather than record a complete performance, he broke the song into sections, recording and rerecording each portion and assembling a collage of his favorite takes into a backing track. At a time when singles were routinely cut in an hour or two, "Good Vibrations" was the most elaborate and expensive track pop music had ever seen, recorded in seventeen sessions in four studios over the course of six months, using over ninety hours of tape and racking up a then-unheard-of cost of $50,000.

Although the rest of the band was skeptical about his unconventional recording approach, Brian's painstaking efforts proved worthwhile. "Good Vibrations"—which Brian described as a "pocket symphony"—was unlike any pop single that had come before it, covering a dizzying amount of musical ground in just over three and a half minutes. As on *Pet Sounds*, Brian made extensive use of instruments rarely heard in pop, with cello and electro-theremin prominent in the song's surging, insistent chorus.

Upon its release in October 1966, "Good Vibrations" became the Beach Boys' biggest hit yet; it went to number one on both sides of the Atlantic, and became the group's first million-selling single. With the song's success demonstrating that the general public could embrace his bravest musical adventures, Brian Wilson moved forward with his most ambitious project yet.

TRYING TO SMILE

The artistic and commercial triumph of "Good Vibrations" set the stage for Brian's plans for the next Beach Boys album, an extended suite of musically and thematically linked pieces that would be recorded using his modular technique. The project—initially titled *Dumb Angel* but eventually renamed

Smile—would incorporate a wide array of new sounds, textures, and arrangement ideas, as well as lyrical imagery and themes drawn from American history, with humor as a key element in the material. The idea of assembling an entire album from short musical fragments was a bold undertaking, and *Smile*—which Brian characterized as "a teenage symphony to God"—promised to be as much of a leap forward from *Pet Sounds* as *Pet Sounds* had been from *The Beach Boys Today!*

To provide lyrics for *Smile*'s musical vision, Brian tapped Van Dyke Parks, a young musical wunderkind (and former child actor) who'd already established himself as an up-and-coming figure on the L.A. scene. His new co-writer had come to Wilson's attention via producer Terry Melcher, who'd hired Parks to play on some Byrds sessions. But it was Parks's talent for evocative poetic wordplay, and his abiding interest in Americana, that made him an ideal *Smile* collaborator.

Wilson and Parks quickly formed a productive partnership; between April and September 1966, they wrote a series of songs that formed the foundation of the new album. Many of those tunes were written in the giant sandbox that Brian had had installed in the living room of his Bel Air home, in order to replicate the inspirational feel of the beach. Their pair's first collaboration was "Heroes and Villains," followed by such key *Smile* tracks as "Wonderful," "Cabinessence," and "Wind Chimes." This period also produced "Surf's Up," which would become *Smile*'s spiritual centerpiece; Wilson and Parks reportedly wrote it in a single night.

At a time when rock had come to be dominated by British sensibilities, Brian was determined to create a fundamentally American work. At one point, he described *Smile* as a musical journey across America, beginning at Plymouth Rock and ending in Hawaii, and touching upon key points of history along the way, including the rise of the railroad and automobiles, and the settlement of the West and its effect on Native American civilization.

Brian began cutting tracks for *Smile* in August 1966, using many of the Wrecking Crew regulars and working at Gold Star Studios as well as Sunset Sound, Western Recorders, and Capitol Records' in-house studio. He worked intensively on the album for the next few months. But by the end of the year, his initial exhilaration had taken a darker turn.

Brian encountered resistance from Capitol, as well as the other Beach Boys, who worried that the new music was too radical a stylistic shift and that it would be impossible to reproduce on stage. The group also expressed concerns that Brian's artistic judgment may have been clouded by his growing use of marijuana and psychedelic drugs. Particularly fierce in his opposition was Mike Love, who complained about having to sing such poetic Parks lyrics as "Over and over the crow cries uncover the cornfield" on "Cabinessence"; the growing tensions would eventually cause Parks to leave the project.

The pressures of creating such challenging music in the face of heavy opposition, combined with his increasingly fragile mental state, took a heavy toll on Brian's previously unshakable creative confidence. In late November, while working on "Mrs. O'Leary's Cow"—the "Fire" section of a planned suite encompassing the elements of earth, air, water, and fire—he reportedly became convinced that the music he was creating had been responsible for a series of blazes in the area. For years afterward, it was rumored that Brian (who had built atmosphere during the session by having the musicians wear firemen's helmets) had become so distressed that he burned the tapes; although he did not actually destroy the recordings, he did abandon work on the track.

Brian continued working on *Smile* through the early months of 1967, tinkering with various combinations of takes and mixes. Despite his prior reputation for working efficiently in the studio, he failed to complete the album, missing a series of deadlines for its delivery to Capitol. By then, he'd recorded countless hours of music for the album, although some tracks were still waiting for the Beach Boys to add their vocals. As a series of proposed release dates came and went, Capitol sent out promotional materials to distributors and retailers, and placed ads for *Smile* in *Billboard* and various teen magazines. Meanwhile, 466,000 copies of the gatefold album cover, designed by artist Frank Holmes, sat in a warehouse in Pennsylvania, where they would remain for the next two decades.

In early May 1967—just a few weeks before the release of the Beatles' groundbreaking, *Pet Sounds*–influenced *Sgt. Pepper's Lonely Hearts Club Band*—it was officially announced that *Smile*'s release had been canceled.

In the decades following its non-release, *Smile* became a source of endless speculation and mystique. Its reputation as a lost masterpiece cast a powerful spell over fans, and was further enhanced by the tantalizing evidence provided by the handful of *Smile* tracks that emerged over the years on various Beach Boys LPs.

While he remained reluctant to discuss the traumatic project, Brian insisted in several interviews that *Smile* was unfinished and did not exist in releasable form. When bootleg releases collecting large amounts of unreleased *Smile* material began to appear in the early 1990s, they strongly suggested that the album had been much closer to completion than Wilson had admitted. It also became clear that, even in incomplete form, *Smile* was a profoundly original and deeply moving work. That was confirmed in 1993, when the career-spanning box set *Good Vibrations: 30 Years of the Beach Boys* debuted a treasure trove of rare *Smile* material.

In 1967, though, the *Smile* debacle became the catalyst in Brian Wilson's abrupt and tragic descent into mental illness and drug abuse. When he had begun work on the album, Wilson was at the top of his game and the height of his influence, with seemingly unlimited creative horizons. After the abandonment of *Smile*, he would retreat from the spotlight and abdicate his leadership of the band that he had previously dominated. It would take decades of short-lived comebacks and false starts before Brian would resume a full-time musical career.

While *Smile*'s non-release set its creator on a precipitous decline, its effect upon the Beach Boys' career was almost as damaging. Mike Love had derided Brian's insistence upon subverting the band's winning formula. But it seems likely that, had *Smile* been released at the time, it would have established the Beach Boys in the vanguard of the seismic changes that were about to permanently alter the direction of rock—changes that would render the group's original sound commercially unfashionable. As the Beatles continued to open up new creative vistas, the Beach Boys, who had been making equally adventurous music, would come to be viewed as a relic of a more conservative age. Although they still had a fair amount of worthwhile music in their future, the Beach Boys would spend the rest of their career struggling to regain their lost momentum as a recording act.

The Beach Boys' hip credibility took a further hit when the group withdrew from a commitment to perform at the historic Monterey International Pop Festival in the summer of 1967. That event, on which they would have performed alongside the leading lights of the emerging rock counterculture, may well have given the group a high-profile shot of relevance amidst the social and cultural upheavals of the Summer of Love.

In August 1967, the public got a tantalizing taste of the abandoned *Smile* with the single release of one of the album's key tracks, the Wild West fantasy "Heroes and Villains." Although the truncated single omitted some of the sections recorded for the album version, its multi-part structure still exemplified Brian's *Smile* approach, overlaying a relatively simple song with complicated vocal and instrumental arrangements. "Heroes and Villains" peaked at number twelve on the U.S. pop chart, and made the Top Ten in England.

A month later, fans who'd been primed for the groundbreaking brilliance of *Smile* instead got *Smiley Smile*, a perplexing hodgepodge that included "Good Vibrations" and "Heroes and Villains" along with drastically scaled-down rerecordings of several *Smile* numbers, recorded by the band in Brian's new home studio. Although its newly recorded tracks possessed a certain ramshackle charm, and the album has gained admirers over the years, *Smiley Smile* was released to general incomprehension. While *Smile* might have divided the Beach Boys' fans had it been released, *Smiley Smile* merely baffled them. Although it made the Top Ten in Britain, *Smiley Smile* peaked at an ignominious number forty-one in the United States.

Whatever its musical merits, *Smiley Smile*—the first album to bear the credit "Produced by the Beach Boys"—was significant in that it marked the beginning of the other Beach Boys taking up the creative slack in the face of Brian's diminishing participation. Hereafter, all of the band members would share songwriting duties, with Carl Wilson becoming the band's driving force in the studio, just as he'd stepped up as leader of the live band when Brian quit the road.

Although they were distributed by Capitol, *Smiley Smile* and the "Heroes and Villains" single were the first releases to bear the logo of the Beach Boys' new, band-owned imprint, Brother Records. Brother's formation had originally been motivated by a desire to maintain creative control in the face of Capitol's resistance to Brian's more daring projects, and by a series of financial disputes between the group and Capitol.

Wild Honey, released in December 1967, was considerably more cohesive than *Smiley Smile*. With Brian once again co-writing with Mike Love, the album—again recorded at Brian's house—consisted largely of upbeat, stripped-down rock and roll, whose unpretentious exuberance contrasted *Smile*'s wide-screen grandeur and *Smiley Smile*'s druggy haze. Much of its energy arose from the sound of the Beach Boys playing as a band; indeed, *Wild Honey* marked the first album in several years on which the Beach Boys played the majority of the instruments. Equally notable was Carl's emergence as a persuasive lead vocalist on such tunes as the wailing title track and the catchy "Darlin'," which became a Top Twenty single. *Wild Honey*'s minute-long coda, "Mama Says," was originally recorded as a section of *Smile*'s "Vegetables," making it the first of several *Smile* numbers to appear as the closing track of subsequent Beach Boys albums.

Just as *Pet Sounds* and *Smile* had reflected Brian's preoccupations at the time, *Wild Honey*'s unpretentious simplicity embodied the simpler lifestyle he'd adopted in the wake of *Smile*'s grand failure. The low-key vibe continued with 1968's *Friends*, on which such Brian-led tunes as "Busy Doin' Nothin'," "Wake the World," and the playful title track offered warmly intimate portraits of the artist as gentle homebody.

Notably absent from much of *Friends* was Mike Love, who had recently become a devotee of transcendental meditation, and was away in India studying with the Maharishi Mahesh Yogi (along with the Beatles, Donovan, and actress Mia Farrow) during most of the recording. A more surprising development on *Friends* was the revelation of Dennis Wilson, the Beach Boys' trouble-prone but charismatic dark horse, as a broodingly soulful songwriter and singer on two tracks, "Little Bird" and "Be Still."

Despite the quality of *Friends*, 1968 saw the Beach Boys' popularity dip to perilous new lows. While they remained in demand in England, *Friends* peaked at number 126 in the United States—a humbling comedown for the band that had topped the charts with "Good Vibrations" just two years earlier. An ill-conceived tour pairing the Beach Boys with the Maharishi was a financial disaster, with several dates canceled after the New York show drew a paltry 200 fans.

Coincidentally or not, *Friends* would be the last Beach Boys album to comprise mostly songs written by Brian Wilson, whose participation in the group would grow more limited in the years to come.

Nineteen sixty-eight also saw the release of *Stack-O-Tracks*, which collected the instrumental tracks of fifteen previously released Beach Boys numbers. Although such archival projects would become commonplace in the CD era, *Stack-O-Tracks* was unprecedented at the time, underlining the esteem in which

Brian Wilson's artistry was still held by his peers. Unfortunately, the album's release coincided with the band's decline in popularity, and it became the first Beach Boys LP to fail to reach the charts on either side of the Atlantic.

In contrast to *Friends'* focused intimacy, 1969's *20/20*—assembled mainly to complete the band's contractual obligation to Capitol—was a patchwork of singles, leftovers from other projects (including *Smile*), and solo efforts by various members. The album benefited from the inclusion of "Do It Again," a nostalgic throwback to the band's early fun-in-the-sun style that had had been a Top Twenty single the previous summer. *20/20* spawned another minor hit in Carl's reworking of the Ronettes' girl group classic "I Can Hear Music," whose layered production demonstrated how much he'd learned from observing his big brother's studio methods.

Brian's limited involvement in *20/20* finally gave Bruce Johnston—his replacement in the touring Beach Boys but also an experienced writer and producer—a chance to get his own material onto a Beach Boys LP. Fittingly, Johnston's moody instrumental "The Nearest Faraway Place" was largely inspired by Brian's work on *Pet Sounds*.

20/20 also featured a trio of contributions from Dennis, including the haunting "Be with Me" and the sweet "All I Want to Do," the latter sung by Dennis's frequent nemesis Mike Love. The third song credited to Dennis, "Never Learn Not to Love," was actually a reworking of "Cease to Exist," written by a then-unknown criminal, cult leader, and aspiring songwriter named Charles Manson, whom Dennis had befriended shortly before work on the album began. According to some reports, Manson was incensed when the song was released without his writing credit, and threatened to murder Dennis. Dennis's involvement with Manson caused considerable concern within the Beach Boys camp, and became more frightening after Manson directed a group of his followers to murder seven people, including actress Sharon Tate, on August 9, 1969. It was later theorized that Manson's original target had been the previous tenant of Tate's rented house, record producer (and Bruce Johnston's former recording partner) Terry Melcher, who had apparently rebuffed Manson's earlier attempts to win a record deal.

The Beach Boys followed *20/20* with the non-LP single "Break Away," on which Brian's credited co-writer, Reggie Dunbar, was a pseudonym for none other than Murry Wilson. Although it was one of the band's strongest releases of the period, "Break Away" stalled at number sixty-three (it made the Top Ten in England). The song's commercial failure reportedly had a demoralizing effect on Brian, hastening his retreat from active musical duty.

SAIL ON

With their Capitol commitments complete, the Beach Boys moved to Reprise/ Warner Bros., probably the hippest and most artist-friendly major label of the time. The new deal seemed to offer the prospect of reestablishing the Beach Boys as a relevant musical entity, and the group rose to the occasion with their Brother/Reprise debut, 1970's *Sunflower*, which many fans rate as their best post–*Pet Sounds* album. Brian was only prominent on a handful of *Sunflower* tracks, most notably the magnificent "This Whole World," sung by Carl. But his influence loomed large over the sunny, harmony-driven album, with the other band members coming up with material that merged the group's classic 1960s sound with a more adult sensibility. Despite critical acclaim, *Sunflower* was a commercial disappointment.

During the *Sunflower* sessions, Dennis Wilson recorded his first solo single, the Brian-influenced "Sound of Free," credited to "Dennis Wilson and Rumbo" and released overseas but not in the United States.

As part of the Beach Boys' Reprise deal, the company had expected the band to deliver a releasable version of the already-legendary *Smile*. But Brian, the only person who could reasonably be expected to assemble the mountains of tape into a cohesive work, remained unwilling and/or unable to complete the album.

"Surf's Up," one of *Smile*'s most powerful songs, became the title track of *Sunflower*'s 1971 follow-up. Brian had publicly unveiled the richly poetic epic four years earlier, performing a solo piano rendition on *Inside Pop: The Rock Revolution*, a CBS TV special hosted by conductor Leonard Bernstein, but the track had never been completed for *Smile*. "Surf's Up"—whose 1971 version was completed by Carl—was a major addition to the Beach Boys canon, as was Brian's new "'Til I Die," whose heart-tugging sonic tapestry recalled *Pet Sounds*. *Surf's Up* also included a pair of impressive songwriting contributions from Carl, but lacked the solid group dynamic that had elevated *Sunflower*.

During the *Surf's Up* sessions, Dennis put his hand through a plate glass window, leaving him temporarily unable to play the drums. Early in 1972, the Beach Boys' lineup got some new blood with the additions of guitarist Blondie Chaplin and drummer Ricky Fataar—both former members of the South African band the Flame, for whom Carl Wilson had recently produced an album. The two new members would help to push the band's live shows toward a tougher sound, and would lend a more prominent R&B feel to the next Beach Boys album, the spotty *Carl and the Passions—"So Tough,"* made with minimal participation from the increasingly reclusive Brian. Reprise hinted at its lack of faith in the album by releasing it as half of a two-LP set with a reissued *Pet Sounds*, making the underwhelming new disc sound even weaker in comparison.

Carl and the Passions—"So Tough" marked the departure of Bruce Johnston, who had become so disenchanted with the band's new manager Jack Rieley that he quit the group. Former DJ Rieley won the position with a strategy to reestablish the Beach Boys' hip credibility, but his efforts further divided the already fractious band. Rieley somehow managed to get Reprise to foot the bill to send the Beach Boys, along with family, staff, and a massive amount of recording equipment, to Holland to record their next album. The change of scene was an effort to shake the group out of its creative doldrums and snap Brian out of his unproductiveness. The trip quickly turned rocky, but the resulting album, titled *Holland*, was a modest improvement upon its predecessor, winning the band some FM airplay and spawning a minor hit in "Sail On, Sailor," whose lead vocal was provided by Blondie Chaplin and whose five credited co-writers included Brian and Van Dyke Parks.

Holland was followed by the double album *The Beach Boys in Concert*, which reflected the band's growing emphasis on touring. The live album also marked the final recorded appearances of Chaplin and Fataar, who would depart in late 1973 and late 1974, respectively. By then, the combination of flagging record sales and Brian's growing reclusiveness didn't seem to bode well for the band's future.

But in June 1974, amidst a resurgence of nostalgic interest in vintage rock and roll, Capitol Records released *Endless Summer*, a two-LP compilation of the Beach Boys' surf and car hits. The collection became a surprise pop-culture phenomenon, spending much of that summer at the top of the American album charts and remaining a top seller for the next two years, making it the Beach Boys' longest-charting release.

The success of *Endless Summer* instantly revitalized the Beach Boys' fortunes as a live act, and the group increasingly tailored their concerts to focus on their crowd-pleasing early hits. While some complained that they'd become a pandering human jukebox, their new status as America's highest-grossing concert act spoke more loudly than any criticism.

While the Beach Boys were on the road reaping the benefits of *Endless Summer*'s success, Brian Wilson had fallen deeply into mental illness, spending much of his time in bed and indulging heavily in alcohol, drugs, and binge eating. A series of psychologists were unable to treat him successfully, until Brian began seeing the unconventional therapist Eugene Landy in the fall of 1975. Despite the controversy surrounding Landy's radical twenty-four-hour treatment, Brian seemingly improved substantially under his care.

Although the Beach Boys had more or less retired from recording after *Holland*, the momentum created by *Endless Summer* built demand for a new studio album. Brian's modest upswing was enough to inspire the band and its label to launch a high-profile "Brian's Back" campaign, trumpeting the tragic hero's return to the producer's chair for a new studio LP featuring the Beach Boys' classic lineup. Brian even rejoined the band on stage for several concerts, looking nervous and awkward. He seemed equally uncomfortable in several high-profile TV appearances, including a prime-time NBC-TV special honoring the Beach Boys and a solo performance on *Saturday Night Live*.

The ballyhoo surrounding Brian's return to active duty proved premature when *15 Big Ones* was released in June 1976. Despite the hype, the album was largely a letdown, comprised largely of lackluster remakes of rock and roll oldies, along with a handful of lightweight but charming new songs by Brian. While *15 Big Ones* possessed surprisingly little of the Beach Boys' classic sound, it nonetheless produced a Top Five single in a remake of Chuck Berry's "Rock and Roll Music."

A more rewarding comeback project was *15 Big Ones*' follow-up, *The Beach Boys Love You*. The album was entirely written and played by Brian, whose extensive use of Moog synthesizer gave it a loopy funhouse ambience. The playfully primitive album sharply divided fans and critics, some of whom proclaimed it a work of eccentric genius while others dismissed it as childish and trivial. Like *15 Big Ones*, *Love You* incorporated outtakes originally recorded for prior albums, which resulted in Brian's coarse 1977 voice, ravaged by years of cigarette smoking and other abuse, appearing alongside his sweeter tone on the *Sunflower*-era "Good Time."

Also in 1977, Dennis Wilson became the first Beach Boy to release a solo album with *Pacific Ocean Blue*. Despite the fact that years of hard living had reduced his voice to a throaty croak, the album was an impressive achievement, with lush, imaginative production and a distinctive lyrical vision that surveyed both the California landscape and the artist's own tortured psyche. Dennis began work on a second album, to be titled *Bamboo*, but the distractions of his turbulent personal life, his escalating substance abuse, and his increasingly strained relations with the other Beach Boys would help to keep that project from being completed.

Meanwhile, Brian Wilson once again regressed into drug use and mental illness. He was credited as executive producer of 1978's *M.I.U. Album*, but the album—a lightweight grab-bag of oldies remakes and Brian compositions rejected from earlier projects—was overseen by Al Jardine, with the sessions taking place at Maharishi University in Iowa. Although Brian was present for much of the recording, his participation was minimal. Carl and Dennis were largely absent as well, hinting at the band's internal instability at the time. One of *M.I.U.*'s cover tunes, an energetic Jardine-led revival of the Del-Vikings' doo-wop classic "Come Go with Me," later became a Top Ten hit 1981, when it was included on the compilation *Ten Years of Harmony*.

Despite Brian's perilous condition and the band's general disarray, the Beach Boys signed a new recording deal with Caribou/Epic, a deal that stipulated Brian Wilson's creative involvement in each album. When Brian proved not to be up to the task, Bruce Johnston—who in his years as an ex–Beach Boy had written the MOR smash "I Write the Songs" for pop superstar Barry Manilow—was called in as producer of 1979's *L.A. (Light Album)*.

Despite the fact that relations within the group were severely strained, *L.A.* featured solid work from all five Beach Boys. Contractual commitments aside, Brian's contributions amounted to a pair of older outtakes completed by Carl: the heavenly "Good Timin' " and a tongue-in-cheek reworking of the standard "Shortenin' Bread." The album also found the Beach Boys attempting to jump on the disco bandwagon with a dance-oriented update of the *Wild Honey* tune

"Here Comes the Night"; although the song got as high as number forty-four, it proved so controversial with fans that it was removed from the band's set list after a handful of shows.

Another attempt to coax Brian back as producer for 1980's undistinguished *Keepin' the Summer Alive* proved unproductive, leading to Johnston again taking the reins in the studio. An increasingly volatile Dennis Wilson exited early in the recording; he would never record with the group again.

Keepin' the Summer Alive's lack of success was one indication of the malaise that hung over the splintered Beach Boys in the early 1980s. Although Johnston returned to the performing lineup, Carl Wilson, frustrated with the band's reliance on the oldies, temporarily quit to record a pair of solo albums, and Dennis's unpredictability got him ejected from the band for a while. Meanwhile, Brian Wilson's condition had gone so far downhill that Dr. Eugene Landy was brought back to treat him in 1983. The existence of a touring Beach Boys lineup with no Wilson brothers seemed to suggest that the band's days were numbered.

Although their recording career had grown moribund, the Beach Boys maintained their status as an iconic American institution. That status was demonstrated in 1983, when James Watt, President Ronald Reagan's Secretary of the Interior, canceled the band's annual July 4 concert on Washington, DC's Mall, replacing them with the more ostensibly wholesome Wayne Newton. When Watt's ban caused a media uproar, the image-savvy Reagan proclaimed himself a Beach Boys fan and welcomed the group to the White House for a face-saving visit. The Watt situation proved to be a publicity bonanza for the group, which would be back playing on the Mall on the following July 4.

When the Beach Boys next won national media attention a few months after the James Watt flap, the news was much sadder. On December 28, 1983, Dennis Wilson drowned while diving from a friend's boat, attempting to recover items that he had angrily thrown overboard.

The five surviving band members regrouped and returned to recording with 1985's *The Beach Boys*, recorded with English producer Steve Levine, fresh from his hit work with Culture Club. While longtime admirers bemoaned the album's trendy, synthetic production and noted its paucity of memorable songs, *The Beach Boys* got the band back into the Top Forty—and even onto MTV—with the catchy Mike Love/Terry Melcher song "Getcha Back," whose choruses featured a prominent falsetto part by Brian Wilson. In an omen of things to come, two of Brian's four new compositions credited Dr. Eugene Landy as co-writer.

Despite the relative success of *The Beach Boys*, the band did not record a follow-up album. Instead, they continued working as a lucrative touring act while recording individual songs for a series of film soundtracks and various-artists albums. The most successful of these was the Love/Melcher tune "Kokomo," which appeared in the Tom Cruise vehicle *Cocktail*. Although undeniably catchy, "Kokomo" was derided by purists as evidence of Mike Love pushing the band toward shallowness and irrelevance. But in the summer of 1988, "Kokomo" became the Beach Boys' first number one single since "Good Vibrations" twenty-two years earlier.

The fact that Brian Wilson's voice did not appear on "Kokomo" was reportedly the result of Dr. Landy forbidding him to attend the session. Many questioned the ethics of Landy's unorthodox and expensive treatment, in which his patient was monitored twenty-four hours a day by the doctor's staff, who apparently controlled nearly every aspect of Brian's life. But Landy did manage to curb Brian's drug use and get him into physical shape, making it possible for him to sign a new record deal with Sire/Warner Bros. and release his first-ever solo album, *Brian Wilson*, in the summer of 1988.

Although a somewhat tentative return—thanks in large part to stiff 1980s production that contrasted the organic sound of his vintage work—*Brian Wilson* contained enough moments of emotional and musical truth, such as the open-hearted ballads "Love and Mercy" and "Melt Away," to offer hope to fans.

Indeed, Brian's return seemed almost miraculous, and it seemed likely that Landy had saved his life. But Landy's methods, and the fact that he was now Wilson's personal manager and songwriting partner as well as his doctor, was troubling to many observers. The appearance of impropriety was reinforced by the voluble Landy's tendency to make self-aggrandizing media appearances alongside Brian, who often seemed disengaged.

The situation was apparently a source of concern to Brian's new label, which declined to release a second Landy-influenced Wilson album, *Sweet Insanity*. The apparent conflicts of interest inherent in Landy's medical, musical, and business relationships with his patient/client, soon came under legal and media scrutiny. Brian's family took legal action, leading to Landy being forced in 1991 to sever his relationship with Brian, and to surrender his license to practice psychology in California. By then, Landy had already reportedly received one third of the $250,000 advance for Brian's ghostwritten autobiography *Wouldn't It Be Nice*, which portrayed Landy in glowing terms—and which Brian later claimed not to have even read.

Free of Landy's influence, Brian Wilson turned to more conventional psychiatric treatment, and tentatively resumed his solo career in the 1990s. He participated in *I Just Wasn't Made for These Times*, a 1995 film documentary tribute directed by musician/producer Don Was. The same year, Brian rekindled his collaboration with his *Smile*-era collaborator Van Dyke Parks on *Orange Crate Art*, a collection of California-themed Parks compositions with Wilson providing lead vocals.

Two years later, Brian teamed with his daughters Carnie and Wendy— who had already tasted pop stardom as members of Wilson Phillips, a slick vocal trio that also included Chynna Phillips, daughter John and Michelle Phillips of 1960s stars the Mamas and the Papas—on the one-off album *The Wilsons*.

Roy Orbison: Pop Vocal Pyrotechnics

Roy Orbison (1936–88) recorded for five years with only modest success until hitting his artistic and commercial stride in 1960 with "Only the Lonely." This number two hit was the Texas-born singer's first in a series of beautifully produced pop classics (many of which he co-wrote) that set his towering tenor within a seamless backdrop of rhythm, strings, and voices. Inducting Roy into the Rock and Roll Hall of Fame in 1987, Bruce Springsteen invoked the near-operatic emotional power of songs like the 1961 number one "Running Scared" and 1964's Top Ten hit "It's Over." While in planning for his own landmark album *Born to Run*, Springsteen admitted, "most of all, I wanted to sing like Roy Orbison."

The hits dried up after 1964, although Orbison was still a charismatic live performer. In early 1988, Roy formed the Traveling Wilburys with such long-time admirers as George Harrison and Tom Petty; he was in the midst of a major comeback when he suffered a fatal heart attack in December. Roy Orbison's posthumous honors included the highest-charting album of his career (*Mystery Girl*, at number five), the Top Ten single "You Got It," and a 1990 Grammy Award for Best Pop Vocal Performance, Male.

A. S.

Meanwhile, the Beach Boys remained a highly profitable touring machine. 1992 saw the band, without Brian, release the oppressively electronic *Summer in Paradise*, which served mainly to confirm fans' darkest fears of what the Beach Boys would sound like with Mike Love in charge.

Brian participated in 1996's equally ill-advised *Stars and Stripes, Vol. 1*, a collection of country artists covering Beach Boys songs, with the band providing backup harmonies. Brian and the Beach Boys also discussed the possibility of reuniting for an album of new Wilson songs, but that plan faded when Carl Wilson died in February 1998, following a long battle with lung cancer.

Brian's next solo release was 1998's *Imagination*, which featured a few bright spots but suffered from soupy overproduction. More notable than the album was the fact that, more than three decades after he'd sworn off touring, Wilson conquered his fears to reinvent himself as a live performer. Fronting a sympathetic live band that included former Beach Boys sideman Jeffrey Foskett and the members of the Wilson-influenced L.A. alt-pop quartet the Wondermints, Brian undertook a series of well-received tours, including full performances of *Pet Sounds*.

By 1999, no fewer than three Beach Boys–related acts were on the road, with Brian competing for ticket sales with Mike Love and Bruce Johnston, who continued to tour under the Beach Boys name, and Al Jardine, performing with his own group.

In 2004, Brian Wilson shocked even his most optimistic fans by reviving *Smile*. Although he'd long declined to discuss his mythic lost album, other than to insist that it would never be released, Brian and band debuted *Smile* in concert at London's Royal Festival Hall on February 20. He released *Smile* in a rerecorded studio version recorded with his touring group and incorporating some newly penned Van Dyke Parks lyrics.

The reappearance of *Smile* on record and on stage—and the rapturous response of fans and critics—vindicated Brian Wilson's expansive musical vision. Released thirty-eight years after its creator had begun working on it, *Smile* still sounded ahead of its time while maintaining a timeless emotional resonance. The same can be said of all of Brian Wilson and the Beach Boys' best work.

TIMELINE

October 3, 1961
The Beach Boys record their first single, "Surfin'," at World Pacific Studios in Hollywood.

December 31, 1961
The Beach Boys make their first major public appearance, performing at a Ritchie Valens Memorial Concert at the Long Beach Civic Auditorium.

May 25, 1963
The Beach Boys score their first Top Ten hit with "Surfin' USA," Brian Wilson's reworking of Chuck Berry's "Sweet Little Sixteen."

December 23, 1964
Brian Wilson suffers an anxiety attack on a flight to Houston. He will soon announce that he will no longer tour with the Beach Boys and will concentrate on writing and recording.

May 16, 1966
Pet Sounds is released.

August 1966
Brian Wilson begins recording tracks for the projected next Beach Boys album, *Smile*.

December 10, 1966
"Good Vibrations" tops the U.S. pop charts.

May 1967
It is officially announced that the release of *Smile* has been canceled.

September 18, 1967
Smiley Smile is released in place of *Smile*.

August 31, 1970
Sunflower, the first album under the Beach Boys' new deal with Reprise/Warner Bros., is released.

June 24, 1974
Capitol Records releases *Endless Summer*, a compilation of vintage Beach Boys hits that will spend the next two years on the charts.

June 28, 1976
15 Big Ones, the first Beach Boys album in a decade to be completely produced by Brian Wilson, is released.

July 12, 1988
Brian Wilson releases his first-ever solo album, simply titled *Brian Wilson*.

February 20, 2004
Brian Wilson debuts the resurrected *Smile* in concert at the Royal Festival Hall in London.

September 28, 2004
Brian Wilson's newly recorded edition of *Smile* is released.

SELECTED DISCOGRAPHY

The Beach Boys

Surfin' USA, 1963

Surfer Girl, 1963

All Summer Long, 1964

The Beach Boys Today!, 1965

Pet Sounds, 1966

Wild Honey, 1967

Friends, 1968

Sunflower, 1970

Surf's Up, 1971

The Beach Boys Love You, 1977

Good Vibrations: Thirty Years of The Beach Boys (box set), 1993

The Pet Sounds Sessions (box set), 1997

Brian Wilson

Brian Wilson Presents Smile, 2004

FURTHER READING

Doe, Andrew and John Tobler. *The Complete Guide to the Music of the Beach Boys.* London: Omnibus Press, 1997.

Gaines, Steven. *Heroes and Villains; The True Story of the Beach Boys.* New York: Dutton/Signet, 1986.

Leaf, David. *The Beach Boys and the California Myth.* New York: Grosset & Dunlap, 1978.

Priess, Byron. *The Beach Boys.* New York: Ballantyne, 1979.

Priore, Domenic, ed. *Look! Listen! Vibrate! Smile!* San Francisco: Last Gasp, 1995.

White, Timothy. *The Nearest Faraway Place: Brian Wilson, the Beach Boys and the Southern California Experience.* New York: Henry Holt, 1994.

Courtesy of Photofest.

James Brown

Andy Schwartz

THE LAST SHOW

On the morning of December 28, 2006, dawn in Harlem broke cold and damp under cloudy skies. But the bleak weather had not kept hundreds of people from lining up, beginning shortly after midnight, at the entrance to the historic Apollo Theater on West 125th Street.

They were mostly black, mostly between the ages of thirty and sixty. They waited patiently and good-naturedly to bid a final farewell to the man whose body would soon rest in an open casket on the Apollo stage. That stage had been the site of some of his greatest career triumphs—the same stage where he had ruled, with fiery music and matchless showmanship, on so many nights down through the decades.

Hours later, the lines from the Apollo extended both east and west, down both ends of the long block, and then around the corners of Adam Clayton Powell and Frederick Douglass Boulevards. All along the route, the dead man's recordings poured forth from makeshift sound systems attached to stores and restaurants: "Try Me," "I Feel Good," "I'll Go Crazy," "Papa's Got a Brand New Bag," "Sex Machine," "Living in America." The police had closed 125th Street to traffic, and the crowds strained against the temporary metal barriers erected at the edge of the sidewalk.

At a few minutes past 1 P.M., a white carriage turned onto the thoroughfare. It was drawn by a pair of plumed white horses, driven by two men wearing formal dress and top hats, and bore a gold-painted coffin built of sixteen-gauge steel. It held the body of a man known by many appellations: "Soul Brother Number One," "The Hardest-Working Man in Show Business," "The Godfather of Soul." But as the carriage moved slowly and solemnly down the street toward the doors of the Apollo, a chant rose up from the throng and his real name rang out:

"James Brown! James Brown! James Brown!"

Born into abject poverty in the segregated South, possessed of both immense talent and indomitable will, James Brown is one of a handful of twentieth-century artists of whom it can truthfully be said that they changed music—not just *black* music, not just *American* music, but the sound of popular music around the world.

In the 1920s another African American genius, Louis Armstrong, defined the role of the instrumental soloist and forever changed the sound of jazz. In the 1960s, James Brown transformed rhythm and blues into funk and thereby laid the sonic groundwork for virtually all subsequent rhythm-based pop music forms. The critic Robert Palmer wrote: "The chattering choke-rhythm guitars, broken bass patterns, explosive horn bursts, one-chord drones, and evangelical vocal discourses he introduced in the mid-sixties became the *lingua franca* of contemporary Black pop, the heartbeat of the discotheques and a primary ingredient in such far-flung musical syntheses as Jamaican reggae and Nigerian Afro-beat."[1]

In Brown's best and most influential recordings, the *song* was virtually inseparable from his *sound*. That sound was raw, intense, and indisputably black in its diction and delivery, and it could not be easily emulated or copied by white performers.

Much more than a singer, James Brown conceived and commanded a complete stage show involving crucial elements of timing and sequence. It encompassed a large instrumental group, backing vocalists, and dancers, all of whose roles were endlessly rehearsed and revised. The James Brown Show functioned as a quasi-religious revival meeting, a variety show, and a communal tribute to both Brown's innate talent and his relentless striving for success. Along with his recordings, album covers, publicity photos, and television appearances, the James Brown Show served as a forum through which he introduced new dances, slogans, and hair and clothing styles. All of these changes were closely followed, especially in the 1960s and early 1970s, by an international fan base that stretched from Manhattan to Mali.

The James Brown story is a classic American saga of upward mobility from impoverished origins to the pinnacle of pop stardom. At the peak of his influence, Brown was a figure of profound social significance in black America whose actions and statements inspired admiration, controversy, and derision. He freed himself from record company interference to gain creative control over his music and established a diversified business enterprise that included record labels, publishing companies, and radio stations.

The story also reveals the limits of the singer's real power within the music industry; it is marred by personal tragedy, professional decline, and numerous acts of willful egomania. None of these things have diminished the global impact of James Brown's greatest music, or the pleasure and inspiration that generations of listeners have taken from it.

COMING UP HARD

Although varying dates and locales have been reported over the years, today it is generally accepted that James Joseph Brown Jr. was born on May 3, 1933, in rural Barnwell, South Carolina, the only child of Joe and Susie Brown. Four years later, James's mother abandoned the family; he would not see her again for twenty years. Joe Brown, with only a second-grade education, toiled for meager wages on farms and plantations, in turpentine camps, and later as a gas station attendant. Driving a vegetable delivery truck, he earned $4 per week.

Father and son, along with a succession of Joe's female companions, "lived about as poor as you could be," James later recalled. Their unpainted wooden shack in the woods outside of town "didn't have windows except for shutters that you could pull together; and there was no electricity or indoor plumbing. . . . We ate black-eyed peas and lima beans, fatback [dried and salt-cured pork fat] and syrup, polk salad that we picked in the woods, and cornbread."[2]

Joe Brown was overwhelmed by the responsibilities of single fatherhood and at age five, James was sent to live with his aunt Handsome "Honey" Washington in the black section of Augusta, Georgia, known as "The Terry" (for "territory"). Her two-story dwelling at 944 Twiggs Street was in fact a working brothel presided over by Honey and her bootlegger brother, Jack Scott. Often as not, James was forced to fend for himself in this house full of adult strangers coming and going at all hours, which was raided regularly by the local police.

Trombonist and arranger Fred Wesley Jr., who served two lengthy stints with the James Brown Show, later explained to writer Cynthia Rose: "We're talking about a three, four-year-old child who actually didn't live anywhere. Nobody fed him, nobody bathed him. He didn't *have* a place to live. He survived on sheer guts."[3] When beds were scarce in the overcrowded house, James slept on a wooden pallet on the floor. He did not own a pair of store-bought underwear until he started school at age seven; at times he was sent home from class, humiliated, for having "insufficient clothes."

Much later in life, Brown cited music as "one of the things that helped me to survive . . . It was just there in the community and I fell into it, the way you will."[4] He heard the country and pop tunes played on local radio stations and tried his hand at any instrument within reach, including harmonica, piano, and guitar. (James also claimed to have taken a few lessons from Hudson Whittaker, the legendary blues singer and guitarist known as Tampa Red.)

But what most impressed the eager adolescent were the shouting, ecstatic crowds and blaring brass bands that, every Sunday, filled the "sanctified" churches like Bishop "Daddy" Grace's House of Prayer in Augusta. Back at Aunt Honey's house, James and his cousin Willie "Junior" Glenn, along with other friends, would try to imitate the singing of such popular male gospel groups as the Five Trumpets and the Golden Gate Quartet.

In his eponymous 1986 autobiography, James recalled attending revival services where the preacher "was just screaming and yelling and stomping his foot, and then he dropped to his knees. The people got into it with him, answering him and shouting and clapping time. After that . . . I watched the preachers real close. Then I'd go home and imitate them, because *I* wanted to preach."

Brown continued: "Audience participation in church is something the darker race of people has going [*sic*] because of a lot of trials and tribulations, because of things that we understand about human nature. It's something I can't explain, but I can bring it out of people. I'm not the only person who has the ability, but I *work* at it, and I'm sure a lot of my stage show came out of the church."[5]

Before he reached the age of twelve, James had dropped out of school and into the world of low-wage, unskilled labor. He picked cotton, cut sugarcane, and washed cars. After his day's work was done, he'd set up a shoeshine stand outside radio station WRDW; to attract customers, James would dance on the sidewalk, sometimes singing to accompany himself. That part of his earnings not contributed to his extended family was often spent at the local colored movie theater. James was thrilled by the performances of 1940s rhythm and blues star Louis Jordan, in such all-black-cast screen musicals as *Reet Petite & Gone* and *Look Out, Sister*.

The odd jobs mixed with small-time crimes and street hustles: "The reality of black existence at this time, when Georgia vied with Mississippi for the national lynching championship, was that in any attempt to be something besides a subservient menial worker, one could hardly avoid breaking the law, and even that didn't make life easy."[6] In 1949, sixteen-year-old James Brown was convicted on four counts of breaking and entering (into cars), and given eight to sixteen years in a state penitentiary. When this draconian sentence was reduced, James was transferred to the Alto Reform School in Toccoa, Georgia. He became popular among the inmates for his gospel singing in chapel and trained as a boxer although he was only five feet, six inches tall and weighed 137 pounds. James also played baseball and showed impressive pitching skills until injuries put an end to his dream of a career in the Negro Leagues.

When a young gospel singer-pianist named Bobby Byrd came to perform at Alto, the two teenagers struck up an acquaintance. On June 14, 1952, James was paroled after serving three years and went to live with the Byrd family temporarily while he looked for a place to stay in Toccoa. (As a condition of his parole, James could not return to the county where his family resided.) When not working a variety of low-paying jobs, he sang with Bobby in the Ever Ready Gospel Singers. This group was affiliated with the Mount Zion Baptist Church, where James met Velma Warren—the first of his four wives. They were wed in Toccoa on June 19, 1953, and settled down there; within five years, Velma had given birth to Teddy, Terry, and Larry, the couple's three sons.

James's local performances brought him to the attention of Clint Brantley, the manager of Little Richard (not yet nationally famous), who urged Brown to relocate to Richard's home base in Macon. Soon, Brown had moved into a room above the Two Spot nightclub in Macon and found a day job with the Lawson Motor Company. In his off hours, he sang with such locally popular groups as the Gospel Starlighters and the R&B-oriented Four Steps of Rhythm (James also played piano and drums).

Bobby Byrd also moved to Macon and formed a new gospel outfit with Nafloyd Scott and Sylvester Keels called the Three Swanees. When first Johnny Terry and then James Brown joined the group, it became the Swanee Quintet; after switching to secular music, over the next year their name was changed to the Flames and then again to the Famous Flames. Whatever the name or style, Brown seems destined to have become the de facto leader and on-stage focus of this group, as he eventually did. He may or may not have been the best pure singer in the Flames, but he was almost certainly the most distinctive. Even at this early stage, James combined raw talent with a determined work ethic and an outsized ego fueled, in part, by envy and insecurity.

"He has no real musical skills," trombonist Fred Wesley Jr. told Cynthia Rose, "yet he could hold his own on stage with any jazz virtuoso—because of his guts. Can you understand that? James Brown cannot play drums at all. But he would sit down on drums and get that look on his face like he's playin' 'em, and you would just play along with him. . . . He doesn't understand losing and he *truly* understands surviving. It's not that James wants to win every time—it's that he will not *lose*."[7]

BREAKING THROUGH

Without a record contract, the Famous Flames worked hard to build up their reputation on a black club circuit that extended from Chattanooga, Tennessee, south to lower Florida and west from Savannah, Georgia, into Mississippi. Their career at this stage was characterized by long hours, low pay, and exhausting, sometimes dangerous travel conditions across the segregated South. Macon disc jockey Ray "Satellite Poppa" Brown sometimes traveled with James in these early days. "Finding a motel room—that was unheard of, man," he later recalled. "You'd sleep in your car or stay at the club until daybreak."[8]

Mostly the group sang other people's hits, including "Please Don't Go," a Top Ten R&B entry for the Orioles in 1952. The Famous Flames' extended live version of this song became an audience favorite and gradually evolved into "Please, Please, Please," a hypnotically repetitive ballad credited to James Brown and Johnny Terry that pitted James's raspy, emotive lead vocal against the Flames' doo-wop background. In late 1955, the group recorded a rough version of the song at Macon radio station WIBB in a session overseen by disc jockey Hamp "King Bee" Swain: "I put it on the air and we got a tremendous reaction. *Immediately.* The phone lines just lit up."[9]

In January 1956, A&R man Ralph Bass heard the song on an Atlanta station while traveling through the South on a talent-scouting trip for King Records of Cincinnati. He tracked down the Famous Flames at a small club near Milledgeville, Georgia, and promptly signed the group for an advance of $200, then brought them to the King studios to re-cut the song with professional studio players. King's rotund, cigar-smoking founder Syd Nathan declared "Please, Please, Please" to be one of the worst songs he'd ever heard and told Ralph Bass he was crazy to have even paid James's train fare from Macon to Cincinnati. But Nathan changed his tune when the record began to sell throughout the South.

"Brown was way ahead of his time," Ralph Bass later recalled. "He wasn't really singing R&B. He was singing gospel to an R&B combo with a real heavy feeling. . . . He wasn't singing or playing music—he was transmitting *feeling*, pure feeling."[10]

"Please, Please, Please" was released in March 1956 on Federal Records (a King subsidiary) with label credit inscribed to "James Brown & the Famous Flames." The disc hung on the *Billboard* R&B singles chart for nineteen weeks, peaking at number five; over time, it sold more than a million copies. The group's success attracted the interest of Ben Bart, the white founder and head of the potent New York booking agency Universal Attractions. Previously, Bart had managed the careers of swing bandleader Jimmy Lunceford, singer Dinah Washington, and a pioneering vocal group the Ravens; it was a big step up for the Famous Flames when he agreed to become their booking agent. Ben Bart later became the singer's manager, business partner, and beloved father figure, and the only person ever to refer to James Brown as "Jimmy" (Brown called him "Pop"). Their close and complex relationship lasted until Bart's death in 1968.

Nine more single releases followed, yet not one reached the *Billboard* R&B chart—perhaps because most were overly derivative of recent hits by better-established performers, including Little Richard ("Chonnie-On-Chon") and Ray Charles ("That Dood It"). Syd Nathan's personal distaste for Brown's music and his tight-fisted attitude toward promotional expenditures on behalf of any King artist also may have been significant factors. This string of failures, combined with Ben Bart's expressed desire to make James its front-and-center star, caused the original group to dissolve in 1957. Later, Bobby Byrd returned to Brown's organization for the long haul through the 1960s with the trio of male singer-dancers always billed as the Famous Flames—but always in a supporting role to Brown himself.

STAR TIME

By the fall of 1958, Syd Nathan was ready to drop James Brown from the King/Federal roster when the singer came up with another slow, bluesy ballad, "Try Me." To the surprise of all concerned, the song shot to number one R&B in early 1959—and from that time until 1982, a year would not pass in which James Brown didn't place at least one song on the *Billboard* R&B chart. ("Try Me" also crossed over to the Hot 100, peaking at number forty-eight.)

Brown became increasingly conscious of the need to maintain his own permanent road band. It was a bold and expensive move that harkened back to the big bands of Count Basie and Duke Ellington as well as Louis Jordan's Tympani Five. Many leading R&B performers of the period, including Sam Cooke and Jackie Wilson, traveled with just a guitarist and a drummer while recruiting other players as needed. But a James Brown *band* could be trained to play his music the James Brown way, night after night. It would also be available around the clock for spontaneous recording sessions in any studio convenient to the singer's never-ending tour itinerary. Among his first recruits (circa 1959) were bassist Bernard Odum, drummer Nat Kendrick, and saxophonists J.C. Davis and Albert Corley.

When James had regained his footing on the charts with "Try Me" and "Think" (number seven R&B), he moved from Federal to the parent King label.

Now commanding a degree of grudging respect from Syd Nathan, he was free to write and produce his own material with his own musicians. Brown had no say over King's release schedule, however, and it was not unusual for six months or more to pass between the recording and the release of a new song like "Night Train." (In 1962, "Night Train" became James's eighth Top Ten R&B hit and his second Top Forty Pop entry.) When Brown suggested the idea of an instrumental based on a dance he called the mashed potatoes, Nathan told him to forget about it. James cut the track at his own expense (dubbing disc jockey King Coleman's voice over his own vocal interjections) and licensed the song to Henry Stone's Dade Records in Miami. Credited to Nat Kendrick and the Swans, "(Do The) Mashed Potatoes (Pt. 1 & 2)" reached number eight R&B in 1960.

Another, more significant confrontation between the artist and his label resulted in one of the key albums of James Brown's entire career. By 1962, his skin-tight, endlessly rehearsed live show was tearing up audiences across the country. Even James's best studio recordings couldn't capture the intensity of his on-stage delivery and the fervor of his fans' collective response. He needed a live album, and Ray Charles had shown the way with *Ray Charles in Person*, a Top Fifteen bestseller in 1960.

James proposed the idea to Syd Nathan—and was turned down flat. The label chief simply didn't believe that fans would buy an album of songs they'd already purchased in studio versions, and he was loath to pay the costs of location recording. In the fall of 1962, James opened the fifth extended engagement of his career at the Apollo Theater in Harlem—the premier showplace in "The Capital of Black America." On October 24, the performance was recorded at Brown's own expense for $5,700. The tapes were pared down to a thirty-two-minute LP so carelessly edited that the break between the first and second sides came right in the middle of the climactic track, an intense 11-minute version of "Lost Someone." When the album was released in January 1963, King initially pressed just 5,000 copies.

Live at the Apollo was an immediate and unprecedented smash. It made no stylistic concessions to the pop mainstream, simply capturing a typically heated James Brown performance before an enraptured black audience. Yet *Live at the Apollo* rose all the way to number two among *Billboard* Top Pop Albums and hung on the chart for sixty-six weeks—in a year when the top-selling album artists included musical humorist Allan Sherman, folk trio Peter Paul and Mary, and crooner Andy Williams. Reaction among black radio listeners was so intense that disc jockeys would often play both sides of the album in full, with commercial spots inserted in the break.

Forty years later, *Live at the Apollo* was ranked at number twenty-four on *Rolling Stone* magazine's list of the 500 Greatest Albums of All Time. In 2004, it was one of fifty recordings added to the National Recording Registry at the Library of Congress, alongside *Pet Sounds* by the Beach Boys and the Vladimir

Horowitz/Arturo Toscanini recording of Tchaikovsky's *Piano Concerto No. 1, Pp. 23, Bb minor.*

MAKE IT FUNKY

James Brown's music continued to evolve as new personnel came into his band. Among the key additions of the early 1960s were saxophonists Maceo Parker and St. Clair Pinckney, guitarist Jimmy Nolen, and drummers Clyde Stubblefield and John "Jabo" Starks. Stubblefield is often credited with a crucial shift in emphasis from the second and fourth beats (as in traditional blues) to the first and third beats—"The One," as this rhythm dynamic became known in the lexicon of funk. Alfred "Pee Wee" Ellis, a saxophonist and arranger who joined Brown's revue in 1965, explained the importance of Clyde Stubblefield's "New Orleans beat" to Cynthia Rose:

> If, in a studio, you said "Play it funky," that could imply almost anything. But "give me a New Orleans beat"—you got exactly what you wanted. And Clyde Stubblefield was just the epitome of this funky drumming. There was a way his beat was broken up—a combination of where the bass and the snare drums hit—which was topsy-turvy from what had been goin' on.[11]

With the success of *Live at the Apollo*, James felt compelled to relocate to the center of the American music business; with Velma and their children, he moved into a twelve-room Victorian house in Queens, New York. Brown and Ben Bart formed an independent company called Fair Deal Productions. The singer's attorney, Marty Machat, took the position that James's agreement with King had expired and signed him, through Fair Deal, to a lucrative new contract with Smash, a subsidiary of Mercury Records. Syd Nathan promptly filed suit, alleging breach of contract, but Brown recorded prolifically for Smash while the case wended its way through the legal system.

In the summer of 1964, his Smash recording "Out of Sight" became James's tenth Top Ten R&B hit and a number twenty-four Pop entry. On this track, "you can hear the band and me start to move in a whole other direction rhythmically," Brown later wrote. "The horns, the guitar, the vocals, everything was starting to be used to establish all kinds of rhythms at once. . . . I was trying to get every aspect of the production to contribute to the rhythmic patterns."[12]

In October 1964, he appeared at the Santa Monica Civic Auditorium in Los Angeles before a predominantly white audience as a part of a star-studded cast assembled to film *The T.A.M.I. [Teen Age Music International] Show*, a concert documentary that was released to theaters the following year. The bill included the Beach Boys, Marvin Gaye, the Supremes, and the Rolling Stones but James pulled out all the stops in an explosion of song and dance.

Motown Records

The Sound of Young America

Berry Gordy Jr. was a former prizefighter and auto plant worker turned song-writer who co-wrote Jackie Wilson's first solo hit "Reet Petite" (1957). Like Stax, Motown Records began as a small family affair: Berry's sisters, Esther, Anna, Gwen, and Loucye, were all early Motown employees, as was his second wife, Raynoma Liles. But in the crossover appeal of its black artists to white audiences, the young company quickly surpassed Stax Records, its Memphis counterpart. The Motown Sound brought rhythm and blues to new heights of polish and sophistication; in the process, Berry Gordy built one of the most important black-owned businesses in American history.

This sound was perfected through a style of record production modeled on a Detroit automobile assembly line. Motown staff writers would compose a song that was then registered with Motown's publishing company, Jobete Music. Motown staff producers worked with the Motown house band in the Motown studio to create a finished instrumental track. Only then would the new song be presented to the Motown artist or group whose vocals would be added to the song. Record production was a seven-day-a-week, nearly around-the-clock operation, conducted in an atmosphere of intense competition—both with other record labels and within Motown itself, where everyone seemed to be striving for Berry Gordy's approval.

Motown Records relocated from Detroit to Los Angeles in 1972, by which time the label's first golden era of explosive growth and unsurpassed creativity was several years in the past. But individual artists like Marvin Gaye and Stevie Wonder were making the most important music of their careers; a youthful group called the Jackson 5, fronted by preternaturally gifted Michael Jackson, had scored seven Top Ten Pop hits (including four consecutive number ones) in three short years. Berry Gordy Jr.—the tough, canny visionary—was still in control, and Motown still had musical history to make.

The Hitmakers of "Hitsville"

The Miracles, the Marvelettes, and Mary Wells were among Motown's leading hit makers in the company's first five years. The Miracles' superb lead singer, William "Smokey" Robinson, was also a gifted songwriter who wrote or co-wrote all of the group's biggest hits from their first R&B number one ("Shop Around," 1960) through their last ("The Tears of a Clown," 1970). In 1961, the Marvelettes' "Please Mr. Postman" became the first single on any Motown-affiliated label (in this case, Tamla) to reach number one on both the R&B *and* Pop charts. Sweet-voiced Mary Wells had the first number one R&B/Pop single on Motown proper in 1964 with Smokey's lilting song "My Guy."

But Mary Wells and the Marvelettes were pushed aside when the Supremes (Diana Ross, Mary Wilson, and Florence Ballard) broke through with "Where

Did Our Love Go" in the summer of 1964. The trio's unprecedented run of twelve number one Pop hits included "Come See About Me," "Stop! In the Name of Love," and "You Can't Hurry Love"—all written and produced by the team of Eddie Holland, Lamont Dozier, and Eddie's brother Brian Holland. The Supremes became the most successful African American group of the 1960s. Florence Ballard, who left in 1967, later died in poverty at age thirty-two; Diana Ross became a top-selling Motown solo artist and an Oscar-nominated film star (*Lady Sings the Blues*).

Holland-Dozier-Holland's most successful Motown act after the Supremes was the Four Tops. When the producers prodded the Tops' lead vocalist Levi Stubbs into singing at the top of his range, a bland supper-club act was transformed into a powerhouse soul group on the R&B/Pop number one hits "I Can't Help Myself" (1965) and "Reach Out I'll Be There" (1966).

Founded in 1960, the Temptations struggled with personnel changes and mediocre material until their first number one R&B/Pop hit in 1965. "My Girl" is *the* classic "Tempts" song, a Smokey Robinson composition sung by Melvin Franklin, Otis Williams, David Ruffin, Eddie Kendricks, and Paul Williams. The Temptations were legendary for their immaculate stagecraft and luxuriant vocal blend, the leads alternating between Ruffin's grainy tenor and Kendricks's ethereal falsetto. After Dennis Edwards replaced David Ruffin in 1968, the group rebounded with two more number one songs, "I Can't Get Next to You" (1969) and "I Wish It Would Rain" (1971). Among Rock and Roll Hall of Fame inductees, Motown is well represented by the Four Tops, the Temptations, Smokey Robinson, the Supremes, Holland-Dozier-Holland, and Berry Gordy Jr.

Andy Schwartz

"[I] hit the stage on fire, just because I was told by so many people not to push my heat button too hard. I mean, I torched those songs. . . . The minute we kicked in with our opening number, 'Out of Sight,' all those white kids in the audience went crazy!" It was, he recounted proudly, "the first time anybody in that neck of the woods had got a dose of real soul, James Brown style."[13]

The T.A.M.I. Show captured on film the so-called cape routine, a key ritual of James's live performance. "In a drama that would play itself out many times during the course of a single concert, Brown, supposedly overcome by torturous emotional and physical cravings, would drop prayerfully to his knees, unable to continue. Only when his seconds, the Famous Flames, draped a velvet cape across his shoulders and led the shambling singer from the stage would he again find the strength to continue."[14]

James's career took a curious turn when King obtained a court injunction which dictated that he release *instrumentals* on Smash and *vocals* on King. Mercury was forced to withdraw the *Out of Sight* album and instead put out instrumental sets like *Grits and Soul* and *James Brown Plays New Breed*, all featuring Brown on organ. Meanwhile, Syd Nathan delved into the King vaults and cobbled together "new" James Brown vocal releases from tapes recorded years earlier.

Stax Records

Soulsville USA

No one can say for certain just when "rhythm and blues" became "soul." By about 1960, the word "soul" was frequently used in the lexicon of African American music: in 1958, for example, Ray Charles and jazz vibraphonist Milt Jackson released an album titled *Soul Brothers*. Nor is it easy to describe the musical elements that differentiate soul music from earlier styles of R&B. James Brown's hard-hitting, syncopated rhythms marked one evolutionary change; so did Jerry Butler's deep, gospel-infused lead vocal with the Impressions on their 1958 ballad hit, "For Your Precious Love."

Once soul music took hold, small and large record companies in urban centers across the nation began pumping out countless records in the new style. In 1959, Jim Stewart and his older sister Estelle Axton created Stax Records (initially as Satellite Records) in Memphis, Tennessee.

Unusually for its time and place, Stax Records was an integrated operation. Its white partners built their offices and recording studio in a converted movie theater in the heart of Memphis's black community. The artist roster was virtually all black, but Booker T. and the MGs—the house rhythm section that played on most of the label's greatest hits—comprised two black musicians (drummer Al Jackson Jr., keyboards player Booker T. Jones) and two white ones (guitarist Steve Cropper, bassist Donald "Duck" Dunn). Black producer/songwriters like Isaac Hayes and David Porter worked alongside the white recording engineer Ron Capone.

In 1959, Rufus and Carla Thomas provided the fledgling company with its first national hit, " 'Cause I Love You." Rufus's daughter Carla became the label's most popular female artist with such songs as "B-A-B-Y" and "I Like What You're Doing to Me." In 1967, she recorded a humorous, funky duet called "Tramp" with Otis Redding, whose music epitomized the Stax sound.

Otis Redding was a classic "down home" soul singer whose gritty voice sounded older than his years, especially on pleading ballads like "I've Been Loving You Too Long." He sang with a pronounced Southern accent, punctuating the lyrics with trademark phrases like "GOT-ta, GOT-ta" and "my-my-my." Otis wrote or co-wrote many of his best-known songs, including "Respect" (later a career-making hit for Aretha Franklin) and "Pain in My Heart" (which was covered by the Rolling Stones). Redding died at age twenty-six in a plane crash in Madison, Wisconsin, on December 10, 1967, soon after recording an unusual new song. With its prominent acoustic guitar and surf sound effects, "(Sittin' on) the Dock of the Bay" was a striking but wholly natural departure from Redding's usual down-home style. Released posthumously, it became his first and only number one hit (on both the Pop and R&B charts) and won two Grammy Awards.

After Otis Redding's death, soul-blues man Johnnie Taylor brought Stax back to the top of the charts in 1968 with "Who's Making Love" (number one R&B/number five Pop). The Staples Singers' blend of social consciousness and funky gospel fervor on "I'll Take You There" and "Respect Yourself" made them one of the most popular R&B groups of the early Seventies.

Sam and Dave and Isaac Hayes

Sam Moore and David Prater Jr., known as Sam and Dave, recorded some of the most enduring songs in the Stax catalog: "Hold On, I'm Coming," "Soul Man," "I Thank You." These discs were written and produced by Isaac Hayes and David Porter—a top Stax production team until 1969, when Isaac's *Hot Buttered Soul* album propelled him into a hugely successful solo career as soul music's first "underground" artist. With some tracks running as long as eighteen minutes, *Hot Buttered Soul* became the first Stax album to sell over one million copies.

"Up to this point," wrote Stax historian Rob Bowman, "virtually everyone in the record industry simply assumed that the black audience was neither economically equipped nor aesthetically interested in purchasing LPs in large numbers . . . *Hot Buttered Soul* unquestionably proved that black artists could sell LPs, and singlehandedly revolutionized the notion of the length and musical palette appropriate for black artists" (p. 184). In 1971, Hayes's Stax soundtrack for the Gopalon parks film *Shaft* shot to number one, and its proto-disco title song won an Academy Award—the first ever earned by an African American composer.

Today, the Stax Museum of American Soul Music commemorates the label's historic achievements. Isaac Hayes, Otis Redding, Sam and Dave, Booker T. and the MGs, and Jim Stewart all have been inducted into the Rock and Roll Hall of Fame.

A. S.

A BRAND NEW BAG

The year of the Beatles' American breakthrough, 1964, visited setbacks and tragedy upon a number of James's fellow soul stars. His friend and former King Records label mate, Little Willie John, was charged with assault in Miami; he died in a Washington State prison in 1968. In October, Ray Charles was arrested for possession of marijuana and heroin in Boston. In December, Sam Cooke was shot and killed by a motel owner in Los Angeles. Jackie Wilson did not have one Top Ten R&B hit in 1964; Solomon Burke had several, mostly sung in a smooth ballad style. Wilson Pickett was between record contracts and Otis Redding had not yet emerged as a national star from his Southern base.

All of these circumstances reinforced James Brown's position as the preeminent soul singer of the day. He criss-crossed the continent at the head of a troupe that now numbered nearly two dozen musicians and vocalists. When James's musical career began, the conditions of his parole prohibited him from remaining within the Augusta city limits for more than twenty-four hours. Now he could, by his insistence on playing to mixed audiences, effectively integrate first the Macon City Auditorium and then Bell Auditorium in Augusta—months before President Lyndon Johnson signed the Civil Rights Act into law on July 2, 1964.

Under a renegotiated contract with King, James was releasing a new single every few weeks. Two of these—"Papa's Got a Brand New Bag" and "It's a Man's Man's Man's World"—were among the best-selling and most influential songs of his entire career.

"Papa's Got a Brand New Bag" is a blues in form but with a sound far removed from the deliberate, Mississippi-bred style of Muddy Waters or Jimmy Reed. Brown's brusque vocal rides a taut, hard-hitting beat as he namechecks various dance crazes like the twist, the jerk, and the boomerang. At the end of each verse, everything drops away for a few seconds of jazzy chickenscratch chording by guitarist Jimmy Nolen and a blast of horns, signaling a repeat of the chord sequence. Like another world changing hit from the summer of 1965, Bob Dylan's "Like a Rolling Stone," "Papa" feels like it could go on for a very long time. In fact, the complete original recording is over seven minutes in length: King's two-minute single edit was only part one of a three-part track.

"Papa" became the first James Brown single to reach the Top Ten of the *Billboard* Hot 100 and held the R&B number one position for eight weeks; it spawned a best-selling album of the same title that reached number two R&B and number twenty-six Pop. In 1999, "Papa's Got a Brand New Bag" was given a Grammy Hall of Fame Award as a recording "of lasting qualitative or historical significance."

"It's a Man's Man's Man's World" was the stylistic opposite, a slow minorkey ballad co-written by Brown and songwriter Betty Jean Newsome. James had produced an earlier version of the song for Tammi Terrell, a singer with his touring revue; it passed unnoticed when released under the title "I Cried." But Brown's own rendition is a moody masterpiece, with dark clouds of orchestration shadowing his lead vocal and the almost inaudible rhythm section. His tormented delivery, with its dramatic sobs and shouts, infused the lyrics with deeper, more universal emotions. Perhaps the depiction of "a man's world" that "would be nothing without a woman or a girl" reflected the pain of James's breakup with Velma, from whom he separated in 1964 (they divorced in 1969).

Released in April 1966, "It's a Man's Man's Man's World" topped the R&B chart and cracked the Pop Top Ten, peaking at number eight. The chord sequence and melody of "Fallin'," Alicia Keys's massive Grammy Award–winning hit of 2001, are startlingly similar to James's song—even though "Fallin'" is credited only to Keys.

BLACK AND PROUD

Brown enjoyed his greatest crossover success in the period 1967–68, when three of his number one R&B hits all reached the Pop Top Ten. "Cold Sweat" and "I Got the Feelin'" were funk masterpieces, but "Say It Loud – I'm Black and I'm Proud" was that and something more. The song was released in September 1968, a year in which the United States was rocked by political assassinations, the Tet offensive in South Vietnam, widespread protests against the Vietnam War, and the violence that erupted during the Democratic National Convention in Chicago.

On April 4, Dr. Martin Luther King Jr. was assassinated in Memphis, Tennessee. The next night, Brown was scheduled to headline Boston Garden in Boston, Massachusetts. At first, Mayor Kevin White wanted to cancel the show. Instead, a plan was formulated to broadcast the show live over Boston's public television station WGBH. A few thousand ticket-holders showed up that night; on stage, James paused several times in the course of his show to speak to the audience, cooling tempers and heading off confrontations between young blacks and the police stationed inside the arena. His words were heard by a much larger audience that had stayed home to watch the show for free— and although civil disturbances broke out that night in nearly 100 cities across the nation, Boston remained calm.

In June, James flew overseas to entertain U.S. troops in Korea and Vietnam—an opportunity he'd been denied, despite his repeated requests to the USO, until Vice President Hubert Humphrey interceded on the singer's behalf. Brown and his band (stripped down to just five musicians for the trip) often played several shows in a day; they traveled in military helicopters that came under enemy fire on several frightening occasions.

James returned to the United States and in August recorded "Say It Loud" in Los Angeles. For the session, he recruited an amateur chorus of schoolchildren and adults to chant the title phrase. His lead vocal is quite literally a "rap," a string of spoken couplets, while the horn section and an unforgettable bass line provide the melodic content.

"Say It Loud—I'm Black and I'm Proud" became a rallying cry and a powerful expression of self-affirmation. Almost overnight, it seemed, terms like "colored" and "Negro" fell out of the African American lexicon. Through the expressive power of this song and its constant airing on black radio, James Brown "named an entire people: *Black* Americans,"[15] wrote journalist

Glen Ford, whose first full-time radio news job was on WRDW Augusta, one of three radio stations owned by Brown in the late 1960s.

"The phenomenon built upon, but was more far-reaching than, Stokely Carmichael's popularization of 'Black Power' two years earlier. Carmichael's slogan called for—demanded—power for Black people. But James Brown's anthem actually empowered ordinary Black folks to signal to their leaders and oppressors—the whole world, in fact—the fundamental terms of any dialogue: how they were to be addressed."[16]

Brown's politics were complicated, contradictory, and rooted in personal experience. He was a member of the National Association for the Advancement of Colored People. In the summer of 1966, he performed in Tupelo, Mississippi, in support of James Meredith, who'd been shot in the back while making his March Against Fear from Memphis, Tennessee, to Jackson, Mississippi. But racial pride didn't prevent James from hiring white musicians or working with white managers and agents. Later in life, he even spoke of George Wallace and Lester Maddox with admiration and forgiveness despite the fact that both men had bitterly opposed the civil rights movement when they served as the governors of, respectively, Alabama and Georgia.

The title of a 2006 book by business author Tyrone L. Cypress—*Say It Loud . . . I Sell and I'm Proud*—may have been a crude manipulation of the song's true historical meaning. But it was also consistent with the recurring theme of black capitalist uplift that ran through Brown's worldview and public rhetoric. For proof that America was indeed a land of opportunity in which hard work and determination could pay off beyond anyone's wildest dreams, James Brown needed to look no further than the nearest mirror. His economic philosophy might have been summed up by the title of his number three R&B/number twenty Pop hit of 1969: "I Don't Want Nobody to Give Me Nothing (Open up the Door, I'll Get It Myself)."

In a real-life demonstration of the song's credo, Brown faced down a local campaign to prevent his realtor from closing on a large house that the singer intended to purchase in Walton Way, an upscale white section of Augusta. In October 1969, following his divorce from Velma, James married Deidre "Deedee" Jenkins and moved into the new home with his new wife who later gave birth to their daughters Deanna and Yamma.

LARGE AND IN CHARGE

Republican President Richard Nixon "made Brown feel he was a key example of black capitalism at work, which appealed to the singer's gigantic ego," wrote Nelson George. "Brown didn't understand the nuances of Nixon's plan—reach out to showcase some black business efforts while dismantling [Lyndon] Johnson's Great Society programs, which for all their reputed mismanagement had helped a generation of blacks begin the process of upward mobility."[17]

James endorsed Nixon in his 1972 re-election campaign—one of the few black entertainers to do so, besides Lionel Hampton and Sammy Davis Jr. In May 1973, during a return engagement at the Apollo Theater, black demonstrators picketed the theater with signs that read "James Brown, Nixon Clown" and "Get That Clown Out of Town."

James was a temperamental and often vindictive employer of musicians and other personnel. Underlying nearly all his actions was, as Arthur Kempton noted, "his conviction that every inch of his way up had been bought and paid for by his own unreasonably hard effort"[18] as well as "the classic Napoleonic little man's disposition to take any subordinate's challenge as a towering affront."[19]

When trombonist Fred Wesley Jr. joined James's organization in early 1968, he was grateful to receive a salary of $350 per week regardless of whether "Mr. Brown" (as he demanded to be addressed by everyone, at all times) was working or not. Wesley soon found out that this system was stacked in favor of the boss, who regularly worked 300 days of the year. The same weekly salary could cover multiple shows in the same venue or gigs in two cities in the same day; the musicians received nothing extra for recording sessions or television appearances. The payroll remained at about $6,000 a week, a paltry sum given Brown's earning power, "and he acted like he didn't want to give you that."[20]

In addition, band members were forced to endure "horror rehearsals" during which James would harangue and insult them for hours on end. He also imposed fines for on-stage offenses ranging from wrong notes to unshined shoes. Fred felt deeply that such manipulation was "unnecessary to the creation of an act as exciting as the James Brown Show. But, on the real side, there has never been a show that exciting, that tight, that completely entertaining. There also has never been a man so dedicated, so determined, so focused."[21]

In 1970, just hours before a show in Columbus, Georgia, the musicians threatened to quit unless Brown promised to change his ways. Instead, he summarily fired most of the band including Maceo Parker, Clyde Stubblefield, and Jabo Starks. James then dispatched his Lear jet to Cincinnati to pick up a local group called the Pacesetters, led by eighteen-year-old William "Bootsy" Collins on bass and his brother Phelps "Catfish" Collins on guitar. They arrived in Columbus, were driven directly to the venue, and carried their equipment on stage as the other musicians were removing their own. Despite a few hours' delay, the James Brown Show went on as scheduled.

James changed the Pacesetters' name to the JBs. It was this group—later rejoined by Parker, Starks, and Fred Wesley Jr.—that provided the backing for many of his best and biggest funk hits of the Seventies. This series of inspired singles included "Get Up—I Feel Like Being Like a Sex Machine," "Super Bad," "I'm a Greedy Man," "Soul Power," and "Get On the Good Foot—Part 1." In 1974 alone, James scored three R&B number one hits with "The Payback—Part 1," "My Thang," and "Papa Don't Take No Mess—Part 1."

The relentless repetition of beats, riffs, and vocal phrases, over tracks that (in their album versions) sometimes ran for ten minutes or more, was not a drawback but an essential element of the James Brown sound. The individual songs seemed to form a non-stop and continuously evolving jam, with the leader verbally cuing one of the tightest and most versatile bands in all of popular music through the chord changes, horn solos, and drum breaks.

After nearly twenty years on the road, James remained a galvanizing live performer whose volcanic intensity and spontaneous eruptions could provoke near-hysterical reaction from audiences throughout Europe, Africa, and North America. In 1970, at a huge outdoor sports arena in Dakar, Senegal, "James demonstrated his endurance . . . by jumping off the ten-foot-high stage and running a lap around the stadium, wearing his 'Please, Please, Please' robe, after singing and dancing for two hours."[22] In Lagos, Nigeria, James communed with Nigerian superstar Fela Kuti. In the fall of 1974, the singer performed in Kinshasa, Zaire, as part of an African American music festival attached to the heavyweight title fight between Muhammad Ali and George Foreman.

Syd Nathan, the founder of King Records, died March 5, 1968, and in October his company was sold to Starday Records of Nashville. Starday itself was then sold to Lin Broadcasting, which sold James Brown's contract and catalog to Polydor Records of Germany in July 1971. James was a vital addition to the Polydor roster as the company sought to establish itself in the all-important U.S. market. In addition to Brown's own unending flow of singles and albums (including the two-LP sets *Revolution of the Mind*, *The Payback*, and *Get On the Good Foot*), he founded a new label, People Records, to distribute his productions of other artists: Hank Ballard, Bobby Byrd, Lyn Collins, and assorted instrumental configurations of the JBs.

TRIALS AND TRIBULATIONS

In his off-stage life, however, the singer was under increasing personal strain. Beginning in 1968, he became embroiled in protracted disputes with the IRS, which claimed that he owed millions in back taxes. Eventually, Brown lost ownership of his three radio stations, his two private planes, and even his Augusta home to the agency. At times, he felt certain he was under government surveillance.

In August 1973, James's eldest son Teddy, age nineteen, was killed in a car accident in upstate New York, leaving his father "on my knees with grief." In his darkest moments, Teddy's death felt like "a kind of punishment for me that I could never be pardoned or paroled from, or a sin I could never properly atone for."[23] His marriage to Deedee began to disintegrate, although they were not legally divorced until 1981.

But the greatest threat to Brown's career was the advent of a kind of music—disco—that could never have existed without him. His complex polyrhythms were smoothed out into one metronomic dance beat; his jazzy horn riffs were replaced by sweeping string arrangements. In general, the new style was more adaptable to the melodic voices of female singers like Donna Summer and vocal groups such as the O'Jays. James derided disco as "a very small part of funk, like a vamp. The difference is that in funk you dig into a groove, you don't stay on the surface. Disco stayed on the surface."[24]

Competition arose on another front from Parliament-Funkadelic, the extravagant "funk mob" led by George Clinton and featuring such former JBs as Bootsy Collins and Fred Wesley Jr. P-Funk's sprawling, wildly costumed live shows were filling the sports arenas and municipal auditoriums that had been Brown's live domain a few years earlier. Meanwhile, Stevie Wonder and Marvin Gaye were selling millions of copies of their progressive soul master-pieces like *Talking Book* and *What's Going On*. In contrast, James's albums seemed to be assembled from a stockpile of recordings while he was on tour or otherwise engaged; the paintings that adorned some of his LP covers had the weirdly sincere look of what later became known as "outsider art." In the course of his career, Brown placed forty-nine releases on the Billboard Top 200 Albums chart but only one—*The Payback*, from 1974—has been certified gold by the Recording Industry Association of America.

REJUVENATION

Toward the end of the 1970s, the singer began to encounter a new and enthu-siastic audience in new wave rock clubs, where hip young whites hailed him as influence and innovator. In 1980, diehard James Brown fans John Belushi and Dan Aykroyd cast him in the role of a singing sanctified preacher in their hit movie *The Blues Brothers* (which also featured appearances by Aretha Franklin and Ray Charles). That same year Brown recorded "Rapp Payback (Where Iz Moses)," one of his best late-career tracks. With his Polydor deal now expired, James licensed the song to T.K. Records, a label run by Henry Stone—the same Miami music entrepreneur who'd picked up "(Do The) Mashed Potatoes (Pt. 1 & 2)" two decades earlier. "Rapp Payback" only reached number forty-five among Billboard R&B Singles but it would be a long time before James Brown again attained even this modest level of chart success.

Two years later, the singer met makeup artist Adrienne Rodriguez on the set of the TV show *Solid Gold*. She moved into James's new South Carolina home a few months later and they were married in 1984. In the same year, Brown released "Unity," a new single and video performed with Afrika Bam-baataa—a Bronx DJ and rapper whose position in New York's hip-hop nation was comparable to Brown's role in traditional R&B.

In 1985, James's career was revitalized temporarily by his recording of "Living in America," the theme song from the movie *Rocky IV*. He had no hand in writing or arranging the song, which others had completed by the time James cut his lead vocal. Nonetheless, "Living in America" went all the way to number four to become the highest-charting Pop hit of his career as well as a number ten R&B entry, and won the Grammy Award for Best Rhythm & Blues Recording.

As the song climbed the Hot 100, James Brown was among the inaugural group of musicians to be inducted into the Rock and Roll Hall of Fame. He attended the black-tie ceremony at the Waldorf-Astoria in New York on January 23, 1986, and later "spoke of it as the culmination of his career."[25] On the morning of January 28, the space shuttle *Challenger* exploded, killing the seven astronauts on board. Twelve hours later, James's first headlining appearance at New York's prestigious Radio City Music Hall began with a solemn invocation offered by Reverend Al Sharpton, the New York political activist who'd become the singer's close friend and confidant after Teddy Brown's death. James Brown then went through the motions of his performance in a manner that suggested either deep despair over the *Challenger* disaster or the fogged-in condition of drug use. Rather than a celebration of a triumphant comeback, the Radio City show was a harbinger of worse things to come.

Nonetheless, the *Rocky IV* soundtrack sold over a million copies and led to a new recording contract with Scotti Brothers Records. *Gravity* (1986), produced by pop hit-maker Dan Hartman, was described by critic Robert Christgau as "not a James Brown album—a James Brown–influenced Dan Hartman record, with James Brown on vocals."[26] *I'm Real* (1988) was a more artistically successful collaboration with the producer/performers of New York hip-hop group Full Force. The album yielded Brown's final number one R&B hit ("I'm Real") and a number five follow up ("Static") but only reached number ninety-six on the *Billboard* Pop Albums chart. If contemporary listeners were no longer receptive to new James Brown songs, perhaps it was because *old* James Brown songs were saturating the radio and MTV airwaves in the form of JB samples on innumerable rap hits.

James Brown: The Godfather of Soul, the first and best of the singer's two memoirs, appeared in 1986. Even if some of the reconstructed conversations didn't ring true, Brown's capacious memory created a richly detailed narrative that blended personal history with philosophical musings on poverty, politics, racism, marriage, and stardom.

CRIME AND PUNISHMENT

Financial pressures, career decline, marital strife, and drug use all came to a head for James Brown in 1988. He was arrested repeatedly on charges ranging from leaving the scene of an accident to domestic violence involving Adrienne. In September, attendees at an insurance seminar in Augusta were confronted by a shotgun-wielding James Brown who demanded to know if anyone had used his office's private restroom on the same floor. He then fled the building and a high-speed police chase ensued, back and forth across the Georgia–South Carolina state line. James's arrest resulted in multiple charges including assault on a police officer, possession of the animal tranquilizer PCP, and carrying an unlicensed pistol.

The singer later insisted that "I never did anything the police said I did. It was simply a vengeance sentence, made worse by my celebrity. Because I was a famous black performer, busted roadside in the South, I had to pay the price."[27] Refusing to plead guilty, Brown was sentenced to a total of six years but served only fifteen months in a South Carolina prison. Even as he protested his innocence, James admitted that his incarceration was "a much-needed break from the crazy merry-go-round of booze and drugs. . . . I was tired, my resistance was low, and I needed a place to get myself together."[28]

After ten more months in a work-release program, Brown was paroled in February 1991. (Later the singer was arrested a few more times—for drug possession and domestic violence—but never re-incarcerated.) In June, he returned to public performance with a show at the Wiltern Theater in Los Angeles. Still on board were such longtime allies as manager Charles Bobbitt and emcee Danny Ray, whose immortal line "Are you ready for star time?" had kicked off the first *Live at the Apollo* in 1963. The James Brown Show was now a slicker, more Las Vegas–style affair that incorporated, among other bits of razzle-dazzle, a troupe of female singer-dancers. One of them, Tomi Rae Hynie, became the fourth Mrs. James Brown—and the mother of his son, James Brown II—after Adrienne Rodriguez died in 1996 while undergoing cosmetic surgery.

Novelist Jonathan Lethem witnessed the spectacle in the course of writing a lengthy, revealing, and often hilarious profile of the artist for *Rolling Stone* magazine. A James Brown performance, he wrote, is

> the ritual celebration of an enshrined historical victory, a battle won long ago, against forces difficult to name—funklessness?—yet whose vanquishing seems to have been so utterly crucial that it requires incessant restaging in a triumphalist ceremony. The show exists on a continuum, the link between ebullient big-band "clown" jazz showmen like Cab Calloway and Louis Jordan and the pornographic parade of a full-bore Prince concert.[29]

In 1991, James's recording career was surveyed on *Star Time*, a carefully compiled and critically acclaimed four-CD box set; new albums such as *Universal James* (1992) and a fourth *Live at the Apollo* set (1995) came and went without much media attention or commercial impact. But at this point—forty-five years after "Please, Please, Please" first hit the charts—it really didn't matter. A Kennedy Center honoree, the winner of a Grammy Lifetime Achievement Award, with his own star on the Hollywood Walk of Fame, the ragged boy from Twiggs Street was now an icon of global pop culture—and the show would go on. "We could work for a hundred years," one member of his Soul

Generals band told Jonathan Lethem. "Because he's James Brown. It's like we're up there with Bugs Bunny, Mickey Mouse. There's no other comparison."[30]

When not on the road, the singer—diabetic and in remission after a bout with prostate cancer—retreated to his home in Beech Island, South Carolina. It was just across the Savannah River from Augusta, where Ninth Street was now James Brown Boulevard and where the civic center was renamed the James Brown Arena in August 2006.

FINAL DAYS

Brown's final tour was a two-week trek across Eastern Europe that included a private fiftieth birthday party in Moscow (the other "entertainment" was Jennifer Lopez). The concluding show, in Croatia, was the last he ever played with his own band. The musicians flew home to the United States but James traveled to London. On November 14, 2006, he was honored by the U.K. Music Hall of Fame in a televised ceremony; backed by a stage band, he sang "I Got You (I Feel Good)." Four decades earlier, in 1965, the song had topped the Billboard R&B Singles chart for straight six weeks. No one could have predicted that it would be James Brown's last live performance.

On the Friday before Christmas, James Brown participated in his fifteenth annual holiday toy giveaway, at the Imperial Theater in Atlanta, Georgia. On Sunday, he was admitted to Emory Crawford Long Hospital in Atlanta with a diagnosis of pneumonia. A show in Connecticut was canceled but the singer told associates that he looked forward to performing at B.B. King's Club in New York on New Year's Eve, as he'd done annually for several years. At 1:45 A.M. on December 25, 2006, James Brown died of congestive heart failure.

LEGACY

The news of James Brown's death prompted a flood of tributes from his contemporaries and admirers. Soul queen Aretha Franklin said, "He was an original, [like] a Rembrandt or a Picasso."[31] "For oppressed people," rap star Common declared, Brown's music "was the light at the end of the tunnel."[32] In the *Village Voice*, writer/musician Greg Tate hailed James Brown as "the embodiment of all the working-class African blood that got us through . . . all our collective love, joy, ingenuity, and indefatigability, all our spirited and spiritual survivalist complexity, all our freedom jazz dance. . . . In a nutshell, JB was our grand black unifier."[33]

At a time when even such soul music pioneers as Ray Charles were moving toward a smoother, more pop-oriented sound, James Brown brought American black music back to its African-derived polyrhythmic roots even as he pushed it forward into the future. Although he never scored a number one Pop hit, Brown is one of an elite group of artists to have placed a song in the

Top Ten of the *Billboard* Hot 100 and/or Top R&B Singles chart in each of four decades from the 1950s through the 1980s. He holds the Billboard R&B Singles record for Most Chart Hits (118), Most Top 40 Hits (100), Most Top Ten Hits (60), and Most Crossover Hits (88), that is, songs that "crossed over" from the R&B chart to the Hot 100.

Traces of James Brown's sound can be heard in the music of Sly and the Family Stone, Talking Heads, Parliament-Funkadelic, Fela Ransome-Kuti, Miles Davis, and Public Enemy, to name but a few. Hip-hop producers and MCs have sampled his recordings countless times, creating new contemporary hits from his classic beats, horn lines, and vocal refrains.

"Funky Drummer," one of Brown's lesser hit singles from 1970, contains a drum break played by Clyde Stubblefield that is probably the most sampled beat in hip-hop history. It has been used in songs by A Tribe Called Quest, the Beastie Boys, George Michael, Public Enemy, and Sinead O'Connor, among others. Additional James Brown samples were employed by Biz Markie on "Vapors" ("Papa Don't Take No Mess"), by Gang Starr on "Words I Manifest" ("Bring It Up"), and by Rob Base and D.J. E-Z Rock on "It Takes Two," which sampled James's production of "Think (About It)" by Lyn Collins.

"He was dramatic to the end—dying on Christmas Day," the Reverend Jesse Jackson told the Associated Press. "Almost a dramatic, poetic moment. He'll be all over the news, all over the world today. He would have it no other way."[34]

TIMELINE

May 3, 1933
James Brown is born in Barnwell, South Carolina. He is raised in poverty in Augusta, Georgia, forty miles away.

1949
At age sixteen, Brown is convicted on four counts of breaking and entering (into cars) and sentenced to a term of eight to sixteen years in a Georgia state penitentiary. The sentence is later reduced and James is transferred to the Alto Reform School in Toccoa, Georgia.

June 14, 1952
Brown is paroled and remains in Toccoa, where he sings with the Gospel Starlighters, a vocal quartet led by his friend Bobby Byrd.

June 19, 1953
James Brown and Velma Warren are married in Toccoa. The couple will have three sons: Teddy, Terry, and Larry.

November 1, 1955
As lead singer of the Famous Flames, a secular vocal group, Brown records the original version of his song "Please, Please, Please" at radio station WIBB in Macon, Georgia. The song receives considerable regional airplay.

January 23, 1956
Producer and A&R man Ralph Bass travels to Macon to sign James Brown to King Records.

February 4, 1956

James Brown and the Famous Flames re-record "Please, Please, Please" at King/Federal studios in Cincinnati.

March 3, 1956

"Please, Please, Please" is released as the group's debut single on Federal Records, a King subsidiary.

April 11, 1956

"Please, Please, Please" by James Brown and the Famous Flames reaches number six on the *Billboard* R&B Singles chart. The single sells over one million copies.

April 1957

The original Famous Flames disband when nine follow-up singles fail to make the charts.

November 10, 1958

"Try Me" by James Brown enters the *Billboard* R&B Singles chart and eventually becomes the best-selling R&B single of 1958. It is the first of the singer's seventeen R&B number one hits, his first song to make the Hot 100 (at number forty-eight), and his second million-seller.

October 24, 1962

Using $5,700 of his own funds, Brown records his live performance at New York's Apollo Theater.

June 15, 1963

James Brown hits number eighteen with "Prisoner of Love," the peak Hot 100 listing of his career thus far.

June 30, 1963

James Brown's *Live at the Apollo* is released and reaches number two on the *Billboard* Pop Albums chart. It becomes the most successful LP ever released on the King label.

September 1963

With manager Ben Bart, Brown forms his first record label, Fair Deal, and a song publishing company, Jim Jam Music.

October 28–29, 1964

The T.A.M.I. Show, a concert documentary, is filmed in Santa Monica, California. It features live performances by James Brown, the Beach Boys, Chuck Berry, the Rolling Stones, and the Supremes.

February 1, 1965

James Brown records "Papa's Got a Brand New Bag." Released in July, the song tops the R&B chart for eight weeks and reaches number eight on the Hot 100—the singer's first Top Ten Pop hit.

March 15, 1966

"Papa's Got a Brand New Bag" wins the award for Best New R&B Recording in the eighth annual Grammy Awards.

May 1966

The singer makes his prime-time network TV debut, appearing on *The Ed Sullivan Show*.

June 4, 1966
James Brown's number one R&B hit, the orchestrated ballad "It's a Man's Man's Man's World," peaks at number eight on the Hot 100.

August 1967
Alfred (Pee Wee) Ellis joins the James Brown Show as musical director. As one of Brown's chief collaborators, Ellis is crucial to the singer's transition from gospel-influenced R&B to a harder-edged and more dynamic funk sound.

April 5, 1968
After Dr. Martin Luther King Jr. is assassinated in Memphis, James Brown appears on WGBH-TV in Boston to appeal for calm in the streets and headlines that night at Boston Garden.

September 14, 1968
"Say It Loud – I'm Black and I'm Proud (Pt. 1)" enters the *Billboard* R&B Singles chart. It becomes Brown's seventh number one R&B hit and reaches number ten on the Hot 100.

July 23, 1969
The City of Los Angeles declares James Brown Day in honor of his sold-out show at the Great Western Forum in Inglewood. When Mayor Sam Yorty arrives late to the ceremony, Brown walks out.

July 1, 1971
James Brown's King Records contract and back catalog of master recordings are sold to Polydor Records. He continues to record for Polydor for the next decade.

August 12, 1972
"Get On the Good Foot" enters the R&B chart and soon reaches number one (for four weeks) and number eighteen Pop. It is Brown's first single to be certified gold for sales of more than one million copies by the Recording Industry Association of America (RIAA).

January 5, 1974
The Payback debuts on the *Billboard* album chart. The most successful of James Brown's 1970s LPs, it becomes the only album of his career to be RIAA-certified gold for sales of more than 500,000 copies.

September 1, 1974
Brown performs at a music festival in Kinshasa, Zaire, staged in tandem with the Muhammad Ali/George Foreman heavyweight championship fight.

June 1, 1980
James Brown appears with stars John Belushi and Dan Aykroyd in the John Landis film *The Blues Brothers*.

January 11, 1986
"Living in America," the theme song from the movie *Rocky IV* reaches number four on the Billboard Hot 100 and number ten R&B. The song becomes James Brown's highest-charting Pop hit and wins the Grammy Award for Best Rhythm & Blues Recording.

January 23, 1986
James Brown is inducted into the Rock and Roll Hall of Fame during the organization's first induction ceremony, held at the Waldorf-Astoria in New York City.

July 23, 1988
"Static" enters the *Billboard* R&B Singles chart. Peaking at number five, it becomes James Brown's final Top Ten R&B hit.

December 15, 1988
In South Carolina, James Brown is sentenced to a six-year prison term on charges of assaulting a police officer, drug possession, and carrying an unlicensed handgun.

February 27, 1991
Brown leaves prison on parole after serving fifteen months and spends the next ten months in a work-release program.

May 7, 1991
Star Time, a four-CD box set surveying the singer's career, is released on Polydor/Universal.

February 25, 1992
The National Academy of Recording Arts and Sciences (NARAS) presents James Brown with a Lifetime Achievement Award during the thirty-fourth annual Grammy Awards.

February 25, 1993
MC Hammer presents James Brown with a Lifetime Achievement Award at the fourth annual Rhythm & Blues Foundation Pioneer Awards.

December 1, 2003
Brown is honored at the Kennedy Center in Washington, DC.

November 14, 2006
In London, James Brown performs "I Got You (I Feel Good)" on the telecast of the U.K. Music Hall of Fame Awards—his final live performance.

December 25, 2006
After being admitted with a diagnosis of pneumonia, James Brown dies of congestive heart failure at Emory Crawford Long Hospital in Atlanta.

SELECTED DISCOGRAPHY

Star Time (four-CD box set spanning James Brown's career)

Roots of a Revolution (two CDs; covers 1956–64)

Foundations of Funk: A Brand New Bag, 1964–1969 (two CDs)

Funk Power 1970: A Brand New Thang

Make It Funky—The Big Payback: 1971–1975 (two CDs)

Dead on the Heavy Funk, 1975–1983 (two CDs)

Messin' with the Blues (two CDs)

Live at the Apollo

Say It Live and Loud: Live in Dallas 08.26.68

Soul Pride: The Instrumentals (1960–69) (two CDs)

Funky Good Time: The Anthology (two CDs; covers 1970–76)

NOTES

1. Robert, Palmer, "James Brown," *Rolling Stone Illustrated History of Rock & Roll* (New York: Random House, 1992), pp. 163–64.

2. James Brown, with Bruce Tucker, *James Brown: The Godfather of Soul* (New York: Macmillan, 1986), p. 3.

3. Cynthia Rose, *Living in America: The Soul Saga of James Brown* (London: Serpent's Tail, 1990), p. 22.

4. Brown and Tucker, p. 17.

5. Ibid., p. 18.

6. Stanley Booth, "The Godfather's Blues," in *Rhythm Oil* (London: Jonathan Cape, 1992), p. 232.

7. Rose, p. 22.

8. Ray Brown quote from "James Brown: Soul Brother No. 1" by Scott Freeman, *Atlanta Creative Loafing,* January 11–17, 2007.

9. Ibid.

10. Arnold Shaw, *Honkers and Shouters: The Golden Years of Rhythm & Blues* (New York: Collier Books, 1978), pp. 241–42.

11. Rose, p. 47.

12. Brown and Tucker, p. 149.

13. James Brown, *I Feel Good: A Memoir of a Life of Soul* (New York: New American Library, 2005), pp. 126–27.

14. Bob Merlis and Davin Seay, *Heart & Soul: A Celebration of Black Music Style in America 1930–1975* (New York: Stewart, Tabori and Chang, 1997), p. 51.

15. Glen Ford, "James Brown: The Man Who Named a People," available online at www.countercurrents.org/ford090107.htm.

16. Ibid.

17. George, Nelson, *The Death of Rhythm & Blues* (New York: Pantheon Books, 1988), pp. 103–104.

18. Kempton, Arthur, *Boogaloo: The Quintessence of American Popular Music* (New York: Pantheon Books, 2003), p. 145.

19. Ibid., p. 394.

20. Fred Wesley Jr., *Hit Me, Fred: Recollections of a Sideman* (Durham: Duke University Press, 2002), p. 95.

21. Ibid., p. 99.

22. Wesley, p. 175.

23. Brown, pp. 178–79.

24. Brown and Tucker, pp. 242–43.

25. Booth, pp. 236–37.

26. See www.robertchristgau.com/get_artist.php?id=631&name=James+Brown.

27. Brown, p. 209.

28. Brown, p. 210.

29. Jonathan Lethem, "Being James Brown," available online at www.rolling-stone.com/news/story/10533775/being_James_Brown (June 12, 2006).

30. Ibid.

31. Aretha Franklin quote from "James Brown, 1933–2006," *Entertainment Weekly* (January 12, 2007).

32. Ibid.

33. Greg Tate, *www.VillageVoice.com* (January 2, 2007).

34. See chronicle.augusta.com/stories/122606/met_109964.shtml.

FURTHER READING

Booth, Stanley. "The Godfather's Blues." *Rhythm Oil.* London: Jonathan Cape, 1992.

Bowman, Rob. *Soulsville, U.S.A.: The Story of Stax Records.* New York: Schirmer Books, 1997.

Brown, James. *I Feel Good: A Memoir of a Life of Soul.* New York: New American Library, 2005.

Brown, James, with Bruce Tucker. *James Brown: The Godfather of Soul.* New York: Macmillan, 1986.

Hirshey, Gerri. "Superbull, Superbad." *Nowhere to Run: The Story of Soul Music.* New York: Times Books, 1984.

Palmer, Robert. "James Brown." *Rolling Stone Illustrated History of Rock & Roll.* New York: Random House, 1992.

Rose, Cynthia. *Living in America: The Soul Saga of James Brown.* London: Serpent's Tail, 1990.

Wesley, Fred Jr. *Hit Me, Fred: Recollections of a Sideman.* Durham: Duke University Press, 2002.

Courtesy of Photofest.

The Beatles

Scott Schinder

THE FOUR AND ONLY

It's nearly impossible to overstate the magnitude of the Beatles' influence—not just on music, but upon virtually every aspect of popular culture in the years since the band's worldwide breakthrough in 1964. In their initial incarnation as cheerful, wisecracking moptops, the Fab Four revolutionized the sound, style, and attitude of popular music and opened rock and roll's doors to a tidal wave of British rock acts.

Their initial impact would have been enough to establish the Beatles as one of their era's most influential cultural forces, but they didn't stop there. Although their initial style was a highly original, irresistibly catchy synthesis of early American rock and roll and R&B, the Beatles spent the rest of the

1960s expanding rock's stylistic frontiers, consistently staking out new musical territory on each release. The band's increasingly sophisticated experimentation encompassed a variety of genres, including folk-rock, country, psychedelia, and baroque pop, without sacrificing the effortless mass appeal of their early work. Although they scored their initial success with an unprecedented run of classic hit singles, the Beatles were instrumental in establishing the long-playing album as rock's chief creative medium.

The Searchers: Needles and Pins

In the spring of 1964, the Searchers brought folk-rock to the American Top Twenty with their first hit, "Needles and Pins." But three years later, the group had vanished from the charts. Today, the Searchers—first-rate musicians who never developed as songwriters—are perhaps the most underrated band of the British Invasion.

Three years after guitarist/vocalists John McNally and Mike Pender founded the Searchers in 1959, their lineup stabilized with the addition of Tony Jackson (bass, vocals) and Chris Curtis (drums, vocals). Signed to Pye Records by producer Tony Hatch, the Searchers had their first U.K. number one in the spring of 1963 with a cover of the Drifters' "Sweets for My Sweet."

The next single, "Needles and Pins," released in early 1964, was the group's real breakthrough. The Searchers' ringing electric twelve-string guitar lines and ethereal harmonies propelled the song to number one in the United Kingdom and number thirteen in the United States—and invented the folk-rock sound later advanced and popularized by the Byrds.

Jackie DeShannon's original version of "Needles and Pins" had only reached number eighty-four on the Hot 100 and never charted in the United Kingdom at all. But the Searchers had a persistent knack for reinventing obscure songs, many by female artists: "Don't Throw Your Love Away" (the Shirelles), "Some Day We're Gonna Love Again" (Barbara Lewis), "Bumble Bee" (Lavern Baker), and the beautiful anti–nuclear testing ballad "What Have They Done to the Rain" (Malvina Reynolds). The Searchers' clean-cut look and seasoned professional attitude were also crucial to their early success. As time went on, however, these same qualities made them appear stolid and un-hip.

Tony Jackson, who'd sung lead on "Sweets for My Sweet," didn't take kindly to sharing this key role with Mike Pender (the voice of "Needles and Pins"). He left the group in August 1964 and was replaced by Frank Allen. From behind the drum kit, Chris Curtis became the Searchers' dominant personality until he too left in March 1966. It's difficult to say just what effect these departures had on the Searchers' musical creativity and career momentum. In the end, they proved unable to adapt to rock's post-1967 evolution.

Andy Schwartz

In 1964, the Beatles captured the world's imagination, and carried their public along on a six-year adventure whose artistic developments paralleled the social and cultural changes of those tumultuous years. The group managed to simultaneously be their era's preeminent musical innovators as well as the most popular recording act of their time, and their status remains unchallenged to this day.

Their adventurous experimentalism established the Beatles as pied pipers of the Aquarian age, shepherding rock's maturation from blues-based forms to a more eclectic and self-consciously serious approach. The band members' interest in political and spiritual consciousness influenced many of their listeners to explore those areas, cementing the Beatles' status at the center of the social revolutions of the 1960s. As their music grew more adventurous and experimental, the Beatles' humor and charisma made it easy for mainstream audiences to embrace even their most eccentric experiments.

Although each Beatle was a notable talent in his own right, the band was more than the sum of its parts. Although the bandmates' differences would fuel tension later on, for most of the group's history, the four diverse characters complemented one another brilliantly. As a songwriting team, John Lennon and Paul McCartney maintained levels of craftsmanship and melodic invention that were unprecedented in rock, and their vocal harmonies were equally distinctive.

Upon their arrival in America in February 1964, the Beatles' sound and spirit seemed to hint at a brighter, more enlightened future—a welcome source of positivity for a country still reeling from the assassination of President John F. Kennedy just two months earlier.

The Beatles' initial success attracted outrage and derision from various representatives of public morality, as well as the old-guard pop mainstream that these outsiders would soon make obsolete. Such resistance quickly proved futile; the appeal of the Beatles' music and personalities was too strong to deny. Even adults who typically scorned and dismissed teenage music had to acknowledge the Beatles' substance and spirit, and couldn't help but be charmed by the musicians' effervescent energy and cheeky humor.

Beyond their musical achievements and their influence in such areas as hair length and fashion sense, the Beatles' runaway commercial success played a pivotal role in the music business's growth into a multimillion-dollar industry. By many estimates, the band remains the best-selling recording act of all time, and the Beatles catalog continues to spin massive sales, captivating new generations of listeners.

BIRTH OF THE FAB

The basic facts of the Beatles' history have been retold so many times that they have attained mythic status. But the story remains a profoundly compelling one, and the band's achievements are no less powerful for their familiarity. By the time the world at large had heard of the Beatles, the core of the band had already been a performing unit for several years, honing its musical chemistry and songwriting craft far from the mainstream spotlight.

John Lennon, Paul McCartney, George Harrison, and Ringo Starr, like the rest of the generation of British rock musicians who would rise to prominence in the 1960s, grew up in an England still recovering from the devastating social and economic effects of World War II. England in the 1950s was still largely a socially and culturally conservative society; that description certainly applied to Liverpool, the Merseyside port town where the future Beatles grew up in largely working-class surroundings. During the war, the area had been hit by Nazi air raids, killing 2,500 people and damaging nearly half of the area's homes.

So it's not surprising that the early stirrings of American rock and roll captured the imagination of British kids, to whom the music represented a vibrant alternative to the grey everyday reality of British life. While Elvis Presley, Buddy Holly, Bill Haley, Eddie Cochran, Little Richard, Chuck Berry, Bo Diddley, and Gene Vincent became major stars in Britain in the late 1950s, the United Kingdom failed to produce much credible homegrown rock and roll during those years. Most British rockers in those years were pale approximations of their Stateside counterparts, with only a handful—for example, dreamy but edgy Billy Fury, pirate-garbed Johnny Kidd, and Cliff Richard, whose backup band the Shadows was England's first notable English instrumental rock and roll combo—making remotely credible music.

Liverpool teens John Lennon and Paul McCartney were both committed rock and roll fans, but they first came together to play skiffle, the homemade folk-blues hybrid that had taken the youth of Britain by storm in the late 1950s. Since it was played on such instruments as acoustic guitar, washboard, and homemade tea-chest bass, skiffle was easily accessible to working-class kids who had no access to electric instruments, and the music's simplicity and energy offered an entry point for numerous young musicians who would graduate to rock and roll.

In March 1957, Lennon formed a skiffle group called the Quarrymen, named after Quarry Bank Grammar School, where he was a student. That July, he met Paul McCartney at the Woolton Garden Fête, where the Quarrymen were performing. Although Paul was two years his junior, Lennon was impressed with McCartney's superior guitar abilities, and invited him to join the Quarrymen. The following March, George Harrison—a year younger than McCartney and even more adept on guitar—was invited to join, overcoming Lennon's initial reservations over the fifteen-year-old axman's youth.

Although the Quarrymen's shifting membership included various Lennon pals who drifted in and out of the lineup, the group eventually solidified around the core of Lennon, McCartney, and Harrison and moved toward electric instruments and rock and roll. As their sound evolved, the band went through a succession of new names —including Johnny and the Moondogs and the Silver Beatles—before settling on the Beatles, the name being a subtle nod to Buddy Holly's Crickets.

In January 1960, Lennon's art-college classmate Stuart Sutcliffe—a prodigiously talented painter but a rudimentary musician—joined on bass. The band played with a series of drummers before Pete Best joined that summer. In addition to brooding good looks that would endear Best to local female fans, his mother Mona owned the Casbah Club, a small basement club in Liverpool where the Beatles had often played.

In May 1960, the Beatles (with short-term drummer Tommy Moore) had gotten their first touring experience, playing a series of gigs in Scotland as backup band for British teen-idol singer Johnny Gentle. Later that year, the band traveled to Hamburg, Germany, where manager Allan Williams had gotten them work playing at the Indra, Kaiserkeller, and Top Ten clubs, located on that city's notorious red-light district, the Reeperbahn.

The extended Hamburg engagement was a punishing one, requiring the Beatles to perform seven nights a week, for six or seven hours per night, entertaining rough-and-tumble crowds that were demanding and often abusive. But the grueling experience proved invaluable in turning the Beatles into a tight, exciting performing unit, and forcing them to expand their repertoire of American rock and roll, R&B, and pop covers. The experience also introduced the musicians to drugs, specifically the amphetamines that they would take to maintain their energy during their endless hours on stage.

The band's first Hamburg visit was cut short after the underage Harrison was deported for lying about his age to German authorities, and McCartney and Best were sent home after being arrested for starting a small fire in their squalid living quarters.

Despite their scrapes with the law, the five Beatles returned to Hamburg in April 1961. While performing at the Top Ten club, they were hired by Tony Sheridan, an English singer/guitarist who'd achieved popularity in Germany, to back him on a set of recordings for the German Polydor label. During the sessions, producer Bert Kaempfert allowed the Beatles to cut two tracks without Sheridan: a rocked-up take on the 1920s novelty tune "Ain't She Sweet" and the instrumental "Cry for a Shadow," which would be the only Beatles tune to credit Harrison and Lennon as co-writers. Although those two tracks were not released at the time, they would be pulled out of mothballs in the wake of the band's subsequent success.

At the end of the second Hamburg engagement, Stu Sutcliffe chose to quit the band and remain in Hamburg with his new German fiancée, Astrid Kirchherr, intending to pursue his budding career as an artist. Beyond her relationship with Sutcliffe, photographer Kirchherr—one of a group of young local Bohemians who'd become Beatles admirers—is notable for taking some iconic photos of the leather-clad, dangerous-looking early Beatles, and suggesting that the band members trade their slicked-back quiffs for soon-to-be-famous moptop hairstyles that were adopted by all of the band members except Pete Best.

Sharpened and toughened by their experiences in Hamburg, the Beatles—with McCartney taking over on bass—returned home a changed band. Where they had previously been just another combo on Liverpool's booming beat scene, they were now one of the hottest acts in town. Their increased local popularity was reflected in the large crowds that turned out for the band's local performances, including a lunchtime residency at Liverpool's Cavern Club—a club located in a dank cellar—that quickly became a local institution.

The Beatles returned to Hamburg one more time, for a six-week engagement during the spring of 1962. Upon their arrival, they were informed of Stu Sutcliffe's death from a brain hemorrhage.

Meanwhile, a rock and roll reworking of the Scottish folk song "My Bonnie," from the Beatles' Tony Sheridan sessions, had become a hit in Germany. Although the primitive disc was hardly an appropriate showcase for the Beatles' rapidly developing talents, it was instrumental in bringing the band to the attention of Brian Epstein. Epstein was manager of the record department at NEMS (North End Music Store), a subsidiary of his family's furniture store. When a young Beatles fan came into NEMS seeking the "My Bonnie" single, which had not been released in Britain, Epstein was intrigued enough to attend one of the band's Cavern Club gigs. Shortly thereafter, Epstein signed on as the Beatles' manager.

Epstein set about fine-tuning his new clients' image, getting them to trade their leather jackets for stylish tailored suits. Epstein also took advantage of his contacts in the music business, using his status as a prominent retailer to gain access to various record-company executives, most of whom turned him down flat.

Decca Records was interested enough to have the band record an audition session in January 1962. With Decca staffer Mike Smith, the band cut fifteen songs in a one-hour session—a trio of Lennon/McCartney originals, plus a dozen covers drawn from their live set, including material by Chuck Berry, Buddy Holly, Carl Perkins, and the Coasters. Although Decca ultimately passed on the Beatles, the audition tracks, which have circulated on bootleg releases for decades, offer a fascinating glimpse of the band at a transitional stage.

The Hollies: Look Through Any Window

The Hollies proved highly adaptable to the rapidly changing sounds and styles of rock and roll in the 1960s. Graham Nash (vocals, guitar) and Allen Clarke (vocals) were grade-school friends in Manchester who began performing together in the mid-1950s, much influenced by the Everly Brothers. In 1962, they formed the Hollies with bassist Eric Haydock, and later recruited guitarist Tony Hicks—the "bottom third," with Nash and Clarke, of the group's trademark vocal harmony—and drummer Bobby Elliot.

The Hollies made an immediate and lasting impact in Britain: After "Stay" reached number eight in January 1964, all but two of the group's singles from 1964–69 reached the U.K. Top Ten. They were less successful in the United States but still scored seven Top Forty hits in the same time period. Significantly, two of their Top Ten songs—"Stop Stop Stop" (1966) and "Carrie-Anne" (1967)—were composed by Graham Nash, Allen Clarke, and Tony Hicks, a team sometimes credited as "L. Ransford." The Hollies' sound progressed rapidly from jumpy beat-group covers of American R&B songs ("Stay," "Just One Look") to a more mature and confident style that blended pure pop with touches of folk-rock and early psychedelia ("I'm Alive," "Look Through Any Window," "Bus Stop," "Pay You Back with Interest").

When Bernie Calvert replaced Eric Haydock in 1966, the Hollies could boast one of the best, most flexible rhythm sections in British pop. But they were typecast as a "singles band" at a time when rock was moving in a more exploratory, album-oriented direction. In 1968, Graham Nash left the Hollies in a dispute over their decision to release an ill-conceived album of Bob Dylan songs. Replaced by Terry Sylvester, he later formed the hugely successful Crosby, Stills and Nash with Stephen Stills and David Crosby.

In 1969 the Hollies released "He Ain't Heavy, He's My Brother," a rather ponderous orchestrated ballad (with an uncredited Elton John on piano) that became their first U.S. Top Ten hit in two years. In 1972, the group suddenly came on like Manchester's answer to Creedence Clearwater Revival with the bluesy guitar rocker "Long Cool Woman (In a Black Dress)." The Hollies' highest-charting American hit, it peaked at number two.

In 1974, another romantic ballad "The Air That I Breathe" breached the Top Ten—the group's last hurrah as contemporary hit makers. But the Hollies' back catalog continues to exert a timeless appeal: "Their longevity is assured," declared the *Guinness Encyclopedia of Popular Music*, "as their expertly crafted, harmonic songs represent some of the greatest music of all mid-1960s pop."

A. S.

Despite multiple rejections, Epstein persisted, and his perseverance paid off when George Martin, producer/A&R for the EMI subsidiary Parlophone, signed the Beatles (after three other EMI execs passed) in mid-1962. Although Martin had little experience with rock and roll, his seasoned studio skills would prove crucial in the Beatles' development as a recording act. His expertise as an arranger, keyboardist, and sonic manipulator would enable the band to execute their most ambitious ideas on record, and Martin would remain a key factor in the Beatles' artistic progression for the remainder of their career.

Martin was adamant in his lack of regard for Pete Best's percussive abilities, and insisted that a session drummer replace him in the studio. Apparently, this was all that was needed for Lennon, McCartney, and Harrison to fire Best from the band, leaving Epstein to deliver the news. It has been speculated that Best's dismissal was hastened by his bandmates' resentment over his popularity with female fans, or his refusal to adopt the distinctive hairstyle, although a more likely explanation seems to be simple personal incompatibility.

Best's replacement was Ringo Starr, then a member of the popular Liverpool outfit Rory Storm and the Hurricanes, and a longtime friend who'd sat in with the Beatles on several occasions in Hamburg. Beyond Starr's superior drumming, his addition gave the band a fourth strong personality.

By then, Lennon and McCartney had become prolific songwriters, but it was still rare at the time for recording artists to write their own material. Martin initially wanted the Beatles' debut single to be "How Do You Do It?," a lightweight ditty by English tunesmith Mitch Murray. But Martin relented after the Beatles cut a lackluster version of the song, and allowed the band to record the Lennon/McCartney original "Love Me Do" as their debut A-side ("How Do You Do It?" subsequently became a hit for Liverpool's Gerry and the Pacemakers, who were also managed by Epstein and produced by Martin).

Starr had only been a Beatle for a few weeks when the group recorded "Love Me Do" and its B-side, Lennon and McCartney's "P.S. I Love You," in September 1962. Martin was still skeptical about Starr's abilities, so he brought in session drummer Andy White to play on "Love Me Do," with Ringo relegated to tambourine; an alternate take with Ringo on drums would become a U.S. hit eighteen months later. Lennon and McCartney would continue to provide most of the Beatles' material for the rest of its existence, and would continue to share composing credits even after they began writing individually.

The energetic but relatively primitive "Love Me Do" became a minor British hit, peaking at number seventeen in October 1962. The Beatles fared far better with their superior second single "Please Please Me," which reached the number two spot on the British charts early in 1963.

The infectious, insistent "Please Please Me" set off a massive wave of Fan hysteria in Britain. The phenomenon was soon dubbed Beatlemania, with the band regularly performing in front of crowds of screaming, hysterical female fans. The commercial momentum continued through 1963, with four consecutive chart-topping singles: "From Me to You," "She Loves You," "I Want to Hold Your Hand," and "Can't Buy Me Love," all Lennon/McCartney originals.

The Beatles first British LP *Please Please Me*—most of which was recorded in a single day—was released in March 1963. It topped the U.K. album charts for thirty weeks, a feat that confirmed the band's status, not just as England's biggest rock act but as a singular phenomenon with no precedent in the annals of the British entertainment industry. A second album, *With the Beatles*, was released in November, and made it clear that the Beatles' songwriting and musical abilities were progressing at an accelerated pace.

While the Beatles were becoming teen idols in Britain during 1963, they remained largely unknown in America. EMI's U.S. arm, Capitol Records, had first refusal on the Beatles' recordings, but declined to pick up the band's initial output. Instead, the Beatles' early singles were licensed variously to the small independent labels Vee-Jay, Swan, and Tollie. Vee-Jay also released *Introducing the Beatles*, a slightly reworked version of the *Please Please Me* album.

In retrospect, it's hard to think of such classic Beatles singles as "Please Please Me," "From Me to You," and "She Loves You" as flops. But despite some airplay on such influential Top Forty stations as New York's WINS and Chicago's WLS, the Beatles' early non-Capitol U.S. releases received little attention.

The Beatles' Stateside fortunes reversed decisively in late 1963, when Brian Epstein managed to get Ed Sullivan—a savvy talent-spotter who'd seen Beatlemania in action during an overseas visit—to book the band for three appearances on his hugely popular Sunday night TV variety show the following February. Epstein parlayed the promise of this high-profile exposure into a commitment from Capitol to release the band's next single, "I Want to Hold Your Hand," with a massive promotion campaign to prime American audiences for the Beatles' arrival.

On December 7, 1963—two weeks after President John F. Kennedy's assassination—a clip of a Beatles performance was shown on the *CBS Evening News*. The clip inspired a teenager in Washington, D.C., to request a Beatles song from a local radio station. After obtaining an import copy of "I Want to Hold Your Hand," the station began playing the song to overwhelming listener response, prompting Capitol to rush-release the single on December 26. The song took off in New York and quickly spread to other markets, selling a million copies in its first ten days of release. By the end of the month, it was the number one song on the U.S. pop charts.

Beatlemania was a transatlantic phenomenon by February 7, 1964, when a crowd of 4,000 fans turned up at Heathrow Airport to see the Beatles off on their first trip to America. Also on the flight were various photographers, reporters, and seminal American record producer Phil Spector, who'd made a point of booking himself on the same flight. Upon their arrival at the recently renamed Kennedy International Airport, the band was met by 3,000 screaming fans. At an airport press conference, the four musicians' spirited banter disarmed many of the reporters who'd previously dismissed the Beatles as a flash-in-the-pan fad. Later, the band's hotel was overrun by fans and media.

The Beatles' first performance on *The Ed Sullivan Show*, broadcast live on February 9, was a landmark event, giving kids across the country their first exposure to the sound that would soon change popular culture forever. Two days later, the band began its first American concert tour at the Washington Coliseum in Washington, D.C.

Capitol Records moved swiftly to capitalize on the buzz by releasing *Meet the Beatles*, an LP comprising recent British singles and tracks from *With the*

Beatles, in early February. *Meet the Beatles* began Capitol's long-standing practice of reworking—and, to many ears, mangling—the band's albums for U.S. release. While their British LPs generally included fourteen songs, Capitol's American editions usually held twelve. Capitol reshuffled and remixed album tracks and added others from British singles and EPs, often with little regard for cohesive sequencing or appropriate packaging. In so doing, the company managed to spin the Beatles' first seven British albums into ten American ones. As a result, the band's American discography often gave a muddled and inaccurate portrayal of their actual artistic progress. (In the CD era, Capitol would reconfigure the Beatles' album catalog to correspond with the original British versions.)

With teenage America now firmly in the grip of Beatlemania, the U.S. labels that had previously released unsuccessful early Beatles singles found themselves with late-blooming hits. The extent of the Beatles' dominance of the American marketplace was demonstrated in the first week of April 1964, when the top five slots of the *Billboard* singles chart were completely occupied by Beatles singles, with "Can't Buy Me Love" at number one, followed by "Twist and Shout," "She Loves You," "I Want to Hold Your Hand," and "Please Please Me." The following week, the Beatles held fourteen positions in *Billboard*'s Top 100.

The market was soon flooded with all manner of products designed to cash in on the Fab Four phenomenon. Other record companies sought to get in on the act by releasing all manner of Beatles-related discs, recycling the band's press interviews and their Tony Sheridan sessions, along with countless Beatles-inspired novelty discs and blatantly deceptive releases hinting falsely at some Beatles connection. Discarded drummer Pete Best found himself with a solo recording deal, and even John's long-estranged father Freddie Lennon got to release his own single.

Meanwhile, the shelves were flooded with all manner of officially sanctioned and unauthorized Beatles-related merchandise, with the band's name and likeness attached to an array of products, from lunchboxes to candy to Beatle wigs.

A more productive result of the Beatles' U.S. breakthrough was rock's British Invasion, as record labels scrambled to sign anything with an accent. Soon the American charts were dominated by English acts, with domestic artists finding it increasingly difficult to gain airplay. Arriving in the Beatles' wake were the Liverpool combos Gerry and the Pacemakers, the Searchers, and Epstein protégés Billy J. Kramer and the Dakotas, whose access to unreleased Lennon/McCartney songs gave them a shortcut to chart success, along with the Rolling Stones, the Dave Clark Five, the Kinks, the Animals, the Hollies, Herman's Hermits, Chad and Jeremy, the Yardbirds, the Zombies, the Who, Donovan, Freddie and the Dreamers, Wayne Fontana and the Mindbenders, Manfred Mann, the Spencer Davis Group, and Peter and Gordon, who scored their biggest hit with the Lennon/McCartney composition "A World Without Love."

The Dave Clark Five: Catch Us If You Can

During a two-year period beginning in February 1964, no British group could top the Beatles for American chart dominance—but the Dave Clark Five (DC5) came close. Drummer Dave Clark formed the London-based group in 1962 with Mike Smith (lead vocals, keyboards), Denny Payton (saxophone, harmonica, vocals), Rick Huxley (bass, vocals), and Lenny Davidson (guitar, vocals).

Clark was a good drummer but an even better businessman. He produced the DC5's records, published their original songs, owned the rights to their master recordings, and managed the band as well. In January 1964, "Glad All Over" by the Dave Clark Five reached number one in the United Kingdom—supplanting the Beatles' "I Want to Hold Your Hand" at the top of the chart—and became the first of the group's *seventeen* American Top Forty hits. In contrast to the melodic, guitar-based sound of most early British rock, "Glad All Over" was a crude but infectious blare with Payton's honking sax, Smith's hoarse lead vocals, and Clark's loudly thumping drums all prominent in the reverb-laden mix.

Throughout 1964-1965, the group dutifully returned to this formula on "Bits and Pieces," "Catch Us If You Can," "Any Way You Want It," and a cover of the Contours' "Do You Love Me" (although the appealing ballad "Because" is among their most-heard songs today). The DC5 made several hugely successful U.S. tours, a surprisingly good dramatic feature film (*Catch Us If You Can* aka *Having a Wild Weekend*), and a record-setting eighteen appearances on *The Ed Sullivan Show*. Musically, however, Clark couldn't keep pace with his former rivals the Beatles (or even the Hollies), and he disbanded the group in the summer of 1970.

A. S.

THEY'RE GONNA PUT ME IN THE MOVIES

Those who continued to dismiss the Beatles as an insubstantial flash in the pan were handily refuted by the band's first feature film, *A Hard Day's Night*, released in the summer of 1964. Based around a fictionalized day in the band's life, the faux cinema vérité comedy cemented the Fab Four's cheeky, breezy image as well as the four Beatles' individual personae, that is, sardonic iconoclast Lennon; sunny diplomat McCartney; thoughtful, dry-witted Harrison; and happy-go-lucky yet melancholy Starr.

A Hard Day's Night had been designed as a low-budget quickie prior to the Beatles' U.S. breakthrough, with the intention of reaching theaters before the band's popularity faded. But its gritty black-and-white immediacy worked in its favor, thanks in large part to the talents of director Richard Lester, who gave the film a kinetic pace that was well suited to the band's energy, and Liverpudlian screenwriter Alun Owen, whose script brilliantly captured the band's humor and attitude. Owen made excellent use of the Beatles' individual personalities, giving each musician memorable solo scenes that showcased their impressive comic skills. The result was an instant hit with critics and audiences alike.

Beyond it cinematic qualities, *A Hard Day's Night* also featured an album's worth of impressive new songs, including "Can't Buy Me Love," "And I Love Her," "If I Fell," and the film's insistent title song. Many of the tunes featured strong twelve-string guitar leads by Harrison that would soon prove influential on such American folk-rock acts as the Byrds, the Turtles, the Lovin' Spoonful, and the Beau Brummels.

The Beatles returned to the big screen with 1965's *Help!* Again directed by Lester, *Help!* traded its predecessor's documentary-style grit for a globe-trotting comic-book romp that pitted the Fab Four against a fanatical religious cult.

In mid-1964, the Beatles launched their first tour of Australia without Ringo Starr, who'd been sidelined by tonsillitis and was replaced on stage by session drummer Jimmy Nicol. Ringo rejoined in time for the band's subsequent dates in New Zealand. On August 15, the Beatles performed rock's first major stadium concert at New York's Shea Stadium, playing to a crowd of 55,600 fans.

Nineteen sixty-four also saw the publication of Lennon's book *In His Own Write*, a collection of his surreal short stories and line drawings. Lennon's prose reflected his love for absurd puns, nonsensical wordplay, and free association. It would be followed in 1965 by a second volume of Lennon prose, *A Spaniard in the Works*.

The Beatles' growing respectability was further demonstrated in October 1965, when England's Queen Elizabeth II awarded the prestigious Order of the British Empire, popularly known as the MBE, to John, Paul, George, and Ringo. The honor, which was usually bestowed upon military officers and civic leaders, sparked protest among several conservative MBE recipients, who returned their awards in protest.

The Beatles' productivity between 1964 and 1967 was uncanny. Between a series of hectic international tours, the band released a remarkable stream of classic singles and albums. *Beatles for Sale*, *Help!*, *Rubber Soul*, and *Revolver* (and their American counterparts) showed the band consistently raising the musical stakes, exploring new sounds and lyrical subject matter. "I Feel Fine" featured some revolutionary guitar feedback, while the muscular folk-rock tunes "Ticket to Ride" and "Paperback Writer" demonstrated how forceful and creative a guitarist Harrison had become, and "Rain" and "Tomorrow Never Knows" exemplified the band's excursions into studio-manipulated psychedelia.

Lennon, McCartney, and Harrison (who had begun to contribute his own compositions to the band's albums) quickly moved beyond the simple romantic concerns of the band's early songs to explore more complex emotional territory. McCartney's "Yesterday" and "Eleanor Rigby" invoked remorse and regret, and diverged from the band's musical format to employ melancholy string quartets. Lennon, meanwhile, had begun to write introspective, Dylan-influenced lyrics on such numbers as "Help!," "I'm a Loser," and "You've Got to Hide Your Love Away." By this point, the Beatles' commercial supremacy—and their bond with their audience—was such that their fans enthusiastically went along with the band's experiments, ensuring that each adventurous new release would be a sales smash.

Despite their worldwide popularity, the Beatles still managed to stumble into controversy. When the band toured the Philippines in July 1966, they unintentionally snubbed Imelda Marcos, wife of the country's despotic president Ferdinand Marcos, when Epstein politely declined an invitation to a breakfast reception at the Presidential Palace. The incident resulted in the band being denounced on Philippine television and radio, and losing its police protection. Upon their arrival at the airport to leave the country, the band was attacked by a hostile crowd, and Epstein and road manager Mal Evans were forced by authorities to return the tour's cash receipts before the band and its entourage could leave.

Almost immediately upon the band's return from the Philippines, a comment that Lennon had made in a British interview a few months earlier launched a noisy anti-Beatles backlash in the United States. Lennon had opined that mainstream religion was losing influence, and casually mentioned that the Beatles were "more popular than Jesus now." When news of Lennon's comment reached America's Bible belt, conservative church groups organized mass burnings of Beatles records. The resulting media furor resulted in Lennon apologizing for his remark in a Chicago press conference on the eve of what would be the Beatles' final tour.

Another controversy arose during the summer of 1966 over the cover photograph for the band's U.S.-only album *Yesterday . . . and Today*. The shot depicted the band surrounded by raw meat and dismembered dolls. Capitol manufactured thousands of copies of the original sleeve, but destroyed most of them before releasing the album with a more conventional cover photo. A handful of original copies reached the public nonetheless, making the "butcher cover" (whose imagery has often been interpreted as the band's comment on Capitol's butchery of their albums) one of the most sought-after Beatles collector's items.

Such petty controversies may have contributed to the Beatles' decision to quit touring at the end of their 1966 tour. The choice was borne largely of their frustration at trying to be heard over the screams of their female fans over the primitive public-address systems of the time, as well as their inability to reproduce their increasingly complex and sophisticated studio recordings as a four-piece live band.

At the time, there was widespread speculation that the Beatles were disbanding. The rumors were fueled by the fact that the four musicians spent a post-tour hiatus engaging in separate pursuits, with McCartney writing and recording (in collaboration with George Martin) the musical score for the English film *The Family Way*, and Lennon making a well-received solo acting debut in Richard Lester's anti-militarist satire *How I Won the War*.

The rumors ended with the February 1967 release of the "Penny Lane"/ "Strawberry Fields Forever" single. The disc featured some of the band's most ambitious work yet, venturing into moody Lennon psychedelia on the latter track, and McCartney's bright orchestral pop on the former. The single helped to set the stage for *Sgt. Pepper's Lonely Hearts Club Band*, a musical watershed that revolutionized the rock album's status as a creative vehicle. One of the first rock albums to be constructed as a cohesive listening experience from start to finish—as well as the first Beatles LP to be released in its original form in America—*Sgt. Pepper* was a giddy bundle of styles and sounds, self-consciously arty but still full of energy, emotion, and humor.

Loosely built around an imaginary concert by the fictional title ensemble, *Sgt. Pepper's Lonely Hearts Club Band* ranged from the candy-colored psychedelia of "Lucy in the Sky with Diamonds" to the cheery sing-along pop "With a Little Help from My Friends" to the multi-tracked cacophony of "Good Morning Good Morning" to the sentimental balladry of "She's Leaving Home," to the operatic grandiosity of the album-closing "A Day in the Life." The album's cutting-edge recording approach was complemented by some modern takes on antiquarian styles, like McCartney's bucolic music-hall excursion "When I'm Sixty-Four" and Lennon's loopy circus tale "Being for the Benefit of Mr. Kite!," while Harrison's recent fascination with Eastern spirituality and Indian sitar music was reflected on "Within You Without You."

Sgt. Pepper's audacious production was all the more impressive in light of the fact that the band and George Martin were working with four tracks, making the album's adventurous use of overdubbing all the more of a technical milestone.

For many, *Sgt. Pepper* served as an unofficial soundtrack to the Summer of Love, and the Beatles' status as spiritual avatars of the hippie movement was confirmed when they premiered their flower-power anthem "All You Need Is Love" on June 25, 1967, via worldwide TV satellite hook-up as part of the TV special *Our World*. Broadcasting from EMI's Abbey Road Studios, where the band had recorded all of its EMI releases, the Beatles were joined by a chorus of friends including Mick Jagger, Marianne Faithfull, Eric Clapton, and Keith Moon.

The creative highs of 1967 were tainted by Brian Epstein's death of a prescription drug overdose in August at the age of thirty-two. The loss of Epstein's stabilizing influence helped to set the band on a less focused course that would gradually lead to the Beatles' unraveling.

In the wake of Epstein's death, the Beatles' lengthy streak of commercial and artistic successes was broken by their next attempt at filmmaking, *Magical Mystery Tour*. Shot with no script and no director, the hour-long film was a self-indulgent mishmash that received a single BBC broadcast in December

1967, before scathing U.K. reviews caused ABC to cancel a planned U.S. telecast; it would not reach America for nearly a decade. Not surprisingly, *Magical Mystery Tour* was partially redeemed by the new songs that the band recorded for it.

Another Beatles-inspired film, the animated feature *Yellow Submarine*, was far better received in 1968, although the Beatles themselves had little involvement with the project apart from contributing a handful of new songs.

FOUR BITES OF THE APPLE

In the wake of *Sgt. Pepper*, the four Beatles began to splinter somewhat, moving in directions that reflected their individual interests and tastes. But the group spent the early part of 1968 together in Rishikesh, India, studying transcendental meditation with the Maharishi Mahesh Yogi, although each of the four would depart the course prior to its completion. The experience led a disillusioned Lennon to write the vitriolic "Sexy Sadie"—originally titled "Maharishi," until the more reverent Harrison prevailed upon Lennon to rename it.

Upon their return from their Indian retreat, Lennon and McCartney flew to New York to announce the formation of Apple Corps, an idealistic but disastrously impractical attempt to launch an egalitarian entertainment empire. The Beatles' attempt to build a utopian commercial enterprise and take control of their economic destiny would soon become a financial and logistical nightmare.

One positive result of the band's trip to India was that they used the time to write a wealth of new material. The songs formed the basis of the two-LP, thirty-song *The Beatles*, commonly known as the White Album for its unadorned cover. In contrast to *Sgt. Pepper*'s densely overdubbed tracks, the White Album was largely a return to spare, guitar-based rock.

The White Album—on which the band graduated to eight-track recording—featured some of the Beatles' most mature and accomplished songwriting and performances yet, but it sounded less like the work of a cohesive band than of four talented individuals with divergent interests and temperaments.

Lennon's compositions, including the fatalistic "Yer Blues," the harrowing "Happiness Is a Warm Gun," and the psychedelic spoof "Glass Onion," were noticeably more edgy and personal than his previous work, previewing the direction that he would pursue in his solo career. Lennon's "Julia" was particularly affecting, evoking his feelings over the his childhood loss of his mother, while the sound collage "Revolution 9" reflected the influence of his new girlfriend, avant-garde artist Yoko Ono (whom he would marry in March 1969). McCartney's songs on the album alternately showcased him as a romantic balladeer ("I Will"), pop craftsman ("Blackbird"), heavy rocker ("Helter Skelter"), retro revivalist ("Back in the U.S.S.R."), and campy faux vaudevillian ("Honey Pie"). Harrison made his presence felt with the epic "While My Guitar Gently Weeps" (with guest Eric Clapton on lead guitar), the languid ballad "Long, Long, Long," and the withering social commentary "Piggies." Even Starr, who'd previously stepped forward for the occasional lead vocal, received his first solo songwriting credit with the country-rocker "Don't Pass Me By."

Although they yielded much enduring music, the White Album sessions—which also produced the classic non-LP single "Hey Jude"/"Revolution"—saw deep divisions arise within the Beatles. One source of tension was a general feeling that McCartney had been taking too dominant a role in the band's affairs in Brian Epstein's absence. Another was the presence of Yoko Ono at most of the sessions. The increasingly prolific Harrison, meanwhile, had grown frustrated with his difficulty in getting the band to record his songs. The situation grew so uncomfortable that the dependable, unassuming Starr walked out at one point, leaving McCartney to handle the drumming on some tracks; the band talked him into returning two weeks later. George Martin and longtime engineer Geoff Emerick also quit the sessions at other points.

Meanwhile, the four Beatles continued to clash over business issues, particularly their choice of a new manager. McCartney wanted to turn the band's affairs over to Lee Eastman, father of his wife Linda. That suggestion didn't sit well with the other Beatles, who wanted to hire fearsome New York music-biz vet Allen Klein. After Klein was hired, he initially impressed the band by renegotiating their contract with EMI, winning them the highest royalty rate paid to artists at that time. But Klein's abrasive style alienated many in the band's inner circle, as did his severe cost-cutting measures at Apple Corps. Klein's stewardship of the band's career would remain controversial, particularly with subsequent allegations of financial irregularities.

In early 1969 the Beatles began working on a new recording project, initially titled *Get Back*. An outgrowth of McCartney's unsuccessful attempts to push the band to return to live performing, *Get Back* was an effort to recapture the Beatles' earthy roots and shake the group out of its recent malaise. Accompanied by American keyboardist Billy Preston, the band recorded in an informal live-in-the-studio setting, running through new material as well as classic cover tunes from the band's early days. The sessions were recorded for a proposed album and filmed for a prospective TV special.

The recording climaxed with the band playing an impromptu set on the roof of Apple's London headquarters, before being shut down by the police. But the sessions were otherwise marred by unfocused performances and inter-band squabbles, with Harrison quitting for a few days at one point. Not surprisingly, the band was unhappy with the recordings and the project was temporarily shelved.

Despite the negative feelings that surrounded the *Get Back* project, the Beatles managed to rally and wrap their recording career on a high note with their studio swan song *Abbey Road*, recorded in the summer of 1969 and released that September. Remarkably enough, the album—named after the EMI studio where the band had done most of its recording—was one of their most unified and sophisticated efforts, boasting some of the most arresting melodies and ambitious arrangements in the band's catalog. *Abbey Road* also continued George Harrison's emergence as a significant songwriter; his songs "Something" and "Here Comes the Sun" were among the album's most popular. The former became the first Harrison composition to occupy the A-side of a Beatles single.

But *Abbey Road*'s musical unity didn't reflect the mood within the band. After finishing the album, Lennon released some singles with various friends as the Plastic Ono Band, Harrison toured with American country-rock duo Delaney and Bonnie, Starr teamed with Peter Sellers to star in the film comedy *The Magic Christian*, and McCartney began working on a solo album. Lennon had announced his intention to quit the Beatles in September 1969, but was persuaded not to make the news public.

So the public was largely shocked in April 1970, when McCartney, on the occasion of the release of his debut solo LP *McCartney*, announced that he was no longer a Beatle. At the end of 1970, McCartney sued his bandmates to dissolve their partnership; the issue would drag through the courts for years, sowing long-term ill will between various members and negating any chance of a reunion.

One factor that pushed McCartney toward the announcement was his refusal to delay *McCartney*'s release date to avoid conflicting with *Let It Be*, an album drawn from the *Get Back* recordings, and a same-titled feature film documentary drawn from the footage originally shot for the unfinished TV special.

The *Let It Be* album was assembled by American producer Phil Spector, who had produced Lennon's solo single "Instant Karma!" and who'd long coveted an opportunity to work with the Beatles. Spector did substantial overdubbing, adding various vocals and instrumentation to several of the band's unadorned live tracks. McCartney was incensed by Spector's post-production tinkering, particularly his addition of a choir and orchestra to his "The Long and Winding Road." But the *Let It Be* film, complete with scenes documenting the band's strained relations and the triumphant Apple rooftop performance, was recognized as a compelling document of the Beatles' dissolution.

SOLO IN THE 1970s

Although fans would spend much of the 1970s waiting in vain for a Beatles reunion, the four ex-Beatles wasted no time in establishing productive solo careers. Perhaps the Beatle who immediately benefited the most from his new solo status was George Harrison, whose subordinate position within the band had allowed him to accumulate a large body of unreleased songs.

Harrison's backlog of quality material was sufficient to fill a double album, *All Things Must Pass*, which was augmented by a third LP of informal studio jams. The album boasted rich, layered production by Phil Spector, and revealed a distinctive sound spotlighting Harrison's eloquent guitar work and lyrics showcasing his abiding sense of spirituality and whimsical sense of humor. The album produced a major hit in the prayerful "My Sweet Lord," which had the distinction of being the first recording by an ex-Beatle to top the American singles charts.

Harrison followed *All Things Must Pass* by spearheading rock's first major charity event, the Concert for Bangladesh, a pair of all-star concerts at New York's Madison Square Garden to raise money to aid that famine-ravaged nation. The shows, which also featured Ringo Starr, Eric Clapton, and Bob Dylan, produced a movie and a live triple album. Harrison continued to record steadily through the 1970s, before settling into a more leisurely pace in subsequent decades, keeping a relatively low public profile and making a surprise return to the top of the charts with 1987's *Cloud Nine*. In 1988, he scored more sales success as a member of the tongue-in-cheek supergroup the Traveling Wilburys, alongside Dylan, Jeff Lynne, Roy Orbison, and Tom Petty. Harrison also appeared frequently as a guest musician, contributing his distinctive guitar work to albums by such friends as Eric Clapton, Leon Russell, and Harry Nilsson, as well as projects by his early rock and roll idols Carl Perkins and Duane Eddy. Harrison also successfully branched out into film production via his company Handmade Films.

John Lennon took advantage of his new freedom as a solo artist to establish a standard of uncompromising personal and political forthrightness that he would maintain for the rest of his career. Lennon was the first Beatle to record outside the group, releasing the singles "Cold Turkey" (a brutally frank account of his battle with heroin addiction) and "Power to the People," the raw album *Live Peace in Toronto*, and a trio of avant-garde collaborations with Yoko Ono (including *Two Virgins*, whose nude cover photo predictably raised a media outcry). In 1970, he released his first solo studio album, *John Lennon/Plastic Ono Band*, whose unflinching, often harrowing introspection instantly established Lennon as a major solo voice. He continued to produce compelling, highly personal work on such subsequent releases as *Imagine*, *Mind Games*, and *Walls and Bridges*.

Lennon, who settled in New York in the early 1970s, became active in anti-war activism and dabbled in radical politics, using his visibility to speak out about various social and political issues. His activism earned Lennon the enmity of President Richard Nixon. As files released under the Freedom of Information Act would later reveal, Nixon feared that Lennon would continue to use his influence with America's youth to turn them against the Vietnam War, and attempted to have Lennon deported or arrested on drug charges. After releasing 1975's *Rock 'n' Roll*, an album of oldies covers paying tribute to his early musical roots, Lennon took an extended hiatus from recording, embracing domestic family life in New York.

If Lennon used his solo work to exorcise his personal and political demons, Paul McCartney's post-Beatles output often seemed designed to establish him as a crowd-pleasing all-around entertainer, indulging the mainstream showbiz impulses that had been held in check during his Beatles years. McCartney's melodic skills and commercial instincts allowed him to maintain the most consistently successful career of any ex-Beatle, scoring nine number one singles and seven number one albums in the United States during the first dozen years of his solo career.

After releasing the charmingly rustic solo efforts *McCartney* and *Ram*, McCartney formed the new group Wings with his wife Linda and ex–Moody Blues frontman Denny Laine. Wings scored massive commercial success (and general dismissal from critics) through the 1970s, before McCartney reverted to solo status at the end of the decade. In the years since, he's continued to record steadily, sporadically earning renewed critical respect with such albums as 1982's *Tug of War*, 1989's *Flowers in the Dirt*, 1997's *Flaming Pie*, and 2007's *Memory Almost Full*. McCartney's periodic tours since then have invariably been greeted as major events, but his 1984 attempt at directing and starring in the feature film *Give My Regards to Broad Street* was roundly dismissed as an ill-conceived vanity project and was a resounding commercial flop.

At the time of the Beatles' breakup, few would have expected Ringo Starr, neither a prolific songwriter nor a conventionally gifted vocalist, to carve out a durable solo career. Yet the beloved drummer's self-effacing charm, and his knack for getting by with a little help from his famous friends, have consistently carried him through.

Starr launched his solo recording career in 1970 with a pair of esoteric projects, the lushly arranged collection of 1930s and 1940s pop standards *Sentimental Journey* and the Nashville-recorded country effort *Beaucoups of Blues*. He subsequently hit Top Ten pay dirt with a pair of self-written 1971 singles "It Don't Come Easy" (whose B-side "Early 1970" offered Ringo's good-natured perspective on the Beatles' breakup) and "Back Off Boogaloo." Those were followed by 1973's *Ringo*, which featured songwriting and instrumental contributions from his three former bandmates and spawned three more Top Ten hits, including the Harrison/Starr-penned "Photograph."

While he has continued to release new albums, Ringo's amiability and comic skills also allowed him to carve out a productive acting career. In the 1990s, he reinvented himself as a frontman and touring artist, fronting various editions of his All-Starr Band, in which he's shared the spotlight with a shifting cast of fellow classic-rock veterans.

John Lennon emerged from his extended hiatus in 1980, releasing *Double Fantasy*, a collaboration with Yoko Ono. Despite their slick pop production, there was no doubting the sincerity of Lennon's heartfelt new odes to love and fatherhood. While the John Lennon of *Double Fantasy* was a far cry from the boundary-pushing rabble-rouser that fans had come to know, the new material showed him to be passionate and reenergized, having found fulfillment in the stable family life that he'd been deprived of in his own youth.

The Kinks: Well-Respected Men

The Kinks' thirty-three-year career was marked by intense internal conflict (sometimes expressed physically), periods of commercial decline, and a live show that often bordered on chaos. Through it all, they remained a "real-time" rock and roll band, never degenerating into a cabaret act or a greatest-hits machine.

Ray Davies (vocals, guitar), his younger brother Dave Davies (guitar, vocals), and Peter Quaife (bass) formed the Kinks in 1963; Mick Avory (drums) joined the group just prior to their signing with Pye Records. In 1964, the group shot to number one in the United Kingdom and into the United States Top Ten with "You Really Got Me," a raw, dynamic rocker (written by Ray Davies) with an overdriven two-guitar sound that verged on heavy metal.

The Kinks' third Top Ten hit, "Tired of Waiting for You" (1965), was slower-paced, almost wistful, and revealed Ray Davies as a songwriter of unusual insight and compassion. "Well-Respected Man" was a sharply observed piece of class-conscious social commentary; "Dead End Street," a moving but unsentimental depiction of English working-class poverty. The Kinks' 1966 LP, *Face to Face*, was hailed by some critics as rock's first concept album.

In 1968–69 The Kinks hit a peak of creativity that produced *Something Else by the Kinks* (featuring "Waterloo Sunset," one of Ray Davies's most poignant and evocative songs) and the superb concept albums, *The Kinks Are the Village Green Preservation Society* and *Arthur, Or the Decline and Fall of the British Empire*. Despite laudatory reviews, none of these albums reached the American Top 100. In 1969, John Dalton replaced Peter Quaife and the Kinks resumed U.S. touring after a four-year hiatus.

The Kinks' comeback began in 1970 with "Lola," a song about a transvestite that became their first U.S. Top Ten hit in five years. In 1973, Ray Davies began creating a sequence of ambitious "story-song" albums including *Preservation: Act One*, *Preservation: Act Two*, and *The Kinks Present a Soap Opera*. The band's live show turned into an extravagant evening of musical theater with horn players, female vocalists, and spoken dialogue.

With *Sleepwalker* in 1977, the Kinks shed their excess baggage and returned to straightforward rock and roll, seeming to draw renewed energy and inspiration from the nascent punk rock movement. The 1981 single "Come Dancing" was the group's first U.S. Top Ten hit since "Lola," and 1983's *State of Confusion* reached number twelve among *Billboard* Pop Albums.

But relations within the group now were badly frayed. Mick Avory quit in 1984 and was replaced by Bob Henrit; album sales and concert attendance gradually declined. A 1993 call-and-response duet between the Davies brothers evoked the emotion of its title: "Hatred." Three years later, in Oslo, Norway, the Kinks played their last concert. But the masterful songs of Ray Davies and a half-dozen great albums make this band one of the greatest to emerge from the original British Invasion, along with the Beatles, the Rolling Stones, and the Who. In 1990, the Kinks were inducted into the Rock and Roll Hall of Fame.

A. S.

The fact that Lennon had achieved personal contentment intensified the crushing sense of tragedy of his death. On December 8, as *Double Fantasy* and its first single "(Just Like) Starting Over" were climbing the charts, Lennon was assassinated by deranged Beatles fan Mark David Chapman, as he and Ono were returning home from a recording session.

The event inspired a worldwide outpouring of shock, grief, and mourning. Of the countless tributes that followed in the wake of Lennon's death, one of the most poignant came from George Harrison, who sang the praises of his fallen ex-bandmate on the song "All Those Years Ago." The song, which appeared on Harrison's album *Somewhere in England*, featured guest appearances by Paul McCartney and Ringo Starr.

More than two decades after Lennon's death, it was revealed that George Harrison was suffering from an inoperable form of brain cancer. He passed away on November 29, 2001, leaving the material world with the same low-key dignity that he'd maintained even amid the madness of Beatlemania.

AND IN THE END . . .

The former Beatles' long-standing legal disputes prevented any unreleased Beatles studio recordings from being released to the public for nearly two decades following the band's breakup, although a massive amount of rare Beatles tracks emerged on bootleg releases. The situation changed with the 1994 release of *Live at the BBC*, which collected the best of the band's vintage radio sessions, and the subsequent release of the epic multi-part documentary *The Beatles Anthology*, broadcast on network TV in early 1995 and subsequently released in expanded form on DVD. Assembled with the surviving band members' active participation, the mini-series spawned a trio of double-CD soundtrack compilations containing a wealth of rare and previously unissued material (including the first official release of some of the band's early Decca demos, resulting in Pete Best receiving his first royalties for Beatles recordings).

But the most newsworthy aspect of the *Anthology* discs was the presence of two songs; "Free as a Bird' and "Real Love," on which McCartney, Harrison, and Starr recorded new studio tracks to accompany a pair of 1970s-era Lennon demos. The hybrid tracks sharply divided the opinions of fans and critics, but both became hits, with radio programmers jumping at the chance to play the first "new" Beatles songs in a quarter-century.

While each of the former Beatles experienced commercial ups and downs in their respective solo careers, the Beatles as a group entity has never lost its appeal, continuing to be discovered and embraced by new generations of fans. Ironically, the band's premature breakup spared it from experiencing an artistic decline, leaving the mystique of their body of work intact. The Beatles' vintage work maintains an ageless, timeless appeal, and the band's impact on music and popular culture remains as strong as ever.

TIMELINE

July 6, 1957
John Lennon meets Paul McCartney at the Woolton Garden Fête at St. Peter's Church in Liverpool, during a performance by Lennon's group the Quarrymen. Impressed by Paul's ability to tune a guitar and by his knowledge of song lyrics, John asks him to join the group.

February 1, 1958
Paul McCartney introduces George Harrison to the Quarrymen at the basement teen club the Morgue. He will be invited to join the group the following month.

August 1, 1960
The Beatles make their debut in Hamburg, West Germany, with Stu Sutcliffe on bass and Pete Best on drums.

January 1, 1961
The Beatles make their first appearance at the Cavern Club in Liverpool.

November 1, 1961
Local record store manager Brian Epstein attends a Beatles performance at the Cavern Club.

January 1, 1962
The Beatles record fifteen songs in a one-hour studio audition session for Decca Records, which will eventually pass on the band.

March 7, 1962
The Beatles make their radio debut performing three songs on the BBC.

April 10, 1962
Stu Sutcliffe dies of a brain hemorrhage.

June 1, 1962
The Beatles audition successfully for George Martin at Parlophone/EMI Records. He agrees to sign the band, but insists that Pete Best be replaced on recording sessions.

August 16, 1962
At the behest of Lennon, McCartney, and Harrison, Brian Epstein informs Best that he has been fired from the band.

September 4, 1962
The Beatles record their first single, "Love Me Do" and its B-side, "P.S. I Love You," at EMI's Abbey Road studios in London.

December 1, 1963
"I Want to Hold Your Hand," the Beatles' first American single, is released by Capitol Records.

February 7, 1964
The Beatles arrive in America.

February 9, 1964
The Beatles make their first appearance on the *Ed Sullivan Show*.

February 11, 1964
The Beatles begin their first U.S. tour at the Coliseum in Washington, D.C.

April 4, 1964
The Beatles hold the top five slots on the *Billboard* pop chart.

July 6, 1964
The Beatles' first feature film, *A Hard Day's Night,* has its world premiere in London.

July 29, 1965
The Beatles' second film, *Help!,* is released.

August 15, 1965
The Beatles play in front of almost 60,000 fans at Shea Stadium in New York City.

August 27, 1965:
The Beatles visit Elvis Presley at his home in Bel Air, California.

October 26, 1965
The Beatles are awarded England's prestigious MBE (Members of the Order of the British Empire).

March 1, 1966
London's *Evening Standard* publishes an interview with John Lennon in which he comments that the Beatles are "more popular than Jesus now." Months later, the quote will inspire protests in America, including the burning of Beatles records.

August 11, 1966
Lennon apologizes for his "Jesus" remarks at a press conference in Chicago, on the eve of what will be the Beatles' final tour.

August 29, 1966
The Beatles play their final concert in front of a paying audience at San Francisco's Candlestick Park.

June 1, 1967
Sgt. Pepper's Lonely Hearts Club Band is released in Britain.

June 25, 1967
The Beatles become the first band to stage a global satellite broadcast, performing their new song "All You Need Is Love" at Abbey Road studio as part of a TV titled *Our World*.

August 1, 1967
George Harrison and his wife Patti stroll through the streets of Haight-Ashbury, bringing international media attention to the budding hippie scene.

August 27, 1967
Manager Brian Epstein dies of an accidental prescription drug overdose.

September 1, 1967
John Lennon writes "I Am the Walrus" while under the influence of LSD.

February 15, 1968
The Beatles depart for Rishikesh, India, for an advanced course in transcendental meditation with the Maharishi Mahesh Yogi.

May 1, 1968
Apple Corps opens its doors in London.

January 30, 1969
The Beatles' final public performance as a band takes place on the roof of the Apple building during the filming of the documentary film *Let It Be*.

August 20, 1969
The Beatles finish recording "I Want You (She's So Heavy)" for their *Abbey Road* album, marking the last time that all four Beatles would be together in the same studio.

September 20, 1969
John Lennon announces his resignation to the rest of the group, but agrees not to make his departure public.

April 10, 1970
Paul McCartney becomes the first Beatle to publicly acknowledge the band's breakup, via a self-written interview included with pre-release promotional copies of his first solo album *McCartney*.

May 8, 1970
Let It Be, recorded live in the studio prior to *Abbey Road*, with additional overdubs by producer Phil Spector, is released, followed by the documentary film of the same name.

December 8, 1980
In New York, John Lennon is shot dead by Mark David Chapman as he and Yoko Ono return from a recording session.

November 19, 1995
"Free as a Bird," the first new Beatles single in twenty-five years, premieres as part of the television broadcast, *The Beatles Anthology*. The song, a 1977 John Lennon demo with new vocal and instrumental tracks by the three surviving Beatles, will reach number six on the U.S. singles chart in early 1996.

March 23, 1996
"Real Love," a 1979 John Lennon demo completed in 1995 by the other Beatles, reaches the charts, where it will peak at number eleven.

November 29, 2001
George Harrison dies at the age of fifty-eight after a long battle with cancer.

SELECTED DISCOGRAPHY

The Beatles

Please Please Me, 1963
With the Beatles, 1963

A Hard Day's Night, 1964

Beatles for Sale, 1964

Help!, 1965

Rubber Soul, 1965

Revolver, 1966

Sgt. Pepper's Lonely Hearts Club Band, 1967

Magical Mystery Tour, 1967

The Beatles (aka the White Album), 1968

Yellow Submarine, 1969

Abbey Road, 1969

Let It Be, 1970

1962–1966, 1973

1967–1970, 1973

Past Masters, Vol. 1, 1988

Past Masters, Vol. 2, 1988

Live at the BBC, 1994

Anthology 1, 1995

Anthology 2, 1996

Anthology 3, 1996

John Lennon

John Lennon/Plastic Ono Band, 1970

Imagine, 1971

Mind Games, 1973

Walls and Bridges, 1974

Paul McCartney

McCartney, 1970

Ram, 1971

Red Rose Speedway (with Wings), 1973

Band on the Run (with Wings), 1973

George Harrison

All Things Must Pass, 1970

Living in the Material World, 1973

Dark Horse, 1974

Extra Texture, 1975

Ringo Starr

Ringo, 1973

Goodnight Vienna, 1974

Blast from Your Past, 1975

FURTHER READING

Carr, Roy and Tony Tyler. *The Beatles: An Illustrated Record*. New York: Harmony, 1975.

Coleman, Ray. *Brian Epstein: The Man Who Made the Beatles*. New York: Viking, 1989.

Davies, Hunter. *The Beatles*. New York: McGraw-Hill, 1985.

Emerick, Geoff and Howard Massey. *Here, There and Everywhere: My Life Recording the Music of the Beatles*. New York: Gotham, 2006.

Lennon, Cynthia. *John*. London: Hodder and Stoughton, 2006.

Lewisohn, Mark. *The Beatles Recording Sessions: The Official Abbey Road Studio Session Notes 1962–1970*. New York: Harmony, 1988.

Lewisohn, Mark. *The Complete Beatles Chronicle*. New York: Harmony, 1992.

Martin, George. *Summer of Love: The Making of* Sgt. Pepper. New York: Macmillan, 1994.

Miles, Barry. *Paul McCartney: Many Years from Now*. New York: Henry Holt, 1997.

Norman, Philip. *Shout!: The Beatles in Their Generation*. New York: Fireside, 1981.

Schaffner, Nicholas. *The Beatles Forever*. New York: McGraw-Hill, 1977.

Spitz, Bob. *The Beatles*. New York: Little, Brown, 2005.

Stokes, Geoffrey. *The Beatles*. New York: Times Books, 1980.

Sulpy, Doug and Ray Schweighardt. *Get Back: The Unauthorized Chronicle of the Beatles'* Let It Be *Disaster*. New York: St. Martin's, 1997.

Weiner, Jon. *Come Together: John Lennon in His Time*. Chicago: University of Illinois Press, 1990.

Courtesy of Photofest.

Bob Dylan

Jesse Jarnow

ROCK AND ROLL POET

It is impossible to conceive of rock and roll's maturation from teenage recreation into intellectually expressive music without Bob Dylan. Comparable only to the Beatles in influence, Dylan brought poetry to rock. More impressive, though, is the massive body of music Dylan has written, performed, and recorded over his unparalleled half-century career.

Often called "the voice of his generation," Dylan's actual voice was instantly identifiable for its nasal qualities. With it, he created and shed a half-dozen musical identities, each a phase in a relentless artistic development. Dylan was a hard-core folkie who imitated Woody Guthrie and learned songs from ancient records, a protest singer who sang against injustice, a confessional songwriter who poured his heart out onstage, a confrontational rock icon in dark sunglasses who played stinging blues, a country crooner, a mysterious figure in white makeup, a born-again Christian who testified for Jesus, and an old-time bandleader in a suit and cowboy hat. In nearly every capacity, Dylan broke new ground. Rock and roll, in a sense, transformed around him, and Dylan's sometimes confounding actions gained praise and acceptance years later.

Idiosyncratic and unpredictable, Dylan changed directions in an effort to escape the labels placed on him by fame. At nearly every turn, Dylan's moves were designed to provoke, as when he plugged in an electric guitar at the Newport Folk Festival, directed a four-hour movie with no discernible plot, released an all-country album sung and written in an unrecognizable voice, or allowed one of his songs to be used in a lingerie advertisement. In his autobiography, Dylan even admitted to recording several intentionally inferior albums in order to lessen the burdens of his popularity.

One obsessive fan who combed through Dylan's trash claimed that his science of "Dylanology" would reveal the true meaning of the artist's cryptic lyrics. Since the 1960s, the songwriter has led an extremely private life. After a very public divorce in the late 1970s, Dylan secretly remarried, only acknowledging it in passing references to "my wife" in his autobiography.

At the center, however, has always been Bob Dylan's songwriting. Throughout every stage of his career, he has employed a musical language drawn from his encyclopedic knowledge of traditional folk, country, and early rock. This strength has enabled Dylan to tap into the deep wellspring of American music and invested his creative endeavors with a sense of timelessness. It has also served as a bedrock for the songwriter, helping him to rebound after a motorcycle accident in the 1960s, as well as rejuvenating his career in the early 1990s.

Dylan combined this vocabulary with poetry that could be surreal, tender, hilarious, biting, oblique, and perfectly obvious—sometimes simultaneously. Though many of his early followers complained that Dylan stopped writing political songs when he "went electric" in 1965, Dylan's lyrics frequently included elements of social commentary, whether direct or hidden. Writers and professors have made a cottage industry of Dylanology, from examinations of Dylan's views on religion to multi-volume studies of Dylan's live performances to an historical treatise on how Dylan relates to "the old, weird America."

"Songs, to me, were more important than just light entertainment," Dylan wrote in 2004. "They were my preceptor and guide into some altered consciousness of reality, some different republic, some liberated republic. . . . Whatever the case, it wasn't that I was anti-popular culture or anything and I had no ambitions to stir things up. I just thought of mainstream culture as lame as hell and a big trick."[1]

Despite writing an autobiography and being interviewed for a major documentary, Dylan remains elusive, the result of a lifetime of self-mythologizing. "I was with the carnival off and on for six years," he told radio host Cynthia Gooding in 1962, at the start of his career. "I was clean-up boy. I was mainliner on the Ferris wheel. Do the shoreline thing. Use to do all kinds of stuff like that. . . . I didn't go to school for a bunch of years, skipped this, skipped that."[2]

None of what Dylan told her was true. His name wasn't even Bob Dylan. It was Robert Zimmerman, and he was from Minnesota.

FROM HIBBING TO HIGHWAY 61

Robert Allen Zimmerman was born in Duluth, Minnesota, on May 24, 1941, to Abraham Zimmerman and Beatrice Stone. Abe was the son of Russian immigrants and worked for the Standard Oil Company. At the end of World War II, as the work force swelled, Abe lost his job. After the birth of Bobby's brother David, in 1945, their father was stricken with polio. As Abe recovered, the family moved seventy-five miles east to Beatrice's hometown, Hibbing. Duluth was several hours north of Minneapolis, a port city on the shore of Lake Superior. Hibbing was smaller, an Iron Range town once known for its mineral deposits. Abe joined his brothers at their furniture and appliance business.

Bobby sang from an early age. He was four when he performed "Some Sunday Morning" and "Accentuate the Positive" at a Mother's Day gathering. Far from the childhood circus career he later invented for himself, Bobby's childhood was quite normal. He and his friends stole crabapples from neighbors' yards, played on Pill Hill (the site of an ore dump), and built clubhouses. When Bobby was in kindergarten, Abe bought a house on Seventh Avenue. In the house, Dylan claimed to have found something of great significance. "[It] has kind of mystical overtones," he recalled many years later.

> The people who had lived in the house previous to that time, they had left some of their furniture, and among that furniture was a great big mahogany radio, like a jukebox. It had a 78 turntable when you opened up the top. And I opened it up one day and there was a record on there, a country record. It was a song called "Drifting Too Far from the Shore." I think it was the Stanley Brothers, if not Bill Monroe. I played the record and it brought me into a different world.[3]

Thus began a lifelong romance with music.

Though boxers, wrestlers, circuses, and stock car races came to Hibbing, it was the movies and the radio that gave young Bobby glimpses of the world outside the Iron Range. His great uncle owned the Lybba Theater, a ten-minute walk from the Zimmerman house, and Bobby was a regular. The radio was different. Late at night, after the serials ended, Bobby could pick up powerful AM signals that traveled north up the Mississippi River from as far away as Louisiana and Mexico. Through this music, Dylan began to yearn for the world outside Hibbing.

Bobby discovered early rock musicians Bill Haley, Buddy Holly, Little Richard, and Elvis Presley, as well as country legends like Hank Williams. He began to collect records. Now proficient on piano, Bobby formed his first band, the Golden Chords. At their appearance at Hibbing High's Jacket Jamboree Talent Festival, the Golden Chords were cut off mid-set as Bobby pounded the piano and emulated the raucous vocals of Little Richard. Under the influence of bluesmen like Muddy Waters and Jimmy Reed, Bobby switched to an electric guitar and formed several other bands. None lasted very long.

On January 31, 1959, he and his friends traveled to the Duluth Armory, where he saw Buddy Holly perform. Standing in the front row, Dylan made eye contact with his hero, an event he remembered vividly forty years later. Three days later, Holly died in a plane crash, along with fellow musicians Ritchie Valens and the Big Bopper. It became known as "the Day the Music Died," but for Bobby Zimmerman, music was busy being born.

That same spring, Bobby discovered folk music, via a high school graduation gift: a set of records by Leadbelly, the great country blues singer and guitarist who'd served time in prison for murder. By the fall, Bobby Zimmerman escaped Hibbing. When he arrived in Minneapolis, he was Bobby Zimmerman no longer.

The Folk Revival

The emergence of Bob Dylan marked a turning point in a large-scale revival of interest in "folk music." In the years 1955–65, this term would encompass everything from protest numbers by youthful singer-songwriters to the classic blues and mountain music of rediscovered performers from the 1920s and 1930s.

In 1950, an urban folk group called the Weavers—Pete Seeger, Ronnie Gilbert, Lee Hayes, and Fred Hellerman—scored two massive left-field hits with "Tzena Tzena Tzena" (number two) and "Goodnight Irene" (number one). But in less than two years' time, the group was blacklisted when its members were accused of having been either Communist Party members or so-called fellow travelers. Their music disappeared from the airwaves and the group disbanded. In September 1955, a Weavers reunion sold out Carnegie Hall and led Vanguard Records to release a best-selling live album from the concert. These events helped to "rehabilitate" folk music in the eyes of a once-wary music industry and, by extension, the general public.

Folk song collectors Harry Smith and Alan Lomax played a crucial role in documenting the music's past. In 1952, Smith compiled the multi-volume *Anthology of American Folk Music*—a hugely influential collection of hillbilly, blues, and sacred songs commercially recorded between 1927 and 1932, all long out of print. Alan Lomax released such albums as *Negro Prison Songs* (1958), which was recorded in a notorious Mississippi penitentiary. Moses Asch released Smith's *Anthology* and many of Lomax's recordings on his scrappy Folkways label; he also kept in print the music of Woody Guthrie and Leadbelly, two founding fathers of American folk music.

Impromptu gatherings of singers and musicians called "hootenannies" were held on weekends in New York City's Washington Square Park; soon, the concept spread to summer camps and college campuses. Non-alcoholic "basket houses" in Greenwich Village offered the promise of exposure to untried performers who played for tips. In 1957, Izzy Young opened the Folklore Center in Greenwich Village. The small storefront sold folk albums, sheet music, and used instruments, and hosted many informal performances over the next decade (including the New York debuts of Tim Buckley and Emmylou Harris).

In 1959, the first Newport Folk Festival was held in Newport, Rhode Island. It became an important annual gathering that brought together young folk fans and musicians with rediscovered traditional performers like the Mississippi bluesman Skip James, born 1902; and the Tennessee mountain singer Clarence Ashley, born 1895. Folk music magazines like *Sing Out* and *Broadside* gained in circulation and advertising.

Elektra and Vanguard were two of the most active labels in the folk field. Elektra Records was launched by founder Jac Holzman on the sales of folk albums by Theo Bikel, Josh White, and Oscar Brand. These 1950s artists were succeeded by new Elektra signings: the gifted singer Judy Collins, topical songwriters Patrick Sky and Tom Paxton, and the seminal white blues group (John) Koerner, (Dave) Ray, and (Tony) Glover. Maynard Solomon founded Vanguard Records as a classical label, but he successfully pursued folk veterans Odetta and Ramblin' Jack Elliot, new voices Joan Baez, Eric Andersen, Ian and Sylvia, and Buffy Sainte-Marie, and the aging but still vital country blues singers Reverend Gary Davis and Mississippi John Hurt.

Andy Schwartz

"The first time I was asked my name in the Twin Cities, I instinctively and automatically without thinking simply said, 'Bob Dylan,'"[4] Dylan wrote in his autobiography. Initially, he'd meant to call himself Robert Allyn, a variation on his middle name. "Unexpectedly, I'd seen some poems by Dylan Thomas. Dylan and Allyn sounded similar."[5] For many years, Dylan denied taking his name from the Irish poet. He told some that it was his uncle's name, his mother's maiden name, or a town in Oklahoma. It was the first of many myths Dylan would create for himself.

In Minneapolis, he worked hard to become Bob Dylan. First, he traded his electric guitar for an acoustic. Then, he learned as much as he could about folk music. Though Bob barely attended classes, he studied for hours in the Bohemian neighborhood Dinkytown. He exchanged songs with local musicians like John Koerner and expanded his repertoire. Quickly, Dylan developed the skill to memorize a song after only one listen, either from a fellow performer or a recording. He listened to Blind Lemon Jefferson, John Jacob Niles, the New Lost City Ramblers, and countless others. Stories abound of Dylan's outright thefts of friends' record collections.

He also discovered Woody Guthrie, the author of "This Land Is Your Land," "Pretty Boy Floyd," "Pastures of Plenty," "Hard Travelin'," and literally hundreds of other songs. "They had the infinite sweep of humanity in them," Dylan later declared. He became obsessed with the itinerant Oklahoma-born folksinger and read Guthrie's autobiography, *Bound for Glory*. "I went through it cover to cover like a hurricane," Dylan wrote, "totally focused on every word, and the book sang out to me like a radio."[6] He now predominantly performed Guthrie songs, dressed like Guthrie in a cowboy hat, and even began to talk like his hero, with a thick Okie accent.

Guthrie's records were rare, so Dylan could only learn songs from other musicians.

> I'd always be checking the repertoires of every out of town performer who came through to see what Guthrie songs they knew that I didn't, and I was beginning to feel the phenomenal scope of Woody's songs—the Sacco and Vanzetti ballads, Dust Bowl and children songs, Grand Coulee Dam songs, venereal disease songs, union and workingman ballads, even his rugged heartbreak love ballads. Each one seemed like a towering tall building with a variety of scenarios all appropriate for different situations.[7]

Informed that a musician named Ramblin' Jack Elliott had already made a career of being a second Woody, Dylan varied his act slightly. He learned harmonica from Tony Glover. Though there was a left-wing political scene around the Dinkytown folk circles, Dylan was uninterested. He only cared about music. In 1960, he decided he'd outgrown Minneapolis. He spent the summer in Denver, where he met guitarist Jesse Fuller, and spent time in Chicago and Madison before he caught a ride to New York with a friend of a friend.

Dylan arrived in Manhattan on January 24, 1961, a bitter night. "Coldest winter in 17 years," he would sing on "Hard Times in New York Town." According to the *New York Times*, it was actually twenty-eight years. Within days, Dylan had left Manhattan and crossed the Hudson River to meet his hero, Woody Guthrie, in an unlikely place: Greystone Hospital in north central New Jersey.

Guthrie was the victim of a rare degenerative disease, Huntington's chorea. By 1961, he lived permanently at Greystone, his body crippled. Dylan became a regular visitor. With his guitar he played Woody's requests, usually for Guthrie's own songs. Though the older folksinger was fatally ill, he immediately liked the scrawny kid with the chubby cheeks and the black corduroy hat. Through Guthrie, Dylan met Sidsel and Bob Gleason of East Orange, one of many couples who took Dylan in after he arrived in New York. Dylan relied on these older patrons, as well as a series of girlfriends, for places to sleep.

Empowered by Guthrie's approval, Dylan took to the famed folk clubs of Greenwich Village. He immediately secured a residency at Cafe Wha?, where he played harmonica alongside Fred Neil. The folk scene in New York was large and had an established hierarchy of clubs, performers, and labels. With a boyish charm that many compared to Huckleberry Finn, Dylan won friends and rose through the ranks. He passed time at Izzy Young's Folklore Center near Washington Square Park, an archive of recordings, instruments, and folk music literature that was a hub for musicians.

Another Bohemian couple Bob stayed with, boasted a massive library. "You couldn't help but lose your passion for dumbness," Dylan remembered. "I usually opened up some book to the middle, read a few pages and if I liked it went back to the beginning."[8] Dylan read political philosophy like Niccolò Machiavelli's *The Prince*, gothic horror writers like Edgar Allen Poe, populist autobiographies of American heroes like Davy Crockett, Romantic poets such as Byron and Shelley, psychotherapist Sigmund Freud, Russian revolutionary Alexander Pushkin, and hundreds of others. He also spent time in the New York Public Library, poring over microfilm of Civil War–era newspapers.

Dylan wrote his first songs, including "Talkin' Hava Negila" and "Talkin' Bear Mountain Picnic Massacre Blues," in a style derivative of Woody Guthrie. He gigged wherever he could, at the Commons, the Gaslight, Gerde's Folk City, and elsewhere. He jammed with Village musicians, and served as an opening act for several artists, including blues legend John Lee Hooker. He was also hard at work inventing his persona, such as when he told Woody Guthrie's wife, Marjorie, that he was from New Mexico, or when he introduced a song by saying he'd learned it on the Brazos River in Texas. Onstage, Dylan perfected a wry presence that recalled Charlie Chaplin. He slipped between stories and songs in a style he learned from hipster monologist Lord Buckley.

On September 29, 1961, the *New York Times* published Robert Shelton's review of one of Dylan's performances at Folk City, titled "Bob Dylan: A Distinctive Stylist." That same month, Dylan participated in his first recording session, where he accompanied Carolyn Hester on harmonica. At a rehearsal, Dylan met John Hammond, the legendary producer who signed jazz great Billie Holiday in 1933. Hammond signed Dylan to Columbia Records.

In November, Dylan joined Hammond in Columbia's Studio A to record his first album. On *Bob Dylan*, released in March 1962, Dylan performed almost all traditional folk songs, including "Man of Constant Sorrow," "Pretty Peggy-O," and "House of the Rising Sun." Also included was Dylan's first completely original composition, "Song to Woody." The album sold poorly. Dylan was referred to within Columbia as "Hammond's folly," but the producer defended his protégé.

In early 1962, Dylan got his own apartment, and started to date Suze Rotolo. A vivacious intellectual, Suze (pronounced "Suzy") turned Bob on to art and awakened his political consciousness. Dylan contributed topical songs to *Broadside,* a new magazine dedicated to spreading new songs, including the satirical "Talkin' John Birch Society Blues," about the right-wing political organization. Suze worked behind the scenes at Theatre de Lys when it presented a program of songs by German musician/playwright Bertolt Brecht.

One song in particular, "Pirate Jenny," took hold of Dylan. "Woody had never written a song like that," he remembered.

> It wasn't a protest or topical song and there was no love for people in it . . . I took the song apart and unzipped it—it was the form, the free verse association, the structure and known disregard for the known certainty of melodic patterns to make it seriously matter, give it its cutting edge. . . . I wanted to figure out how to manipulate and control this particular structure and form which I knew was the key that gave "Pirate Jenny" its resilience and outrageous power.[9]

The songs began to pour from him, many based on traditional tunes but with a new strength in them. "The Ballad of Emmitt Till" was dedicated to a black adolescent killed in Mississippi in 1955.

In April, Dylan wrote "Blowin' in the Wind," based on the slave spiritual "No More Auction Block." Comprising a series of rhetorical questions, the song framed the civil rights struggle in nearly biblical terms, but was general enough to be applicable to any strife. "How many roads must a man walk down before you call him a man?" Dylan asked in the first line.

In September, he penned "A Hard Rain's A-Gonna Fall," which dealt with the Cuban missile crisis and the imminent threat of nuclear war, with much the same strategy as "Blowin' in the Wind." "I saw a highway of diamonds with nobody on it," he sang, describing his vision of a post-nuclear America, "I saw a black branch with blood that kept drippin'." Determined not to be known merely as a protest singer, he also wrote love songs, both tender, like "Girl of the North Country," and bitter, like "Don't Think Twice, It's Alright," the first of Dylan's many so-called put-downs. Anchored by these songs, *The Freewheelin' Bob Dylan* was released in May 1963, reaching number twenty-two on the *Billboard* albums chart. The cover depicted Bob and Suze walking arm-in-arm down a snow-lined 4th Street.

The Protest Song

During the period leading up to the Revolutionary War, many protest songs were written in defiance of British policies in the American colonies. Composers set new words to familiar British/Celtic tunes to create "The Liberty Song" (from 1768, decrying new import taxes imposed by the Crown) and "Free America" (1774). Slaves brought from West Africa contributed to the development of protest songs when they transformed the church hymns of their white masters into work songs and emancipation anthems.

In the twentieth century, the songs of the civil rights movement encouraged its supporters through hazardous, sometimes deadly marches and demonstrations. The most popular anthem of the era, "We Shall Overcome," was crafted from Charles Tindley's circa 1900 gospel song, "I'll Overcome Some Day." Another movement standard, "No More Auction Block for Me," was derived from "Many Thousands Gone"—a post–Civil War song popularized by Negroes who had fled to Canada, where slavery was abolished in 1833.

Folksinger/activist Joan Baez credits Bob Dylan for expanding the lyrical scope of the protest song. Dylan's "North Country Blues" (1963), for example, was one of the first works by a singer-songwriter to decry the negative effects of globalization, with "words which would move me out of the ethereal but archaic ballads of yore and into the contemporary music scene of the 1960s."[1] Singing an international repertoire in several languages, Baez went on to amass a devoted international following that persists to this day.

When Dylan's song "Blowin' in the Wind" became a number two Pop hit for Peter, Paul, and Mary in 1963, the former gospel singer turned R&B idol Sam Cooke felt personally challenged by "a white boy writing a song like that."[2] Cooke quickly wrote and recorded "A Change Is Gonna Come," a hymn-like soul ballad that touched on the hardships of African American life and the struggle for racial justice in the era of segregation. He sang the song on national television during an appearance on *The Tonight Show* in February 1964 and it became a Top Ten R&B hit after his death in December.

Phil Ochs (1940–76) was among the foremost writers of folk protest songs of the 1960s: The title of his 1964 debut album was *All the News That's Fit to Sing*. The assassination of President Kennedy ("That Was the President"), the U.S. Marines' invasion of the Dominican Republic ("Santo Domingo"), the plight of immigrant farm workers ("Bracero")—all were grist for his compositional mill. Ochs's public profile far exceeded his modest record sales, and he struggled with this contradiction throughout a career in which he helped to organize protests and support left-wing political causes both in the United States and abroad. The singer struggled with alcoholism, depression, and disillusionment brought on by the decline of the New Left; during a trip to Africa, a brutal mugging damaged his vocal chords. Phil Ochs committed suicide on April 9, 1976.

Diverse voices and political orientations entered into the protest music of the Vietnam War era: rowdy folk-rooted satire (the Fugs' "Kill for Peace"), apocalyptic electrified rock songs ("Machine Gun" by Jimi Hendrix), and funky R&B hits (Edwin Starr's "Stop the War Now"). The protest current in pop music reached a chilling dénouement of sorts in 1970 when "Ohio" by Crosby, Stills, Nash, and Young commemorated the killing of four Kent State University students by the Ohio National Guard on May 4, 1970. In subsequent decades, a new style of topical song—from Jackson Browne's anti–mass media "Information Wars" to Steve Earle's pro-democracy call to arms, "The Revolution

Starts Now"—would attempt to speak inclusively and globally to a new popular consciousness.

A. S.

1. Joan Baez, And a Voice to Sing With (New York: Summit Books, 1987), p. 92.
2. Daniel Wolff, You Send Me: The Life and Times of Sam Cooke (New York: William Morrow, 1995), p. 291.

In August 1962, Dylan signed with a new manager, Albert Grossman. The owner of the Gate of Horn, a folk club in Chicago, and a savvy businessman, Grossman transformed Dylan from a folk sensation into an international superstar. In July 1963, Peter, Paul, and Mary—a group masterminded by Grossman—released their single of "Blowin' in the Wind." It sold over a million copies and charted at number two.

Another new friend was Joan Baez, the most famous folk singer in the country. Introduced in early 1963, as Dylan's relationship with Suze crumbled, Baez and Dylan began a romance. Dylan would join her onstage frequently over the next two years, starting in July at the Newport Folk Festival in Rhode Island, as well as on an August tour. On August 28, Dylan and Baez played in front of the Lincoln Memorial as part of the March on Washington, singing "When the Ship Comes In" in front of some 150,000 people from the same podium where Dr. Martin Luther King Jr. would deliver his famous speech. It had been barely three years since Bobby left Hibbing.

Dylan remained busy in Manhattan, penning dozens of songs for *Broadside*, contributing columns to *Hootenanny*, and writing freeform poetry. Much of the latter was published in concert programs and liner notes for himself and others, including Baez. He wrote "The Times They Are A-Changin'," another biblically influenced anthem, which became the title of his third album. Released to wide acclaim in February 1964, *The Times They Are A-Changin'* announced Dylan to the world, charting at number twenty. It featured a similar mix of socially aware ballads, such as "With God on Our Side" and more personal numbers, like "Boots of Spanish Leather."

But Dylan did not want to be hemmed in by the demands of his followers. On one side were associates from Dinkytown, such as Paul Nelson, who told Bob that topical songs did not make good art. On the other were politically engaged folksingers and their fans, who wanted Dylan to be their new poster boy. In December, Dylan accepted the Tom Paine Award from the Emergency Civil Liberties Union, an organization of New York's wealthy, old-guard liberals. Dylan was uncomfortable. Slightly drunk, he berated them obscurely. "There's no black and white, left and right to me anymore; there's only up and down,"[10] he told them.

In spring 1964, Dylan and three friends drove coast to coast in a station wagon. Dylan played several shows along the way, but mostly he went to see the country. When he returned, he declared he was going to only write songs for himself. At the Newport Folk Festival that summer, where he played to 15,000 fans, he debuted "Mr. Tambourine Man," a powerful, surreal epic. Under the influence of marijuana, Dylan's phrases and rhymes swelled, giving the lyrics a magical feel.

In the fall, he invited a group of friends into the studio. With a bottle of red wine at his side, Dylan recorded a dozen new songs live for *Another Side of Bob Dylan*. Some, such as "Chimes of Freedom," were politically aware as well as poetic. Others, like "Motorpsycho Nitemare" and "I Don't Believe You (She Acts Like We Never Have Met)" were more social comedy than social consciousness, filled with biting one-liners. Though the album didn't sell as well as his two previous releases, only reaching number forty-three, Dylan continued to expand his following, and grew further apart from the Greenwich Village scene. Bob spent more and more time staying with Albert Grossman in Woodstock, an idyllic town 100 miles north of Manhattan. By 1965, he'd moved there full-time.

Dylan's music continued to evolve at a rapid rate. Though he had recorded two songs with a backing band in December 1962, Bob had not played rock and roll since he left Hibbing. In spring 1965, he recorded *Bringing It All Back Home*. The first side featured Dylan backed by a blues band put together by producer Tom Wilson. Though many folk purists decried the harder sound, defiant songs like "Maggie's Farm" were no less protests than "Blowin' in the Wind." "I thought I'd get more power out of it with a small group in back of me," Dylan said simply of his decision to employ the combo.[11]

The second side featured four long acoustic ballads, including "Mr. Tambourine Man" and "Gates of Eden," as well as the pointed "It's Alright Ma (I'm Only Bleeding)" which spawned such aphorisms as "money doesn't talk, it swears" and "even sometimes the president of the United States has to stand naked." It was the first Dylan album to break the Top Ten, reaching number six.

In April 1965, the Byrds' rock adaptation of "Mr. Tambourine Man" hit number six on the *Billboard* chart. It brought Dylan's name to further millions, and began a national folk-rock craze. Bob traveled to England for a ten-show tour, during which he broke up with Joan Baez. Documented by filmmaker D.A. Pennebaker in *Don't Look Back*, the film opened with an early video for "Subterranean Homesick Blues," the first song on *Bringing It All Back Home*, which Dylan delivered in a near-rap over a Chuck Berry beat. Dylan performed well on the tour, though he grew bored playing the same songs over and over. He told others he was on the verge of quitting.

THIN WILD MERCURY MUSIC

The week after he returned to the United States, Dylan wrote what he described as "a long piece of vomit." "It wasn't called anything, just a rhythm thing on paper all about my steady hatred directed at some point that was honest."[12] Affixed with a chorus, the song became "Like a Rolling Stone." A few weeks later, producer Tom Wilson convened a new band for Dylan. Relying on serendipity, Bob barely gave the musicians any instructions. Despite the fact that it was over six minutes in length, Columbia released "Like a Rolling Stone" as a single on July 20. It instantly went to number two on the Hot 100, Dylan's first appearance there. Almost forty years later, the editors of *Rolling Stone*—a magazine named in part for the song—ranked it the greatest song of all time.

On July 25, 1965, Dylan made his third and final appearance at the Newport Folk Festival. Though "Like a Rolling Stone" blasted from radios around the country, Bob had never performed live with an electric guitar. With members of his studio band, including guitarist Mike Bloomfield and guitarist Al Kooper, Dylan's brief set was greeted with both boos and cheers. He left the stage after only three songs. When he returned, he performed "It's All Over Now, Baby Blue," the final song from *Bringing It All Back Home*, alone on acoustic guitar. He enunciated the lyrics clearly, saying goodbye to the folk scene that had made him famous.

With a new producer, Bob Johnston, Dylan recorded eight more songs to complete *Highway 61 Revisited*, named for the road that—like the Mississippi River—connected the singer's North Country home to the Deep South. It was, in Dylan's words, "the main thoroughfare of the country blues." Even in 1965, "it was the same road, full of the same contradictions, the same one-horse times, the same spiritual ancestors."[13] Dylan used his poetry to update the swinging blues he'd heard years before on the radio. Driven by the guitar lines of Mike Bloomfield and the rich organ of Al Kooper, the album was an instant hit that reached number three.

Backed by a rhythm and blues bar band known as the Hawks, Dylan toured across the country. In the first half of the show, Bob played by himself to rapturous silence from the audience. In the second half, joined by the Hawks, he was met nearly every night with jeers. Interviews and press conferences were theaters of the absurd, in which Dylan often made fun of the journalists. In San Francisco, a reporter requested that Bob "define folk music," to which Dylan responded, "a constitutional replay of mass production."[14]

Dylan was a cult hero. Because listeners found so much meaning in his lyrics, they expected Dylan to have the answers to the world's problems. Dylan continued to tour, though his physical state worsened as he grew dependent on amphetamines. "It takes a lot of medicine to keep up this pace," he admitted to journalist Robert Shelton.[15] In the same interview, he all but admitted to using heroin.

Besides touring, Dylan also wrote a "novel." Published six years later as *Tarantula*, it was actually a sprawling jumble of fragments. In spring 1966, he traveled to Nashville with Al Kooper and Hawks' guitarist Robbie Robertson, and recorded a new album—his third in under a year. With country session musicians at his call, Dylan wrote much of the double-LP *Blonde on Blonde* in the studio.

"The closest I ever got to the sound I hear in my mind was on individual bands in the *Blonde on Blonde* album," Dylan said in 1978. "It's that thin, that wild mercury sound. It's metallic and bright gold, with whatever that conjures up."[16] Dylan continued to draw inspiration from folk music, fashioning lyrics from Bascom Lamar Lunsford's "I Wish I Was a Mole in the Ground" into a verse of "(Stuck Inside of Mobile with the) Memphis Blues Again." Dylan's songs grew even longer, including the seven-and-a-half-minute urban drama of "Visions of Johanna," and "Sad-Eyed Lady of the Lowlands," which took up the entirety of the album's fourth side.

The "Sad-Eyed Lady" was Sara Lowndes. A friend of manager Albert Grossman's wife, Bob had met Sara in Woodstock. She was an actress and occasional hostess at the Playboy Club. The two were married on November 22, 1965, in a private ceremony. On January 3, 1966, Sara give birth to their first child, Jesse Dylan. Bob went to great lengths to protect his wife and child from the press, and until February it was not known that he'd even married. Dylan spent the first months of his son's life touring, with no end in sight: Albert Grossman had booked several years worth of engagements.

In April, Dylan traveled to Australia, France, and England with the Hawks. Drummer Levon Helm had quit in frustration, sick of being booed, and was replaced by Mickey Jones. Dylan had grown musically tight with the quintet, especially guitarist Robbie Robertson. Still, the jeers continued. On the second to last night of the tour, May 25, they played the Royal Festival Hall in Manchester, England. The day before, Bob had celebrated his twenty-fifth birthday.

Before the encore, a fan stood up and shouted at Dylan: "Judas!"

"I don't believe you," Dylan sneered back. "You're a *liar*." He turned to the Hawks. "Play fucking *loud*," he told them. The band blasted into "Like a Rolling Stone."[17]

Two months later, back in Woodstock on July 29, the brakes of Dylan's Triumph 650 locked up, throwing Bob over the bike's handlebars. He would perform in public only a half-dozen times over the following eight years.

IN THE BASEMENT AND BEYOND

Rumors circulated that Bob Dylan was seriously crippled, and that he had retired from music. Other gossip suggested that Dylan had a severe drug problem. Dylan did nothing to clarify the situation. He suffered a mild concussion and cracked vertebrae. He canceled all of his tour dates and future plans. He was only twenty-five. With Sara at his side, he recovered. The *Tarantula* manuscript, overdue to his publisher, gathered dust. He relaxed and took up painting. The following summer, when he started to make music again, it wasn't on a stage, or even in a studio, but in a basement.

Big Pink was a house in nearby West Saugerties rented by members of the Hawks. In Woodstock, rejoined by drummer Levon Helm, they became known simply as The Band. In the spring of 1967, Dylan and The Band fell into a routine: smoke a joint and jam in the basement. At first, they just played old folk, blues, and R&B songs, but Dylan quickly began writing again, composing lyrics on a typewriter at the kitchen table. He was just as prolific as ever, recording up to fifteen songs a day, some of them improvised over traditional chord changes. Organist Garth Hudson captured the proceedings on Robbie Robertson's Uher multi-track tape recorder.

Over the course of several months, Bob Dylan and The Band recorded over thirty new originals, as well as literally hundreds of tossed-off covers. When they were done, the songs spanned a phenomenal range, the covers alone comprising a thorough tour of American music. Dylan's new originals ranged from novel jokes such as "See You Later, Allen Ginsberg" to major statements like "I Shall Be Released" and "I'm Not Here (1956)."

Some were recorded as demos for other artists to cover. Manfred Mann scored a number ten single with "The Mighty Quinn" in January 1968. As the acetates circulated, bootleggers got hold of them. A steady stream of illicit Dylan records could now be found at record shops around the country, containing many songs from the basement sessions, as well as private tapes Bob had made for friends over the years.

In October 1967, Dylan returned to Nashville and cut *John Wesley Harding* with a stripped-down band of session musicians. With a sparse, stark backing and a muted gray LP cover, the lyrics were filled with oblique morality tales. A hungry public sent the album to number two. Jimi Hendrix covered "All Along the Watchtower" within the year. Dylan has often announced his preference for the guitarist's rendition.

Though Dylan stayed out of the public eye, his following was undiminished. People started arriving at his Woodstock sanctuary. Where he had once sought to mythologize himself, Dylan now wished to make himself plain. Besides a tribute concert to Woody Guthrie, who died in October 1967, Bob did not perform. He wanted a normal life. In 1969, he recorded a country album, *Nashville Skyline*. The lyrics were as simple as possible, and Dylan sang in a voice all but unrecognizable to longtime listeners. Johnny Cash, a Dylan fan and one of Bob's heroes, guested on a remake of "Girl of the North Country," and wrote the liner notes.

The album charted at number three and the harassment from fanatics did not stop. "I was sick of the way my lyrics had been extrapolated, their meanings subverted into polemics," Dylan wrote.[18] Indeed, the Weathermen, one of the most renowned and violent radical groups of the 1960s, took their name from a lyric in "Subterranean Homesick Blues," from *Bringing It All Back Home*.

The Dylans, with new baby Jakob, moved back to Manhattan, where self-proclaimed "garbologist" A.J. Weberman rifled through the family's trash, looking for "clues" as to Dylan's state of mind. Convinced Dylan was a junkie, Weberman staged protests outside his front door, and demanded that Bob make a statement. When A. J. harassed Sara, it was too much. Bob found Weberman on Elizabeth Street and beat him up.

Though Dylan still enjoyed playing and recording, he put less of himself into his music. In 1970, he issued another double album, boldly titled *Self Portrait*. It was filled with stray covers, live recordings from a disastrous set with The Band at the Isle of Wight festival in the summer of 1970, and other odds and ends. Greil Marcus began his *Rolling Stone* review by asking: "What is this shit?" Simply by virtue of being new Bob Dylan product, *Self Portrait* made it all the way to number four. Though 1970's *New Morning* (*Billboard*, number seven) reunited Bob with organist Al Kooper, and featured a bright accessible sound that expressed Dylan's own personal happiness, the songwriter soon all but stopped recording. He was content to rest.

In 1973, Dylan freed himself from both Albert Grossman and Columbia Records. He signed with David Geffen's fledgling Asylum imprint, and the Dylans relocated to Malibu, California, north of Los Angeles. With his new record contract, Dylan called on The Band, who'd achieved a remarkably successful career on their own. After a preliminary session at Robertson's Malibu studio, Dylan and the group decided they could record and tour. In November 1973, they recorded *Planet Waves*, which became Dylan's first number one album.

On January 3, 1974, at Chicago Stadium, in front of an audience of 18,500, Bob Dylan and The Band began a forty-show cross-country tour. Though Dylan had played big shows before, most of his tours had concentrated on theaters. Now, he was in an arena every night. The shows were rapturously received and Asylum issued a double live album, *Before the Flood* (*Billboard*, number three). Dylan, however, was far from satisfied. "When [Elvis] did 'That's All Right, Mama' in 1955, it was sensitivity and power," he explained later. "In 1969, it was just full-out power. There was nothing other than just force behind that. I've fallen into that trap, too."[19]

After the tour, Dylan returned to Manhattan. Since returning to the road, Bob had recommitted himself to his music. His marriage felt the strain. Temporarily separated from Sara in New York, he once again became a regular on the Village folk scene, sitting in with old friends at old haunts. He also studied with painter Norman Raeben, who—according to Dylan—taught the songwriter a new way to look at the world. Inspired, Dylan began a new batch of songs, many of them character-driven narratives.

The first of the new songs was titled "Tangled Up in Blue." In it, Bob was

trying to tell a story and be a present character in it without it being some kind of fake, sappy attempted tearjerker. I was trying to be somebody in the present tense, while conjuring up a lot of past images. . . . I wanted to defy time, so that the story took place in the present and the past at the same time. When you look at a painting, you can see any part of it, or see all of it together. I wanted that song to be like a painting.[20]

Back on Columbia, Dylan recorded *Blood on the Tracks* at Studio A in the fall of 1974. On many of the tracks, at first, he recorded only with bassist Tony Brown. Bob deemed the album complete, and had vinyl pressings made. Over the holidays in Minnesota, he played a test copy for his brother David, who pronounced it too glum. The two rounded up a band of local folk musicians, who re-recorded a number of the tracks, including "Tangled Up in Blue" and "Simple Twist of Fate."

Released in January 1975, *Blood on the Tracks* reached number one and began Dylan's busiest year in nearly a decade. He spent the spring and summer in New York, where he reestablished old creative relationships and forged new ones. Introduced to theater director Jacques Levy, the two bonded. Several times, they retreated to Levy's house in South Hampton, on the east end of Long Island, to write songs that ventured further into Dylan's new interest in narrative. Dylan tried new genres, from cowboy tales ("Romance in Durango") to gypsy fantasies ("One More Cup of Coffee [Valley Below]") to gangster biographies ("Joey"). They also penned a song dedicated to Rubin "Hurricane" Carter, a boxer serving time in jail for what many believed to be a racially motivated murder frame-up. After rewriting several lyrics to avoid legal liability, Dylan rush-released it as a single. "Hurricane" only reached number thirty-three, though it helped Carter secure a mistrial. That summer, Columbia also released a cleaned up version of *The Basement Tapes* (*Billboard*, number seven).

In a whirlwind, Bob assembled musicians for his next album. They included everybody from legendary rock guitarist Eric Clapton to harmonica player Sugar Blue, who ordinarily played on a Village street corner. They also featured Scarlett Rivera, a mysterious-looking violinist Dylan had spotted on the street and immediately recruited. The sessions maintained a spontaneous feel, and *Desire* reached number one.

The spontaneity carried over into the organization of the tour, the Rolling Thunder Revue. Wary of the giant operation the tour with The Band had been the previous year, Bob sought to keep it looser. Shows were booked in small theaters under assumed names, and not announced until a week previous. Bobby Neuwirth, a painter and folk musician who served as Dylan's right-hand man and road manager in 1965 and 1966, rounded up a troupe. When the buses rolled into Plymouth, Massachusetts, in October 1975, the assembled included Dylan, Neuwirth, Scarlett Rivera, poet Allen Ginsberg (a friend since the 1960s), Ramblin' Jack Elliott, and Joan Baez. Along with another dozen musicians and hangers-on, they criss-crossed New England.

During the tour, Dylan decided to film a movie, improvising scenes with the musicians. When Sara Dylan joined her sometimes-wayward husband on tour, and acted opposite Baez on screen, the results were sometimes uncomfortable. Wearing whiteface make-up, both onstage and on camera, Bob Dylan became a character named Renaldo. Playwright Sam Shepard was brought in to help write dialogue, though he did not compose much. Between the chaos of the film, which Dylan called *Renaldo and Clara*, the shows were an incredible success. They also staged two shows billed as "Night of the Hurricane," at Boston Garden in Massachusetts and Madison Square Garden in New York City, to draw attention to Rubin Carter's case.

The tour resumed in 1976, though the shows did not have the same spark. Dylan's marriage finally ended when Bob and Sara were divorced on June 28, 1977. Over many hours in the studio, Dylan and producer Howard Alk edited *Renaldo and Clara*. When they were done, the film was four hours long. Bob tried to explain the movie in several interviews. "It's about the essence of man being alienated from himself and how, in order to free himself, to be reborn, he has to go outside himself."[21] He did not try to explain the plot. The film bombed, and was never released on video.

Embittered, Dylan recorded a new album, *Street-Legal* (*Billboard*, number eleven), and formed a new band for what many critics dubbed "the alimony tour." Where the Rolling Thunder Revue was loose, the new group was as rehearsed as a Las Vegas stage show. With an eleven-piece band behind him, including three back-up vocalists, Bob recast 1965's acoustic love song "Love Minus Zero/No Limit" as calypso and turned the plaintive blues of "Don't Think Twice, It's Alright" into reggae. Like *Renaldo and Clara*, both the 115-show tour and the album were panned by critics. Dylan had reached another breaking point. On tour in late November, in an Arizona hotel room, Bob Dylan saw Jesus and was reborn.

SLOW TRAIN COMING

"There was a presence in the room that couldn't have been anybody but Jesus," Dylan said two years later. "Jesus put his hand on me. It was a physical thing. I felt it. I felt it all over me. I felt my whole body tremble. The glory of the Lord knocked me down and picked me up."[22] "I truly had a born-again experience. If you want to call it that. It's an over-used term, but it's something that people can relate to."[23]

After the tour, Dylan attended classes four days a week at the Vineyard School of Discipleship in Tarzana, California, near Malibu. The church included several members of the Rolling Thunder Revue, including guitarist T-Bone Burnett and mandolinist David Mansfield. In April, Dylan contacted veteran Atlantic Records producer Jerry Wexler. He told Wexler he wanted a more modern sound. It would be the first Dylan album to feature extensive use of overdubbing, a technique he'd largely eschewed in the ten years since it had become commonplace. Wexler assembled a band that included Dire Straits guitarist Mark Knopfler.

Despite its evangelical overtones, "Gotta Serve Somebody," *Slow Train Coming*'s first single, was as packed with put-downs as "Like a Rolling Stone."

Released in August 1979, the album peaked at number three. "Gotta Serve Somebody" earned Dylan his first Grammy Award, for Best Vocal Performance. In November, a year after his conversion, Dylan began to perform again. He started with a fourteen-night run at San Francisco's Warfield Theater. Setting the pattern for the next year, Bob played only his Christian material. He preached from the stage. "If you want rock and roll, you go down and rock and roll," he told a restless audience in Tempe, Arizona. "You can go and see Kiss and you can rock and roll all the way down to the pit!"[24]

Shortly after the Warfield shows, longtime fan Paul Williams published a book titled *Dylan—What Happened?*, articulating possible reasons for the singer's conversion. Dylan bought over 100 copies to give to his friends to explain his newfound beliefs. "We talk about him, we listen to his music, and all our friends want to talk about him too," Williams theorized. "So much attention directed at one man! Maybe he turned to Christ so he'd have somewhere to refer all this energy that gets thrown at him. If you don't want to be the messiah, and people keep treating you like one anyway, it makes sense to hook up with somebody who's willing to accept that karma."[25]

In 1980, Dylan released *Saved* and returned to the Warfield. At the urging of promoter Bill Graham, Dylan added secular songs back into his set list. *Saved* (*Billboard*, number twenty-two) was the first Bob Dylan album since *Another Side of Bob Dylan* not to make the Top Twenty. In 1981, he released his final religious album, *Shot of Love* (*Billboard*, number thirty-three). It concluded with "Every Grain of Sand," in which Dylan questioned his faith. By the fall of 1981, Bob was back to playing much of his pre-religious material. Keyboardist Al Kooper even joined Dylan for the first time in over a decade. He'd reached another end.

"Too many distractions had turned my musical path into a jungle of vines," Dylan wrote of his experience during the 1980s. "I'd been following established customs and they weren't working . . . Many times I'd come near the stage before a show and would catch myself thinking that I wasn't keeping my word with myself. What that word was, I couldn't exactly remember, but I knew it was back there somewhere."[26]

Dylan released four albums of new songs, though what was left off was often better than what was issued. Like many of his contemporaries, Dylan's 1980s albums were mired in excessive use of synthesizers, which buried his distinct guitar playing deep in the mix. He never publicly announced the end of his Christian period, though his songs were no longer evangelical. In 1989, he participated in a telethon raising funds for Chabad Lubavitch, a Hasidic Jewish group, playing recorder and flute alongside actor Harry Dean Stanton.

In 1987, Dylan toured with the Grateful Dead. Longtime fans, the Dead wanted to play *their* favorite Dylan songs. Bob observed that the Dead were more familiar with his songs than he was. In long rehearsal sessions they played a broad array of material, but the actual concerts stuck mostly to the classics and were less than satisfactory. Still, during the rehearsals, Dylan had a musical revelation.

During a break, Dylan entered a nearby jazz club, where he suddenly remembered a style of singing taught to him by blues guitarist Lonnie Johnson in the 1960s. It was a mathematical technique. "It's a highly controlled system of playing and relates to the notes of a scale, how they combine numerically, how they form melodies out of triplets and are axiomatic to the rhythm and the chord changes,"[27] Dylan described later. It allowed Dylan to improvise his vocals in the way a jazz musician might solo over a set of chord changes. Though the song might be unrecognizable to the audience, Bob was enthralled.

Inspired by the Grateful Dead, Dylan encouraged his manager to book him on extensive tours that would return him to the same towns year after year. He wanted to build a new following, separate from those who knew him only for his 1960s persona. Dylan established a semi-permanent road band. Though the members rotated, they did so over a long period of time. As of 2007, bassist Tony Garnier had served with Dylan for nineteen years, the longest musical partnership of Dylan's career. Other long-standing accompanists included *Saturday Night Live* bandleader G.E. Smith, roots-rock guitarists Larry Campbell and Charlie Sexton, as well as former Jerry Garcia Band drummer David Kemper. The Never-Ending Tour—as it was semi-officially known—began June 7, 1988, at the Greek Theater in Berkeley, California.

Dylan recorded a new album with producer Daniel Lanois in New Orleans. Bolstered by Lanois's textured arrangements, and accompanied by local musicians, 1989's *Oh Mercy* (*Billboard*, number thirty) was Bob's strongest effort in years. On stage, Dylan dipped into a seemingly endless well of songs by other artists. He played folk songs like "House of the Rising Sun" and "Pretty Peggy-O" that he'd not performed since his Greenwich Village days. He also covered material by contemporaries like the Grateful Dead, the Beatles, Van Morrison, Bruce Springsteen, and others. He performed country by Johnny Cash and Hank Williams, as well as early rock and roll by Chuck Berry and Buddy Holly.

In the early 1990s, the now fifty-year-old Dylan released two solo acoustic albums of folk songs. The first time he'd recorded alone since 1964, 1992's *Good As I Been to You* (*Billboard*, number fifty-one) and 1993's *World Gone Wrong* (*Billboard*, number seventy) featured songs from the age "before the Children of the Sun—before the celestial grunge, before the insane world of entertainment exploded in our faces," Dylan wrote in his cryptic liner notes to the latter.

Snowed in at his Minnesota farm in 1996, Dylan wrote a new batch of songs, soon recorded with Daniel Lanois, this time in Miami. The album *Time Out of Mind,* concluded with "Highlands," a sixteen-minute half-spoken blues narrative. On May 29, however, before the album could be released, Bob was admitted to the hospital with histoplasmosis, a heart infection. He was back on the road by August 3.

Time Out of Mind was released in September 1997 to critical acclaim and impressive sales. Charting at number ten, it was Dylan's first Top Ten entry in almost twenty years and won three Grammy Awards including Album of the Year. Dylan's touring continued unabated. He had evolved into an old-time country bandleader, wearing a suit, tie, and cowboy hat on stage. On September 11, 2001, he released "*Love and Theft,*" another album of Americana-informed rock. Its title referenced *Love and Theft: Blackface Minstrelsy and the American Working Class*, a 1995 book by historian Eric Lott about minstrelsy, and some lyrics were adapted from Japanese author Dr. Junichi Saga's *Confessions of a Yakuza*.

Bob Dylan also became involved in a number of extra-musical projects. In 2003, he starred in *Masked & Anonymous,* a movie he co-wrote with director Larry Charles under the pseudonyms Sergei Petrov and Rene Fontaine. Dylan played Jack Fate, a washed-up caricature of himself in a dystopian United States, sprung from jail to play a dubious benefit concert. With co-stars John Goodman, Jeff Bridges, Luke Wilson, and Jessica Lange, the film was a modest cult success. Two years later, Dylan published *Chronicles, Volume One,* the first part of a proposed three-volume autobiography. Non-linear in structure and divulging little with regard to divorce, marriage, and the lives (or even the names) of his children, *Chronicles* reads like a road trip of Dylan's psyche. Vivid recollections of the sights, sounds, and scene-makers of 1960s New York mark the path of his artistic development; poets and songwriters, both past and present, serve as guides to the singer's creative process, with evocative side trips to New Orleans, Woodstock, and Hibbing. Whether or not Dylan told the whole truth was, as always, a matter for debate but *Chronicles* was the most successful non-musical endeavor of his career. The book reached number two on the *New York Times* best-seller list and was nominated for a National Book Award.

Bob also sat for extensive interviews with manager Jeff Rosen for Martin Scorsese's *No Direction Home,* a 2005 documentary for PBS's *American Masters* series. In 2006, he launched a weekly radio show on XM Satellite Radio, *Theme Time Radio Hour*. He devoted each episode to playing songs about a specific subject, such as baseball, spring cleaning, friends and neighbors, and others.

During shows on the Never-Ending Tour, an announcer introduced Dylan nightly with a summary of his career:

> "Ladies and gentleman, please welcome the poet laureate of rock 'n' roll. The voice of promise of the sixties counterculture. The guy who forced folk into bed with rock, who donned makeup in the seventies and disappeared into a haze of substance abuse, who emerged to find Jesus, was written off as a has-been, and who suddenly shifted gears, releasing some of the strongest music of his career beginning in the late nineties. Ladies and gentlemen, Columbia Recording artist Bob Dylan!"

In 2006, Bob Dylan released *Modern Times*, his thirty-second studio album, and his first number one album since 1976's *Desire*. The Never Ending Tour rolled on down the highway.

Inducting Bob Dylan into the Rock and Roll Hall of Fame in 1988, Bruce Springsteen recalled the initial impact of "Like a Rolling Stone":

"The first time I heard Bob Dylan, I was in the car with my mother listening to WMCA, and on came that snare shot that sounded like somebody'd kicked open the door to your mind . . . "

"Bob freed your mind the way Elvis freed your body. He showed us that just because music was innately physical did not mean that it was anti-intellectual. He had the vision and the talent to make a pop record that contained the whole world."[28]

TIMELINE

September 1959
Robert Zimmerman enrolls in the University of Minnesota and begins to call himself Bob Dylan.

January 24, 1961
Bob Dylan arrives in New York City.

March 1962
Columbia Records releases *Bob Dylan*.

July 1963
Peter, Paul, and Mary's version of "Blowin' in the Wind" charts at number two Pop.

July 20, 1965
Bob Dylan's "Like a Rolling Stone" charts at number two.

July 25, 1965
Bob Dylan "goes electric" at the Newport Folk Festival in Newport, Rhode Island.

July 29, 1966
Dylan is hurt in a motorcycle accident in Woodstock, New York, and temporarily retires from live performance.

May 17, 1967
Don't Look Back, D.A. Pennebaker's documentary of Dylan's 1965 tour of England, premieres in San Francisco.

April 1967
With The Band, Bob Dylan begins to record music in the basement of a house in Saugerties, New York.

November 1971
Macmillan publishes *Tarantula*, Dylan's experimental novel, written in 1965 and 1966.

January 3, 1974
With The Band, Dylan begins his first concert tour in eight years.

December 8, 1975
As part of the Rolling Thunder Revue, Bob Dylan stages "Night of the Hurricane" at New York's Madison Square Garden, a benefit for jailed boxer Rubin "Hurricane" Carter.

January 25, 1978
Renaldo and Clara, Bob Dylan's directorial debut, is released theatrically.

November 1978
Bob Dylan experiences a religious revelation in Arizona and becomes a born-again Christian.

July 1987
Dylan tours with the Grateful Dead as his backing band.

June 1988
Bob Dylan begins the Never-Ending Tour.

May 29, 1997
Dylan is admitted to a hospital with a heart infection.

February 25, 1998
Bob Dylan wins three Grammy Awards for *Time Out of Mind*.

October 5, 2004
Simon & Schuster publishes *Chronicles, Volume One*, the first part of a proposed three-book autobiography.

SELECTED DISCOGRAPHY

The Freewheelin' Bob Dylan, 1962

The Times They Are A-Changin', 1963

Another Side of Bob Dylan, 1964

Bringing It All Back Home, 1965

Highway 61 Revisited, 1965

Blonde on Blonde, 1966

John Wesley Harding, 1968

Blood on the Tracks, 1975

The Bootleg Series, volumes 1–3: Rare & Unreleased, 1961–1991, 1991

World Gone Wrong, 1994

Time Out of Mind, 1997

The Bootleg Series, volume 4: Live 1966, 1998

The Bootleg Series, volume 5: Live 1975, 2002

The Bootleg Series, volume 6: Live 1964, 2003

NOTES

1. Bob Dylan, *Chronicles, Volume One* (New York: Simon & Schuster, 2004), pp. 34–35.

2. Jonathan Cott, ed., *Bob Dylan: The Essential Interviews* (New York: Wenner Books, 2006), pp. 4–5.

3. Robert Santelli, *The Bob Dylan Scrapbook* (New York: Simon & Schuster, 2005).

4. Dylan, *Chronicles*, p. 79.

5. Ibid., p. 78.

6. Ibid., pp. 244–45.

7. Ibid., p. 247.

8. Ibid., pp. 35–36.

9. Ibid., pp. 275–76.

10. Clinton Heylin, *Bob Dylan: Behind the Shades Revisited* (New York: HarperCollins, 2001), p. 137.

11. Santelli.

12. Paul Williams *Performing Artist, 1960–1973: The Early Years* (London: Omnibus Press, 1994), p. 148, 151.

13. Dylan, *Chronicles*, p. 241.

14. Cott, p. 65.

15. Robert Shelton, *No Direction Home: The Life and Music of Bob Dylan* (New York: Ballantine Books, 1986), p. 395.

16. Cott, p. 208.

17. Bob Dylan, *Live 1966* (Columbia Records, 1988).

18. Dylan, *Chronicles*, p. 120.

19. Heylin, p. 363.

20. Ibid., p. 370.

21. Cott, p. 217.

22. Heylin, p. 491.

23. Cott, p. 281.

24. Heylin, p. 517.

25. Paul Williams, *Watching the River Flow: Observations on His Art-in-Progress, 1966–1995* (London: Omnibus Press, 1996), p. 131.

26. Dylan, *Chronicles*, pp. 146–47.

27. Ibid., p. 157.

28. Elizabeth Thomson and David Gutman (editors), *The Dylan Companion* (New York: Delta, 1990), pp. 286–287.

FURTHER READING

Cott, Jonathan, ed. *Bob Dylan: The Essential Interviews.* New York: Wenner Books, 2006.

Dylan, Bob. *Chronicles, Volume One.* New York: Simon & Schuster, 2004.

Heylin, Clinton. *Bob Dylan: Behind the Shades Revisited.* New York: HarperCollins, 2001.

Marcus, Greil. *Invisible Republic: Bob Dylan's Basement Tapes*. New York: Henry Holt, 1997.

Marcus, Greil. *Like a Rolling Stone: Bob Dylan at the Crossroads*. New York: Public Affairs, 2005.

Santelli, Robert. *The Bob Dylan Scrapbook*. New York: Simon & Schuster, 2005.

Shelton, Robert. *No Direction Home: The Life and Music of Bob Dylan*. New York: Ballantine Books, 1986.

Williams, Paul. *Performing Artist, 1960–1973: The Early Years*. London: Omnibus Press, 1994.

Williams, Paul. *Watching the River Flow: Observations on His Art-in-Progress, 1966–1995*. London: Omnibus Press, 1996.

© AP/Wide World Photos.

The Rolling Stones

Scott Schinder

ALL BOW TO THEIR SATANIC MAJESTIES

The Rolling Stones may have demonstrated a certain lack of modesty when they anointed themselves the World's Greatest Rock and Roll Band in the late 1960s. But the title was no idle boast. In their early days as the British Invasion's foremost exponents of bad attitude, the scruffy quintet embodied all that was dangerous and transgressive about rock and roll. In the decades that followed, they managed to maintain their defiant aura, even after they became a stadium-filling, profit-spinning institution.

Adults who were initially resistant to the Beatles couldn't help but surrender to the Fab Four's cheeky charms. But there was never anything cuddly about the Rolling Stones. While the relatively clean-cut Beatles and their Merseybeat contemporaries were souping up the country/rockabilly-derived sounds of Buddy Holly, the Everly Brothers, and Carl Perkins, the Stones took a darker approach, launching their career with unruly variations on black American blues and R&B. Even after they began writing their own songs and downplaying the cover material that had comprised their early repertoire, the band maintained its rebellious stance, while indulging an abiding fascination with darkness and sleaze, along with an air of world-weary decadence that suited their status as jet-setting libertine superstars.

Like the Animals, the Yardbirds, Them, and the Pretty Things, the Rolling Stones embodied the rougher, rootsier end of the British Invasion. But the Stones' commercial appeal and musical influence quickly put them in a class of their own. Mick Jagger is probably rock's most imitated frontman, embodying a singular mix of macho swagger and campy flamboyance that's been emulated by multiple generations of rock singers. Beyond his stage presence, Jagger quickly emerged as an original, inventive songwriter as well as a canny packager of his band's mystique.

Jagger's long-standing bandmate, writing partner, and onstage alter ego Keith Richards is an equally seminal figure. In addition to being one of rock's most influential rhythm guitarists, Richards is an ageless, seemingly indestructible icon whose unflappable rock and roll cool has remained intact through all manner of personal, chemical, and legal problems. Richards is also unusual among rock guitar heroes in that he's always been more concerned with riffs and grooves than flashy solos, while maintaining a deep connection to his blues roots.

Richards and fellow founding member Brian Jones were an extraordinarily in-sync guitar duo, setting a remarkable standard for interlocking ax interplay that was extended by Jones's successors Mick Taylor and Ron Wood. The band's stellar guitarists were complemented by the rock-solid, subtly inventive rhythm section of bassist Bill Wyman and jazz-loving drummer Charlie Watts, who gave the music a propulsive punch as well as a subtle sense of swing.

The Rolling Stones were initially the product of a groundswell of interest in vintage American blues among a generation of young British men in the early 1960s. That movement would spawn many of the musicians who would become leading lights in the U.K. rock scene in the coming decade. The Stones rose from a small but thriving London-based electric blues revival, and began their career playing music that merged the raw sound of Chess Records' urban blues artists with the propulsive rock and roll style of Chuck Berry's classic

Chess sides. But the Stones' derivative early efforts quickly gave way to a distinctive musical persona.

By the late 1960s, the Rolling Stones were the Beatles' only serious competitor, in terms of popularity, prestige, and musical influence. By then, the Stones had already built a body of work as original and accomplished as anything to emerge from the decade's fertile rock scene, integrating country blues, baroque folk, and psychedelia into their sound. After Brian Jones's death in 1969, the band downplayed its more experimental elements to re-embrace rock and roll basics. They largely stuck to that stylistic template, with brief detours into reggae and disco, for the next four decades. If the music they made didn't always live up to the act's legendary status, it rarely detracted from their legendary aura.

LITTLE RED ROOSTERS

Precocious blues and jazz enthusiast Brian Jones was the Rolling Stones' founder and, in its early days, main motivating force. But the team of Mick Jagger and Keith Richards (aka the Glimmer Twins) quickly emerged as the Rolling Stones' musical and conceptual focal point. The pair first met as childhood schoolmates, and became reacquainted again in 1960. Depending upon which source one believes, they either reconnected while both were waiting on a train platform and Richards noticed that Jagger was carrying some American blues LPs, or they were reintroduced by mutual friend Dick Taylor. Taylor, also a budding musician and blues convert, was then attending Sidcup Art School with Richards. At the time, Jagger was a student at the London School of Economics, and playing the blues with Taylor in a combo known as Little Boy Blue and the Blue Boys. Richards joined soon after.

By the time he met Jagger and Richards, Brian Jones had already led an eventful life. He'd quit school and run away to Scandinavia when he was sixteen, by which time he'd already mastered several instruments and fathered two illegitimate children. After returning, he played in some local bands before moving to London, where he became a member of Blues Incorporated, an outfit led by blues revival godfather Alexis Korner.

Deciding to form his own group, Jones advertised for musicians; among those he recruited was pianist Ian Stewart. Jones also performed solo, playing Elmore James–style blues under the pseudonym Elmo Jones. While playing at the Ealing Blues Club, he shared a bill with Blues Incorporated, which by now included Charlie Watts on drums as well as auxiliary members Jagger and Richards.

The Rolling Stones—with a lineup consisting of Jagger, Richards, Jones, Ian Stewart, Dick Taylor on bass, and drummer Mick Avory—made their public debut at London's Marquee Club on July 12, 1962. Taylor left a few weeks later to attend the Royal College of Art; he would soon form the Pretty Things, in which he would play lead guitar for much of the next four and a half decades. Avory exited as well; he would soon join the Kinks, with whom he would spend more than thirty years.

Taylor's eventual replacement, joining in December 1962, was Bill Wyman. At twenty-five, Wyman was a few years older than the rest of the Stones, but the fact that he owned his own amplifier helped him to clinch the gig. The following month, the band convinced Charlie Watts, who had quit Blues Incorporated and taken a job at an advertising agency, to join on drums.

In February 1963, the Rolling Stones began a now-legendary eight-month residency at London's Crawdaddy Club, located at the Station Hotel, across from the Richmond railway station. The band's high-energy performances became so popular that the club was forced to move to a larger venue, the Richmond Athletic Ground. By April, the Stones were playing two nights a week at the Crawdaddy as well as doing a weekly gig at Eel Pie Island, two miles away in Twickenham.

The Yardbirds: Beyond the Blues

When the popularity of the Rolling Stones exceeded the cramped confines of the Crawdaddy Club, Crawdaddy impresario Giorgio Gomelsky found another blues-based London quintet, the Yardbirds, to take their place. Keith Relf led the group on vocals and harmonica, backed by Chris Dreja (rhythm guitar), Paul Samwell-Smith (bass), and Jim McCarty (drums). But it was their fast, fiery lead guitarist Eric Clapton who—although not yet the awe-inspiring virtuoso he would soon become—won the immediate attention of fans and critics.

Five Live Yardbirds, their 1964 U.K. debut album, captured the spontaneous excitement of a typical live set, this one at the fabled Marquee Club in London. It went unreleased in the United States, but the group made an immediate impact in 1965 with its first American LP, *For Your Love*, and the title hit single. This minor-key song by an outside composer (Graham Gouldman), with its prominent harpsichord and bongos, took the group in a pop direction that blues purist Clapton declined to follow. He left the Yardbirds in March 1965, a few months before "For Your Love" reached number six on the U.S. Hot 100—the first of the band's five consecutive U.S. Top Twenty singles.

Clapton's replacement was Jeff Beck, an equally gifted blues guitarist with a penchant for sonic experimentation. Cranking the volume and pushing the tempos, Beck galvanized listeners with fuzztone, feedback, and slide (bottleneck) guitar. In the studio, the Yardbirds incorporated Indian and Arabic strains, Gregorian chants, and European folk music on such influential hit singles as "Heart Full of Soul" (another Graham Gouldman song), "Shapes of Things," and "Over Under Sideways Down."

By mid-1966, the touring grind had begun to take a psychological toll on Jeff Beck, and Paul Samwell-Smith had left the band to pursue record production. Chris Dreja switched to bass and an experienced session musician, Jimmy Page, was brought in to play second lead guitar with Beck. This potentially devastating lineup lasted less than six months, long enough to make a memorable appearance in the film *Blow Up* (performing "Stroll On" aka "The Train Kept A-Rollin'") and release one brilliant single, the apocalyptic "Happenings Ten Years Time Ago," which stalled at number thirty in the United States and number forty-three in the United Kingdom.

By the end of the year, Jeff Beck was gone for good and the Yardbirds were reduced to a quartet. But Jimmy Page's prodigious technique and on-stage flair were nearly enough to carry the whole band. Page sometimes played electric guitar with a violin bow, and his instrumental showcase "White Summer" popularized the acoustic folk-raga style of Bert Jansch and Davy Graham. A live set album in March 1968 at New York's Anderson Theater would have positioned the Yardbirds squarely on the U.S. rock ballroom circuit, but the band rejected the performances as below par. (They were later issued as the quasi-bootleg *Live Yardbirds! Featuring Jimmy Page.*) Meanwhile, managers and producers repeatedly directed the Yardbirds toward the pop charts, resulting in such feeble efforts as "Ten Little Indians."

The Yardbirds played their last gig in Luton, England in July 1968. Contractually committed to a Scandinavian tour, Jimmy Page recruited Robert Plant (vocals), John Paul Jones (bass), and John Bonham (drums). Initially billed as the New Yardbirds, the group would soon adopt a new name: Led Zeppelin.

Andy Schwartz

A key component in the Stones' early sound was the bracing guitar interaction of Richards and Jones, which blurred the traditional distinctions between the guitarists' lead and rhythm parts. It was Keith Richards who was responsible for introducing Chuck Berry and Bo Diddley songs to their initial repertoire of blues and R&B material, facilitating the band's eventual embrace of rock and roll.

After briefly being handled by Crawdaddy founder Giorgio Gomelsky, the Rolling Stones gained a new manager in Andrew Loog Oldham, a flamboyant hustler who'd worked as a press agent for Beatles manager Brian Epstein, among others. The promotion-savvy Oldham consciously played up the Stones' bad-boy mystique, packaging the quintet as the unsavory, rebellious answer to the Beatles, who by then were drastically altering the face of the British pop scene.

One of Oldham's first moves in establishing the Stones' image was forcing the talented but unglamorous Ian Stewart out of the band. The unpretentious Stewart would nonetheless remain a beloved fixture of the group's organization until his death in 1985, serving as road manager as well as sideman in the studio and on stage.

After George Harrison recommended the Stones to Decca Records' A&R head Dick Rowe (who had infamously turned down the Beatles not long before), Oldham secured a recording deal for the band with Decca Records. June 1963 saw the release of the Rolling Stones' debut single, a cover of Chuck Berry's "Come On," backed by the Willie Dixon–penned "I Want to Be Loved." The disc became a minor hit, reaching number twenty-one on the U.K. charts, and the group promoted it by performing on a series of British package tours.

In November, the Stones released a second single, a cover of the Lennon/McCartney composition "I Wanna Be Your Man. The song was perhaps a curious choice, given the band's supposed rivalry with the Beatles, but it reached number twelve on the British pop chart. Its B-side was the instrumental "Stoned," written by Jagger and Richards but credited to the fictitious "Nanker/Phelge." The second half of the pseudonym referred to James Phelge, a friend with whom Jagger, Richards, and Jones shared a squalid Chelsea flat for most of 1963.

In February 1964, the Rolling Stones achieved a commercial breakthrough with their third single, a Bo Diddley–inflected reading of Buddy Holly's "Not Fade Away." The song reached number three in Britain. Its U.K. success was enough to win the band its first release in the United States, where "Not Fade Away" squeaked into the Top Fifty.

Although it would take a while longer for the Stones to make a substantial impression in America, they quickly became a sensation in Britain. The group's surly, dangerous vibe was enhanced by a series of minor scandals, like the band members being busted in March for public urination (they were fined £5 each).

April 1964 saw the release of the band's self-titled U.K. debut album, released in the United States in slightly altered form as *England's Newest Hitmakers*. The LP's American edition combined three Jagger/Richards compositions with covers of tunes by Chuck Berry, Muddy Waters, Slim Harpo, Rufus Thomas, and Marvin Gaye.

In June 1964, the Rolling Stones undertook their first U.S. tour. While the eight-city visit included a pair of sold-out shows at New York's Carnegie Hall in front of screaming, enraptured crowds, the band encountered less enthusiastic reactions in other cities. Haphazard promotion, combined with the fact that the band had yet to score a major U.S. hit, resulted in lukewarm crowds and cancellations.

The tour allowed the band members to visit several landmarks of the American music that had influenced them, including Chicago's legendary Chess Records—home of such seminal performers as Chuck Berry, Bo Diddley, Muddy Waters, and Howlin' Wolf, all of whose material the Stones had covered. At Chess's studio, they recorded the British EP *Five by Five*, which spawned another British number one with an appropriately raw reading of Howlin' Wolf's "Little Red Rooster."

The tour preceded the American release of the band's reading of Bobby Womack's "It's All Over Now," which was the Stones' first number one single in the United Kingdom and reached number twenty-six in the United States.

The Stones had already achieved substantial commercial success by covering outside material, playing to crowds of screaming teenagers in the United Kingdom and Europe. But Andrew Oldham recognized the value of songwriting royalties and publishing copyrights, and pushed Jagger and Richards to pursue their budding writing partnership. At one point, he reportedly locked them in a room until they came up with a usable song.

In August 1964, "Tell Me (You're Coming Back)" became the first Jagger/ Richards composition to see release as an A-side. It was a Top Thirty hit in the United States, but it took another cover—a rugged reading of New Orleans soul queen Irma Thomas's "Time Is on My Side"—to get the Stones into the American Top Ten. It was followed by a pair of memorable Jagger/Richards-penned hits, the Top Twenty "Heart of Stone" and the Top Ten "The Last Time."

It was "(I Can't Get No) Satisfaction," released as a U.S. single in May 1965, that established the Rolling Stones as both commercial superstars and an important musical force. The song—driven by Richards's commanding fuzz-guitar riff and Jagger's wry social commentary—offered bracing evidence that Jagger and Richards had developed into distinctive songwriters.

"Satisfaction" (which appeared on the U.S. version of the album *Out of Our Heads*) spent four weeks at number one in the United States. The song began a remarkable two-year string of Top Ten Stones singles that established the band as one of the British Invasion's most popular acts, while maintaining a steady creative growth. The streak encompassed the swaggering rockers "Get Off of My Cloud" and "Have You Seen Your Mother, Baby, Standing in the Shadow?," the bittersweet ballads "As Tears Go By" and "Ruby Tuesday," the menacing, exotic "Paint It, Black," and the social-commentary "19th Nervous Breakdown" and "Mother's Little Helper."

One Stones single that didn't fare as well on the U.S. charts during this period was the early 1967 release "Let's Spend the Night Together," whose title was judged to be a bit too risqué for U.S. sensibilities by radio programmers—as well as Ed Sullivan, who had Jagger sing the title phrase as "Let's spend some time together" when the band appeared on Sullivan's influential Sunday night variety TV show.

Aftermath, 1966, was the first Rolling Stones LP comprising entirely original compositions. The material showcased the Jagger/Richards writing team's increasing sophistication, even if the misogynistic lyrical sentiments of "Under My Thumb" and "Stupid Girl" demonstrated that they hadn't exactly grown up. The album also reflected Brian Jones's stylistic sense of adventure: it was Jones who played sitar on the psychedelic "Paint It, Black," marimba on the jazzy "Under My Thumb," and dulcimer on the medieval-flavored ballad "Lady Jane." Jones's influence was also prominent on the droning eleven-minute blues jam "Going Home," whose length was a daring move at the time.

The move toward more exotic sounds continued with 1967's *Between the Buttons*, which matched the Stones' budding penchant for experimentation with an ironic pop sensibility. While some fans complained that the stylistic departures diluted the band's original appeal, such tunes as "My Obsession," "Connection," and "Yesterday's Papers" found the Stones rocking with wit and style.

While their music may have been moving in a more cerebral direction, the Stones' decadent image remained as strong as ever, making the band members inviting targets for British law enforcement officials. In February 1967, a month after the release of *Between the Buttons*, Jagger and Richards were busted when police raided a party at Redlands, Richards's estate in Sussex, and found four amphetamine pills in Jagger's possession. The pair was convicted of the charge in June, when Jagger and Richards, respectively, were sentenced to three months and a year in prison. But public outcry over the blatantly trumped-up charges and the excessive sentences—including a now-famous *London Times* editorial headlined "Who Breaks a Butterfly Upon a Wheel?"—prompted their sentences to be reversed.

Meanwhile, Brian Jones was arrested in May for possession of cannabis, cocaine, and methamphetamine. He escaped with a fine, probation, and an admonition to seek professional help.

Their legal travails informed the next Rolling Stones single, "We Love You." In addition to being the band's strongest stab at psychedelia yet, the song was both a thank-you to fans for their loyalty through their legal difficulties, and a pointed jab at the Metropolitan Police and the British tabloid press, which had relentlessly sensationalized their coverage of the drug busts. "We Love You" also featured guest vocals by John Lennon and Paul McCartney and opened with the sound of a cell door banging shut. It was accompanied by a promotional film that paralleled the Stones' trials and the legal persecution of Oscar Wilde seventy years earlier, with Jagger portraying Wilde. Despite (or because of) its topical nature, "We Love You" proved a bit too heady for U.S. radio; its gentler flip side "Dandelion" became a hit in the United States.

"Dandelion" and "We Love You" set the stage for the Rolling Stones' full-on embrace of psychedelia on their next LP *Their Satanic Majesties Request*, released in December 1967. Ostensibly the Stones' darker answer to the Beatles' *Sgt. Pepper's Lonely Hearts Club Band*, the album (complete with 3-D cover depicting the Stones dressed as wizards amidst a mystical landscape) was vilified by many fans and savaged by many critics. But it's far better than its reputation suggests, with tunes such as "She's a Rainbow," "Citadel," and "2000 Light Years from Home" carrying an earthy, menacing undercurrent that balanced their spacier pretensions. The songs' exotic arrangements gave Jones a chance to try out a variety of offbeat instruments, and Jones's interest in Moroccan music is manifested in the album's prominent Eastern rhythms.

The legal threats hanging over the band members' heads were such a distraction during the making of *Their Satanic Majesties Request* that Bill Wyman finally managed to get one of his own compositions, the playfully woozy

"In Another Land," onto the album. The song, on which Wyman sang lead, even saw release as a single and slipped into the lower reaches of the U.S. Top 100.

The Stones' psychedelic flirtation was a short one. The band soon returned to basics with the anthemic May 1968 single "Jumpin' Jack Flash," whose intimations of rebellion were well suited to the era's turbulent political mood. It was followed in August by "Street Fighting Man," whose rabble-rousing stance expanded its predecessor's air of provocation.

Early in 1968, the band had parted ways with Andrew Oldham and turned their business affairs over to tenacious American music-industry hustler Allen Klein. Klein had earned a fearsome reputation within the American music industry for his ability to extract payment from record companies. He also controlled the U.S. rights to albums by such artists as Sam Cooke, Herman's Hermits, and the Animals, and would eventually gain control of the Rolling Stones' London LPs.

"Street Fighting Man," released in August 1968, previewed the Stones' next LP *Beggar's Banquet*, which wouldn't be released until December. The delay was largely due to disputes over the album's original cover art, which pictured a graffiti-covered men's room wall. When finally released, it bore a simple white cover. *Beggar's Banquet* was quickly recognized as a creative rebirth for the band, mixing raucous rock ("Sympathy for the Devil") with rootsy departures into Delta blues ("No Expectations") and British folk ("Factory Girl"). It also spotlighted Richards's distinctive use of open guitar tunings, which would soon emerge as one of the band's most recognizable musical elements.

DARK CIRCUS

Although it reestablished the Rolling Stones as a vital creative force, *Beggar's Banquet* also marked the end of Brian Jones's participation in the group that he originally founded and led. While the band had never recorded any of his compositions, Jones's iconoclastic spirit and charismatic presence had been key elements in the Stones' unruly public persona, and his musical knowledge and multi-instrumental abilities had been crucial to their artistic progress. But Jagger and Richards's dominance of the band restricted Jones to an increasingly marginal role.

Jones had put some of his creative urges to use on a pair of extracurricular projects: his musical score for the 1967 German film *A Degree of Murder*, which starred his then-girlfriend Anita Pallenberg, and his 1968 recordings of traditional Moroccan musicians, which would be released in 1971 as *Brian Jones Presents the Pipes of Pan at Joujouka*. He also contributed a jazzy saxophone solo to the Beatles' "You Know My Name (Look Up the Number)," recorded in 1967 but not released until 1970, when it became the B-side of their "Let It Be" single.

As Jones grew alienated from his bandmates, he retreated into drug use and became increasingly unreliable. His participation in *Beggar's Banquet* had been minimal, and in June 1969, Jagger, Richards, and Watts paid a late-night visit to inform Jones that he was no longer a member of the band he'd founded.

Jones's final public appearance with the band was in *The Rolling Stones Rock and Roll Circus*, a star-studded variety extravaganza shot in December 1968 but never broadcast. The show was conceived by Jagger and director Michael Lindsay-Hogg (who had previously shot conceptual promo clips for two Stones songs), and used a circus setting as a backdrop for performances by the Stones, John Lennon and Yoko Ono, the Who, Eric Clapton, Marianne Faithfull, Taj Mahal, and Jethro Tull. But Jagger was dissatisfied with the results—according to some accounts, he felt that that the Who's powerful performance had stolen the Stones' thunder—and the show was shelved. It would finally be released on CD and DVD in 1996.

Following his dismissal, Jones retreated to his rural home—Cotchford Farm, formerly owned by *Winnie the Pooh* author A.A. Milne—and planned to launch a new, blues-based band. But on July 3, less than a month after his dismissal and two days before the Stones were scheduled to play a free outdoor concert in London's Hyde Park, Jones was found dead in his swimming pool. While his demise was officially ruled "death by misadventure," its cause has been the subject of various rumors and theories, many of them involving foul play.

The Stones, meanwhile, went ahead with their Hyde Park concert as a tribute to Jones. Performing in front of a crowd of 200,000, Jagger read from Shelley's *Adonais* and released hundreds of butterflies (most of which were dead by the time he turned them loose) in Jones's memory. The band's under-rehearsed set—later broadcast on British TV as *Stones in the Park*—marked the debut of Jones's replacement, Mick Taylor.

Fleetwood Mac: Green's Blues

Few fans of the group responsible for such multi-platinum pop-rock albums as *Rumours* (1977) will recall that Fleetwood Mac was founded with a very different musical mission: to play classic Chicago blues regardless of the commercial consequences. In July 1967, inspired by B.B. King, Otis Rush, and Elmore James, ex-Bluesbreakers guitarist/vocalist Peter Green joined forces with Jeremy Spencer (slide guitar, vocals), John McVie (bass), and Mick Fleetwood (drums) to form Fleetwood Mac. In March 1968, the band's debut album reached the British Top Five—the commercial apex of the British blues boom. The band's second U.S. album *English Rose* included "Black Magic Woman," a haunting minor-key blues written by Peter Green that became a massive hit for Santana in 1970.

Fleetwood Mac's restless creativity inevitably led them beyond the twelve-bar blues form into progressive rock, especially after the addition of Danny

Kirwan on guitar and vocals. In December 1968, Peter Green's moody instrumental "Albatross" shot to the top of the U.K. singles chart and eventually sold over one million copies. "Man of the World," his pained meditation on the emptiness of stardom, made it to number two. Meanwhile, on tour in the United States, Fleetwood Mac were hailed not as Top Forty hit makers but as an FM rock radio favorite whose powerful three-guitar jams rivaled in exploratory intensity those of the Grateful Dead and the Allman Brothers Band.

Then Play On (1969) captured Fleetwood Mac at its creative peak. But two further Top Ten U.K. hits, the two-part "Oh Well" and "The Green Manalishi (With the Two-Pronged Crown)," offered lyrical evidence of Green's increasing spiritual turmoil. Disenchanted with the music business, disoriented by his experiments with LSD, he left Fleetwood Mac in May 1970. The following year, the guitarist briefly filled in for Jeremy Spencer when the latter suddenly defected to a religious cult, the Children of God, in the midst of an American tour. Peter Green did not appear with the group again until 1998, when he played "Black Magic Woman" on stage in New York during the ceremony marking Fleetwood Mac's induction into the Rock and Roll Hall of Fame.

A. S.

Taylor was a prodigiously talented player who'd made a name for himself as teenage guitar wunderkind in British kingpin John Mayall's Bluesbreakers. The Bluesbreakers' guitar slot had previously been occupied by two U.K. guitar legends—Eric Clapton and Fleetwood Mac founder Peter Green—but Taylor nonetheless established himself as one of Britain's finest young axmen. Taylor's addition to the lineup introduced a somewhat more conventional separation of lead and rhythm guitar parts.

John Mayall: Godfather of British Blues

The opening of Alexis Korner's London Blues & Barrelhouse Club in 1954 and Muddy Waters's first U.K. tour in 1958 had been seminal events for a small but dedicated number of English musicians committed to playing and popularizing the blues. Among those who followed the trail blazed by Alexis Korner and his band, Blues Incorporated, was John Mayall. Born in 1933 near Manchester, Mayall was an independent thinker with a strong do-it-yourself ethic. In addition to playing harmonica, guitar, piano, and organ, the former commercial graphic artist designed his own album covers, produced most of his own sessions, and lugged his own equipment on tour (as did his band members, a condition of their employment).

In January 1963, John Mayall moved to London and formed the Bluesbreakers, with seventeen-year-old bassist John McVie among his first recruits. The new group struggled for two years until Eric Clapton joined in April 1965, bringing with him a reputation from his former group, the Yardbirds, as the finest blues guitarist in Britain. Faster, louder, and more aggressive than any of his prede-cessors, he stayed long enough to record *Blues Breakers: John Mayall with Eric Clapton* (1966)—a landmark album in British blues and the leader's first disc to reach an American audience. On the 1967 album *Crusade*, featuring new guitarist Mick Taylor, Mayall paid musical homage to his African American blues heroes including Sonny Boy Williamson II, Freddy King, and J.B. Lenoir.

John Mayall's five-decade career has been characterized by an unwavering dedication to his own muse and an ever-changing lineup of musicians. A seven-piece band with horns recorded the jazz-influenced *Bare Wires* in 1968; the next year, a drum-less acoustic group recorded *The Turning Point*, Mayall's first gold disc. The highest-charting U.S. album of Mayall's career—*USA Union*, from 1970—featured an all-American lineup with guitarist Harvey Mandel and R&B veteran Don "Sugarcane" Harris on electric violin.

The Bluesbreakers "school" has offered rigorous on-the-job training to scores of musicians who went on to greater glory including Mick Taylor with the Rolling Stones, John McVie and guitarist Peter Green with Fleetwood Mac, and drummers Keef Hartley and Jon Hiseman as leaders of their own bands. In July 2003, the "Godfather of British blues" celebrated his seventieth birthday with a gala concert in Liverpool where John Mayall and Eric Clapton performed together for the first time in thirty-eight years.

A. S.

The Stones' next single "Honky Tonk Women"—released on the day of Jones's death—was a tough, raunchy evocation of the Stones' new rock sound, and went to number one on both sides of the Atlantic.

The next Rolling Stones album *Let It Bleed* had been started prior to Jones's departure; Jones and Taylor appear on two tracks each. It also continued in its predecessor's rootsy vein, while indulging a lyrical fascination with sex and sleaze. The band's interest in the dark side was manifested on such tunes as "Midnight Rambler," "Monkey Man," and the apocalyptic "Gimme Shel-ter." The title track embodied the elegantly wasted ambience that the Stones would maintain for much of the 1970s, while "You Got the Silver" marked Keith Richards's first recorded lead vocal. Elsewhere, "You Can't Always Get What You Want" employed lush orchestrations and a surging vocal choir, while an edgy invocation of the Robert Johnson classic "Love in Vain" invokes their American blues influences.

In late 1969, the Rolling Stones mounted their first U.S. tour in three years. In the time since the band's last visit, the American rock scene had changed drasti-cally. The emergence of such popular live acts as Cream and Led Zeppelin had raised the stakes of the concert business, putting the Stones in the position of hav-ing to once again prove their mettle as a live act. Furthermore, this time they'd be playing to attentive audiences who were actually listening to the music, rather than the screaming teens they'd played for on previous American visits.

As it turned out, the Stones tour (which would yield the 1970 concert LP *Get Yer Ya-Yas Out!*) was a massive success, breaking attendance records across the country. Rather than playing in front of crowds of screaming teenagers, the band performed for young adults who actually listened—and thus were able to appreciate the strength of the new lineup, and the richness of the guitar interplay between Richards and Taylor.

But the triumphant return took a tragic turn when the tour climaxed with a free concert on December 6 at Altamont Speedway, near San Francisco, with a bill that also included Jefferson Airplane; Crosby, Stills, Nash and Young; Santana; and the Flying Burrito Brothers. Unlike the Stones' peaceful Hyde Park show, the poorly organized Altamont event was chaotic and fraught with violence from the start.

At the suggestion of the Grateful Dead, the Stones had hired the local chapter of the Oakland chapter of the Hell's Angels motorcycle gang as security, but that move backfired tragically. At one point, Jefferson Airplane singer Marty Balin was knocked unconscious during his band's set, when he attempted to stop some Hell's Angels from beating up an audience member. Later, during the Stones' headlining set, eighteen-year-old Meredith Hunter was fatally stabbed by an Angel as the Stones performed "Under My Thumb."

Filmmakers Albert and David Maysles, who'd been documenting the tour, caught the murder on film, and it became the disturbing centerpiece of their documentary *Gimme Shelter*. Upon its release in 1970, the film, and the Altamont show, were widely cited as marking the end of the 1960s, indicating that the innocence and idealism of the Woodstock era was now a thing of the past.

Gimme Shelter wasn't the first Stones-related project to hit the big screen. In 1969, Jagger had launched an acting career by starring in the Australian film *Ned Kelly*, portraying the nineteenth-century outlaw of the title. He then co-starred in the 1970 cult classic *Performance*, co-directed by Donald Cammell and Nicolas Roeg and featuring Anita Pallenberg in a key role.

Richards, meanwhile, spent time hanging out with country-rock pioneer Gram Parsons, whose band the Flying Burrito Brothers had performed at Altamont. In the process, he absorbed many of Parsons's country influences, which would be reflected in some of the Stones' subsequent output.

Get Yer Ya-Ya's Out! marked the expiration of the Rolling Stones' contract with Decca/London. Contractually obligated to provide Decca with one more single, the band delivered its parting shot with "Cocksucker Blues," a profane ballad whose bawdy lyrical content made it unreleasable.

In the years since they first signed to Decca, the Rolling Stones had gone from little-known local heroes to world-class superstars. Their commercial status gave the Stones—largely motivated by the business-minded Jagger—the clout to launch their own label. Their new venture, Rolling Stones Records, was initially distributed by Atlantic Records, and allowed the band ownership and control of its own master recordings, and thus a greater share of the profits. To set up and run the new company, they appointed old friend Marshall Chess, son of Chess Records co-founder Leonard Chess, who'd spent most of his adult life helping to run the label that was a key influence in the Stones' early days.

Unlike such artist-run labels as the Beatles' Apple and Led Zeppelin's Swan Song, Rolling Stones Records stuck mainly to releasing Stones albums and Stones-related side projects, making little effort to sign outside acts. There was some talk of the company releasing a Richards-produced solo LP by Richards's pal Gram Parsons, who'd left the Flying Burrito Brothers, but that collaboration never materialized. In 1973, Jagger would sign ex–Mamas and the Papas leader John Phillips to a solo deal, and Jagger and Richards produced several Phillips sessions. But runaway expenses—partially related to excessive drug use by Phillips and Richards—caused that album to be shelved by Jagger and Atlantic Records head Ahmet Ertegun. One of the few non-Stones successes on Rolling Stones Records was reggae star Peter Tosh's 1978 album *Bush Doctor*, which featured a popular Tosh/Jagger duet on a version of the Temptations' "Don't Look Back."

The Rolling Stones' first release on their own label was *Sticky Fingers*, released in March 1971. The album—whose cover design incorporated an actual metal zipper, inconveniencing record store clerks for years to come—continued where *Let It Bleed* had left off. The songs' drug subtext was hard to miss—more than half of them contained explicit drug references—and the resulting mix of malevolent decadence and folk-blues roots set the pattern that the Stones would follow for years to come.

Sticky Fingers featured a trio of memorable rockers, "Bitch," "Can't You Hear Me Knocking," and the number one U.S. hit "Brown Sugar"—whose upbeat chorus and surging guitar riffs assured that its lyrical themes of racism and slavery were lost on most listeners. The material otherwise struck a bluesy, world-weary tone, exemplified by the heartbreaking ballad "Wild Horses," the yearning, orchestrated album-closer "Moonlight Mile," and the emotionally naked "Sister Morphine," whose harrowing autobiographical lyrics were written by Marianne Faithfull.

On May 12, 1971, Jagger married Nicaraguan model Bianca Perez Morena de Macias, who was pregnant with their daughter Jade at the time, in St. Tropez. The couple's jet-set lifestyle would soon make them a gossip column staple.

Following the release of *Sticky Fingers*, the Stones went into tax exile and retreated to France. There, Richards rented a gothic chateau, Villa Nellecote, which had been used as the headquarters of the local Nazi SS during World War II. The band, along with an assortment of technical crew and various hangers-on, moved into Villa Nellecote to record their next album in the house's basement, with the band's own mobile studio park outside.

The result was the two-LP, eighteen-song *Exile on Main St.*, released in the spring of 1972. The sprawling but inspired epic was loose and organic, seamlessly integrating the country, soul, and gospel influences that the band had begun to explore on *Beggar's Banquet*, *Let It Bleed*, and *Sticky Fingers*, while amplifying those albums' dark, druggy lyrical undercurrent. Jagger's vocals were noticeably lower in the mix, which emphasized the band's dense, soulful ensemble playing and the riveting chemistry between Richards's eloquently basic, Chuck Berry–inspired rhythm work and Taylor's incisive, intricate solos.

While it contained several Stones classics—including "Tumbling Dice," "Rocks Off," "Shine a Light," "Torn and Frayed," "Rip This Joint," and the Richards-sung "Happy"—*Exile on Main St.* is less about individual songs than a sustained ambience, and its relatively muddy, cluttered sound rewards multiple listens with a wealth of sonic riches. Although it's now acknowledged as one of the Rolling Stones' greatest works, *Exile on Main St.* was initially dismissed by many critics as spotty and self-indulgent.

The Stones supported *Exile on Main St.* with a highly anticipated, highly publicized North American tour—their first Stateside performances since the Altamont debacle. The tour's rampant drug use and debauchery was captured in Robert Frank's cinema vérité documentary *Cocksucker Blues*. Frank's candid footage proved so incendiary that the band, which had originally commissioned the film, worked to have Frank's work suppressed, resulting in an unusual court order that barred it from being shown unless the director is physically present. Like the song with which it shares it name, the film was never officially released, but bootleg copies have circulated widely among fans and collectors.

Nineteen seventy-two also saw the release of *Jamming with Edward!*, a bluesy jam session cut during the *Let It Bleed* sessions by Jagger, Richards, Watts, American guitarist Ry Cooder, and veteran session pianist Nicky Hopkins. The impromptu recording reportedly occurred one day when Richards failed to show up at the studio.

ONLY ROCK AND ROLL

The Rolling Stones had made some of their best, most original music in the late 1960s and early 1970s. But following the ragged tour de force of *Exile on Main St.*, the Stones quickly lost focus, resulting in a series of competent but uninspired releases that maintained the band's crowd-pleasing sound, while adding little of substance to their recorded legacy. Many of their post-*Exile* albums would be recorded in bits and pieces rather than as concerted creative efforts, with various band members working in various combinations when schedules permitted.

It probably wasn't a coincidence that the Stones' descent into the musical doldrums coincided with a growing rift between the band's principal members, as Richards's drug dependency deepened and Jagger continued to pursue the high-society lifestyle that, in the eyes of many, distanced him from his musical roots and alienated him from his longtime musical partner.

The Rolling Stones nonetheless remained as popular as ever through the 1970s, and became bigger than ever, as the record and concert industries expanded during the decade. But while fans continued to embrace their albums and turn out in huge numbers for their tours, it was hard to ignore the general air of excess and indifference that pervaded such LPs as 1973's *Goats Head Soup* and 1974's *It's Only Rock 'N Roll*, whose spotty contents supported the widely held belief that the band members' various indulgences had adversely affected the quality of their musical output.

Goats Head Soup was memorable mainly for the heartrending hit ballad "Angie," which many fans interpreted as a paean to David Bowie's new wife Angela. The song was actually Richards's ode to Anita Pallenberg, who'd left Jones for Richards in 1967, and with whom the guitarist had a lengthy relationship that would last for a decade and produce three children (one of whom died in infancy). Another standout was the menacing urban nightmare "Doo Doo Doo Doo (Heartbreaker)" and the compellingly nasty "Star Star" (originally known as "Starfucker" but retitled for mass consumption). But most of the album suffered from indifferent songwriting, as evidenced by such tunes as "Dancing with Mr. D," on which Jagger's satanic posturing was more feeble than frightening.

It's Only Rock 'N Roll spawned a catchy, if somewhat obvious, anthem in its title track, as well as the catchy "If You Can't Rock Me," the paranoid "Fingerprint File," and a respectable reading of the Temptations' 1960s hit "Ain't Too Proud to Beg." But, like its predecessor, it was weighed down by a surfeit of obvious filler—an issue that would be a recurring problem for the band in years to come.

One factor in the Stones' uninspired output during this period was Richards's heroin addiction, which may have enhanced his outlaw image but did little for his musical consistency. Richards's French villa had been the subject of a drug raid in 1972, and his British home had been raided the following year. The guitarist's drug use took on such a mythic aura that it gave rise to all manner of urban legends, including the memorable (but untrue) rumor that he'd had all of his blood replaced during one effort to clean up.

Richards wasn't the only one in the Stones camp whose chemical dependency affected the quality of his work. Producer Jimmy Miller, who'd been a key member of the band's creative team since "Jumpin' Jack Flash" and *Beggar's Banquet*, was fired from *It's Only Rock 'N Roll* due to his own drug use.

Richards's unreliability reportedly led Jagger to co-write several songs with Mick Taylor during this period. But those compositions nonetheless bore the familiar Jagger/Richards credit when they were released. Taylor's frustration over the situation—and his impatience over the band's failure to tour in 1974—contributed to his surprise decision to quit the band.

Nineteen seventy-four also saw the release of Bill Wyman's first solo LP *Monkey Grip*, which he would follow two years later with *Stone Alone*.

With Taylor gone, the Rolling Stones used the Munich recording sessions for their next album, *Black and Blue*, as an opportunity to audition for his replacement. The candidates included a pair of Americans, ex–Canned

Heat/Bluesbreakers member Harvey Mandel and Muscle Shoals session man Wayne Perkins, who ended up appearing on the album, as well as ex-Yardbird Jeff Beck and former Humble Pie member Peter Frampton, who didn't.

The winner was Ron Wood, a former member of the Faces and the Jeff Beck Group who'd also guested on *It's Only Rock 'N Roll*. Wood, coincidentally, had first been introduced to the Stones by his longtime friend Mick Taylor. While Wood may not have possessed his predecessor's technical chops, his spiky, rhythmic style perfectly complemented Richards's playing, and the pair's sympathetic instrumental rapport would quickly become a crucial element in the Stones' sound.

Prior to *Black and Blue*'s release, Wood made his public debut with the Stones on the band's 1975 North American tour. In addition to introducing the new lineup, those shows also marked the first time that the Rolling Stones had augmented their live act with an elaborate theatrical presentation, including such unsubtle visual props as an inflatable giant phallus and a cherry picker that would hoist Jagger over the audience.

The retooled stage show was Jagger's effort to stay competitive with the overblown extravaganzas that had become standard for touring rock superstars at the time. But it also created another source of tension in his increasingly fractious relationship with Keith Richards, who considered the onstage frills to be an unnecessary distraction.

Black and Blue, released in April 1976, was a marginal improvement over *Goats Head Soup* and *It's Only Rock 'N Roll*. The album's emphasis on loose, funky grooves—like those of the disco-leaning "Hot Stuff" and the reggae-ified "Cherry Oh Baby"—rather than concise songs wasn't surprising, in light of the fact that most of the material was derived via casual studio jams. But *Black and Blue*'s standout tracks were a pair of moody ballads, "Fool to Cry" and "Memory Motel."

Black and Blue did little to reverse critics' assertions that the Stones had grown stagnant. But Keith Richards had bigger problems than musical direction. Although he'd gone through a series of therapies attempting to cure his heroin addiction, in February 1977 he and Anita Pallenberg were arrested for heroin and cocaine possession in a room at Toronto's Harbour Castle Hotel. Richards was charged with importing narcotics, an offense that carried a minimum prison sentence of seven years.

Jagger, meanwhile, continued to play the role of glamorous globe-hopping celebrity to the hilt. The singer, whose marriage to Bianca would end in 1977, was a regular at the notorious New York disco Studio 54, often in the company of his new girlfriend, model Jerry Hall. Jagger would marry Hall in 1990; the couple would have four children before divorcing in 1999.

By now, the punk rock movement had emerged as a significant force, rebelling against entrenched millionaire rock stars who'd lost touch with their original inspiration. That description certainly applied to the Rolling Stones at the time, and was confirmed when the Clash's Joe Strummer sang "No

Elvis, Beatles or Rolling Stones" in the song "1977." The rote performances on the Stones' 1977 double concert set *Love You Live* supported the band's growing reputation as a spent force coasting on past glories.

But the Stones made an unexpected return to form with 1978's *Some Girls*. That album recaptured the raw, rude spirit of the band's best work, channeling its recent internal turmoil into raucous, spirited music, and drawing energy from punk as well as the then-ubiquitous disco explosion. The result was their most focused and consistent music in years, music that instantly made the Rolling Stones seem current once again.

Along with the disco-inflected number one single "Miss You," the punchy mid-tempo "Beast of Burden," and the droll country parody "Far Away Eyes," *Some Girls* was loaded with tough, witty rockers that showcased Jagger's reenergized presence and the solid guitar rapport of Richards and Wood, for example, "Shattered," "Respectable," "When the Whip Comes Down," and the Richards-sung outlaw anthem "Before They Make Me Run."

The latter track was a liberating shout of defiance in the face of Richards's recent problems with drugs and the law. The song held particular resonance, since the guitarist was still under the threat of imprisonment when it was recorded and released. Richards ultimately escaped serving time, and instead was sentenced to play two benefit concerts in Toronto for the Canadian National Institute for the Blind.

For that purpose, Richards put together the New Barbarians, a short-lived supergroup that also included Ron Wood, ex-Faces keyboardist Ian McLagan (who'd been working with the Stones as a studio and stage sideman), jazz-fusion bassist Stanley Clarke, drummer Zigaboo Modeliste of fabled New Orleans funk combo the Meters, and frequent Stones saxophonist Bobby Keys. Following the court-mandated Toronto shows on April 22, the ensemble did a month-long U.S. tour, ostensibly to promote Wood's then-current solo album *Gimme Some Neck*, to which Richards, McLagan, and Keys all contributed.

His legal problems apparently motivated Richards to successfully overcome his heroin addiction, after multiple attempts. At around the same time, he ended his relationship with Anita Pallenberg. 1979 also saw the first official Richards solo release, a Christmas single combining covers of Chuck Berry's seasonal tune "Run Rudolph Run" and Jimmy Cliff's reggae classic "The Harder They Come."

In addition to making the Rolling Stones artistically relevant again, *Some Girls* restored their commercial status. It became their best-selling album in years, topping the American charts and reaching number two in punk-gripped Britain.

But the band was unable to maintain that level of quality with 1980's *Emotional Rescue*. That disc, partially comprising *Some Girls* outtakes, had an unmistakable throwaway feel, with such numbers as "She's So Cold," "Send It to Me," and the reggae-flavored title track sounding like pale reworkings of older, better Stones songs.

Emotional Rescue's lackluster quality betrayed the Stones' unstable internal state. With Richards having curbed some of his drug excesses, he began to become a more active and assertive participant in the studio, leading to personal tensions and creative power struggles with Jagger.

The Stones' 1981 release *Tattoo You* was also largely assembled from leftover tracks from prior recording projects, some of them nearly a decade old, but was a substantial improvement over *Emotional Rescue*. Divided into separate sides of rockers and ballads, its rock half featured such highlights as the insistent "Start Me Up," the self-mocking "Hang Fire," and one of the band's best Richards-fronted tracks, the cheerfully sleazy "Little T & A." The Richards-sung ballad "Worried About You" was another standout, as was the hit ballad "Waiting on a Friend," which caught Jagger in an uncharacteristically reflective mood and featured a sax solo by jazz great Sonny Rollins. Rollins overdubbed his part years after the original track was recorded; it and "Tops" had both been cut during the *Goats Head Soup* sessions and featured the guitar work of the long-departed Mick Taylor.

Tattoo You was followed by a stadium tour that was captured on the 1982 live album *Still Life* and shot by director Hal Ashby for the concert film *Let's Spend the Night Together*. That tour also marked the introduction of American pianist Chuck Leavell, formerly of the Allman Brothers Band and Sea Level, to the Stones' stage lineup.

In 1982, Bill Wyman, who rarely got the chance to display his songwriting abilities within the Stones, achieved a surprise European solo smash with "(Si Si) Je suis un Rock Star," a playful, new-wavey pop novelty that spoofed his status as a French tax exile.

ACHING IN THE 1980s

The Rolling Stones continued to tour and record consistently through the 1980s. While their tours continued to be tremendous money makers, their albums were largely disappointing, both musically and commercially. The creative rut was widely assumed to be the result of the ongoing strained relations between Jagger and Richards. One source of disagreement was Jagger's desire to take the band in a direction more in keeping with contemporary pop trends and Richards's insistence on sticking with rock and roll basics.

Nineteen eighty-three's *Undercover* is generally regarded as Jagger's attempt to give the Rolling Stones a more modern sound, integrating a variety of then-contemporary beats and flashy production techniques. But the ionic frills felt awkward, and the songs' self-consciously nasty, nihilistic lyrics—manifested in the tawdry images of kinky sex, sleazy violence, and political corruption on such numbers as "Undercover of the Night," "Pretty Beat Up," and "Too Much Blood"—seemed less like musical growth and more like a forced attempt to give the band an edgy veneer.

The ill will between Jagger and Richards was exacerbated when Jagger signed a solo deal with Rolling Stones Records' new distributor, CBS. Richards, who'd largely refrained from extracurricular musical pursuits, resented Jagger's apparent lack of commitment to the group. The public feuding between the two longtime bandmates seemed to cast serious doubt on the Stones' future.

The much-ballyhooed 1985 release of Jagger's first solo effort *She's the Boss* seemed to confirm the widely held assumption that the Stones were nearing the end of their run. But the album—recorded with a sprawling cast of players that included Jeff Beck, Pete Townshend, Herbie Hancock, and the reggae rhythm section of Sly and Robbie—was a flimsy collection of trendy, lightweight 1980s pop, with nary a trace of stonesy spirit.

To help promote *She's the Boss*, Jagger shot a series of elaborate promotional videos that received heavy MTV airplay. Although the exposure pushed the album to platinum status and helped to send its first single "Just Another Night" into the Top Twenty, the public response seemed muted in comparison to the promotional hype that had accompanied the project. That summer, Jagger teamed up with David Bowie to record a cover of Martha and the Vandellas' 1964 Motown classic "Dancing in the Street" to benefit the Live Aid organization. The single reached number seven in the United States.

A further blow to the Stones' stability came when beloved pianist and band retainer Ian Stewart—whose calming influence had long had a stabilizing effect on the group's internal conflicts—died of a heart attack in December 1985. A set at a Stewart tribute concert in February 1986 was the Rolling Stones' only public appearance during that period.

The Stones paid further tribute to their fallen comrade by including a snippet of a Stewart boogie-woogie piano solo in the final fadeout of 1986's *Dirty Work*. That troubled album represented a conscious attempt to return the Stones to their rock and roll roots. But the largely Richards-penned album suffered from a paucity of memorable songs, and the lukewarm performances—not to mention the lightweight 1980s production—did little to put the subpar material across.

Despite its musical deficiencies, *Dirty Work*'s relatively lackluster sales probably had as much to do with Jagger's decision that the Stones not tour to promote it. The growing perception of his lack of interest in the band was supported by the release of his solo title song for the film *Ruthless People* concurrently with *Dirty Work*.

Also in 1986, the Rolling Stones were honored with a Grammy lifetime achievement award. But that honor was undercut by the spectacle of Jagger and Richards frequently sniping at each other in interviews. The pair would have little contact over the next few years.

With no *Dirty Work* tour to keep him busy, Richards found an even more stubborn musical partner in his idol Chuck Berry, when Richards volunteered to serve as musical director for a pair of concerts in Berry's hometown of St. Louis to honor the legendary singer/guitarist on his sixtieth birthday. The turbulent process of staging those shows was chronicled in the documentary film *Hail! Hail! Rock 'n' Roll.*

Rather than touring with the Stones, Jagger continued to put his energies into establishing his individual career. He teamed up with producer Dave Stewart, of Eurhythmics fame, to record a second solo album, 1987's *Primitive Cool.* Like *She's the Boss*, it was another attempt to reinvent the once-rebellious rock icon as a state-of-the-art 1980s pop star. Minus the curiosity factor and corporate hype that had accompanied its predecessor's release, *Primitive Cool* was a commercial bust.

Ironically, the lower-profile Richards—who had long been reluctant to record without the Stones, but was motivated to strike out on his own by Jagger's extracurricular ambitions—fared much better than Jagger as a solo artist. Richards's 1988 release *Talk Is Cheap* contrasted his bandmate's work by concentrating on spare, no-frills rock and roll. The album mixed catchy, Stones-style grooves and the guitarist's own enthusiastically ragged vocals, to make music that rocked harder than anything the Stones had done in years.

Richards proved a capable frontman when he supported *Talk Is Cheap* by doing a brief tour with a backup combo he dubbed the X-Pensive Winos. That lineup included veteran session guitarist Waddy Wachtel, bassist Charley Drayton, keyboardist Ivan Neville, and drummer Steve Jordan; Jordan had done some playing on *Dirty Work* and was part of the band that Richards had assembled to back Chuck Berry. That tour yielded the album *Live at the Hollywood Palladium, December 15, 1988*, released in 1991.

Charlie Watts, the Rolling Stones' most low-key member, used the band's frequent hiatuses to indulge his lifelong love for jazz. In 1986, he recorded and toured with the Charlie Watts Orchestra, the first of a series of instrumental groups that included many of England's top jazz players.

The Rolling Stones' 1989 induction into the Rock and Roll Hall of Fame set the stage for the band's studio reconciliation on *Steel Wheels*. If not in the same league as their best work, the album at least found Jagger and Richards working in relative harmony again. Although *Steel Wheels* was generally well received, the world tour that accompanied it was bigger news. The tour grossed over $140 million and spawned yet another live album, *Flashpoint.*

The success of the *Steel Wheels* tour demonstrated that public demand for the Rolling Stones remained as high as ever. For years to come, the band would follow a similar pattern, releasing a new album, followed by a high-profile tour, with both events routinely accompanied by widespread media speculation over whether they would be the band's last.

Those projects would proceed without founding bassist Bill Wyman, who quit the band following the *Steel Wheels* tour. Although he'd never had the high media profile of Jagger and Richards, Wyman had recently received much unwelcome publicity regarding his marriage to the thirty-four-years-younger

Mandy Smith, whom Wyman had begun dating when she was thirteen (the couple divorced after a year). The tabloid stories grew juicier when Wyman's thirty-year-old son Stephen became romantically involved with Mandy's forty-six-year-old mother.

The Stones did not announce an immediate replacement for Wyman, since various members were all working on individual projects in the period following *Steel Wheels*. In 1991, Wyman published a frank tell-all autobiography, *Stone Alone*, which recounted a litany of his randy exploits during his years with the band. In the years to come, Wyman would also publish books of his photography and his cartoon drawings, as well as launching the all-star R&B-oriented cover outfit Bill Wyman's Rhythm Kings, featuring such notable contemporaries as Gary Brooker, Eric Clapton, Georgie Fame, Peter Frampton, George Harrison, Albert Lee, and even fellow ex-Stone Mick Taylor.

The Stones' return to active duty with *Steel Wheels* was apparently enough to satisfy Richards's musical urges, and he put his solo career on hold after releasing a second studio solo outing, *Main Offender*, in 1992. Jagger, meanwhile, recorded a third slickly produced solo release, *Wandering Spirit*, with Beastie Boys/Red Hot Chili Peppers producer Rick Rubin in 1993.

Although *Steel Wheels* had apparently helped to mend the Jagger/Richards feud, it took five more years—two years longer than the gap between *Dirty Work* and *Steel Wheels*—for the Rolling Stones to reconvene for 1994's *Voodoo Lounge*.

Voodoo Lounge's producer, versatile American Don Was, was noted for helping veteran acts recapture their original essence. The album did, indeed, retain much of the stones' classic sound, with some additional nods to their *Beggar's Banquet/Let It Bleed*–era folk and blues excursions. But as with many of the recent Stones releases, *Voodoo Lounge*'s songwriting was more functional than inspired.

To fill the void left by Wyman's departure, the band, at Chuck Leavell's suggestion, tapped bassist Darryl Jones, a seasoned jazz/funk player whose credits included work with Miles Davis and Sting. Although Jones was hired as a sideman rather than a full member, he would continue as the Stones' touring bassist for the next dozen years as well as doing the lion's share of the bass work on their future recordings.

Whatever its flaws, *Voodoo Lounge* sold in higher quantities than its predecessor, and its accompanying tour was even more successful than the *Steel Wheels* extravaganza. *Voodoo Lounge* also won the Stones their first-ever Grammy award, in the Best Rock Album category.

Following the *Voodoo Lounge* tour, the Rolling Stones jumped on the "unplugged" bandwagon by releasing *Stripped* in the fall of 1995. Recorded during rehearsals and low-key club gigs in Amsterdam and Paris, the album recast an assortment of Stones classics, fan favorites, and blues covers—plus a punning but not altogether inappropriate reading of Bob Dylan's "Like a Rolling Stone"—with spare, largely acoustic arrangements. The concept had grown out of the acoustic sets that the band had introduced during the *Voodoo Lounge* tour. As promising as the concept was, the performances were unremarkable, adding little to the familiar material.

A much bigger windfall for the Stones in 1995 was the band's licensing of "Start Me Up" to Microsoft to advertise the company's Windows 95 operating system for the tidy sum of $14 million. The Microsoft campaign marked the first time the group had allowed its music to be used in a commercial.

According to legend, Microsoft boss Bill Gates had asked Jagger how much he'd want for the rights to use the song. Rather than refuse, the singer facetiously named the $14 million figure—which he considered to be ridiculously high—and Gates readily agreed. Four years later, Apple Computers would use the *Their Satanic Majesties Request* tune "She's a Rainbow" to promote the introduction of multicolored iMacs.

The Stones worked with Don Was again on 1997's *Bridges to Babylon*. But while *Voodoo Lounge* attempted to reclaim the band's classic style, *Bridges to Babylon* made a concerted—and somewhat forced—effort to update their sound. With trendy alt-hitmakers the Dust Brothers and Danny Saber producing individual tracks, it augmented the band's familiar sound with samples and drum loops. Despite the postmodern gimmicks, the album—which featured a higher than usual vocal presence by Richards, who sang lead on three standout tracks—didn't sound all that different from *Voodoo Lounge*, with its solid execution compensating for the forgettable material.

Although ex–Sugarhill Gang/Living Colour vet Doug Wimbish played most of the album's bass parts, Wimbish reportedly turned down the offer of becoming the Stones' touring bassist, and Darryl Jones was back for the epic *Bridges to Babylon* world tour. This time, the shows included a segment during which a metal bridge unfolded from the stage, from which the musicians walked to a smaller stage set up in the middle of the audience to play a stripped-down mini-set. Not surprisingly, the tour spawned yet another live album, *No Security*, whose main selling point was that none of its songs had appeared on any of the band's six previous live releases.

In 2001 Jagger took another crack at his solo career with *Goddess in the Doorway*, whose sprawling roster of guest stars—including Pete Townshend, Bono, Joe Perry, Lenny Kravitz, Missy Elliot, Wyclef Jean, and Matchbox 20 singer Rob Thomas—smacked of commercial desperation rather than sound aesthetic judgment. Jagger also continued to take occasional acting assignments, earning positive notices for his roles in 1997's *Bent* and 2001's *The Man from Elysian Fields*.

In 2002, Allen Klein's label ABKCO, which controlled the Rolling Stones' pre–*Sticky Fingers* catalog, finally released upgraded, remastered editions of all of those albums, including separate versions of their U.S. and U.K. variants. The refurbished discs were welcomed by fans, who for years had had to make do with the inferior versions that ABKCO had issued early in the CD era. The remastered editions were initially released in the high-tech SACD format, but were re-pressed as conventional CDs after the SACD format failed to catch on with consumers.

The belated reclamation of the Rolling Stones' best recorded work coincided with the band's rebirth as a performing unit. A 2002 tour—in conjunction with the career-spanning compilation *Forty Licks* rather than a new studio release—found the band playing with renewed fire and a heightened sense of purpose. This time around, the de rigueur concert album, *Live Licks*, was a worthy addition to the Stones' catalog.

On July 30, 2003, the Stones headlined a benefit concert in Toronto, in front of an audience estimated at 490,000, to help the city—which the band regularly used as a base for pre-tour rehearsals—recover from the effects of the recent SARS epidemic. On November 9, 2003, the Stones played their first-ever Hong Kong concert, a show staged as part of that city's post-SARS recovery effort.

The same month, the band released the four-DVD set *Four Flicks*, recorded on their most recent tour. In the United States, the package was distributed exclusively to the Best Buy retail chain, leading several other music retail chains to retaliate by temporarily removing all Rolling Stones merchandise from their shelves.

THE LAST TIME?

By this point, the Rolling Stones had fallen into an familiar (if undeniably profitable) pattern: release an album that's routinely hyped as a return to form, followed by an epic stadium tour, with both accompanied by intimations that they might be the band's last. The fact that the Stones can continue to reap massive rewards from this strategy every few years is powerful evidence of their bigger-than-life status as one of rock's few living legends.

So it was that in 2005, after countless false alarms and supposed artistic resurrctions that never quite panned out, the Rolling Stones surprised even their most skeptical fans with their best and hardest-rocking album in years, *A Bigger Bang*. Eight years had passed since *Bridges to Babylon*—the longest-ever gap between new Stones discs—but the new disc embodied much of the revived spirit that the band had demonstrated on the *Forty Licks* tour. Where *Steel Wheels* and *Voodoo Lounge* had been consciously designed to resurrect the familiar Stones sound, *A Bigger Bang* (produced once again by Don Was) sounded more like the band had stopped considering audience expectations and just set out to make a good record.

Whatever the intentions, *A Bigger Bang* found the Stones sounding tougher and greasier than they had in a couple of decades, boasting a spacious sound that provided a solid framework for the revitalized band's tough, sinewy playing. The album's sixteen new originals represented their strongest batch of new material since *Some Girls*, including such venomous rockers as "Rough Justice," "Look What the Cat Dragged In," and "Oh No Not You Again," as well as some convincing ballads and blues tunes and Keith's after-hours lament "This Place Is Empty." *A Bigger Bang* briefly stirred some pre-release controversy over "Sweet Neo Con," a pointed Jagger jab at the Bush administration's recklessness. The song was reportedly almost left off the album due to the objections of the staunchly apolitical Richards.

The band began its tour in support of *A Bigger Bang* in August 2005, covering North America, South America, and East Asia in a mixture of venues. By the end of that year, the tour had racked up a record-setting $162 million in gross receipts, breaking the record that the Stones themselves had set in 1994.

In February 2006, the Stones performed in the high-profile halftime slot of the Super Bowl. On April 27, while vacationing on the island of Fiji following some concerts in Australia, Richards suffered a head injury after a fall from a coconut tree. A few days later, he underwent successful brain surgery in Auckland, New Zealand, to relieve a blood clot. One of rock's most durable anti-heroes was back on stage within a few months.

Whether *A Bigger Bang* signaled a long-term return to form or merely a fond farewell, it made the point that it's possible to age gracefully and still make great rock and roll. Nearly four and a half decades after their formation, the Rolling Stones had successfully defended their status as the World's Greatest Rock and Roll Band.

TIMELINE

July 12, 1962
Billed as The Rollin' Stones, the band plays its first gig at London's Marquee club, with a lineup composed of Mick Jagger, Keith Richards, Brian Jones, Dick Taylor on bass, Ian Stewart on piano, and Mick Avory on drums.

December 1962
Bill Wyman joins the Rolling Stones as bassist.

January 1963
Charlie Watts joins the Rolling Stones as drummer.

February 1963
The new Rolling Stones lineup begins an eight-month residency at London's Crawdaddy Club. The band's performances there will become so popular that the club is eventually forced to move to a larger location.

June 1963
The Rolling Stones' first single, consisting of cover versions of Chuck Berry's "Come On" and Willie Dixon's "I Want to Be Loved," is released in Britain.

January 18, 1964
Gene Pitney's version of "That Girl Belongs to Yesterday" enters the *Billboard* Hot 100, becoming the first Jagger/Richards composition to chart in the United States.

February 1964
The Rolling Stones' third single, a cover of Buddy Holly's "Not Fade Away," becomes the band's commercial breakthrough in Britain, reaching number three on the U.K. pop chart.

June 1, 1964
The Rolling Stones begin their first North American tour, which will include appearances on *The Ed Sullivan Show* and Dean Martin's *Hollywood Palace*, as well as a visit to Chicago's legendary Chess studio. At Chess, the band will record the EP *Five by Five*.

June 1966
The Stones release *Aftermath*, their first album consisting entirely of Jagger/Richards originals.

June 19, 1965
"Satisfaction" becomes the Rolling Stones' first number one hit in the United States.

February 1967
Mick Jagger and Keith Richards are arrested on drug charges when the police raid a party at Richards's estate in Sussex, and find four amphetamine pills in Jagger's possession. The pair will be convicted of the charge in June, but public outcry over the trumped-up charges and excessive sentences will prompt the reversal of their sentences.

May 1967
Brian Jones is arrested for the possession of cannabis, cocaine, and methamphetamine. He will escape with a fine and probation, but is ordered to seek professional help.

December 1967
The Stones release their controversial psychedelic album *Their Satanic Majesties Request*.

May 1968
The single "Jumpin' Jack Flash" is released.

July 26, 1968
Decca withdraws the original version of the Stones album *Beggars Banquet* due to its controversial cover art.

December 11–12, 1968
The Rolling Stones film their TV special *Rock and Roll Circus*, with guest appearances by John Lennon, Eric Clapton, Jimi Hendrix, the Who, and others.

June 8, 1969
Brian Jones is fired from the Rolling Stones.

July 3, 1969
Brian Jones is found dead in his swimming pool.

July 5, 1969
The Rolling Stones play a previously scheduled free concert in London's Hyde Park, in front of a crowd of 200,000, as a tribute to Brian Jones. The show is the debut of new guitarist Mick Taylor.

August 23, 1969
The Rolling Stones reach number one with "Honky Tonk Women."

November 1969
The band plays its first U.S. tour in three years.

December 6, 1969
The Stones headline an all-star free concert at Altamont Speedway in California. The event becomes a disaster when it's disrupted by violence from Hell's Angel members, with one audience member stabbed to death. The event will be documented in the feature film *Gimme Shelter*.

March 1971
Sticky Fingers, the band's first album on their own Rolling Stones Records label, is released.

February 1977
Keith Richards and Anita Pallenberg are arrested for heroin and cocaine possession in a Toronto hotel room. Richards will receive a suspended sentence and be ordered to play two free concerts for a local charity. The sentence sparks the formation of Richards's temporary supergroup the New Barbarians, which plays some U.S. dates as well as the court-ordered concerts.

1993
Bill Wyman quits the Rolling Stones.

SELECTED DISCOGRAPHY

The Rolling Stones (England's Newest Hitmakers), 1964

12 × 5, 1964

The Rolling Stones, Now!, 1965

Out of Our Heads, 1965

December's Children (And Everybody's), 1965

Aftermath, 1966

Between the Buttons, 1967

Flowers, 1967

Their Satanic Majesties Request, 1967

Beggars Banquet, 1968

Let It Bleed, 1969

Get Yer Ya-Ya's Out!, 1970

Sticky Fingers, 1971

Exile on Main St., 1972
Some Girls, 1978

FURTHER READING

Booth, Stanley. *Dance with the Devil: The Rolling Stones and Their Times*. New York: Random House, 1984.

Booth, Stanley. *The True Adventures of the Rolling Stones*. Chicago: Chicago Review Press, 2000.

Carr, Roy. *The Rolling Stones: An Illustrated Record*, New York: Harmony Books, 1976.

Dalton, David. *The Rolling Stones; The First Twenty Years*. New York: Alfred A. Knopf, 1981.

© Chris Walter/WireImage/Getty.

The Who

Alan Bisbort

WHO ARE THEY?

In their lengthy career, the Who have been many things. They began as a mascot of England's Mod movement, recording a string of savage, anthemic singles that defined rock's rebellious adolescent edge. They then became a key force in rock's shift in emphasis from singles to albums, pioneering the idea of the concept album with their seminal rock operas *Tommy* and *Quadrophenia*. The thematic and musical complexity of those albums reflected leader Pete

Townshend's restless drive to conquer new musical territory, as well as his equally relentless instinct for self-examination. In later years, the band would be a vehicle for Townshend's introspective wrestling with the deeper meanings of rock and roll and the psychic demands of his role as an artist.

The Who has always been an unwieldy yet fascinating mass of complementary contradictions, with the four band members' divergent personalities lending depth and dimension to their musical output. Strutting, microphone-twirling singer Roger Daltrey set the standard for macho rock frontmen for decades to come. Swaggering guitar hero Townshend played his instrument with such abandon that his hands were often bloody by the end of the show. Townshend's violent performing style was matched by that of drummer Keith Moon, who flailed away at—and sometimes demolished—his drum kit with a manic madness that matched his lovably unhinged off-stage persona. Meanwhile, strong, silent bassist John Entwistle stood quietly at the eye of the sonic hurricane, anchoring the maelstrom with his thunderous bass lines.

While the band's live shows attained a heroic, bigger-than-life scale, Townshend's identity as one of the most cerebral and introspective rock songwriters of his era gave his songs a rare emotional and rhetorical depth. Townshend was also one of the first rock songwriters to wrestle with the thorny topic of the aging process, as it relates to the creators and consumers of rock and roll.

For all of their contradictions and misadventures—some of which manifested themselves in the premature deaths of Moon and Entwistle—the Who have made music that's often been magnificent and never been less than interesting. Indeed, even the band's musical failures have been fascinating and edifying ones.

TALKIN' 'BOUT THEIR GENERATION

Roger Daltrey, John Entwistle, and Pete Townshend all grew up in the same West London district of Shepherd's Bush. They were acquaintances at Acton County Grammar School, and Entwistle and Townshend became close friends, bound by their common musical interests. Entwistle performed with the Middlesex Youth Orchestra, gaining notice for his abilities on trumpet, French horn, and piano. Townshend came from a musical family; his mother Betty was a singer with the Sidney Torch Orchestra and his father Clifford was a clarinetist and sax player who led the Squadronaires, a Royal Air Force dance band. In their early teens, Entwistle and Townshend—then playing banjo—performed in traditional and Dixieland jazz combos, and in the rock and roll outfits the Confederates, the Aristocrats, and the Scorpions.

While Townshend and Entwistle were natural musicians, Daltrey was a natural leader. Blessed with a strong constitution and matinee-idol looks but cursed with a hair-trigger temper, Daltrey had been kicked out of school for smoking and was already working by the time Townshend and Entwistle joined his band, the Detours. The Detours played covers of American blues, soul, and R&B standards, with Daltrey playing lead guitar, as well as booking the gigs and providing transportation with a company van borrowed from his job as a sheet-metal worker. Although Daltrey would soon drop guitar to concentrate on singing, Townshend later stated that at the time they met, Daltrey was a more accomplished instrumentalist than himself or Entwistle.

The Detours' original drummer, Doug Sandom, quit in March 1964, and the band recruited a temporary replacement to fulfill their prior live commitments. It was at one of those shows that Keith Moon—then playing in the London surf-covers outfit the Beachcombers and working in a cement plant—announced to Townshend that he was more capable than the band's replacement drummer. After sitting in with the Detours, Moon—who already had a reputation as London's loudest drummer—secured the job permanently.

With their soon-to-be-famous lineup in place, the Detours acquired a well-connected manager in Peter Meaden. Meaden was a prominent figure in London's Mod scene, a subculture comprising largely disaffected working-class youths fond of American rhythm and blues, French fashions, Italian motor scooters, Pop Art imagery, pills, and occasional punch-ups with their nemeses, the Rockers.

Although both groups were composed largely of working-class youths, the Mods and Rockers were bitter rivals. The rough-edged Rockers were descended from the Teddy Boys of the 1950s, working stiffs who affected Edwardian styles in a parody of the aristocracy. Sporting leather jackets and slicked-back hair, the Rockers rode motorcycles and favored the early rock and roll of Elvis Presley, Eddie Cochran, Gene Vincent, and Chuck Berry. The Mods, by contrast, viewed themselves as sophisticates, riding imported motor scooters and conforming to elaborate codes of style and behavior, and listened to American rhythm and blues.

The first of several widely publicized Mod/Rocker confrontations took place on March 27, 1964, in the coastal resort town of Clacton-on-Sea, when a group of local Rockers took umbrage at a group of Mods who'd ridden their scooters from London. The two factions' initial scuffling was exaggerated by the national press as a "teenage riot." The media frenzy became self-fulfilling prophecy to larger, weekend-long riots in various locations through the spring and summer of 1964 (the riots would later help to inspire the Who's rock opera *Quadrophenia*).

With an eye toward courting the Mod audience, Peter Meaden reinvented the Detours. He convinced the band to change its name to the High Numbers—"high" in honor of the Mods' penchant for amphetamines and "Numbers" being Mod slang for "the crowd." Since the Mods favored American R&B, Meaden sought to create an explicitly British variation to appeal to mod tastes.

For the High Numbers' first single, Meaden had the band cut two of his own derivative compositions, "I'm the Face" and "Zoot Suit." The tune of the former was appropriated from American bluesman Slim Harpo's "Got Love If You Want it," and the latter borrowed liberally from "Misery" by the Dynamics. Both songs were filled with Mod terminology designed to appeal to the disc's target demographic. Despite Meaden's canny marketing, the single failed to catch on.

Although Peter Meaden's machinations had failed to yield hit results, the struggling quartet—which had rechristened itself the Who shortly after the release of the High Numbers single—soon found a more productive association with the duo of aspiring filmmakers Kit Lambert and Chris Stamp. Lambert was the son of classical composer Constant Lambert, while Stamp was the brother of actor Terence Stamp, whose performances in such films as *Billy Budd* and *The Collector* had established him as an icon of 1960s British cinema. Lambert and Stamp had planned to make a film that would feature an unknown pop group. But after encountering the Who, they abandoned their film project and instead became the band's managers, purchasing their management contract from Meaden.

As it happened, the night that Lambert and Stamp first saw the Who, at the Railway Tavern in Harrow, Middlesex on July 14, 1964, was also the first time that Townshend smashed his guitar on stage. This destruction initially occurred by accident, when his guitar slammed against the club's low ceiling, cracking the neck. Angered by the damage to his precious ax, Townshend ritually disemboweled it, inducing ear-splitting feedback from his amplifier in the process.

Word of the incident soon spread through the Mod scene. Before long, audiences expected to witness similar chaos whenever the Who performed. When Townshend learned that a Who gig was to be covered by the London tabloid the *Daily Mail*, he made a point of destroying another guitar at the set's climax. Guitar-smashing soon became a regular feature of the band's shows, and Moon began to join in the destruction, kicking over his drum kit at the end of shows. Later, he added smoke bombs and explosives. Townshend augmented the pyrotechnics by adding a stack of Marshall amplifiers to achieve additional volume and more intense feedback. The excessive on-stage volume would have a long-term effect on Townshend's hearing, resulting in the chronic tinnitus that would plague him for the rest of his career.

Townshend later explained that his guitar-smashing was partially motivated by his frustration at the technical limitations of his own playing. But the act was also informed by Townshend's art school training. While attending Ealing Art College, he'd learned about "auto destruction" from instructor Gustav Metzger, who'd published a manifesto on the subject in 1959. Metzger's idea was to create art objects only to publicly destroy them, thus rendering them unexploitable, and Townshend viewed his ritual onstage destruction within that context.

After taking over the Who's management, Kit Lambert and Chris Stamp recognized and nurtured Townshend's nascent songwriting abilities and nurtured his talent, encouraging the twenty-year-old guitarist to write original material, in contrast to the covers of American R&B and rock and roll that still dominated the repertoire of most British bands.

Lambert and Stamp moved Townshend and his art-school classmate Richard Barnes into a flat above their offices, and plied Townshend with money, equipment, and intellectual stimulation. With access to a small home recording setup, Townshend cut demo tapes of his new songs, meticulously overdubbing all of the instruments and vocals himself, in order to present the material to the band in its most complete and favorable light (years later, Townshend's demo recordings would form the basis of several albums released under his own name).

The Who achieved a crucial breakthrough when they played an extended Tuesday night residency at London's Marquee club, a former jazz club that had become ground zero for the swinging London scene, as well as a popular Mod hangout.

Lambert and Stamp helped to build the Marquee gigs into events by promoting them with distinctive Pop Art graphics. Lambert helped to cement the band's image by designing a poster to promote the shows, picturing Townshend caught in mid-wind-up for one of his fingertip-severing power chords. The poster hung on the walls of virtually every record shop and trendy clothing store in London, building public excitement and curiosity for the gigs. The managers further strengthened the band's mod image by giving the band members money to deck themselves out in trendy Carnaby Street fashions. Moon soon became known for his bull's-eye T-shirts and Townshend for his Union Jack suits.

Lambert's inventive approach to visual presentation would prove crucial in establishing the Who's early identity. But the expense of his and Stamp's promotional efforts, along with the need to constantly replace the musicians' decimated equipment, would cause the band to remain in debt for years.

The managers' confidence in Townshend paid quick dividends. The guitarist's first major composition was "I Can't Explain," an insistent evocation of adolescent dislocation that became the Who's first Top Ten hit single in Britain, and would remain the opening number of the band's concerts for decades to come. Townshend later asserted that he modeled "I Can't Explain" on the Kinks' breakthrough smash "You Really Got Me." The two bands shared a producer in talented, abrasive American transplant Shel Talmy.

On the strength of "I Can't Explain," Lambert and Stamp got the Who a spot on the popular and influential British TV pop show *Ready Steady Go!* The band first appeared on the show on January 29, 1965, and were so well received that that they were invited back eight more times over the next two years.

The Who's next single, "Anyway Anyhow Anywhere," was a swaggering barrage of guitar feedback, cacophonous drumming, and macho lyrics, and followed its predecessor into the U.K. Top Ten. The defiant youth anthem "My Generation" arrived in late 1965, at the height of the excitement surrounding the band's Marquee residency. "My Generation" amplified the rebellious vibe of the Who's prior singles to maximum intensity, with Townshend's and Entwistle's frenzied solos and Daltrey's aggressive, stuttering vocal, while Townshend's lyrics drew a line in the sand with the blunt catchphrase "Hope I die before I get old." Townshend would come to rue the line in future years, but at the time it perfectly encapsulated the in-the-moment spirit of Swinging London in the mid-1960s. Daltrey's memorable stutter was initially the result of his stumbling in his first run-through in the studio, and was kept in at Lambert's suggestion.

"My Generation" was a sensation in Britain, where it reached number two on the singles chart. But its success was not repeated in America, where it stalled at number seventy-four. The song became the title track of the Who's first LP, released in Britain at the end of 1965 and in the United States in early 1966. The album also contained such Townshend-penned teen anthems as "The Kids Are Alright," "Out in the Street," and "Circles" (which was unaccountably deleted from *My Generation*'s U.S. edition). The album reached the Top Five in the band's homeland, but in America it was lost amid a flood of British Invasion acts.

By the end of 1965, the pressures of touring the British Isles and Europe, combined with Townshend assuming the leadership role that had previously been held by Daltrey, took its toll upon the Who. The tensions within the band manifested themselves in Copenhagen, where Daltrey, angered by Moon's jibes at his vocal abilities and by the drummer's prodigious pill-popping, physically attacked the drummer, leaving him nearly unconscious and prompting his bandmates to ask Daltrey to leave the group. Following a cooling-off period, and Daltrey's promise to keep his hands to himself, the hatchet was buried.

NO SUBSTITUTIONS

Frustrated with producer Shel Talmy's dictatorial approach, the Who split from Decca Records and signed to Reaction, a label run by British rock impresario Robert Stigwood. The change in labels resulted in a rash of legal disputes and competing singles releases. Meanwhile, the personal tensions within the band continued to fester. Entwistle and Moon, who'd incurred Townshend's and Daltrey's wrath after failing to show for a gig in May 1966, briefly considered leaving to form their own band. They'd fantasized naming their new group Led Zeppelin, a moniker that noted London session guitarist Jimmy Page would later borrow when forming his own band.

The Who's next single was the self-produced "Substitute," which marked a substantial leap forward for the band. Although Townshend later claimed that the song was a parody of the Rolling Stones' "19th Nervous Breakdown," its lyrics suggest otherwise. Its deceptively simple pop structure actually masked a vivid meditation on pretense and inauthenticity. When Townshend's line "I look all white, but my dad was black" was judged to be too controversial for U.S. airplay, the band re-recorded the line as "I try walking forward but my feet walk back" for Stateside consumption. Despite the revision, the song didn't make the American charts, although it reached the British Top Five.

Kit Lambert took over production duties for the Who's next single, "I'm a Boy," which offered an early glimpse of the band's future conceptual ventures. Townshend had originally written the song as part of a never-completed science fiction concept project. Removed from its original futuristic context, the catchy gender-confusion vignette gave the band another British Top Five hit.

In an effort to defuse tensions within the band, Townshend and Lambert suggested that the other three members try writing songs for the Who's second album, which would be released in the United Kingdom as *A Quick One* and in the United States as *Happy Jack*. Daltrey's and Moon's contributions were serviceable enough, but Entwistle's songs "Boris the Spider" and "Whiskey Man" were genuinely impressive, revealing a macabre sensibility and a dark sense of humor that would remain key elements in his future songwriting efforts.

But it was a Townshend composition, the infectious "Happy Jack," that finally gave the Who the U.S. Top Forty hit that had long eluded them. The song, partially inspired by his recollections of childhood trips to the Isle of Man with his father, managed to capture youth's innocence as well as its casual cruelty, a dichotomy that was further reflected in the track's ironic, sing-songy la-la backing vocals.

Equally significant was Townshend's "A Quick One While He's Away," a multi-part mini-opera that pointed the way toward the larger conceptual projects that the Who would soon pioneer. The piece was originally encouraged by Lambert, who needed more material to fill out *A Quick One*'s second side, and suggested that Townshend try writing a ten-minute song to fill the gap. Townshend balked at that idea, but was more receptive to Lambert's alternate suggestion that he build an extended track out of five shorter pieces.

In its nine-minute length, "A Quick One While He's Away" introduced a series of distinct musical themes and characters, telling the story of a lonely woman who, in her lover's absence, has an affair. On her man's return, she tearfully confesses her infidelity, and is ultimately forgiven.

Townshend would construct another multi-part story-song, "Rael," for the band's third album, *The Who Sell Out*, released in late 1967. Townshend had originally intended "Rael"—which contained some musical themes that would reappear on the Who's subsequent rock opera *Tommy*—as part of another never-completed science fiction concept project. He had originally intended the piece as a vehicle for Arthur Brown, whose flamboyant stage theatrics had won him a deal with Track Records, the new Lambert/Stamp-run label for which the Who now recorded. (Brown didn't end up cutting Townshend material but, recording as the Crazy World of Arthur Brown, he would score a major international hit the following year with the Lambert-produced "Fire.")

"Rael" wasn't the only visionary aspect of *The Who Sell Out*. The album was structured to resemble a radio broadcast, with the songs framed by tongue-in-cheek jingles, advertisements, and public service announcements. The format was patterned after that of Radio London, one of several pirate radio stations that were then popular in England, which themselves emulated the flashy, hyperactive sound of American Top Forty radio.

The Who Sell Out was both conceptually ambitious and sonically compelling, offering a cohesive long-form listening experience as well as a cogent satire of the pandering pop milieu that had given the Who its initial fame. *Sell Out* also offered withering commentary on modern consumerism, via humorous fake commercial spots for deodorant, pimple cream, a body-building course, and Heinz baked beans. Those ads were echoed in the album's memorable cover art, which depicted each band member delivering a cartoonish testimonial for one of the aforementioned products.

Beyond its conceptual and satirical accoutrements, *The Who Sell Out* featured some of the Who's catchiest songs and strongest performances yet, including such memorable Townshend tunes as "I Can't Reach You," "Mary Anne with the Shaky Hand," and "I Can See for Miles." The latter, cited by many fans as the Who's greatest pop single, was a masterpiece of production by Lambert, who seamlessly integrated parts recorded in London, New York, and Los Angeles. "I Can See for Miles" would be the Who's only U.S. Top Ten U.S. single. Despite the song's breakthrough success in America, its disappointing chart showing in Britain was a key impetus in Townshend's decision to stop attempting to write hit singles.

Although they would eventually reap substantial commercial success in America, the Who made relatively little Stateside headway during the mid-1960s British Invasion, watching most of their singles gain little attention while such contemporaries as the Beatles, the Rolling Stones, the Animals, the Kinks, the Hollies, the Searchers, the Yardbirds, and the Zombies stormed the American charts.

Unlike most of those bands, the Who did not undertake a major American tour until the summer of 1967, by which time the British Invasion's unpretentious, singles-oriented sensibility had begun to give way to a more album-oriented, self-consciously serious attitude that would soon manifest itself in the Who's musical output.

The Who's first U.S. tour found them opening for cuddly popsters Herman's Hermits, whose teen fan base was hardly the ideal audience for the confrontational mayhem of the Who's live performances. The trek opened with a week-long run at New York's RKO Theater, as part of an all-star musical extravaganza staged by New York disc jockey Murray the K. The show required the Who to play a ten-minute set three times per day, with each set climaxing in the gear-smashing pyrotechnics that now routinely ended Who performances. Over the course of the week, the band managed to destroy five guitars, four speaker cabinets, twenty-two microphones, and sixteen pieces of percussion equipment.

More prodigious destruction occurred later that summer when Moon, celebrating his twenty-first birthday with members of Herman's Hermits, trashed a meeting room at a Holiday Inn in Flint, Michigan, before driving a Lincoln Continental into the motel's swimming pool. Moon lost one of his front teeth in the melee, and was taken by helicopter to a medical facility. Though the drummer could have drowned or served prison time, the two bands pooled their money to reimburse the hotel for damages.

The Who had actually begun their assault on America in June with a landmark appearance at the historic Monterey Pop Festival, a star-studded event that kicked off the Summer of Love and served as an unofficial death knell for the sort of mainstream gigs that the band would play for most of the summer. The Who's now road-tested visual act came close to stealing the thunder from career-launching performances by Janis Joplin and Jimi Hendrix. In fact, Hendrix was scheduled to perform the same night as the Who. Because Hendrix had now appropriated Townshend's guitar-smashing routine, the two guitarists flipped a coin backstage to determine the running order. Townshend won the toss and the Who played first. Hendrix still managed to wow the crowd, setting fire to his guitar in an effort to top Townshend.

The Monterey International Pop Festival (1967)

"Monterey Pop" (June 16–18, 1967) was the first and perhaps the most successful multi-day rock festival ever held. The festival took place at the Monterey (CA) County Fairgrounds, site of the venerable Monterey Jazz Festival. The festival board of governors—including music executive Lou Adler, John Phillips of the Mamas and the Papas, Paul McCartney, and Paul Simon—announced that all net proceeds would be donated to charity, so thirty acts performed for expenses only (save for Indian sitar master Ravi Shankar, who was paid $3,000). The weather was excellent, and services—including sanitation, security, and medical care—were more than adequate for a crowd estimated at 200,000 spread over three days. Like its jazz predecessor, Monterey offered seats (priced at $3.50–$6.50) as well as a $1 daily general admission; camping was available within a mile of, but not on, the fairgrounds.

Their Monterey Pop performances had a profound impact on the careers of several artists. Soul singer Otis Redding's well-practiced but furiously energetic set brought the largely white crowd to its feet—a potential career breakthrough for this gifted artist, who died in a plane crash the following December. The Jimi Hendrix Experience made its American debut at Monterey, two months before the U.S. release of *Are You Experienced*, and the audience roared its approval as Hendrix set fire to his guitar at the climax of an intense set.

His album reached the Billboard Top Five and remained on the chart for two years.

Janis Joplin trembled with anxiety as her band, Big Brother and the Holding Company, played out of tune on their blues showpiece, "Ball and Chain." They earned a standing ovation anyway, and were promptly signed to Columbia Records by company president Clive Davis, who was in the audience.

The Byrds, Canned Heat, Electric Flag, the Grateful Dead, Jefferson Airplane, Steve Miller Band, Simon and Garfunkel, the Mamas and the Papas, Lou Rawls, and the Who all performed at Monterey. Director D.A. Pennebaker kept the cameras rolling, and his documentary *Monterey Pop* was released the following year. (The original seventy-eight-minute film was expanded later into a multi-disc DVD set with a running time of nearly four hours.)

Andy Schwartz

Comedian/musician Tom Smothers, who'd served as one of the MCs at Monterey, was impressed with the Who and invited them to perform on his and his brother Dick's CBS-TV variety show *The Smothers Brothers Comedy Hour*—by far the hippest and most politically conscious network show of the period—that September.

By now, Moon was routinely packing his drum kit with explosives, in order to blow out the head of his bass drum at the end of the band's shows. Not surprisingly, CBS's fire marshals forbade such shenanigans for the studio taping. Undaunted, Moon convinced a stagehand to pack extra explosives in the drum, in order to end the band's TV performance with an extra flourish. The ensuing blast, occurring soon after Townshend smashed his guitar and shoved its neck through the speaker cabinet, was more than even Moon had bargained for. It deafened Townshend for twenty minutes, sliced open Moon's arm with cymbal shrapnel, blew Daltrey off his feet, and caused veteran actress Bette Davis, waiting backstage, to faint into the arms of fellow guest Mickey Rooney. Meanwhile, the cameras continued rolling as Tom Smothers strolled over for a post-boom interview. A still-dazed Townshend grabbed Smothers's acoustic guitar and smashed it against the floor.

TOMMY, CAN YOU HEAR ME?

The Who attempted to consolidate the success of "I Can See for Miles" and the notoriety from their Monterey Pop Festival and TV appearances, but the subsequent singles "Dogs" and "Magic Bus" failed to generate substantial chart action. The band was also unhappy when their American label, Decca, issued the deceptively titled *Magic Bus: The Who on Tour*—a ragtag assortment of singles tracks that had been issued in Britain as *Direct Hits* the previous month—in November 1968. Despite its scattershot quality, it proved to be their biggest-selling U.S. LP to date, rising to number thirty-nine on *Billboard*'s album chart.

Meanwhile, the Who's creative output was suffering from tour fatigue. Townshend felt desperate to break out of the pop-single mode and record his ambitious "rock opera" about a deaf, dumb, and blind boy who becomes a modern messiah. Frustrated and consuming large quantities of drink and drugs, Townshend found himself unable to work. It was at that point that he became a follower of the Indian spiritual leader Meher Baba, whose teachings would become a key influence on Townshend's life and work.

Baba, who had in 1925 taken a vow of silence that he would maintain until his death in 1969, communicated through writings. He did not proselytize or attempt to convert followers. He taught that life was an "illusion," and that people exist mostly in a dream state, unable to grasp the infinite nature of reality. His followers were asked to deny greed, lust, and anger, in order to begin a journey back to God.

His embrace of Baba's teachings helped to clear Townshend's troubled mind, allowing him to focus on the major project that had been germinating for the prior two years. A newfound spirituality infused Townshend's new rock opera. After toying with such titles as *The Amazing Journey* and *Deaf Dumb and Blind Boy*, he settled on *Tommy*, partially because he thought his main character's name sounded essentially British, and because the name contained the mystical syllable "om."

Kit Lambert gave Townshend a wide berth in order to create his musically and thematically ambitious opus. Meanwhile, Townshend's often fractious bandmates, uncharacteristically, united around the album's creation. To bring the band into the process of constructing what would be their masterpiece, Townshend enlisted Entwistle to write songs for the supporting characters Cousin Kevin and Uncle Ernie, and to utilize his talents on French horn. Moon, meanwhile, was credited with writing "Tommy's Holiday Camp."

The Who interrupted *Tommy*'s eighteen-month recording process to perform at the Woodstock Music and Art Fair on August 17, 1969. Despite the exposure to an audience of over 600,000, the band wasn't happy to be there. They had only agreed to the gig because they needed the money, but when they arrived, they learned that the promoters were unable to pay them. The band refused to perform until cash was procured. By the time the band was asked to take the stage at 4 A.M., the musicians had been surreptitiously dosed with LSD. A seething Townshend knocked over filmmaker Michael Wadleigh, who was shooting a feature documentary on the event, when one of Wadleigh's cameras got too close to the guitarist during the set. He also clobbered Abbie Hoffman with his guitar when the Yippie activist attempted to commandeer a stage microphone.

The Woodstock Music and Art Festival (1969)

The Woodstock Festival (August 15–18, 1969) was the culmination of a two-year period during which such events became a familiar feature of the pop culture landscape. It was held on 600 acres of pastureland in Bethel, New York—50 miles west of the actual town of Woodstock—and drew an estimated 450,000 fans, most without tickets. This was nearly double the number anticipated by promoters Michael Lang, John Roberts, Artie Kornfeld, and Joel Rosenman, the oldest of whom was twenty-six.

The "miracle" of Woodstock was simply that—despite drenching rain, backstage chaos, a seventeen-mile traffic backup, and drug taking on a massive scale— nearly everyone made it through alive. (There were three accidental deaths in the course of the weekend.) The outcome might have been much worse if not for the heroic volunteer efforts of communes like the Hog Farm. These counterculture veterans prepared large quantities of free food, assisted the overtaxed medical staff, and did much to create the festival's near-mythic sense of community.

Richie Havens played the first set at Woodstock, beginning at 5:00 PM on Friday. The festival had been planned as a series of evening concerts but by the second day, to pacify the immense crowd, the organizers decided to have live music played nearly around the clock. Among the thirty-one acts that took the stage were Joan Baez, The Band, Creedence Clearwater Revival, Crosby, Stills, Nash and Young, the Grateful Dead, Arlo Guthrie, Jefferson Airplane, Mountain, Santana, Ravi Shankar, Ten Years After, and the Who. With delays caused by thunderstorms, transportation problems, and disputes over payment, the festival ended up nine hours behind schedule. When Jimi Hendrix finally took the stage at 9 A.M. on Monday, he played to a trash-filled and nearly empty field.

Woodstock, directed by Michael Wadleigh, won the Academy Award for Documentary Feature in 1970. A three-LP soundtrack album topped the *Billboard* chart for four weeks and sold more than two million copies; its two-LP sequel *Woodstock Two* (1971) reached number seven and was certified gold. The festival gave rise to memoirs and photography books, and its signature illustration (a white bird perched on a guitar) has adorned countless T-shirts and coffee mugs. Woodstock '69 brought forth the forgettable Woodstock '89 and the disastrous Woodstock '94, where angry fans set fires and looted concessions. On July 1, 2006, the Bethel Woods Center for the Arts opened on the site of the festival. The inaugural season included a performance by Crosby, Stills, Nash and Young.

A. S.

Despite the less-than-ideal circumstances, the Who's timing could not have been more propitious. As dawn broke over Yasgur's farm, they played "See Me, Feel Me," "Pinball Wizard," and the instrumental "Sparks," from the unreleased *Tommy*. As captured in Wadleigh's hugely successful *Woodstock* film, the scene carried immense resonance, instantly establishing the Who as Aquarian-age icons. Three weeks later, the band reprised most of their Woodstock set list at another gigantic rock festival, this one on the Isle of Wight.

The Who's high-profile, high-energy performance in the *Woodstock* film helped to make the LP *Tommy*, released in May 1969, a massive commercial and critical success on both sides of the Atlantic. The groundbreaking two-LP set closed the door on the Who's days as makers of pop singles, and made the band's Mod epoch seem like a thing of the distant past.

Tommy was hardly the first pop concept album, or even the first to be built around an extended narrative. For example, the Pretty Things' seminal *S.F. Sorrow* had been released the year before, and Townshend admitted that it had influenced him. But *Tommy* was the first album to be billed as a "rock opera," and the first of its kind to make a substantial impression on mainstream popular culture.

Tommy's plotline charts the spiritual journey of Tommy Walker, who becomes deaf, blind, and mute during childhood, after seeing his mother's lover murdered by his father. He becomes a target for abuse and molestation by relatives, endures his parents' misguided attempts to cure him, and becomes a pinball champion. After being cured of his afflictions, he becomes the leader of a messianic cult, but is eventually abandoned by his followers.

Beyond its ambitious lyrical themes, *Tommy* greatly expanded the Who's musical and compositional palette. The album's richly complex, layered arrangements were generally built around Townshend's acoustic guitar and incorporated an assortment of new instrumental textures.

Tommy would have a lengthy shelf life, and would be revived in various incarnations in the years to come. In 1972, rock entrepreneur Lou Reizner staged an all-star version of *Tommy*, as both a new studio recording and a concert presentation at London's Rainbow Theatre. Both featured the London Symphony Orchestra, with various roles performed by such guest singers as Sandy Denny, David Essex, Richie Havens, Ringo Starr, Rod Stewart, and Steve Winwood. That version would subsequently be staged in Australia, with Moon appearing in the role of Uncle Ernie alongside a cast of Australian rock performers.

Controversial filmmaker Ken Russell would turn *Tommy* into a big-budget 1975 feature film, with Daltrey starring as Tommy and Moon reprising his role as Uncle Ernie, along with a cast that included Ann-Margret, Oliver Reed, Jack Nicholson, Eric Clapton, Elton John, and Tina Turner. Townshend substantially reworked and fleshed out the storyline for the film, altering some key plot points and updating the story's time frame. Although the film received mixed reviews, Daltrey's work demonstrated sufficient screen presence to allow the singer to build a prolific and varied acting career.

The Who would also revive *Tommy* on stage in 1989, performing the complete work in concert in Los Angeles and New York, with guest performances by the likes of Elton John, Phil Collins, Billy Idol, and Patti LaBelle. Their performance of *Tommy* became a television special and home-video release.

In 1993, Townshend and playwright Des McAnuff wrote and produced a Broadway musical adaptation of *Tommy* that added a new song, reworked some old lyrics, and substantially altered the story's ending. The stage musical became a Tony Award–winning smash, and was revived for subsequent touring productions.

But in 1969, before *Tommy* became a pop-culture touchstone, it became the focus of the Who's live shows, with its epic narrative condensed into a lean hour-long stage set. The band rose to the challenge of the material, and their dramatic performances helped to establish the foursome's status as a bigger-than-life live act.

One highlight of the *Tommy* tour was a week-long stand at the Fillmore East in New York, capped by an appearance on *The Ed Sullivan Show* on October 5, 1969. On December 14, the band announced its triumphant return to England with a show at the London Coliseum, in which the band played *Tommy* in its entirety, backed by an orchestra.

The Second Atlanta International Pop Festival (1970)

The first "Atlanta Pop," held July 4–5, 1969, was a marginally profitable event that drew 150,000 fans to Atlanta International Raceway. For the June 3–5, 1970 sequel, organizers relocated to Middle Georgia Raceway in Byron, Georgia, ninety miles south of Atlanta and two miles off Interstate 75. This second Atlanta Pop is remembered today as "the Woodstock of the South," but at the time it was largely overlooked by the major media on both coasts.

By dusk of the first day, there were approximately 200,000 people on and around the site and all of the by-now-familiar attributes of a major rock festival—blazing heat, inadequate sanitation, casual nudity, endless traffic backups—were suddenly and startlingly present in conservative rural Georgia. Overwhelmed state and local police made almost no arrests after the first day. On a footpath leading into the site, drug dealers set up tables to hawk their wares as if selling household utensils at a flea market.

Local favorites the Allman Brothers Band played the first set in mid-afternoon on Friday. During a break in their performance, it was announced that the gates had been thrown open and the festival was now free. On Saturday, the temperature hit 115°F: it was literally too hot to play, and the music did not resume until late afternoon.

In the course of the weekend, a crowd that swelled to nearly 500,000 heard performances by (among others) Cactus, Captain Beefheart, the Chambers Brothers, Chicago, B.B. King, Mott the Hoople, Mountain, Poco, Procol Harum, Terry Reid, Ravi Shankar, Spirit, Ten Years After, and Johnny Winter. Shortly before midnight on Saturday, Jimi Hendrix performed for the largest audience of his career. Fireworks lit up the night sky as the guitarist rampaged through his greatest Woodstock hit, "The Star-Spangled Banner."

At 4 A.M. Monday, the Allmans returned to play the last official set of the festival. But other bands continued intermittently into the afternoon, and Atlanta Pop ended only when the Memphis cast of *Hair* led a few hundred stragglers in a sing-along version of "Aquarius (Let the Sunshine In)."

A. S.

The Who followed the groundbreaking, elaborately recorded *Tommy* with its polar opposite, the back-to-basics *Live at Leeds*, an unadorned concert recording which captured the raw crunch of the band's then-current stage act. Rather than the *Tommy* material that had come to dominate their shows, the live disc—recorded on February 14, 1970, at the University of Leeds—combined punchy readings of "Substitute," "My Generation," and "Magic Bus" with thunderous interpretations of Mose Allison's "Young Man Blues," Eddie Cochran's "Summertime Blues," and Johnny Kidd and the Pirates' early Brit rock and roll classic "Shakin' All Over."

Live at Leeds was something altogether different from the quirky pop of the band's early singles and the layered art rock of *Tommy*. Daltrey seemed to explode through the speakers, and Townshend's furious guitar work had evolved tremendously from the days when he claimed to be so self-conscious about his talent that he'd developed his arm-flailing style to mask it. Decades after its release, rock critics continue to list *Live at Leeds* among rock's greatest in-concert albums.

WHO'S BACK

While *Live at Leeds* filled public demand for new Who product, and gave Townshend time to prepare another major thematic work: the futuristic rock opera *Lifehouse*, which he envisioned as both an album and a film. The concept ultimately proved too complex to execute, creating stresses within the band, leading to a falling out with longtime producer/manager Kit Lambert, and driving Townshend to the brink of a nervous breakdown.

Although *Lifehouse* would not be completed, several of its songs formed the basis of *Who's Next*, which is widely considered to be the Who's greatest album. Although ostensibly a collection of unconnected songs, *Who's Next* presented a seamless package of serious rock music that connected with the audience that had grown up with the band. Much of the credit for the album's powerful sound could be attributed to new producer Glyn Johns, who took over after Townshend and Lambert parted ways.

Among the songs rescued from the aborted *Lifehouse* were, "Behind Blue Eyes" and "Won't Get Fooled Again," both of which were hit singles in the United Kingdom and the United States. From the opening synthesizer riff of "Baba O'Reilly" to the screaming dénouement of "Won't Get Fooled Again," *Who's Next* was an inspired blend of emotion, intellect, craft, and raw power.

Townshend didn't allow the non-appearance of *Lifehouse* to keep him from beginning work on another rock opera, this one with an earthier, more auto-biographical edge. The protagonist of the new project, *Quadrophenia*, was a Mod named Jimmy.

Townshend wanted to recapture what it was like to be a teen rebel and simultaneously encapsulate ten years of the Who's existence. The album's title referred to the four-sided personality of the band members. Townshend under-lined the concept in the booklet that accompanied the album insisting the four distinct personalities of Jimmy the Mod actually reflected the four members of the Who.

In some ways, Jimmy's story is like Tommy's, a quest for self-awareness and a sense of place and purpose. Rather than witnessing a murder, Jimmy is trau-matized by everyday life and beginning to suspect that the affectations of his teen-rebel phase were as illusory as his family bond, his girlfriend's constancy, his job and his drug intake. Like Tommy and Townshend, Jimmy wants to discover the meaning of life. After all of his illusions are dashed on a two-day trip to Brighton in 1964 during the height of the Mod-Rockers clashes, he ends up stranded on a rock out at sea, undergoing a spiritual awakening in a drench-ing rain (during the closing cut, "Love, Reign O'er Me").

The material from *Quadrophenia* worked better on the album than on stage, as it necessitated the use of synthesizers, sound effects, and long instru-mental interludes that often meandered in front of the paying customers. Despite its complicated story line and murky themes *Quadrophenia* proved to be one of the Who's biggest selling albums, hitting the number two slot on the *Billboard* album chart.

Although the Who continued to develop as a formidable live act, they would never approach such creative peaks in the studio again. Perhaps the June 1974 departure of Kit Lambert and Chris Stamp as managers (replaced by Bill Curbishley) was more than just an administrative move. It marked the end of one of the most creative and productive management teams in rock and roll history. Meanwhile, on May 31, 1976, the group's show in Charlton entered the *Guinness Book of World Records* as the loudest performance by any rock band.

As a new decade dawned, each member of the Who pursued outside proj-ects. Entwistle released two albums, *Smash Your Head Against the Wall* (1971) and *Whistle Rymes* (1972), spotlighting his sardonic lyrics and voice. Daltrey recorded a series of middling solo efforts, tackling blustery hard rock and lightweight folk-pop. Moon moved to Malibu and led the decadent rock star life.

Only Townshend's solo releases stand alongside the work of the Who. Espe-cially notable was his first solo album, *Who Came First*, a deeply affecting tribute to Maher Baba and his devotees released in 1972. *Rough Mix* (1977), a collaboration with Ronnie Lane, a fellow Baba devotee and member of the Small Faces, was also a fine understated work. *Empty Glass* (1980) was Townshend's hardest rocking solo album, at times bringing a Who-like fury to what turned out to be a commercially viable collection of songs. Townshend even took time to pursue a job in publishing and author a book of his own, *Horse's Neck* (1985) a quirky collection of metaphorical short stories.

In 1975 *The Who by Numbers* produced the humorous hit "Squeeze Box," but was otherwise dominated by Townshend's pensive introspection. And 1978's

Who Are You proved to be the last album by the Who's classic lineup. Just weeks after its release, Keith Moon died, overdosing on the prescription he'd been taking to combat his alcoholism.

With Moon's friend, ex-Small Faces drummer Kenney Jones, taking over his vacant chair, the band went on tour to support *Who Are You*. But disaster struck at a Who concert in Cincinnati on December 3, 1979, when eleven people were killed in a stampede for unreserved "festival seating." The band learned in April 1981 that their former manager, producer, and friend Kit Lambert died from a fall down a flight of stairs at his mother's house. Meanwhile, punk rock had emerged and shunted the Who aside with all the other rock "dinosaurs."

Although a capable drummer, Jones lacked Moon's fiery unpredictability, and for many fans the "real" Who ended with *Who Are You*. Nonetheless, the band recorded two studio albums with Jones on drums—*Face Dances* (1981) and *It's Hard* (1982). Largely on the strength of the opening cut, "You Better, You Bet," *Face Dances* sold well, reaching number four on the U.S. charts and number two in the United Kingdom. *It's Hard*, produced by Glyn Johns, yielded the concert staple "Eminence Front," but critical reaction to the album was lukewarm. It would be another twenty-four years before the Who would release another studio album.

Ironically, it wasn't until after Entwistle died—from a cocaine-induced heart attack on June 27, 2002—that the fire returned for Townshend and Daltrey, now the heart and soul of the Who. Entwistle died on the eve of an American tour, leaving the two survivors to make what they called the hardest decision in Who history: whether to carry on without the "Ox." They weighed the economics, possible lawsuits by promoters, loyalty of, and to, their fans, and their own responsibility, and chose to carry on.

In October 2006, Townshend and Daltrey released a new Who studio album, *Endless Wire*. *Endless Wire* is a fascinating work, pulling fragments from the Who's past out of the fire and recasting them in the Internet age. At the center of the album is yet another mini opera, called "Wire & Glass," which is based on Townshend's then-unpublished novella *The Boy Who Heard Music*. It is both elegiac and innovative reflecting an ending and perhaps a new beginning.

TIMELINE

March 1964
Drummer Doug Sandom quits the Detours, clearing the way for Keith Moon to join Detours members Roger Daltrey, Pete Townshend, and John Entwistle in the band that would eventually become the Who.

July 14, 1964
Pete Townshend smashes his guitar on stage for the first time, at the Railway Tavern in Harrow, Middlesex.

August 1964
The band, now known as the High Numbers, release their unsuccessful first single, "I'm the Face" backed with "Zoot Suit."

September 1964
Filmmakers Kit Lambert and Chris Stamp attend a High Numbers gig and are so impressed that they agree to manage the band.

November 1964
The band changes its name to the Who and begins playing a regular Tuesday night gig at the Marquee in London.

January 1965
The Who record their first single, "I Can't Explain," with producer Shel Talmy.

July 1965
The Who's second single, "Anyway Anyhow Anywhere" becomes the theme song for the popular British pop TV show *Ready Steady Go!*

November 5, 1965
The Who release their single, "My Generation."

December 3, 1965
The group's debut album, *My Generation*, is released in Britain.

February 1966
The Who record "Substitute," their first self-produced single.

June 18, 1967
The Who perform at the Monterey Pop Festival in California.

July 14, 1967
The Who begin their first official U.S. tour, opening for Herman's Hermits.

September 17, 1967
The Who makes a memorably chaotic appearance on TV's *Smothers Brothers Comedy Hour*.

November 25, 1967
"I Can See for Miles" becomes the Who's first American Top Ten hit.

January 1968
The Who Sell Out, the band's first concept album, is released.

February 22, 1968
The group begins a three-night gig at the Fillmore West, becoming the highest-paid act to have played at the venue.

August 7, 1968
The Who perform in New York City's Central Park.

May 1969
The Who's first rock opera, *Tommy*, is released.

August 16, 1969
The Who performs at the Woodstock Music and Art Fair.

August 31, 1969
The Who perform at the Isle of Wight festival, sharing the bill with Bob Dylan.

October 5, 1969
The Who perform on *The Ed Sullivan Show*.

Dec. 14, 1969
The Who performs *Tommy* in its entirety, backed by an orchestra, at the London Opera House.

February 14, 1970
The band performs at Leeds University. A recording of this show will be released in June 1970 as *Live at Leeds*.

August 1971
Who's Next is released.

October–November 1973

Another Pete Townshend–penned rock opera, *Quadrophenia*, is released.

May 31, 1976
The Who's concert at Charlton soccer stadium enters the *Guinness Book of World Records* as the loudest performance ever by a rock band.

August 18, 1978
Who Are You is released. It will be the Who's last album with Keith Moon.

September 7, 1978
Keith Moon dies in London, of an overdose of the drug prescribed to control his alcoholism.

January 1979
Former Faces drummer Kenney Jones replaces Moon as the band's drummer.

December 3, 1979
Eleven audience members are crushed to death at a Who concert in Cincinnati's Riverfront Stadium.

March 1981
Face Dances, the first Who album with Kenney Jones as drummer, is released.

June 27, 2002
John Entwistle dies of a cocaine-induced heart attack while on tour in Las Vegas.

October 31, 2006
Endless Wire, the first album by the surviving duo of Pete Townshend and Roger Daltrey, is released.

SELECTED DISCOGRAPHY

The Who

My Generation, 1965
A Quick One (Happy Jack), 1966
The Who Sell Out, 1967
Tommy, 1969
Live at Leeds, 1970

Who's Next, 1971
Quadrophenia, 1973
The Who by Numbers, 1975
Who Are You, 1978
Thirty Years of Maximum R&B, 1994

Pete Townshend

Who Came First, 1972
Rough Mix (with Ronnie Lane), 1977
Empty Glass, 1980

NOTES

1. Dafydd Rees and Luke Crampton, *Encyclopedia of Rock Stars* (Dorling Kindersley, 1996), p. 923.
2. *Mojo*, December 2006, p. 83.

FURTHER READING

Barnes, Richard. *The Who: Maximum R&B*. New York: St. Martin's, 1982.

Clayson, Alan. *Beat Merchants: The Origins, History, Impact and Rock Legacy of the 1960s British Pop Groups*. London: Blandford, 1996.

Giuliano, Geoffrey. *Behind Blue Eyes: The Life of Pete Townshend*. New York: Dutton, 1996.

Levy, Shawn. *Ready, Steady, Go!: The Smashing Rise and Giddy Fall of Swinging London*. New York: Doubleday, 2002.

Marsh, Dave. *Before I Get Old: The Story of the Who*. New York: St. Martin's, 1983.

Neil, Andy and Matt Kent. *Anyway, Anyhow, Anywhere: The Complete Chronicle of The Who, 1958–1978*. New York: Friedman/Fairfax, 2002.

Courtesy of Photofest.

The Byrds

Scott Schinder

COSMIC TROUBADOURS

As much as any American rock act of the 1960s, the Byrds embodied their era's ideals of creative risk taking, restless experimentation, and artistic evolution. The Byrds' development paralleled a period of massive changes in popular music and culture, and the band remained on rock's cutting edge for most of its existence.

Through a variety of personnel shuffles and stylistic shifts, the Byrds spearheaded more than one movement that altered the course of popular music, and many of the group's innovations have become deeply ingrained into rock's sonic vocabulary.

In their original incarnation, the Byrds were widely celebrated as America's answer to the Beatles, and even acknowledged as such by the Fab Four themselves.

The Byrds pioneered the folk-rock genre by applying jangly twelve-string guitars and organic vocal harmonies to Bob Dylan songs, traditional material, and the band members' own thoughtful compositions.

But the Byrds weren't content to stick with the style that they helped to invent. After scoring a pair of genre-defining folk-rock hits with "Mr. Tambourine Man" and "Turn! Turn! Turn," the band helped to usher in the psychedelic era with the landmark space-rock epic "Eight Miles High." Within a few years, they became the first major long-haired rock act to make the then-radical move of embracing the traditions of country music.

Beyond their immense influence as a group, the Byrds' various lineups hosted a remarkable array of individuals who would continue to make significant music after leaving the group. In addition to singer, guitarist, and sole charter member Roger McGuinn, notable Byrds alumni included Gene Clark, whose broodingly poetic songwriting and frustratingly spotty solo career would make him one of rock's most intriguing cult figures; David Crosby, who would achieve massive commercial success with Crosby, Stills, and Nash and fight a very public battle with drug addiction; and Gram Parsons, the charismatic self-styled cosmic cowboy whose brief but pivotal tenure as a Byrd was instrumental in putting country rock on the map, and whose remarkable post-Byrds career would be cut short by an early drug-induced death.

The Byrds' commercial peak was relatively brief, encompassing their first two years as a recording act, during which they scored seven Top Forty singles. But the band's propensity for rebirth and reinvention resulted in a long and prolific life span, one fraught with frustration, tension, and disappointment but which also yielded a remarkably large and diverse body of music. Although their record sales never matched those of the Beatles and the Beach Boys, history has shown the Byrds' long-term influence to be comparable with those groups.

Despite their crucial role in rock's evolution, none of the Byrds' founding members had much experience playing electric rock music prior to the group's formation. Instead, they graduated to rock from the worlds of folk and bluegrass.

Before launching the Byrds, Jim McGuinn (who would change his first name to Roger in 1965, as part of his conversion to the spiritual sect Subud), Gene Clark, and David Crosby were all young veterans of the folk music world, having performed on the early 1960s coffeehouse scene as well as the more commercial end of the folk world.

Of the Byrds' five founding members, the Chicago-born McGuinn had the most prior show business experience. He became active on his hometown's folk scene during his teens, and later worked as a sideman for the popular mainstream folk acts the Limelighters and the Chad Mitchell Trio. He also backed pop star Bobby Darin as Darin was exploring folk, and found session work with Judy Collins, Hoyt Axton, and Simon and Garfunkel. By the time the Beatles hit the American charts in 1964, folk's popularity was on the wane, and McGuinn was in New York working as a staff songwriter for Darin's publishing company.

The Beatles' arrival ignited McGuinn's imagination, inspiring him to envision a fusion of the Beatles' electric energy and the lyrical substance of folk. By the spring of 1964, he was performing Beatles numbers on acoustic twelve-string guitar at the famed L.A. folk club the Troubadour. While McGuinn's Beatles covers offended some audience members, it thrilled others, including fellow restless folkie Gene Clark, who'd been harboring similar thoughts about breaking out of the acoustic ghetto.

Clark had grown up in Tipton, Missouri, with a love for country and rock and roll. By his early teens, he'd begun writing his own songs and performing with a local rock combo, the Sharks, with whom he recorded one single. When the folk boom arrived in the early 1960s, his interests turned toward acoustic. His work with some Kansas City folk groups led to an offer to join the New Christy Minstrels, an upbeat, unabashedly commercial folk-pop act that had achieved mainstream stardom with a squeaky-clean style that ignored folk's traditional topical and political edge.

After a two-album stint with the New Christy Minstrels, Clark grew frustrated and quit. Determined to play his own songs, he moved to Los Angeles. There, he became a regular at the Troubadour, where he was impressed enough by McGuinn's Beatles act that he approached him and proposed that they join forces. Not long after, McGuinn and Clark were harmonizing in a stairwell at the Troubadour; they were joined by an uninvited third voice, belonging to David Crosby.

The son of Academy Award–winning cinematographer Floyd Crosby, David grew up in Los Angeles and dropped out of drama school to pursue a musical career. He'd developed a local reputation for his beautiful tenor voice and his uncanny facility for vocal harmony—not to mention his outspoken, assertive personality. Like McGuinn and Clark, Crosby had also paid some dues in the commercial folk world, touring as a member of the white-bread act Les Baxter's Balladeers.

Beyond his musical talents, Crosby also had some helpful local connections, including access to free recording time at World Pacific, a Hollywood studio where he'd recently been cutting solo demos with producer Jim Dickson, who would become the Byrds' co-manager and play a key role in helping the band to refine its sound.

Dubbing themselves the Jet Set, the new trio recorded a series of demos that were impressive enough for Elektra Records head Jac Holtzman to offer a deal. Rechristened the Beefeaters by Holtzman in a somewhat feeble attempt to suggest that the group was British, the trio released its first and only Elektra single, "Please Let Me Love You" backed with "Don't Be Long," in mid-1964. Although the disc flopped, it offered an embryonic glimpse of the style that the Byrds would unveil a few months later.

At around the same time, McGuinn, Clark, and Crosby went to see the Beatles' first movie *A Hard Day's Night*. McGuinn later recalled coming away from the theater with a laundry list of the instruments that his band would need to compete, including the Rickenbacker electric twelve-string guitar that George Harrison played in the film—which would soon become one of McGuinn's trademarks.

Soon, the trio expanded to a quintet with the addition of two musicians who, like McGuinn, Clark, and Crosby, also lacked experience playing electric music. Enlisted to play bass was Chris Hillman, a former teenaged blue-grass mandolin prodigy who'd recorded albums as a member of the Scottsville Squirrel Barkers and the Hillmen, and who'd never played bass before. (The Scottsville Squirrel Barkers, whose LP was produced by Jim Dickson, also included guitarist Bernie Leadon, who would later play with Hillman in the Flying Burrito Brothers before becoming a founding member of the Eagles.)

Drafted as drummer was Michael Clarke, whom McGuinn and Crosby had spotted playing congas in a San Francisco coffeehouse. Although he'd never played a full drum kit in public, Clarke reportedly won the job on the strength of his physical resemblance to the Rolling Stones' Brian Jones. Clarke didn't even own a drum kit at the time; in his initial rehearsals with the new band, he kept the beat on cardboard boxes.

Despite their inexperience, the new bandmates quickly mastered their respective instruments and became a cohesive unit, spending much time recording demos and honing their sound at World Pacific. Many of those embryonic recordings would later be released in album form as *Preflyte*.

FINDING THEIR JANGLE

In November 1964, the quintet signed with Columbia Records, with some help from jazz giant Miles Davis, who also recorded for the company and made some phone calls to Columbia execs to praise the band. A few weeks later, the group officially became known as the Byrds.

Although its artist roster included Bob Dylan and the soon-to-be-famous Paul Revere and the Raiders, Columbia had been one of the last major record companies to seriously embrace rock and roll, thanks in large part to former A&R director (and TV sing-along king) Mitch Miller's long-standing aversion to teen music. But the Byrds were fortunate to be assigned to Columbia staff producer Terry Melcher. The twenty-three-year-old son of actress/singer Doris Day, Melcher was the company's resident rock specialist, having already achieved success as producer/songwriter/performer on a series of surf music hits for the company, many in collaboration with future Beach Boy Bruce Johnston. Melcher's recording and arranging skills would play a key role in crafting the Byrds' classic sound.

Paul Revere and the Raiders: Steppin' Out on Network TV

Paul Revere and the Raiders were a proto-garage band whose Revolutionary War costumes and high-stepping choreography earned them a national television audience and a string of Top Ten hits. Founded by Paul Revere (his real name), the son of pacifist Mennonites and a conscientious objector during his Vietnam War draft term, the Portland, Oregon–based quintet worked the Northwest teen dance and frat party circuit.

In 1963, the Raiders became the first rock and roll band signed to prestigious Columbia Records. That same year, Dick Clark moved his *American Bandstand* operation from Philadelphia to Los Angeles. As the group's first Columbia hit, "Steppin' Out," began to climb the charts, Clark offered them a steady gig as the house band on his new ABC network show *Where the Action Is*. It debuted in June 1965 and aired five days each week for nearly two years—not surprisingly, the most successful years of the Raiders' career.

On their Top Ten hits "Just Like Me," "Hungry," and "Kicks," L.A. producer Terry Melcher bolted Mark Lindsay's gritty white R&B voice to a driving guitar and organ instrumental attack as potent as that of British bands like the Kinks and Yardbirds. In 1971, the Raiders scored a left-field hit with "Indian Reservation." Ironically, this million-seller—the group's only number one single—marked the beginning of the Raiders' chart decline. Within a few years, they were playing casinos, state fairs, and "oldies" package shows.

Andy Schwartz

At Jim Dickson's suggestion, the song slated for the Byrds' first single was "Mr. Tambourine Man," an as-yet-unreleased Bob Dylan composition of which Dickson had obtained a demo version. The band converted Dylan's wordy original into a catchy pop tune by eliminating all but one of the verses, and adding warm, angelic harmonies and McGuinn's infectious, Bach-inspired guitar hook.

McGuinn, whose reedy lead vocal would be the track's most Dylan-esque element, would be the only Byrd to play an instrument on "Mr. Tambourine Man" and its Gene Clark–penned B-side "I Knew I'd Want You." With studio time at a premium, Melcher judged the other band members to be a bit too green to be trusted with the task. So when the debut single was recorded at Columbia's Hollywood studio on January 20 and 21, 1965, most of the playing was left to A-list session men Jerry Cole (guitar), Larry Knechtel (bass), Hal Blaine (drums), and Leon Russell (keyboards), with McGuinn playing lead guitar and Clark and Crosby providing the vocals.

Regardless of who played on it, "Mr. Tambourine Man" offered a brilliant crystallization of the Byrds' original sound, with its chiming guitars and luminous vocal blend already in place. The band's distinctive harmonies were achieved by McGuinn and Clark singing the lead in unison, with Crosby providing high harmony. McGuinn credited Columbia staff engineer Ray Gerhardt with helping him to achieve the warm, resonant trademark guitar tone, by applying copious amounts of compression when recording his parts.

At once majestic and earthy, "Mr. Tambourine Man" was unlike anything previously heard in rock. It made an immediate splash upon its release, climbing to the top slot on the U.S. pop charts at the height of the British Invasion. Its B-side was the Gene Clark composition "I Knew I'd Want You," which offered an early example of Clark's ability to merge Beatles-esque songcraft with pensive lyrical melancholy.

In March, the Byrds cut their second single; this time, Melcher was finally confident enough in the band's abilities to allow them to play on the session, which they did brilliantly. The sophomore disc repeated its predecessor's formula of a McGuinn-sung Dylan cover on the A-side and a Gene Clark composition on the flip. The former was "All I Really Want to Do," backed by the Clark original "I'll Feel a Whole Lot Better."

The same month, the Byrds began a now legendary residency at the hip Hollywood club Ciro's, a high-profile event that would cement the band's status as darlings of the emerging Hollywood rock scene. They followed their Ciro's engagement with an extended run of live work that included a series of shows with the Rolling Stones, a nationwide tour with Dick Clark's Caravan of Stars, TV appearances on various teen pop shows, and a somewhat disappointing U.K. visit that was marred by sloppy performances.

Love and the Doors: Sunset Strip Visionaries

The Byrds were not the first rock and roll act to be signed as a direct result of their appearances in the clubs of L.A.'s Sunset Strip. But their rapid rise to stardom was an important catalyst in the transformation of the Sunset scene and, by extension, the West Coast music industry. In 1963, the stages of the Strip were filled with groups in matching suits and pompadours playing generic Top 40 music in teen clubs like Gazzari's and the Whisky A Go Go. Within two years, some of the same clubs had become career launching pads for some of the most adventurous rock groups in the country.

Love was the first prominent integrated rock group of the 1960s. Lead singer and primary songwriter Arthur Lee and guitarist Johnny Echols were playing in an instrumental R&B band when they witnessed a Byrds show at Ciro's. The two black musicians abruptly changed course and recruited blonde, sweet-voiced singer-guitarist Bryan MacLean (1947–98) for their new group called Love. These three were its only constant members in the crucial years from 1965 to 1968. MacLean composed and sang lead on several key album tracks but the mercurial Arthur Lee was the group's acknowledged leader and creative guiding light.

Love's self-titled Elektra debut album, released in May 1966, spun off the mid-chart single "My Little Red Book," a radical remake (both menacing and yearning) of a Burt Bacharach/Hal David pop song. The group expanded to seven pieces on their second album *Da Capo* (January 1967). "Stephanie Knows Who" incorporated a Coltrane-style saxophone solo and "Orange Skies" floated on a light Latin rhythm. "7 and 7 Is," Love's only hit single, was a furious proto-punk rocker that climaxed with the sound of a nuclear blast.

Drug use, lineup changes, and personality clashes brought the group to the brink of dissolution. But Love pulled itself together for one more album: *Forever Changes*. A commercial failure in the United States when issued in November 1967, today it is hailed as a masterpiece of visionary lyrics and prescient musical fusion. The basic band tracks are played with intuitive dexterity, and adorned by stirring horn and string arrangements. In 2003, *Rolling Stone* magazine ranked *Forever Changes* at number forty on its list of the "500 Greatest Albums of All Time."

Lee disbanded Love in 1968 but then reconstituted the group with new members for a few less impressive albums. In the 1990s the singer served a five-year prison sentence following his conviction on a firearms charge—a victim of California's "three strikes" law. Upon his release in 2001, Lee mounted a successful performing comeback with a sturdy new Love lineup that sometimes included Johnny Echols. Arthur Lee died of leukemia on August 3, 2006 at age sixty-one.

After Jim Morrison (vocals), Ray Manzarek (organ), Robbie Krieger (guitar), and John Densmore (drums) formed the Doors, their first career goal was to become as big as Love. The Doors paid their dues on the same L.A. club scene and were signed to the same label, Elektra. Jim Morrison's lyrics, like Arthur Lee's writing on *Forever Changes*, tapped into the undercurrent of dread that ran through American society in a time of war, social unrest, and mass political protest.

But unlike their Sunset Strip predecessors, the Doors worked well with their Elektra producers, played live at every opportunity, and maintained their internal cohesion. In Jim Morrison, the group had a forceful but melodic singer whose intense charisma blended danger and sensuality. In March 1967, the first billboard ever erected on the Sunset Strip advertised their debut album *The Doors*, and in July "Light My Fire" became the band's first Number One single.

Critics derided albums like *Waiting for the Sun* (1968) as pretentious and over-arranged, but the fans didn't care: of the eight Doors albums released between 1967 and 1971, seven reached the Top Ten. In May 1971, the band made a compelling return to basic blues-rock form with *L.A. Woman*, which sold over two million copies. But Jim Morrison was now a confirmed alcoholic whose escapades (including a 1969 obscenity conviction for exposing himself onstage in Miami) threatened to tear his band apart. The singer moved to Paris, where he died of an apparent heart attack on July 3, 1971, at the age of twenty-seven.

A. S.

June 1965 saw the release of the Byrds' first album, *Mr. Tambourine Man*, a remarkably accomplished effort that stands as one of its era's most dynamic debut LPs. The band's dynamic performances belied their producer's early reservations about their ability to cut it in the studio, and the assortment of material was unusually ambitious.

The album featured no fewer than four Dylan covers—the title hit plus "All I Really Want to Do," "Spanish Harlem Incident," and "Chimes of Freedom," the latter three from the *Another Side of Bob Dylan* LP, released the previous fall. All followed the basic "Mr. Tambourine Man" blueprint, with McGuinn's Dylan-esque lead vocal on the verses, uplifting group harmonies on the choruses, prominent guitar hooks, and abbreviated lyrics.

The band tapped another folk icon, Pete Seeger, for one of *Mr. Tambourine Man*'s standout numbers. Seeger originally adapted "The Bells of Rhymney" from a piece by Welsh poet Idris Davies, who borrowed the structure of a well-known British nursery rhyme to craft a mournful lament about a deadly mining disaster. The Byrds' version managed to craft the dour subject matter into a radio-friendly pop song without sacrificing the song's haunting message. McGuinn created a central guitar riff that was so memorable that his hero George Harrison would adapt it for the Beatles' "If I Needed Someone," released six months later.

The album closed with a tongue-in-cheek reading of the World War II–era pop standard "We'll Meet Again," which the band included as a tip of the hat to filmmaker Stanley Kubrick, who had made ironic use of the song in his 1964 doomsday satire *Dr. Strangelove (or How I Learned to Stop Worrying and Love the Bomb)*.

Mr. Tambourine Man's original tunes—three by Clark and two co-written by Clark and McGuinn—were equally notable. Highlights included Clark's "I'll Feel a Whole Lot Better," a rousing pop-rock gem on which Clark brought a subtle sense of poetry to standard teen subject matter. Another standout was the Clark ballad "Here Without You," whose yearning lyric is matched by melancholy melody and unearthly harmonies.

The Byrds once again tapped the Pete Seeger catalog for their next single, "Turn! Turn! Turn!" Released in October 1965 as a last-minute substitution for a shelved version of Dylan's "It's All Over Now, Baby Blue," "Turn! Turn! Turn!" became the band's second number one. The song's lyrics, which Seeger adapted from the Bible's book of Ecclesiastes, embodied a timely message of acceptance and hope that struck a responsive chord with listeners troubled by the turbulent events of the era. Two years earlier, McGuinn had arranged and played on a version of the song for Judy Collins's album *#3*. The Byrds' reading featured distinctive guitar arpeggios and subtle tempo changes as well as some subtly inventive Hillman bass work.

In keeping with previous Byrds singles, "Turn! Turn! Turn!" carried a Gene Clark–penned original on its B-side. "She Don't Care About Time" was his most accomplished effort yet, a lyrical and melodic tour de force that showcased Clark's knack for weaving evocative abstract images with accessible pop lyrics. The song climaxed with a McGuinn guitar solo borrowed from Johann Sebastian Bach's *Jesu, Joy of Man's Desiring*.

"Turn! Turn! Turn!" became the title song of the Byrds' second album, released in time for Christmas 1965. Although it's sometimes dismissed as being weaker than its predecessor, *Turn! Turn! Turn!* featured confident, imaginative performances that demonstrated how much the band had matured in the months since their debut LP.

Clark's songwriting showed increasing assurance and sophistication, with the wordy, Dylan-inspired "Set You Free This Time" becoming the first Byrds original to be released on the A-side of a single. "The World Turns All Around Her" spotlighted Clark's propensity for marrying uplifting melodies to downbeat lyrics. Another Clark-penned highlight was the melancholy "If You're Gone," whose droning harmonies hinted at the raga-rock style that the band would soon unveil.

McGuinn also checked in with a pair of solid pop numbers. "It Won't Be Wrong" was a fizzy reworking of "Don't Be Long," previously heard on the Beefeaters' single. "Wait and See," co-written by McGuinn and Crosby, was the latter's first songwriting credit on a Byrds album.

Elsewhere on *Turn! Turn! Turn!*, the Byrds dipped into the Dylan songbook for "The Times They Are A-Changin'" and "Lay Down Your Weary Tune." Although the former was uninspired and listless by Byrds standards, the latter ranked among the band's best Dylan covers, thanks to a heartfelt McGuinn vocal and anthemic vocal and instrumental arrangements. "He Was a Friend of Mine" was a traditional folk standard that Dylan had adopted early in his career; the Byrds' version featured new McGuinn lyrics paying tribute to John F. Kennedy.

Turn! Turn! Turn! was also notable for the Byrds' first venture into country music, "Satisfied Mind," a homespun message number that was originally a hit for Red Foley in 1955 and subsequently covered by Jean Shepard and Porter Wagoner. The country motif continued with the album's closing number, a somewhat tongue-in-cheek rendition of Stephen Foster's "Oh! Susannah," with McGuinn on banjo. That track's campy presentation contrasted the more respectful attitude that the Byrds would adopt in their future country forays.

FREQUENT FLYERS

Mr. Tambourine Man and *Turn! Turn! Turn!* had established the Byrds as one of rock's most vital creative forces, on a par with the Beatles, the Beach Boys, and the Rolling Stones. But by early 1966, the band's volatile mix of personalities, which had initially been one of their strengths, had begun to take a toll on the Byrds' stability.

The first casualty of the group's turbulent internal chemistry was Gene Clark. The prodigiously talented yet emotionally fragile singer/songwriter had been a magnetic stage presence as well as the band's primary songwriter, but he abruptly quit in February 1966. His departure was officially attributed to his fear of flying—an explanation that held some poetic resonance—but Clark later attributed his decision to a nervous breakdown brought on by a combination of internal and external pressures, including the punishing pace of the band's schedule.

Clark's parting gift to the Byrds was their next single, "Eight Miles High," a landmark track that constituted a radical departure from their established style. The song, the last track Clark recorded with the group, would be widely interpreted—and, in some conservative quarters, vilified—as an ode to psychedelic drugs. But Clark's lyrics, which carried a darker and more menacing tone than anything the group had done previously, were actually inspired by the disorientation he felt during the band's first trip to England, with vivid imagery that referred to their transatlantic flight and the mania that greeted them upon their arrival in London—the "Rain grey town/Known for its sound" referred to in the song.

More significant than the brouhaha over the song's lyrical content was the quantum musical leap that "Eight Miles High" represented. The song dispensed with the standard verse/chorus structure, and the musicians' fiery interplay reflected their recent obsessions with the music of Indian sitar master Ravi Shankar and jazz icon John Coltrane (McGuinn borrowed the central four-note riff from "India," from a track on Coltrane's *Africa/Brass* album). McGuinn and Crosby's stratospheric guitar work made good on McGuinn's stated desire of playing guitar the way Coltrane played saxophone. Hillman and Clarke drove the track with a force and dexterity that belied their status as relative neophytes on their respective instruments.

In addition to heralding the birth of psychedelia, "Eight Miles High" marked the end of the Byrds' days as pop hit makers. It would be their final Top Twenty single, stalling at number fourteen after many radio stations banned it due to its alleged drug references. The disc's B-side was the Crosby/McGuinn composition "Why," whose innovative use of Eastern musical scales won the Byrds notoriety as the creators of "raga-rock."

"Eight Miles High" and "Why" were prominent on the Byrds' third LP, *Fifth Dimension*, released in July 1966. The album found the group adapting smoothly to life as a quartet, with Hillman revealing an angelic singing voice that filled Clark's spot in the band's harmony team, with McGuinn and Crosby stepping forward to fill the songwriting void. Stylistically, *Fifth Dimension* found the Byrds exploring unknown sonic territory with exhilarating urgency— and largely resisting the straightforward pop-song format that they'd perfected on their first two albums. And while *Fifth Dimension* was uneven in comparison with its predecessors, its high points were as original, and as thrilling, as any music being made in 1966.

McGuinn's interests in philosophy and space travel were reflected, respectively, in "5D," which appropriately ponders a reckless leap into the unknown, and the whimsical, countrified alien encounter "Mr. Spaceman." McGuinn and Crosby co-wrote "I See You," a semi-sequel to "Eight Miles High" that featured a crashing modal melody, free-verse lyrics, and more of McGuinn's Coltrane-inspired guitar excursions. Crosby received his first solo songwriting credit for the introspective "What's Happening?!?!"

Although *Fifth Dimension* included no Bob Dylan or Pete Seeger songs, the Byrds updated their approach to folk material with gorgeous adaptations of the traditional standards "Wild Mountain Thyme" and "John Riley," which augmented the band's sound with graceful orchestrations. More disturbing was "I Come and Stand at Every Door," which combined a traditional melody with lyrics adapted by McGuinn from a poem by Nazim Hikmet, narrated by the ghost of a child killed in the Hiroshima atom bomb blast.

Fifth Dimension nonetheless included some fairly obvious filler in the form of the aimless jam "2-4-2 Fox Trot (The Lear Jet Song)" and the R&B-inflected instrumental throwaway "Captain Soul" (featuring harmonica from a visiting Gene Clark), as well as a somewhat redundant Crosby-sung take on the garage-punk standard "Hey Joe." The latter had long been a feature of the Byrds' live sets, but had been recorded in the meantime by fellow L.A. combos Love and the Leaves (the song would subsequently receive a definitive reworking from Jimi Hendrix).

Gene Clark wasn't the only member of the Byrds' original creative team missing from the *Fifth Dimension* sessions. Producer Terry Melcher, who'd played a key role on the first two albums, was out of the picture as a result of disputes with Jim Dickson. Instead, the album's producer was the straightlaced Allen Stanton, Columbia's West Coast head of A&R. Although Stanton had little experience recording rock bands, by now the Byrds had apparently amassed sufficient studio experience—and commercial clout—to be trusted with their own artistic decisions.

While his former band regrouped, Gene Clark launched a promising solo career, remaining with Columbia Records and still working with the Byrds' management team of Jim Dickson and Eddie Tickner. Assembling a new live combo, known as Gene Clark and The Group, he played a series of well-received L.A. shows, including an extended engagement opening for the Byrds at the Whisky A Go Go.

In making his first solo album, Clark didn't stray far from the Byrds' extended circle. Enlisted to sing harmony were siblings Vern and Rex Gosdin, veterans of the California country scene who shared management with Clark and the Byrds, and who'd played with Chris Hillman in his early days. Clark also enlisted Hillman and Michael Clarke to serve as rhythm section on the album sessions, with further support provided by guitarists Clarence White, Glen Campbell, and Jerry Cole, keyboardist Leon Russell, and banjoist Doug Dillard.

Although the album's title, *Gene Clark with the Gosdin Brothers*, blurred his new solo status, it was Clark's show all the way, with catchy, memorable songs, expressive performances, and a distinctive, dynamic sound that fused folk-rock, power pop, and country in a manner that anticipated the Byrds' future explorations of American roots music.

Gene Clark with the Gosdin Brothers confirmed Clark's status as a powerful singer and a highly original songwriter. By all rights, it should have been the start of a stellar solo career. But a variety of factors conspired to keep the album for making much of a public impact. For one thing, its February 1967 release was simultaneous with that of the Byrds' fourth album, *Younger Than Yesterday*, virtually guaranteeing that Columbia would focus its promotional resources on the Byrds disc. Clark's ambitious, orchestrated single "Echoes" received some promising airplay around L.A. but got little attention elsewhere. Although Clark had put together a solid live band that included Clarence White and bassist John York (both of whom would resurface in later Byrds lineups), he did little live work outside of the Los Angeles area. Clark would continue to produce first-rate music that reached a limited audience for the remainder of his career.

Sonny and Cher and the Monkees: Top of the Pops in L.A.

By 1964, a new wave of young producers and songwriters—combined with heightened exposure for rock and roll on network television—was transforming Los Angeles into the capital of American pop music. One familiar figure on the Hollywood recording scene was Salvatore "Sonny" Bono—songwriter, session percussionist, and gofer for super-producer Phil Spector. Born in 1935, Sonny had years of music industry experience under his belt when he met and then married eighteen-year-old singer Cherilyn Lapierre. As Sonny and Cher, they scored their first Top Ten single in 1965 with "Baby Don't Go," which Bono wrote and produced.

For the next year or so, the outlandishly dressed couple with the weirdly similar singing voices epitomized Sunset Strip hippie glamour to middle America. This image was reinforced musically by the chiming folk-rock sound of their number one single "I Got You Babe" and by Cher's hit version of the Bob Dylan classic "All I Really Want to Do." In the early 1970s, Sonny and Cher became a headlining attraction in mainstream show business. The couple hosted a popular comedy-variety TV series and had many more hit records (mostly Cher solo efforts) until they were divorced in 1975.

Television was important to Sonny and Cher's career, but it was the reason that the Monkees *had* a career to begin with. Davy Jones, Mickey Dolenz, Mike Nesmith, and Peter Tork were actors and musicians selected by producers Bert Schneider and Bob Rafelson to play a madcap rock and roll band in a *Hard Day's Night*–inspired TV series. *The Monkees* premiered in September 1966 on NBC and was an immediate hit. Meanwhile, the "band" was brought into the studio where—with the aid of top session players and professional songwriters—they created such catchy number one hits as "I'm a Believer," "Last Train to Clarksville," and "Daydream Believer." The Monkees topped the charts with each of their first four albums; in concert, they performed to sold-out crowds of screaming teenage girls.

Jones, Dolenz, Nesmith, and Tork soon tired of being puppets tied to strings pulled by television and record executives. They demanded to write and produce their own songs (with mixed results), and made a further bid for hip credibility by starring in *Head*, a psychedelic pastiche written by actor Jack Nicholson. The skimpy plot of this 1968 film satirized the corporate mechanisms that had brought the group into existence: "Hey-hey, we're the Monkees, a manufactured image," they sang. *Head* bombed at the box office, *The Monkees* was canceled, and the group disbanded in 1969.

A. S.

Clark's former group, meanwhile, continued to thrive. *Younger Than Yesterday* offered an appealing mix of the spacy experimentalism of *Fifth Dimension* and the sparkling pop sensibility of the first two albums, along with a more pronounced country influence that reflected Hillman's expanded influence in the band. Although the bassist had written no songs and sang no lead vocals on the first three albums, on *Younger Than Yesterday* he emerged as able singer and songwriter, holding his own with the more experienced McGuinn and Crosby.

Hillman's four *Younger Than Yesterday* compositions were among the album's highlights. "Have You Seen Her Face" and "Thoughts and Words" restored the savvy pop craftsmanship that had been largely absent from *Fifth Dimension*, while "Time Between" and "The Girl With No Name" drew upon their author's country background and featured stellar guitar work by guest Clarence White, an old friend of Hillman's from the bluegrass scene.

Hillman and McGuinn co-wrote "So You Want to Be a Rock 'n' Roll Star," a good-natured jab at the pop industry's star-making machinery that was ahead of its time, both thematically and sonically. The track, which became a minor hit when released as a single, featured the sounds of an audience of screaming teenaged Byrds fans, recorded in Bournemouth, England, on the band's 1965 tour by publicist Derek Taylor (who had previously worked with the Beatles) on one of the first commercially available cassette recorders, which had recently been purchased by inveterate gadgeteer McGuinn.

"So You Want to Be a Rock 'n' Roll Star" also featured a guest appearance by noted South African trumpet player Hugh Masekela, with whom the Byrds now shared management. In addition to being the first to add brass to a Byrds record, Masekela was credited with helping to ignite Hillman's burst of song-writing on *Younger Than Yesterday*. The bassist said that he was inspired to step up his writing output after he and Crosby played alongside a group of South African musicians on a demo session for South African singer Letta Mbulu, which Masekela was producing.

McGuinn's fascination with space travel and extraterrestrial contact fueled "C.T.A.-102." Its title referred to a recently discovered object in space, which scientists briefly speculated might be emitting radio transmissions from an alien civilization; it turned out to be the first known quasar. The song was a giddy ode to the prospect of extraterrestrial contact, with a bouncy hook and speeded-up alien voices provided by McGuinn and Crosby. In his book *The Demon-Haunted World: Science as a Candle in the Dark*, astronomer Carl Sagan discussed the discovery of CTA-102 and the media sensation that followed, citing the Byrds' song as evidence.

Crosby's contributions to *Younger Than Yesterday*, meanwhile, found him embracing the emerging hippie counterculture, for better and for worse. His "Renaissance Fair" captured the heady rush of a social revolution in its early stages, maintaining a playful energy that was completely absent from his bloated, pretentious "Mind Gardens." Far more satisfying was Crosby's jazz-tinged "Everybody's Been Burned," which offered a clear-eyed alternative to hippie naiveté.

Younger Than Yesterday also featured one of the band's best Bob Dylan interpretations with "My Back Pages," whose chorus gave the album its title. The song's message, which had originally been interpreted as Dylan's repudiation of his early protest phase, made it a rather paradoxical choice for the Byrds. On one hand, the track found the group reverting to their tried-and-true Dylan cover format on an album on which they otherwise staked out new musical territory. At the same time, the song's examination of the arrogance of youth made it an interesting choice for a group that was, by the standards of the day, entering its middle age. It was also the fifth song from 1964's *Another Side of Bob Dylan* that the Byrds had covered, and it became the band's last U.S. Top Forty single.

Younger Than Yesterday found the Byrds beginning a productive association with a supportive new producer, Gary Usher, who shared the band's passion for experimentation. Like Terry Melcher, Usher had gotten his start in surf music, having co-written several early Beach Boys songs with Brian Wilson. Usher also produced *Gene Clark and the Gosdin Brothers* back-to-back with *Younger Than Yesterday*.

July 1967 saw the release of the Byrds' Crosby-penned non-LP single "Lady Friend." The song was Crosby's most ambitious effort to date, a soaring mini-pop-opera incorporating surging horns and massed harmony vocals, as well as borrowing Gene Clark's old method of marrying sad lyrics to uplifting music. Although it was one of Crosby's finest achievements as a Byrd, "Lady Friend" would not find a home on a Byrds album until the CD era.

"Lady Friend"'s B-side was the Hillman-led "Old John Robertson," which marked the Byrds' most adventurous venture into country music yet, with its rollicking country arrangement punctuated by a bridge that featured a string quartet.

The same month, the Byrds began work on what would become their fifth album, *The Notorious Byrd Brothers*, with McGuinn, Crosby, and Hillman retreating to a beach house on the Hawaiian island of Oahu to recharge their creative batteries and write new material. The bucolic surroundings would help to inspire some of the Byrds' most introspective, thoughtful work to date.

But the idyllic retreat provided only a temporary respite from the turmoil that was brewing within the band. Crosby's combative personality fueled tensions between himself and McGuinn, a situation that was exacerbated that by Crosby's moonlighting with another L.A. outfit, Buffalo Springfield (he'd played with both the Byrds and the Springfield at the historic Monterey Pop festival in June).

Another source of ill feeling was the Byrds' refusal to include Crosby's ménage a trois love song "Triad" on *The Notorious Byrd Brothers*, despite having recorded a compelling version of it during the album sessions. With no outlet for the song, Crosby eventually passed "Triad" on to his friends in Jefferson Airplane, who recorded it on their 1968 album *Crown of Creation*.

In October, more than two months into recording *The Notorious Byrd Brothers*, McGuinn and Hillman informed Crosby that he was out of the band. Gene Clark briefly returned to the lineup for a three-week stint that included some TV appearances but no recording sessions. After Clark departed once again, the Byrds went back to recording as a trio, but Michael Clarke quit in November.

In later years, McGuinn and Hillman would both express regret over their decision to part ways with Crosby. After producing Joni Mitchell's 1968 debut album, Crosby would outpace his former band's commercial success after linking with the Buffalo Springfield's Stephen Stills and former Hollies member Graham Nash to form one of the next decade's most successful musical partnerships.

Although he exited during its former recording, Crosby remained a prominent presence on *The Notorious Byrd Brothers*, which has been described as the best album ever made by a band in the process of breaking up. Despite the bitter turmoil that accompanied its creation, it features some of the most harmonious music the Byrds ever made, brimming with pastoral beauty and utopian optimism.

A seamless weaving of tradition, topicality, and futurism, *The Notorious Byrd Brothers* reflected its era's emerging spirituality, addressing such timely lyrical themes as nature, social harmony, and non-conformity, while acknowledging the worldly horrors that threatened Aquarian idealism.

The fracturing of the Byrds' lineup actually seemed to have a liberating effect on *The Notorious Byrd Brothers*' sonic palette, which featured significant contributions from several outside players, including Clarence White, electronic music pioneer Paul Beaver, steel guitarist Red Rhodes, and ace session drummer Jim Gordon, who supplanted Michael Clarke on about half of the tracks.

With sympathetic support from producer Usher, the tracks employed a variety of studio gadgets and sound effects, with washes of Moog synthesizer and electronic phasing, with subtle fades and segues that linked the individual tracks. But the sonic frills never overshadowed the craftsmanship of the songs or the immediacy of the performances.

The Notorious Byrd Brothers' opening track "Artificial Energy," powered by a spacy-sounding phased horn section, was a gentle repudiation of chemical abuse that seemed to be a pointed response to accusations that the band had advocated drugs in "Eight Miles High" and "5D." Representing McGuinn's science fiction interests was "Space Odyssey," which was released a few months before Stanley Kubrick's film *2001: A Space Odyssey* and inspired by the same source, Arthur C. Clarke's short story "The Sentinel."

While "Dolphin's Smile" and "Natural Harmony" celebrated nature, the darkness of the human world intrudes with Crosby's "Draft Morning," in which a reluctant draftee is torn between his orders and his conscience. The song's gentle, ethereal melody eventually dissolves into a volley of fade-out harmonies and battlefield sound effects (the latter provided by visionary comedy troupe the Firesign Theatre), while McGuinn mournfully picks "Taps."

The band members' own compositions were augmented by a pair of memorable Gerry Goffin/Carole King songs that despite their Tin Pan Alley origins, meshed seamlessly with the Byrds' sound and the album's introspective vibe. The twangy "Wasn't Born to Follow" featured distinctive country picking by Clarence White. "Goin' Back," previously a U.K. hit for Dusty Springfield, was a sweet ode to childhood innocence. Despite its wistful Hillman vocal, the song failed to make the Top Forty when released as a single. Although "Goin' Back" was cut while he was still a Byrd, Crosby hated the song and refused to participate in its recording.

The Notorious Byrd Brothers was released in January 1968, with a front cover shot of McGuinn, Hillman, and Clarke peering out the windows of a stable, with a horse occupying a fourth window, an image which many observers interpreted as a parting shot at the departed Crosby.

In the wake of *The Notorious Byrd Brothers*' free-spirited experimentation, McGuinn began to plan an expansive double album that would explore the entire history of contemporary music, encompassing folk, bluegrass, country, and jazz, as well as the electronic music of the future. But fate would take the Byrds in a very different direction.

With the Byrds down to the core duo of McGuinn and Hillman, the pair set out to rebuild the band. To fill the vacant drum seat, they tapped Hillman's cousin Kevin Kelley, who had previously played alongside Ry Cooder and Taj Mahal in the Rising Sons, an under-recorded L.A. combo whose ahead-of-its-time fusion of blues, folk, and rock would subsequently win them cult-legend status.

The next addition to the Byrds lineup would be a crucial one. Gram Parsons was a twenty-one-year-old trust-fund kid from an affluent Southern family. According to popular legend, Parsons faked his way into the gig by auditioning as a jazz pianist for McGuinn's proposed concept album. But Parsons's real love was country and western music, and his influence would steer the Byrds toward a wholehearted embrace of country on their next album, the seminal *Sweetheart of the Rodeo*.

NASHVILLE SWEETHEARTS

Born in Florida and raised in Georgia, Gram Parsons possessed an intimate knowledge of Southern rock and roll and rhythm and blues as well as country. He'd previously played Buddy Holly covers in his teen combo the Pacers, worked on the Greenwich Village scene with his folk group the Shilohs, and dropped out of Harvard University. He'd moved to L.A. with his group the International Submarine Band, with whom he recorded one album, *Safe at Home*, whose country/rock/soul fusion previewed the direction that the Byrds would pursue on *Sweetheart of the Rodeo*.

Once he'd joined the Byrds, Parsons found a kindred spirit in Chris Hillman. Hillman, who'd initially been the one to bring Parsons into the fold, shared his new bandmate's extensive grounding in country music. Soon Parsons and Hillman had persuaded McGuinn to abandon his grandiose album concept in favor of a full-on plunge into country.

Although the Byrds' embrace of country was not without precedent in rock, it was nonetheless a radical and audacious move. Rock and roll had originally been born as a hybrid of country, gospel, and blues, but by 1968, the divisions in American culture were reflected in the us-versus-them dichotomy that divided rock and country. Rock was the music of the counterculture, while country was the sound of conservative, blue-collar white America.

As the first high-profile long-haired rock act to seriously explore country, the Byrds were entering enemy territory. But while outsiders had tended to treat country music with one-dimensional condescension, *Sweetheart of the Rodeo* embraced the music's emotional honesty as well as its sound, showing young listeners that the alien genre could be both hip and heartfelt.

In March 1968, the Byrds and Gary Usher traveled to Nashville to cut tracks for the album. For the sessions, they were accompanied by such seasoned country session pros as steel guitarist Lloyd Green, pianist Earl P. Ball, and standup bassist Roy Huskey.

During their stay in Music City, the Byrds made a now-legendary appearance on the *Grand Ole Opry*, the fabled bastion of the country-music establishment, where Elvis Presley was reportedly advised to go back to driving a truck. The band's performance outraged influential Nashville DJ Ralph Emery, who gave them a chilly reception when they appeared on his popular late-night radio show. McGuinn and Parsons responded by writing "Drug Store Truck Drivin' Man," which portrayed Emery as a stereotypical redneck bigot; the song would appear on the next Byrds album, *Dr. Byrds and Mr. Hyde*.

Although he'd only been in the band for a few months, Parsons quickly assumed a dominant role on the *Sweetheart of the Rodeo* sessions, singing lead on more than half of the tracks and writing most of the original material. But the vocal spotlight shifted back toward McGuinn and Hillman after artist/producer Lee Hazlewood, for whose LHI label the International Submarine Band recorded, asserted that Parsons was still under contract to his company.

Depending on whose version of events one believes, the LHI situation either forced the removal of several of Parsons's lead vocals, or simply gave McGuinn an excuse to wrest control of his band back from the upstart newcomer. In any event, several of Parsons's vocals were deleted from the album rerecorded by McGuinn and/or Hillman, making the released version of *Sweetheart of the Rodeo* less of a radical departure from the Byrds' established sound than it might have been otherwise.

Even in its ostensibly compromised form, the version of *Sweetheart of the Rodeo* that was released in July 1968—by which time Parsons had already quit the band—was a masterpiece and a potent testament to Parsons's talent. Although his lead vocals remained on only three of its eleven tracks, the album was nonetheless an early manifestation of the expansive vision that Parsons dubbed Cosmic American Music, which encompassed R&B, soul, and early rock and roll as well as country.

Among *Sweetheart of the Rodeo*'s highlights were its two Parsons compositions, "Hickory Wind" and "One Hundred Years from Now." The former is one of his finest songs and most moving performances, a poignant evocation of lost innocence and homesick longing. The latter—on which Parsons's voice was replaced by those of McGuinn and Hillman—is actually the closest the album gets to a conventional pop-rock track, with Clarence White's guitar taking the place of pedal steel (a third Parsons original, "Lazy Days," was cut from the album, and was restored, along with some of the deleted Parsons vocals, on the 1990 box set *The Byrds* and on a 1997 expanded edition of *Sweetheart of the Rodeo*).

Beyond Parsons's new compositions, *Sweetheart of the Rodeo* emphasized interpretations of material drawn from various country traditions, for example, bluegrass, gospel, heart-on-sleeve balladry, and hard-core honky-tonk.

Perhaps as a nod to the Byrds' own history, the album opened and closed with a pair of songs—"You Ain't Going Nowhere" and "Nothing Was Delivered"—from Bob Dylan's then-unreleased "basement tapes," which had become a rich source of material for a variety of performers.

Elsewhere, *Sweetheart of the Rodeo* dipped into country's gospel tradition with the traditional "I Am a Pilgrim," which featured a stripped-down acoustic arrangement and an affecting Hillman vocal. Less moving was a version of the Louvin Brothers' "The Christian Life," on which Parsons's sincere delivery was replaced by a rather cartoonish McGuinn vocal. McGuinn fared better on a banjo-powered reading of Woody Guthrie's outlaw "Pretty Boy Floyd," while the band explored the country-soul connection with a bittersweet reading of Stax singer/songwriter William Bell's "You Don't Miss Your Water." Parsons stepped out front for solid versions of the George Jones hit "You're Still on My Mind" and Merle Haggard's fatalistic "Life in Prison."

Commercially, *Sweetheart of the Rodeo* was probably doomed from the start. Although the album divided critics, alienated some of the band's fans, and failed to win over mainstream country audiences, its popularity and influence in the decades since has vindicated the Byrds' contention that traditional country could be adapted for rock-weaned listeners, without sacrificing the music's timeless emotional appeal.

Gram Parsons was vocal in his dissatisfaction with the released version of *Sweetheart of the Rodeo*, and had ended his six-month stint with the band by the time it was released in July 1968. He abruptly quit in London on July 8, on the eve of a scheduled tour of South Africa. His official reason for leaving was his refusal to perform in the racially segregated country. But many observers, including McGuinn, felt that the tour offered Parsons a convenient excuse to bail out in order to launch his own band, and to pursue his budding friendship with Rolling Stone Keith Richards.

The latter view carries a good deal of weight when one considers the fact that while in South Africa, McGuinn and Hillman (who drafted roadie Carlos Bernal to fill in for Parsons on guitar) were openly critical of the country's apartheid regime, and that the musicians received death threats and were ultimately not paid for their performances. The tour ended prematurely when authorities attempted to arrest the group on bogus drug charges, and the musicians had to charter a plane to escape the country. The South African tour also caused the British Musicians Union to impose a ban on the Byrds, but the prohibition was lifted after the band provided evidence of its anti-apartheid statements during the tour.

PHASE THREE

Their South African experience took a heavy toll on the Byrds, and Kevin Kelley quit soon after. Hillman then left, suprising many by reconciling with Parsons to launch the Flying Burrito Brothers, the fulfillment of a concept—country music played with rock and roll attitude—that they'd kicked around while they were both in the Byrds. The Flying Burrito Brothers signed with A&M Records and made good on Parsons's grand musical ambitions with their landmark debut album *The Gilded Palace of Sin*, released in February 1969. By the time the Burritos delivered their less focused sophomore effort *Burrito Deluxe*, their lineup included a third ex-Byrd, Michael Clarke. But Parsons's drug use and increasing unreliability soon got him kicked out of the band he'd started. He then moved to Warner Bros./Reprise and released a pair of much-celebrated solo efforts, *GP* and *Grievous Angel*, before dying of a drug overdose at the age of twenty-six in a motel room in Joshua Tree, California, on September 19, 1973.

The Flying Burrito Brothers shared a label and some band members with the Dillard and Clark Expedition, a similarly innovative country-rock outfit co-led by Gene Clark and ace banjo player/multi-instrumentalist Doug Dillard, who'd led the noted bluegrass combo the Dillards and worked as a sideman with the *Sweetheart*-era Byrds. They made an impressive debut with 1968's *The Fantastic Expedition of Dillard and Clark*, which featured some of Clark's finest writing and singing. Its 1969 follow-up *Through the Morning, Through the Night* relied a bit too heavily on cover material, and the Expedition folded its tent soon after. Clark resumed his solo career with 1971's *Gene Clark*, aka *White Light*, whose pensive poetry and brooding performances again marked Clark as one of his era's finest and most distinctive singer-songwriters.

Meanwhile, Roger McGuinn picked up the pieces and put a new Byrds lineup together from scratch, recruiting the gifted country guitarist Clarence White, who was a natural choice for the job, having guested on the Byrds' three previous albums. White was a former teen prodigy who'd gotten his start playing with his brothers Eric and Roland in the bluegrass group the Kentucky Colonels. He subsequently went electric and developed a singular flatpicking style that made him a popular session player on the L.A. studio scene.

White brought along drummer/multi-instrumentalist Gene Parsons (no relation to Gram). White and Parsons had played together in the California country-rock outfit Nashville West, as well as collaborating on the development of the Parsons/White String Bender, a device that allowed six-string guitarists to replicate steel-guitar licks, and which became a key tool in White's arsenal.

Before joining the Byrds, White and Parsons had done some informal recording and rehearsing with Gram Parsons and Chris Hillman in an informal aggregation that was a prototype for the Flying Burrito Brothers. But they'd turned down an offer to become founding Burritos members, opting to join McGuinn in the new-look Byrds instead.

Rounding out the new Byrds lineup was bassist John York, who'd played alongside White in the Gene Clark and The Group. York had also done an extended stint with the Mamas and the Papas, and done time with Hollywood proto-punks the Standells and seminal roots rockers the Sir Douglas Quintet.

The new Byrds would never attain the original lineup's commercial success, and McGuinn would later publicly opine that he should have put the band to rest and began a solo career after *Sweetheart of the Rodeo*. But the Byrds still had plenty of worthy and distinctive music ahead of them. The group would also emerge as a formidable live act and a consistently popular attraction on the expanding touring circuit. Evidence of the White-era Byrds' potency would appear on *Live at the Fillmore, February 1969*, a vintage performance that would be released on CD three decades later.

The White-era Byrds debuted with *Dr. Byrds and Mr. Hyde*, which, despite Bob Johnston's murky production, showed the new lineup to be worthy of the Byrds name. As indicated by its split-personality title—and by its cover art, which depicted the band members decked out in spacesuits and cowboy outfits—the album found the band working in two contrasting but complementary modes. While some tracks picked up *Sweetheart of the Rodeo*'s country-rock threads, others carved out a distinctive brand of heavy psychedelic rock, embodying a dark, turbulent vibe that reflected the fatalism and social unrest that were the flipside of the hippie dream.

The latter style was represented by "Bad Night at the Whiskey," which combined a heavy, rumbling bottom, ethereal background vocals, bluesy guitar work by White, and a vitriolic McGuinn vocal. The energetic protest tune "King Apathy III" came close to garage-punk, alternating electric verses with acoustic choruses. The band also applied the hard-edged approach to Bob Dylan on a blistering reading of his "This Wheel's on Fire," with apocalyptic fuzz-tone guitar by White.

The album's country tunes, aside from the aforementioned *Sweetheart of the Rodeo* throwback "Drug Store Truck Drivin' Man," were somewhat less convincing. And there was plenty of obvious filler in the form of a live medley and "Candy" and "Child of the Universe," a pair of McGuinn tunes written for the film disaster *Candy*. Despite its inconsistency, and despite the fact that it was the lowest-charting album of the Byrds' career (peaking at a pallid number 153 on the *Billboard* album chart), *Dr. Byrds and Mr. Hyde* was in many ways a remarkable rebirth.

Following *Dr. Byrds and Mr. Hyde*, the Byrds and Bob Johnston cut a lackluster version of "Lay Lady Lay" (from Dylan's *Nashville Skyline*, which Johnston produced) which was issued as a stand-alone single. Beyond its drab arrangement and uninspired performance, the most memorable thing about the track was its overproduction, including a prominent female backup chorus that Johnston added without the musicians' knowledge. The band was mortified with the result, and vowed to work with a more sympathetic producer the next time around.

For that task, they turned to their original studio mentor, Terry Melcher, for their next album, *Ballad of Easy Rider*. Melcher brought sonic clarity to the album, which otherwise featured a diverse mixed bag of styles. McGuinn's sole songwriting contribution to *Ballad of Easy Rider* was its title song, which he had previously performed in a solo version on the soundtrack of the recent counterculture film smash *Easy Rider* (which also included the *Notorious Byrd Brothers* number "Wasn't Born to Follow").

The song, "Ballad of Easy Rider," which boasted lush orchestrations and one of McGuinn's prettiest melodies, was the result of an offbeat collaboration between McGuinn and Bob Dylan. When *Easy Rider*'s producer/star Peter Fonda asked Dylan to write a theme song for the film, Dylan wrote a few lines on a napkin and told Fonda to pass them on to McGuinn. McGuinn finished the song, using Dylan's lyrics as the first verse. Dylan later insisted on his name being removed from the song's credits.

Beyond its title track, *Ballad of Easy Rider* presented a more democratic Byrds. At the time, McGuinn was devoting much of his attention to *Gene Tryp*, a Broadway rock musical he was co-writing with director/lyricist Jacques Levy. McGuinn's involvement in that project allowed White, York, and Parsons to play more prominent roles on *Ballad of Easy Rider*, with each member taking turns writing and singing.

With its scattershot assortment of styles, *Ballad of Easy Rider* did little to establish a consistent sound for the reorganized Byrds. But the album's best tracks show the band to be tight and in control, tackling diverse material with confidence and verve. McGuinn delivered affectingly melancholy performances on the country-pop number "Tulsa County Blue," and Woody Guthrie's "Deportee (Plane Wreck at Los Gatos)," although his reading of Dylan's "It's All Over Now, Baby Blue" (which the Byrds had previously attempted unsuccessfully in 1965) was one of their weakest Dylan covers.

Elsewhere, White steps out front on the country-gospel tune "Oil in My Lamp," which he wrote with Parsons. York takes the lead on the uncharacteristically funky "Fido." Parsons wrote and sang the catchy pop number "Gunga Din," which describes such autobiographical incidents as an outdoor Byrds concert in New York being rained out and John York being denied entrance to a restaurant for wearing a leather jacket. The band harmonizes mightily on another gospel song, "Jesus Is Just Alright," featuring droning, bluesy guitar by White.

In addition to demonstrating the new Byrds' versatility, *Ballad of Easy Rider* restored some of their commercial momentum, returning the band to the *Billboard* Top Forty. The sales upswing was undoubtedly aided by the band's increased touring activity, as well as their new association with the massively popular *Easy Rider*.

McGuinn's musical *Gene Tryp* would never be staged, due to financing problems and Jacques Levy's impractically grandiose production plans. But several of the twenty-six songs McGuinn and Levy wrote for the show would resurface as highlights of subsequent Byrds albums. The project was the source for much of the McGuinn material on 1970's *Untitled*.

By then, the band included a new bassist, Skip Battin, a music-biz veteran whose résumé stretched back to the late 1950s, when he scored the hits "It Was I" and "Cherry Pie" as half of the teen-pop duo Skip and Flip. He'd since worked extensively as a songwriter and studio musician, as well as forming a writing partnership with notorious L.A.-scene hustler Kim Fowley.

An inconsistent double LP divided between live and studio material, *Untitled* was the late-era Byrds' most popular album. Its best tracks were four McGuinn/ Levy compositions rescued from the stillborn *Gene Tryp*. The wild-west fantasy "Chestnut Mare" recaptured the transcendent, twelve-string-driven beauty of the Byrds' early classics and became an album-rock radio staple, while "All the Things" and "Just a Season" manifested an autumnal reflectiveness, and the live "Lover of the Bayou" found the band working convincingly in greasy swamp-rock mode. White contributed a twangy reading of Little Feat's "Truck Stop Girl," while "You All Look Alike," one of four Battin co-compositions, put a timely hippie twist on the folk murder-ballad tradition.

Untitled's muddy but energetic live disc was alternately self-indulgent and exciting, thanks largely to White's rewiring of songs associated with earlier Byrds lineups, including "So You Want to Be a Rock 'n' Roll Star," "Mr. Tambourine Man," "Mr. Spaceman," and a jam-heavy fifteen-minute version of "Eight Miles High." The band also expands Dylan repertoire with an enjoyably ragged take on his "Positively Fourth Street," featuring an appropriately venomous McGuinn vocal.

The next Byrds release, 1971's *Byrdmaniax*, is generally regarded as their worst album, distinguished mainly by a surfeit of weak material and uninspired performances, as well as extraneous production frills that diluted the album's better songs. The studio tinkering—which drowned the tracks in excessive keyboards, horns, strings, and backup vocals —was done by Melcher and co-producer Chris Hinshaw while the band was out on tour. The morass of overdubs marred two of the album's strongest numbers, McGuinn's lovely, fragile "Kathleen's Song" (a *Gene Tryp* number cut during the *Untitled* sessions) and White's tender reading of Jackson Browne's "Jamaica Say You Will."

The Byrds hated *Byrdmaniax* as much as fans and critics did, and attempted to atone by recording its followup, *Farther Along*, quickly and with a minimum of embellishment. The band produced the sessions themselves using no outside players or singers, and got the album into stores within six months of its predecessor.

The fact that various band members were hoarding their best songs for solo projects ensured that *Farther Along* wasn't exactly a decisive return to form. But it was a consistently spirited, unpretentious evocation of the late-model Byrds' salient qualities. McGuinn's "Tiffany Queen" was his best rocker in ages, while White delivered a heart-tugging performance of the boy-and-his-dog story "Bugler" and some nimble bluegrass licks on the instrumental "Bristol Steam Convention Blues." Another highlight was the title track, a harmony-laden rendition of a country gospel standard. On the whole, though, *Farther Along* was insubstantial enough that no one was particularly surprised to learn that it would be the band's final album, and that McGuinn was already in discussions to reunite the original Byrds lineup.

Following a brief spell with L.A. session man John Guerin replacing Parsons on drums, McGuinn disbanded the Byrds. With several live dates still on the calendar, McGuinn and White honored their commitments using replacement musicians. The Byrds finally limped to a halt in February 1973, playing their final show in Passaic, New Jersey, with a makeshift lineup that included Chris Hillman (who'd left the Burritos in 1972 and joined Stephen Stills's short-lived semi-supergroup Manassas) on bass and Joe Lala on drums.

REUNIONS AND RECRIMINATIONS

After the Byrds' dissolution, Clarence White returned to session work, played some shows with a reunited Kentucky Colonels, formed the new acoustic combo Muleskinner, and began planning his first solo album. But the guitarist's bright future was cut short on July 14, 1973, the twenty-nine-year-old White was killed by a drunk driver while loading his equipment into a van after a show in Palmdale, California. At his funeral, Gram Parsons led the mourners in singing "Farther Along."

Meanwhile, plans to reassemble the five original Byrds had been set in motion by David Crosby and Elektra/Asylum Records chief David Geffen, and had been a factor in McGuinn's decision to break up the then-current version of the band. The buzz surrounding the project built an air of anticipation around the reunion. But the resulting album, simply titled *Byrds*, proved to be a major disappointment.

Although *Byrds* sold well, it added little to the band's legacy or reputation. McGuinn, Clark, Crosby, and Hillman split lead vocal duties on mostly undistinguished originals, along with covers of tunes by Joni Mitchell and Neil Young (but not, surprisingly, Bob Dylan). The album made no effort to recapture the classic Byrds sound, instead pursuing a bland soft-rock approach, and bore little evidence of the collaborative chemistry that had originally helped to make the band special.

McGuinn later speculated that the ill-conceived reunion was motivated by the desire of Crosby—who now possessed considerable music industry clout due to his success with Crosby, Stills, and Nash and Crosby, Stills, Nash, and Young—to return to his old band with a level of control he'd never possessed the first time around. McGuinn, whose presence on *Byrds* is noticeably diminished, also admitted that he'd held back his best songs for his first solo album.

The reunion LP's only compelling moments belonged to Gene Clark, who contributed two worthy originals, "Full Circle" and "Changing Heart," and sang expressive leads on the Neil Young covers "Cowgirl in the Sand" and "See the Sky About to Rain." Otherwise, *Byrds* sounded like competent hackwork from the sort of unremarkable country-rock outfit that were a dime a dozen in the early 1970s, rather than the historic reunion of one of rock's most inventive and influential bands.

One positive result of the reunion is that Clark remained with Elektra/Asylum as a solo artist, releasing the classic *No Other* in 1975. Although it once again failed to substantially expand his audience, the album was Clark's most thematically and musically ambitious work yet—and also featured perplexing cover photos of the artist decked out in glam makeup.

Chris Hillman also stayed with Elektra/Asylum after the Byrds reunion. In 1974, he teamed with singer/songwriter J.D. Souther and ex–Buffalo Springfield/Poco member Richie Furay to form the Souther-Hillman-Furay Band, an underwhelming attempt to launch a Crosby, Stills, and Nash–like supergroup. After two albums with Souther-Hillman-Furay, Hillman went solo with 1976's *Slippin' Away* and 1977's *Clear Sailin'*.

Roger McGuinn launched his solo career strongly with 1973's *Roger McGuinn*, a confidently eclectic effort that was a much stronger showcase for his talents than any recent Byrds album had been. It was followed by the more uneven *Peace on You* and *Roger McGuinn and Band*. McGuinn's high-profile participation in Bob Dylan's Rolling Thunder Revue tour was followed by 1976's *Cardiff Rose*, probably his best solo effort.

In 1977, McGuinn was touring to promote his album *Thunderbyrd*, while Clark was on the road behind his *Two Sides to Every Story* and Hillman was supporting *Clear Sailin'*. The coincidental timing of their respective solo releases inspired a British promoter to book the three ex-Byrds on a package tour. Although the former bandmates hadn't initially intended to perform together, on some nights they would end the show with a short joint set of Byrds hits, backed by McGuinn's band. Their London shows were taped for broadcast by the BBC, and later released on CD as *3 Byrds Land in London*. Although much of the tour ended up being canceled due to financial disputes with the promoter, the experience was apparently satisfying enough for the trio to consider a more permanent collaboration.

In late 1977, McGuinn and Clark toured in the United States as an acoustic duo. Hillman joined them for several shows, and David Crosby sat in for three West Coast performances. The following year, McGuinn, Clark, and Hillman toured as a trio in the United States, Canada, and Australia. In late 1978, the trio signed with Capitol Records. Since they'd informally agreed at the time of the 1973 reunion not to resurrect the Byrds name unless all five original members were involved, they billed themselves as McGuinn, Clark, and Hillman, which was also the title of their 1979 album.

Even more so than the 1973 LP, *McGuinn, Clark and Hillman* went out of its way not to replicate the Byrds' trademark sound. Instead, it was a blatant effort to craft a contemporary commercial product, with slick production that integrated disco beats as well as treacly strings, horns, and synthesizers. Producers Ron and Howard Albert were so intent on downplaying the trio's musical history that they forbade McGuinn from playing guitar on the sessions and wouldn't even allow the three singers to harmonize, instead backing each individually with anonymous session vocalists.

In spite of, or because of, its mainstream production, *McGuinn, Clark and Hillman* was fairly well received. The album made the Top Forty, as did its first single, McGuinn's effervescent "Don't You Write Her Off." Still, the commercial direction may have been short-sighted. At the time, the rise of new wave had made the Byrds' vintage sound hip and fashionable again, and an edgier, more substantial album might have been the basis for a longer-term resurgence, rather than a one-off minor hit.

Despite the project's initial success, McGuinn, Clark, and Hillman quickly lost momentum. Clark began to drift away midway through a second album, 1980's somewhat Byrdsier-sounding *City*. That disc ended up containing a pair of Clark songs, and was released under the unwieldy billing of "Roger McGuinn and Chris Hillman featuring Gene Clark." The remaining duo stuck together for 1981's inappropriately R&B-flavored *McGuinn/Hillman*, produced by soul vets Jerry Wexler and Barry Beckett, before going their separate ways.

McGuinn took an extended break from recording, spending much of the 1980s touring as an acoustic solo performer. Hillman achieved a late-blooming solo breakthrough by returning to his bluegrass and country roots with *Morning Sky* and *Desert Rose*, both released on the independent Sugar Hill label. Those albums would lead to the formation of the Hillman-led Desert Rose Band, which scored a series of mainstream country hits between 1987 and 1994.

McGuinn and Hillman briefly reunited to guest on the Nitty Gritty Dirt Band's all-star *Will the Circle Be Unbroken, Vol. 2*, duetting on a version of "You Ain't Going Nowhere" that became a surprise Top Ten country hit. Considering the unfriendly reaction they'd gotten from the Nashville establishment when they'd first cut the song on *Sweetheart of the Rodeo*, the song's belated success on the country charts must have been a particularly sweet vindication.

During the first half of the 1980s, David Crosby fought a very public battle with drug addiction that included a series of scrapes with the law, including arrests for possession of cocaine and illegal weapons. He eventually conquered his demons and chronicled his experiences in his autobiography *Long Time Gone*. In the 1990s, Crosby would experience two more brushes with death, first suffering severe injuries in a motorcycle accident and later being diagnosed with hepatitis C and undergoing a successful organ transplant. Since then, he's participated in successful reunions with Crosby, Stills, Nash, and Young, both on tour and in the studio.

In 1984, Gene Clark led a tour billed as a "20th Anniversary Tribute to the Byrds," fronting an ensemble that included fellow founding member Michael

Clarke and late-1960s Byrd John York, along with The Band's Rick Danko, ex–Beach Boy Blondie Chaplin, and former Flying Burrito Brother Rick Roberts. Many promoters couldn't resist the temptation to shorten the name of the show and simply bill the aggregation as the Byrds. The opening act on many of those dates was a tenuous incarnation of the Flying Burrito Brothers that included another ex-Byrd, Skip Battin.

Finding continued demand on the club and oldies circuits after the anniversary tour ended, Clark continued to use the Byrds name for subsequent band lineups that at various times included York and even ex-Byrds roadie and short-term Gram Parsons impersonator Carlos Bernal. McGuinn, Crosby, and Hillman were understandably perturbed by Clark's use of the Byrds name—particularly since the members had informally agreed not to revive it again without the participation of all five original members—but grudgingly looked the other way to allow their former cohort to earn a living.

In 1987, Clark recorded *So Rebellious a Lover*, a collection of duets with Carla Olson, leader of L.A.'s Textones. The album was a surprise cult hit, becoming Clark's biggest-selling solo release. In 1988, with election to the Rock and Roll Hall of Fame imminent and public interest mounting for a proper high-profile Byrds reunion, Clark acceded to his former bandmates' wishes and stopped touring under the Byrds banner. At around the same time, he developed health problems aggravated by his years of heavy drinking, undergoing major surgery to treat a stomach ulcer.

A few months after Clark put his "Byrds" to rest, drummer Michael Clarke assembled his own faux Byrds with some little-known players, at various times bringing in Skip Battin, John York, and Carlos Bernal in a feeble effort to boost the act's dubious pedigree.

Clarke's low-rent act prompted McGuinn, Crosby, and Hillman to reunite for a handful of California shows, billing themselves as the Byrds. The move was partially an effort to strengthen the lawsuit that the three were planning in an attempt to stop their former drummer's appropriation of the band's name. The first of these shows was in June 1988 at L.A.'s Ash Grove, with Gene Clark, still recuperating from surgery, in the audience.

In August 1990, McGuinn, Crosby, and Hillman recorded four new studio tracks in Nashville, backed by guitarist John Jorgenson and drummer Steve Duncan of Hillman's Desert Rose Band. These new efforts, along with some tracks recorded at one of the trio's recent reunion shows, appeared on the career-spanning box set *The Byrds*.

In January 1991, the five original Byrds were inducted into the Rock and Roll Hall of Fame. The honor offered a chance for the musicians to set aside their differences and bury the hatchet. But the evening was marred by the news of the first air strikes against Iraq in the Gulf War, and by the condition of an inebriated Michael Clarke. Despite the less-than-celebratory mood, the five original Byrds reunited on stage to perform several of their vintage classics.

The Hall of Fame induction would be the original Byrds lineup's final reunion. On May 24, 1991, forty-six-year-old Gene Clark's declining health caught up with him, and he died from the effects of a bleeding ulcer.

Michael Clarke continued to tour with his ersatz Byrds until December 19, 1993, when he died of liver disease brought on by years of alcohol abuse. Incredibly, Clarke's death didn't stop his unknown cohorts from going ahead with the New Year's Eve gig they'd already booked, or from continuing to bill themselves as the Byrds for years after Clarke's death, until David Crosby's ongoing legal efforts against them finally proved successful in returning the name to the surviving originals.

While the deaths of two founding members killed the prospect of a full Byrds reunion, Roger McGuinn, David Crosby, and Chris Hillman have remained active in their individual musical pursuits. Meanwhile, the body of music that the Byrds produced endures as one of rock's most rewarding catalogs.

TIMELINE

January 20–21, 1965
The Byrds record their first single, "Mr. Tambourine Man" at Columbia Records' Hollywood studio

March 1, 1965
The Byrds begin a residency at Ciro's nightclub in Hollywood, helping to build their local reputation and energize the emerging Sunset Strip rock scene.

June 20, 1965
"Mr. Tambourine Man" hits the number one spot on the *Billboard* Pop chart.

June 21, 1965
The Byrds' first album *Mr. Tambourine Man* is released.

December 4, 1965
"Turn! Turn! Turn!" becomes the Byrds' second number one single.

February 1966
Gene Clark quits the Byrds.

March 14, 1966
"Eight Miles High," Clark's last Byrds composition, is released as a single. It will stall at number fourteen on the pop chart after it's banned by some radio stations due to its lyrics' alleged drug references.

October 1967
Roger McGuinn informs David Crosby that Crosby is no longer a member of the Byrds. Michael Clarke quits the band the following month.

March 1968
The Byrds, with new member Gram Parsons, begin recording their album *Sweetheart of the Rodeo* in Nashville. During their stay, they also make a controversial appearance on the *Grand Ole Opry*, and have a now-infamous on-air confrontation with veteran country disc jockey Ralph Emery.

July 8, 1968
Gram Parsons abruptly quits the Byrds on the eve of the band's tour of South Africa.

September 1968
Chris Hillman quits the Byrds to join Parsons in the Flying Burrito Brothers, leaving McGuinn to regroup with new members Clarence White, Gene Parsons, and John York.

February 24, 1973
The Byrds play their final show at the Capitol Theater in Passaic, New Jersey.

March 5, 1973
Byrds, a one-off reunion album by the five original Byrds, is released.

October 22, 1990
A career-spanning box set titled *The Byrds* is released, including some new studio and live tracks recorded by McGuinn, Crosby, and Hillman under the Byrds name.

January 17, 1991
The five original Byrds reunite on stage for the last time on the occasion of their induction into the Rock and Roll Hall of Fame.

SELECTED DISCOGRAPHY

The Byrds

Mr. Tambourine Man, 1965
Turn! Turn! Turn!, 1965
Fifth Dimension, 1966
Younger Than Yesterday, 1967
The Notorious Byrd Brothers, 1968
Sweetheart of the Rodeo, 1968
There Is a Season (box set), 2006

Gene Clark

Gene Clark and the Gosdin Brothers, 1967
The Fantastic Expedition of Dillard and Clark, 1969
Gene Clark (White Light),1971
No Other, 1974

The Flying Burrito Brothers

The Gilded Palace of Sin, 1969

Roger McGuinn

Roger McGuinn, 1973
Cardiff Rose, 1976

Gram Parsons

The Complete Reprise Sessions, 2006

FURTHER READING

Einarson, John. *Mr. Tambourine Man: The Life and Legacy of the Byrds' Gene Clark*. San Francisco: Backbeat, 2005.

Fong-Torres, Ben. *Hickory Wind: The Life and Times of Gram Parsons*. New York: Atria, 1991.

Rogan, John. *Timeless Flight Revisited*. London: Rogan House, 1998.

Courtesy of Photofest.

Jimi Hendrix

Alan Bisbort

In his all-too-brief four-year recording career, Jimi Hendrix forever redefined the role of the electric guitar in rock, altering the instrument's basic vocabulary while drastically expanding guitarists' technical and creative options for generations to come. Like no other player before or since, Hendrix coaxed a vibrant new universe of sounds from his ax.

Hendrix's technical wizardry and dizzying showmanship continues to overshadow his immense gifts as a songwriter and vocalist, as well as his effortless mastery of a broad range of musical styles, all of which he integrated into music that was wholly his own.

When he rose to international stardom in 1967, Hendrix had no precedent in contemporary music. Although he seemed to have come out of nowhere, Hendrix had actually served a long, unglamorous apprenticeship toiling as a sideman for countless R&B acts. By the time he was spotted by Animals bassist Chas Chandler, who plucked him from the Greenwich Village club scene and brought him to London to groom him for stardom, Hendrix was a seasoned journeyman, albeit one who'd had little chance to spread his creative wings.

Once he gained that artistic freedom, Hendrix built a body of music that instantly took the rock world by storm and has lost none of its transformative power in the years since. Before his death in 1970 at the age of twenty-seven, with just three albums released, Hendrix's musical horizons seemed unlimited, and there's no telling what he might have achieved had he lived.

FIRST RAYS OF A NEW RISING SON

The future Jimi Hendrix was born on November 27, 1942, in Seattle, one of six children of Lucille and James Allen "Al" Hendrix. Although his name at birth was John Allen Hendrix, his father renamed him James Marshall Hendrix when he was four. Neither parent provided a stable home life, and the marriage ended in divorce in 1950. According to biographer Charles Cross, his part Cherokee mother was largely absent and died of alcohol-related health problems in 1958, while his father was abusive and distant.

After their parents divorced, Jimmy and his younger brother Leon were sent to Vancouver, British Columbia, to stay with an aunt and maternal grandmother, a half-Cherokee who lived on a reservation. The four other Hendrix siblings were either placed in foster care or given up for adoption. After returning to Seattle two years later, Jimmy and Leon often had to scrounge for food or shoplift from grocery stores. While attending Garfield High School, he regularly begged for leftovers at a fast food joint across the street. In contrast to his chaotic, impoverished home life, the shy Jimmy would often lose himself in dreams about outer space and Native Americans and fantasized about playing guitar, using a broom as his prop. Friends later quoted the young Jimmy's stated desire to travel far from Seattle and become rich and famous.

Upon receiving a $5 acoustic guitar at the age of thirteen, Jimmy began his unorthodox relationship with the instrument. Since he was left-handed and the guitar was not, he turned it upside down and learned to play it that way, as he would continue to do for the rest of his life. (The approach wasn't unprecedented; famed southpaw bluesmen Albert King and Otis Rush also played "right-handed" guitars). Even then, Hendrix had eclectic musical tastes, maintaining an affinity for such electric blues players as Muddy Waters and Buddy Guy as well as rock and rollers Eddie Cochran and Chuck Berry. He played guitar along with his father's R&B records and the radio hits of Elvis Presley, James Brown, Buddy Holly, and Little Richard. He eventually managed to acquire an electric Silvertone guitar from Sears Roebuck, and became proficient enough to join a local band, the Rocking Kings.

At sixteen, Hendrix was suspended from Garfield High School for disciplinary reasons. With few options—and partly because Rocking Kings leader Fred Rollins had quit school to enlist—Jimmy joined the U.S. Army in May 1961. As a member of the 101st Airborne Paratroopers elite Screaming Eagles squad, he was sent to Fort Campbell, Kentucky. In his free time, Hendrix practiced his guitar, often sleeping alongside the instrument. On furlough, he visited Nashville, where he combed the clubs for live music. He also hung out at the base's service club, strumming the guitar for beer-drinking GIs. It was there that he met bassist and fellow serviceman Billy Cox, with whom he formed a group, the Casuals, that played gigs on the base and in lounges in the area.

Although he'd enlisted for three years, Hendrix was as eager to be free of the military as he had been to escape Seattle. Hendrix would later state that he was honorably discharged after breaking an ankle, or injuring his back, on his twenty-sixth parachute jump. But in his 2005 biography *Room Full of Mirrors*, Charles Cross reported that Hendrix actually won his early release by telling the Fort Campbell psychiatrist that he was homosexual. The ruse worked. Hendrix was honorably discharged in July 1962, and immediately made moves to pursue a musical career. He went to Nashville and hooked up with Cox, who received his discharge soon after.

At the time, Nashville was a crossroads for a number of musical genres, and over the next three years Hendrix (using the stage name Maurice James) found work as sideman with an assortment of rhythm-and-blues acts, including Little Richard, the Marvelettes, the Impressions, Solomon Burke, Hank Ballard, Chuck Jackson, the Supremes, Tommy Tucker, Lonnie Youngblood, Ike and Tina Turner, and King Curtis. He also met and learned from some of his guitar heroes, including Muddy Waters, B.B. King, and Albert King.

Most of Hendrix's early live work took place on the so-called chitlin' circuit, the network of venues in the South and along the East Coast that were safe havens for black entertainers and audiences in the days of segregation. Many of the greatest African American entertainers had launched their careers on the chitlin' circuit, and the experience was invaluable to the young Hendrix, exposing him to a number of musical styles while teaching him invaluable lessons in discipline. Even at this early stage, Hendrix's instrumental showmanship often crossed the line of what was expected from a sideman, and Hendrix was fired from more than one band for excessive flash.

After being dismissed by Little Richard for, among other things, habitually missing tour buses, Hendrix moved to New York City in 1964 and found work as part of the Isley Brothers' band. After eight months, he quit to join another outfit, Curtis Knight and the Squires. Knight, a hard-working soul singer who gigged regularly in the city's nightclubs, saw the young guitarist's potential and encouraged him to stretch out on stage. Hendrix wowed the club crowds, both with his fiery playing and the flashy tricks he'd learned on the chitlin' circuit. Hendrix also recorded several tracks with Knight—tracks that would be reissued endlessly after Hendrix achieved fame.

The Isley Brothers: Fight the Power

Down to two siblings but still going strong in 2007, the Isley Brothers are the longest-lived group in rock and roll history. Ronald, Rudolph, and O'Kelly Isley of Cincinnati, Ohio, made their first recordings in 1957. In the first half of the 1960s, their material was often covered by white artists—including the Beatles ("Twist and Shout") and the Yardbirds ("Respectable")—who had more success than the Isleys had with the same songs. The rewards of crossover acceptance must have been all too apparent to the brothers as they went from label to label, never quite establishing their own musical identity.

During this time, the Isley Brothers played a significant role in the musical development of Jimi Hendrix (still known then as Jimmy James). The Isleys employed Jimi in their touring band and his first significant studio performance was on the group's recording of "Testify" in 1964. When the Brothers found themselves sidelined at Motown and unable to follow up their 1966 hit "This Old Heart of Mine (Is Weak for You)," they followed Hendrix's example and decamped to England, residing there for two years (1967–69).

After their return to the States, the Isleys added brother-in-law Chris Jasper on keyboards, brother Marvin on bass, and brother Ernie on guitar. Suddenly, they were transformed from a traditional R&B vocal group into a self-contained band equipped with a muscular rhythm section and Ernie Isley's Hendrix-influenced lead guitar. In 1969, the group declared its artistic and commercial independence when the first single on their own T-Neck label, "It's Your Thing," became a number one R&B/number two Pop smash.

More hits followed, including "That Lady" and the politically charged "Fight the Power." Reversing the cover-song syndrome that had stymied them ten years earlier, the Isleys recorded rock tunes by Stephen Stills, Bob Dylan, and James Taylor. The Brothers paid homage to their former sideman with two versions (studio and live) of Jimi Hendrix's anti-war epic "Machine Gun." From 1973 to 1978, the Isleys placed five albums in the Top Ten of the *Billboard* Pop Albums chart, going head to head with the best-selling white rock acts of the era.

Andy Schwartz

It was while playing with Knight that Hendrix was spotted by Linda Keith, the British girlfriend of Rolling Stone Keith Richards. She was staying in New York with friends for the summer of 1966 while the Stones were on a U.S. tour. After seeing Hendrix play with Knight's band and deciding that he was destined for bigger things, she befriended the frustrated guitarist and encouraged him to quit to form his own group. Soon, Hendrix was fronting Jimmy James and the Blue Flames, in the clubs of Greenwich Village. (Another member of the Blue Flames was young guitarist Randy Wolfe; Hendrix nicknamed him Randy California, and Wolfe would retain that stage name when he formed the revered cult band Spirit, in which he would carry on his former mentor's stylistic legacy.)

The Blue Flames' career peaked when they were hired to back folk-blues revivalist John Hammond Jr. (son of the legendary record company executive who'd discovered Billie Holiday and Bob Dylan) for a two-week stand at the renowned Café Au Go Go. Each night, Hammond allowed "Jimmy James" to close out the show with Bo Diddley's "I'm a Man," during which Hendrix employed every stage trick he'd learned on the chitlin' circuit—playing guitar behind his back, between his legs, with his teeth. Soon the word was out on the street about this wild new act.

Linda Keith tried to interest Rolling Stones manager Andrew Loog Oldham and Sire Records president Seymour Stein in Hendrix. Though both were impressed with Hendrix's talent, neither pursued him. Keith had more success on her third try, when she convinced Chas Chandler—bassist for English rock-blues sensations the Animals—to check Hendrix out. On August 3, 1966, Chandler accompanied Keith to the Café Wha? in Greenwich Village to see Jimmy James and the Blue Flames. He was so impressed that he vowed to return to New York at the end of the Animals' U.S. tour, quit the band, and make Hendrix a star.

That Chandler, then a member of one of the world's most popular rock and roll bands, was willing to ditch his own performing career to manage the career of an unknown says much about Hendrix's incipient talent and star quality. The fact that Hendrix, at the time, could barely sing above a mumble and had never written a single piece of his own music, made Chandler's faith in him even more impressive. True to his word, Chandler returned to New York on September 3, 1966, to become Hendrix's manager. He got the guitarist a passport, flew him to London, and set out to find the proper musicians to back rock's next superstar.

THE EXPERIENCE BEGINS

On September 23, 1966, Jimi Hendrix—he had decided to alter the spelling of his first name during the flight over—arrived in London. He brought only his guitar and the clothes on his back, leaving everything else (including an unpaid hotel bill) behind in New York. His flamboyant fashion sense, which would become one of his visual signatures, was not yet in evidence. Much of his eclectic choices in clothing—including the antique British army coat in which he would later be photographed—were initially dictated by poverty, found in Portobello Road thrift shops or made for him, as a sort of walking advertisement, by hip London clothiers like Granny Takes a Trip.

Once established in London, Chandler and Hendrix quickly began seeking musicians for the band. Chandler approached organist Brian Auger, whose band the Trinity had already had some success. Auger was impressed with Hendrix's skills, but wasn't interested in breaking up his existing band to accommodate an unknown American who'd yet to play a single gig in the United Kingdom.

Chandler then invited Noel Redding, a seasoned guitarist who'd recently failed an audition with the Animals to sign on as Hendrix's bassist. Redding had never played bass, but learned quickly, developing a free-form approach that augmented Hendrix's playing well.

Meanwhile, Chandler showcased his protégé all over London, hitting jam sessions at hot clubs like the Speakeasy and Blaises. On October 1, 1966, Hendrix jammed with Cream—playing Howlin' Wolf's "Killing Floor"—at Regent Polytechnic in London. Cream guitarist Eric Clapton was shocked to encounter a player who could do things he himself never dreamed possible. This was, after all, the era when "Clapton Is God" graffiti was appearing on subways and walls all over London.

A series of auditions failed to turn up a suitable drummer, so Chandler contacted Mitch Mitchell. Though not yet twenty, Mitchell was already a seasoned session player and drummer for Georgie Fame and the Blue Flames. As fate would have it, Fame had laid off his band the week before Chandler called.

With Mitchell's ascension to drummer's chair, the Jimi Hendrix Experience was born. The band's name has been credited to Mike Jeffery, the Animals' manager who'd joined Chandler as co-manager (officially "agent") of the Experience. Jeffery, known for some shady connections, managed to secure vital work permits for non-citizen Hendrix.

The new power trio had little time to rehearse or work up original material before they were on their first tour, a two-week stint opening for Johnny Hallyday, France's answer to Elvis Presley.

Before embarking, Hendrix and Redding convinced Chandler to pay for proper equipment. They wanted new Marshall stacks—two amplifiers with four twelve-inch speakers in each—which gave them not only volume but a palpable sense of power. Chandler sold some of his own guitars to pay for the equipment, which they packed up and toted to France. Hendrix would use Marshall amps for the rest of his career; they, in fact, became as synonymous with him as his Fender Stratocaster guitar.

October 13, 1966 marked the first official gig of the Jimi Hendrix Experience, at Novelty, in Eveux, France. Mandated to play a fifteen-minute opening set, the trio ran through R&B standards "In the Midnight Hour," "Land of 1000 Dances," "Have Mercy," and "Hey Joe." By their fourth gig, on October 18 at the prestigious Paris Olympia, the trio had attracted media notice and boisterous fans. Emboldened by the reception, Hendrix began to stretch out on stage, playing on his knees, picking the guitar with his teeth and behind his head. Mitch Mitchell later noted,

> One thing that struck me about Jimi early on was his hands. He had these huge hands; his thumb was nearly as long as his fingers. Like many blues players he could use it to his advantage, hooking it over the neck of his guitar as an extra finger. But we're not talking 'secrets of his success' here because Jimi could, and did, play anything—left-handed, right-handed, upside down, behind his back and with his teeth. He probably could've played with his toe-nails.[1]

On October 23, 1966, the Jimi Hendrix Experience recorded their first two songs, at De Lane Lea Studio in Kingsway, London. In concert, they'd been stretching out on "Hey Joe," a song that had been a hit for American garage-rockers the Leaves the previous year. Hendrix preferred the slow folk-blues arrangement of the song by Tim Rose, so the band simply electrified Rose's version. It became their first hit single upon its release by Track Records on December 16, 1966. The day after recording "Hey Joe," the Experience began work on "Stone Free," which was originally slated to be the B-side to the single (though "51st Anniversary" ended up serving that role). "Stone Free," the first Hendrix original the band recorded, was the result of prodding by Chandler, who was determined to unlock the gift for songwriting that he believed Hendrix possessed.

Between studio sessions the band played a brief residency at the legendary Munich club Big Apple. Here, it is alleged by Redding, Hendrix "accidentally" discovered feedback, yet another weapon in his guitar arsenal. Having left the stage in a hurry, Hendrix tossed his guitar down without unplugging it. By the time he returned to the stage, the guitar was spewing all kinds of noise through the Marshall amps.

Upon returning to De Lane Lea Studio on November 24, 1966, the Experience recorded "Love or Confusion" and "Here He Comes." These song, like the others that would appear on the band's groundbreaking debut album, *Are You Experienced*, were not rehearsed or played live before they were recorded in the studio. Hendrix simply showed Redding the chords, then the trio ran through the song a few times, then recorded the basic instrumental tracks.

The Jimi Hendrix Experience moved to CBS Studios on New Bond Street in London. Here, in a brief but creative burst, their loose recording method paid even quicker dividends. They were able to nail "Purple Haze"—which would become Hendrix's signature song—on only the third take, after having been shown the chords and hummed the melody by Hendrix before the tape began rolling. In the next two days, they also recorded "Red House," "Third Stone from the Sun," "Foxy Lady," and "Can You See Me."

Despite the seeming looseness of their recording regimen, Chandler ruled his protégé with an iron fist. Their bond was so close, in fact, that Hendrix and his girlfriend—a hairdresser named Kathy Etchingham, whom he met on his first night in London—moved into an apartment with Chandler and his girlfriend in Montagu Square, and later into a second flat in Mayfair. Parlaying his contacts from his days with The Animals, Chandler got the Experience gigs on the Ricky Tick circuit, a chain of clubs around England run by Phil Hayward. He also scored higher-profile "showcase" gigs at trendy London clubs like the Bag O' Nails, 7 _ Club, and Blaises.

Through Track Records' Chris Stamp and Kit Lambert—who also managed the Who—the Jimi Hendrix Experience won a guest spot on the British pop music TV institution *Ready Steady Go!*, promoting "Hey Joe," which would peak at number seven on the U.K. charts in January 1967. "Purple Haze," released as a single on March 17, 1967, would peak at number three.

Meanwhile, the reputation of the Jimi Hendrix Experience grew as members of the Rolling Stones, the Beatles, and Cream began to turn up at the band's London gigs and rave about them to the press. Animals frontman Eric Burdon and Paul McCartney, in particular, played key roles in spreading the word. When John Phillips of the Mamas and the Papas, who was helping to organize a three-day pop festival in Monterey, California, called him for advice, McCartney recommended Hendrix. His appearance at the Monterey Pop festival in June 1967 would make Hendrix an overnight superstar.

Stevie Wonder: Living for the City

Seventeen-year-old Stevie Wonder was already a major Motown star in 1967 when he jammed with Jimi Hendrix on a BBC television broadcast. Born Steveland Hardaway Judkins in 1950 in Saginaw, Michigan, and blind since birth, Wonder was a versatile, soulful singer who taught himself harmonica, drums, and piano. At age thirteen, "Fingertips (Pt. 2)" became his first number one Pop/R&B hit, followed by such classic Motown singles as "Uptight (Everything's Alright)" (1965) and "I Was Made to Love Her" (1967).

But Stevie chafed under his label's creative and financial restrictions. His situation stood in contrast to those of Jimi Hendrix and Marvin Gaye, who seemed fully in charge of their music if not their business affairs. Hendrix in particular wrote, arranged, and produced his own songs, recorded in studios of his own choosing, then delivered the finished album to Warner Bros. Records.

Wonder's Motown contract expired in 1971, and he turned twenty-one in May of the same year. He built his own studio and cut two self-financed albums of original material, playing most of the instruments himself. Stevie re-signed with Motown only after the company agreed to release the albums. In 1972 the second disc, *Music of My Mind*, rose to number twenty-one among *Billboard* Pop Albums—his best chart showing since his first LP in 1963. Hendrix and Wonder shared a fascination with recording technology and the desire to reach out beyond their established audience. In Stevie's case, that meant accepting a support slot on the Rolling Stones' 1972 tour rather than headlining his own more lucrative dates.

Some Hendrix songs had reflected the late 1960s climate of war and social protest; a few years later, Wonder's "Living for the City" depicted poverty, joblessness, and police brutality in the American inner city. His albums featured guest appearances by some of rock's top guitarists: Jeff Beck on *Talking Book*, Stevie Ray Vaughan on *Characters*. Surely Jimi Hendrix, had he lived, would have found himself welcome at a Stevie Wonder session—the results of which we can only dream about today.

A. S.

On January 24, 1967, a Jimi Hendrix Experience gig at London's Marquee club attracted all four members of the Beatles, some of the Stones, Eric Clapton, and Jeff Beck. On January 27, 1967, at a Bromley club called Chislehurst Caves, Hendrix talked shop with Roger Mayer, an inventor of guitar gadgets designed to alter and distort and vary the sound of the instrument. Thus began a long relationship with Mayer, who would guide Hendrix into new sonic pastures.

Whatever money the band made from performances went to pay off studio fees, as they continued to record sporadically between gigs. On February 3, Chandler booked the band at Olympic Studios, where they met Eddie Kramer, who would engineer all of Hendrix's subsequent albums. They continued to play nearly non-stop at gigs, and returned to De Lane Lea Studio to try to lay down tracks for "Manic Depression" and Bob Dylan's "Like a Rolling Stone," which they'd been playing as part of their regular live set.

LET ME STAND NEXT TO YOUR FIRE

Having completed most of the tracks for *Are You Experienced*, the Jimi Hendrix Experience embarked on a twenty-four-date package tour visiting backwater British cities, with a mismatched bill that included teen-idol headliners Walker Brothers, a young Cat Stevens, and Englebert Humperdinck as "special guest star."

Beyond its incongrously matched performers, the tour was notable in that it inspired Hendrix to set fire to his guitar for the first time, at Finsbury Park Astoria in London. Although the flaming-guitar trick would become an essential element of Hendrix's image, he would only do this three times in his career. The second time was at the Monterey Pop festival, famously captured on film.

"The Wind Cries Mary," not on the album, was released as the band's third U.K. single on May 5 and the U.K. debut album, *Are You Experienced*, was released on May 12 (it would peak at number two, unable to wrest The Beatles'

Sgt. Pepper's Lonely Hearts Club Band from the top spot). On May 1, "Hey Joe" was released as their first U.S. single, paving the way for their pivotal performance at the Monterey Pop Festival on June 18, 1967, at which the trio was introduced on stage by Rolling Stone Brian Jones.

Before embarking for America, the Experience were on such a roll that they returned to the studio to lay down several tracks that would end up on their second album, *Axis: Bold as Love.*

When they arrived in California for the festival, they learned that they would be sharing the bill with the Who. Much has been made of the standoff between the two bands, but Chris Stamp—who had relationships with both—claimed the two acts' main concern was not competing unnecessarily with one another; following a coin toss, the Who played first, with the Grateful Dead playing in between. The mellowing effect of the Dead was enough to prime the crowd for a Hendrix performance as incendiary as the one they'd witnessed two hours earlier by the Who. It was a quintessential rock and roll moment, and both bands conquered America on the same stage, only hours apart.

Although they captivated the audience, the Experience had no other gigs booked. San Francisco concert promoter Bill Graham changed that, booking the band at the Fillmore Auditorium for six straight nights, while John Phillips—who'd brought Hendrix over for the festival—hired them to open for the Mamas and the Papas at the Hollywood Bowl later that summer. The Fillmore bill paired Hendrix with another performer who'd leaped to stardom on the Monterey stage, Janis Joplin. The visit to San Francisco also found the Experience playing a free afternoon concert in Golden Gate Park for an audience of stoned, gyrating flower people.

The Experience spent the remainder of the Summer of Love touring the United States. In New York, they played upscale discotheques like Ondines, Cheetah, the Salvation, and Steve Paul's Scene Club. They also played an open-air gig in Central Park, as the opening act for the Young Rascals.

The Jimi Hendrix Experience began their first formal tour in July, as the wildly mismatched opening act for prefab popsters, the Monkees, whose teenaged fans were reportedly horrified by Hendrix.

The band managed to cut short their Monkees' tour after five dates—or it was suggested that they do so by tour management.

On September 1, 1967, *Are You Experienced* was released in the United States on the Reprise label, home of Dean Martin and Frank Sinatra. The album's American edition replaced "Red House," "Can You See Me," and "Remember" with the singles "Hey Joe," "Purple Haze," and "The Wind Cries Mary." Although the album did not spawn a hit single, enough ground had already been broken to lift it to number five on the *Billboard* charts.

Their newfound stardom allowed the Experience to record where they liked, rather than scraping together gig money and going where they were told. The band recorded some tracks with engineer Gary Kellgren, before returning to London to continue work on their followup to *Are You Experienced.*

Once money began coming in, Hendrix became extravagant giving away thousands of dollars in cash, buying cars for virtual strangers, covering old debts and new damage to hotel rooms and vehicles. Chandler felt duty-bound to tighten the leash over retakes in the studio. He and Hendrix were still sharing a flat, and tensions were growing between them, exacerbated by Mitchell's and Redding's demands to have a greater voice in how their playing was recorded.

Despite those hassles, the second Jimi Hendrix Experience LP was completed in June 1967 and released the following January.

The Jimi Hendrix Experience was back on the road in America in February 1968, topping a bill that also included the Soft Machine and Eire Apparent. The tour included a trip to Hendrix's old hometown of Seattle, where the guitarist was coaxed into addressing an assembly at the high school that had once made his life so miserable. After cancelling a show in Newark, New Jersey, in the wake of Dr. Martin Luther King Jr.'s assassination, the trio retreated to Manhattan's Record Plant to record tracks for the album that would be their magnum opus.

Meanwhile, Chas Chandler, having grown weary of Hendrix's extravagance and unpredictability, sold his management interest to Mike Jeffery. Chandler returned to England, where he would soon guide another band, Slade, to stardom.

Indeed, Hendrix's monetary excesses were already legendary. Often, he and Mitchell would jam at a New York club and then take limos the few blocks to the studio, which was filled with various friends and hangers-on, and where they would hold jam sessions until the sun came up. The Record Plant was a sophisticated and expensive state-of-the-art studio, decked out with twelve-track and sixteen-track machines. The party atmosphere of the sessions led to endless outtakes and improvisations that would later emerge on various posthumous releases.

No longer under pressure to produce hit singles, Hendrix stretched out to meet the album format. The resulting double album, *Electric Ladyland*, was a sprawling affair; one highlight was a searing cover version of Bob Dylan's "All Along the Watchtower," a haunting aural assault that perfectly embodied the chaotic state of affairs in America during a time of civil unrest and dissent over the Vietnam War. The album topped the *Billboard* charts, the biggest commercial success Hendrix would have in his lifetime.

The Jimi Hendrix Experience spent the rest of 1968 in a blur of concerts and festival gigs across America, Europe and Scandinavia. By the end of the year, without the stabilizing influence of Chandler, the Experience was on the verge of breakup. Redding started his own band, Fat Mattress, in which he played guitar. He agreed to rejoin the Experience for their outstanding commitments on the condition that Fat Mattress be added to the bill.

Manager Mike Jeffery had reason to keep the Experience going. They were the highest-grossing band in the world now, netting as much as $100,000 per show. Their "final" tour took place in America, with Fat Mattress opening the shows. The nadir, legally, was a gig at Toronto's Maple Leaf Gardens, prior to which the band was strip-searched by Canadian authorities. A small vial of heroin was discovered in one of Hendrix's bags, Hendrix was arrested, bail was paid, and a trial date was set. He was later acquitted, after claiming that the heroin had been put there by one of his fans.

The nadir, musically, was the Newport Pop Festival at San Fernando State College. Hendrix's set was so lackluster that he felt compelled to return without the band the next day and play for free, taking part in impromptu jams with other musicians. Despite the subpar performance, Newport was his highest-paying gig ever, at $125,000. The next concert, an open-air concert at Denver's Mile High Stadium, was the final nail in the Experience's coffin with police firing tear gas at the stage when members of the audience rushed it.

BY THE TIME HE GOT TO WOODSTOCK

Redding and Mitchell returned to England, while Hendrix retreated to a house in upstate New York, that had been rented for him by Jeffery. Invited along were musicians with whom he felt comfortable, including old buddy Billy Cox. Jeffery also entertained the idea of Hendrix's dream of building his own recording studio. Despite the projected expense of the project, the choice was actually a pragmatic one, considering the massive studio bills that Hendrix had already racked up. The resulting studio, Electric Lady, was built on West 8th Street in Manhattan, but the facility became a money pit before the doors were opened. Workers hit an underground stream and flooded the building, delaying its opening and inflating the costs. To exacerbate the situation, Hendrix had grown weary of playing his familiar hits, and had expressed an interest in experimenting in more jazz-based directions. It had long been one of his dreams to record with Miles Davis, who had already begun playing on bills with rock bands and would soon release his own groundbreaking jazz-rock album, *Bitch's Brew*. Hendrix envisioned a collaboration with Davis, a project that was discussed but which never came to fruition.

Perhaps needing the advice of a trusted colleague, Hendrix called Mitchell in August and beseeched him to come to his upstate New York lair and rejoin him for an appearance at the Woodstock Music and Art Fair, taking place just down the road in Bethel in August. Although it would be a historic event, for Hendrix the Woodstock festival was a letdown. For Hendrix and his band, Woodstock turned into a meteorological mess and waste of time. It rained buckets on the final day—Hendrix, as its highest paid performer, was slated to close the festival—and the resulting delays pushed Hendrix's scheduled Sunday night slot into Monday morning. They finally hit the stage at 6:00 on Monday morning, with only one-tenth of the festival's audience remaining to hear him. Although the set was generally considered to be subpar, Hendrix's version of "The Star

Spangled Banner" provided an inspired climax to director Michael Wadleigh's successful documentary film of the festival.

An outstanding legal commitment forced Hendrix to produce an album for Ed Chalpin, a New York studio entrepreneur who'd signed him to a contract during his Curtis Knight days. Hendrix agreed to form a band and perform two shows at the Fillmore East on January 1, 1970 to be recorded for an album that would satisfy Chalpin's claims on Hendrix. The result was *Band of Gypsys* an uninspired jam session with Buddy Miles on drums and Billy Cox on bass. Some have suggested that Hendrix formed this all-black band to silence those critics in the black community who complained that Hendrix didn't court a black audience.

With his Woodstock band Sky Church having yielded disappointing results and his expensive lifestyle draining his finances, Hendrix reformed the Jimi Hendrix Experience, with Mitchell back in the drum seat and Billy Cox replacing Noel Redding on bass. The new lineup began a three-month tour on April 25, 1970. They played in Berkeley on May 30, 1970, while mass demonstrations against the Vietnam War were taking place all over the Bay Area. Those events were captured in the documentary *Jimi Plays Berkeley*. The ad hoc Experience made lackluster appearances at two more huge pop festivals, in Atlanta and Randall's Island, New York. They traveled to Maui, Hawaii, on July 30, 1970, to work on a joint film-soundtrack project dubbed *Rainbow Bridge*. The setting of the venue, between two extinct volcanoes, could not have been more stunning, but the musical and cinematic results were less than lovely.

The trio returned to Europe to honor some concert commitments, including the ill-fated and inaccurately named Love and Peace festival on the Isle of Fehmarn in West Germany. Neither love nor peace reigned, as anarchists and neo-Nazis engaged in bloody clashes and a member of the Experience road crew was shot in the leg. Hendrix was showing signs of exhaustion and depression, while the reliable and drug-eschewing Cox drank something that had been spiked with a hallucinogen. The drug initiated a breakdown causing Cox to be hospitalized and two shows to be canceled. Fearing that his old friend was not up to the grind of planned tours of Australia and Japan, Hendrix asked Noel Redding to rejoin.

Hendrix had repeatedly told friends that he wanted to return to the United States to finish work on a massive album tentatively titled *First Rays of a New Rising Sun*. He then aimed to take the demos to Chas Chandler in hopes that his old manager would reconsider renewing their working relationship.

Sly and the Family Stone: I Want to Take You Higher

Formed in 1967, Sly and the Family Stone were the progenitors of "psychedelic soul." For founder and front man Sly Stone (born Sylvester Stewart in 1944 in Denton, Texas), it was a natural evolution. Sly had already moved beyond the conventions of rhythm and blues by 1965, when he produced the Beau Brummels's "Laugh Laugh," a Top Ten hit for the Bay Area folk-rock group. As a disc jockey on KSOL in San Francisco, he injected Bob Dylan and Beatles songs into the station's standard soul fare.

The group's male/female, black/white lineup, unusual for its time, included Sly's brother Freddie Stone (lead guitar), Cynthia Robinson (trumpet), Larry Graham (bass, vocals), Jerry Martini (saxophone), Greg Errico (drums), and later Sly's sister Rose Stone (vocals, keyboards). Sly sang lead and played organ; he also wrote and produced the songs. The Family Stone's fresh, unique sound blended the stabbing horn riffs and danceable beats of contemporary soul music with extended instrumental jams, communal vocal interplay, and an irresistible kinetic energy. Sly's lyrics preached peace, brotherhood, or—as on the group's first hit "Dance to the Music"—simply getting the party started.

The U.S. debut albums of both Jimi Hendrix and Sly and the Family Stone were released in 1967. *Are You Experienced* eventually reached the Top Five, but *A Whole New Thing* didn't even make the chart. The group struggled along on the club circuit until May 1968 when they shared a weekend bill with Hendrix at New York's Fillmore East. Sly pulled out all the stops, and the Fillmore rock crowd was thrilled by his old-school R&B showmanship in a hip new package.

Hendrix's star turn at the 1967 Monterey Pop Festival paved the way for Sly and the Family Stone to appear at subsequent rock festivals where black artists were often under-represented. At Woodstock in 1969, the group went on-stage after 3 A.M. following a drenching rainstorm, but halfway through their set, the bedraggled crowd was on its feet.

In the mid-1960s, the recording of black music (and most rock and roll) was still subject to tight budgets and strictly regulated session hours. Jimi Hendrix again broke this mold by consuming long blocks of unstructured studio time to create his landmark double album *Electric Ladyland* (released September 1968). After the multi-platinum success of *Stand!* and its celebratory number one single "Everyday People" in 1969, Sly Stone would take full advantage of this new creative freedom.

For the follow-up to *Stand!*, Sly began recording (and re-recording) many of the instrumental tracks himself: the Family Stone never knew how or even if their individual parts would be used. Outside musicians—some as well-known as soul singer Bobby Womack and Beatles sideman Billy Preston, others who were complete strangers—came and went through weeks of inconclusive sessions. Finally, *There's a Riot Goin' On* was released in November 1971. Murky and downbeat, *Riot* was the group's first number one album; the strangely mournful "Family Affair" topped the Pop and R&B singles charts. Sly Stone took two years to create this dark masterpiece. In that time, Motown Records had rolled out *ten* albums by the Temptations, including a Christmas collection and a greatest hits package.

A. S.

THE KILLING FLOOR

On the night of September 17, 1970, Hendrix, unable to sleep, took at least six and possibly as many as nine Vesperax, a sleeping medication given to him by Monika Danneman, a German woman he'd only met three days earlier. On top of whatever else he may have ingested, the potent drug sent him into a deep sleep from which he ultimately never awoke. At some point in his deep stupor, Hendrix vomited and, because he was lying on his back, suffocated on his vomit.

Hendrix, it has often been reported, seemed to think that he would not live a long, full life. In March 1967, on the verge of international fame, he was asked to answer a "Life-Line" questionnaire for the British pop magazine *New Musical Express*. For the "Personal ambition" category, Hendrix said, "To have my own style of music; to see my mother again." (His mother, Lucille, died ten years earlier.) For the "Professional ambition" category, he said, "To be a movie and caress the screen with my shining light."[2]

It is safe to say that Jimi Hendrix fulfilled both of these ambitions, and that the continuing worldwide fascination with his life and music—attested by the phenomenal amount of posthumous material released and purchased—proves that his shining light is still bright.

Hendrix never drew up a will and, upon his death, his father Al Hendrix became the main inheritor of his lucrative estate. Thus began a complex quarter-century legal battle over the rights to both Jimi Hendrix's music and his name. The situation was further complicated when Michael Jeffery died in a plane crash in 1973. After this, the lawyer for the Hendrix family, Leo Branton, sold the rights to Jimi Hendrix's music to a number of record companies outside the United States.

The management of the estate then fell to Alan Douglas, a producer who assembled some controversial albums from a backlog of 600 hours of studio tapes that Hendrix had left behind. Prior to tackling the Hendrix archives, Douglas had been instrumental in bringing together rock and jazz figures for some of the first work in what would later become known as fusion, and he was in negotiations with Hendrix to record with legendary jazz arranger Gil Evans. While Jeffery was dead-set against this, it seems plausible that Hendrix, had he lived, would have evolved into a progenitor of a new rock-jazz sound. Hendrix, in fact, died a week before the first rehearsal with Evans for what would have been a Carnegie Hall concert to be recorded live by Douglas.

After Hendrix died, Douglas hired used studio musicians to "complete" some of Hendrix's unfinished tapes, or to overdub parts he deemed inadequate—including parts played by Hendrix himself. While the players were competent enough, the sound was fusion and funk, hybrid genres that did not exist when Hendrix was alive. The two resulting albums, *Crash Landing* and *Midnight Lightning*—both released in 1975—have potentially good compositions that are marred by this awkward studio trickery. At times, the approach created an unpleasantly jarring mish mash, something Hendrix himself would never be accused of doing.

In the early 1990s, Douglas oversaw the CD release of the three original Experience albums, minus their original artwork. In 1995, Al Hendrix regained the rights to his son's music; his legal fees were underwritten by Paul Allen, the Microsoft executive. Since then, under the family-run company, Experience Hendrix LLC, and with the help of Eddie Kramer, Mitch Mitchell, and Billy Cox, much of Hendrix's essential work has been restored and reissued in an appropriate and respectful manner.

In the years following Hendrix's death, literally hundreds of albums composed of the guitarist's early work as a sideman were released. Almost all were blatantly exploitative, and many misrepresented the nature of their musical contents. Meanwhile, it's estimated that anywhere from 500 to 1,000 hours of unreleased material existed at the time of Hendrix's death making it likely that this aural and sonic deluge will continue.

And why not? We still cherish newly unearthed recordings by Charlie Parker, Miles Davis, and Bill Evans, so why shouldn't the same reverence be applied to the man who revolutionized rock and roll in his all-too-brief twenty-seven years?

Meanwhile, the legend of Jimi Hendrix continues to grow. He was inducted into the Rock and Roll Hall of Fame in 1992. The Experience's first album, *Are You Experienced*, was included in the U.S. National Recording Preservation Board's National Recording Registry. Finally, Hendrix took top honors in *Rolling Stone*'s list of 100 Greatest Guitarists of All Time.

Nearly four decades after his death, Jimi Hendrix's influence remains as strong as ever, and his musical legacy continues to beguile and inspire.

TIMELINE

May 1961
Jimmy (not yet "Jimi") Hendrix joins the 101st Airborne Paratroopers and is stationed at Fort Campbell, Kentucky. Here he befriends bass player Billy Cox; they form a group, the Casuals, and play gigs on the military base and in lounges in the area.

July 1962
Hendrix is honorably discharged from the U.S. military and moves to Nashville.

1962–64
Though nominally based in Nashville and Vancouver, Hendrix works the chitlin' circuit for the next two years, playing in the touring bands of the Marvelettes, Curtis Mayfield and the Impressions, Little Richard, Solomon Burke, Hank Ballard, Chuck Jackson, the Supremes, Tommy Tucker, Lonnie Youngblood, Ike and Tina Turner Revue, Joey Dee and the Starliters, and King Curtis.

1964
Hendrix ends up in New York City, playing guitar in the Isley Brothers' band. He meets soul singer Curtis Knight and joins his band.

April 17–18, 1965
As a member of Little Richard's band, Hendrix plays the storied Paramount Theater in New York.

June 1966
Encouraged by Linda Keith, Hendrix forms his own band, Jimmy James and the Blue Flames, and begins playing the Greenwich Village club circuit.

August 3, 1966
Chas Chandler, the Animals' bass player, accompanies Linda Keith to the Café Wha? to see Jimmy James and the Blue Flames. He's impressed enough with the guitarist's potential that he promises to return at the end of the Animals' U.S. tour and take Hendrix to England.

September 3, 1966
Chandler makes good on his promise, returns to New York, and arranges to take Hendrix to England.

September 23, 1966
Newly renamed Jimi Hendrix arrives with Chandler in London.

October 1, 1966
Hendrix jams with Cream at Regent Polytechnic in London. Cream guitarist Eric Clapton—whom fans liken to God—was shocked to encounter a player who could do things he himself never dreamed possible.

October 13, 1966
The newly formed Jimi Hendrix Experience—with Noel Redding on bass and Mitch Mitchell on drums—play their first official gig, at Novelty, in Eveux, France. They are the opening act for French pop star Johnny Halliday.

October 18, 1966
The Jimi Hendrix Experience play the prestigious Paris Olympia. The sensation they cause has the press and new fans buzzing.

October 23, 1966
The Jimi Hendrix Experience record their first two songs, at De Lane Lea Studio in Kingsway, London.

December 16, 1966
"Hey Joe" is released as the first single by the Jimi Hendrix Experience.

March 17, 1967
One of Hendrix's signature songs, "Purple Haze," is released by Track Records.

January 24, 1967
The Experience play the famed Marquee club; among the audience are all four members of the Beatles, some members of the Rolling Stones, Eric Clapton, and Jeff Beck.

May 12, 1967
The debut album of the Jimi Hendrix Experience, *Are You Experienced*, is released in the United Kingdom.

June 18, 1967
The Experience play a career-making set at the Monterey Pop Festival, finally establishing Hendrix as a bona fide star in his home country.

December 1967
The Experience's second album, *Axis: Bold as Love*, is released in the United Kingdom.

June 1968

The Experience begins recording their epochal third album, *Electric Ladyland*, a process that would, off and on, consume the next six months.

June-December 1968

The Experience embark on their first "proper" U.S. tour, an exhausting grind that ends with the group temporarily disbanding. Chandler quits as the band's manager, and all such duties are relegated to Michael Jeffery.

February 1969

Reunited Experience play two dates at the famous Royal Albert Hall in London.

April–June 1969

The Experience tour the United States.

June 29, 1969

The Experience's set at the Denver Pop Festival is their final gig together.

August 18, 1969

As the sun rises, Hendrix and his new assemblage of musicians perform the show-ending set at the Woodstock Music and Art Fair in upstate New York.

January 1, 1970.

Hendrix and the Band of Gypsys (Billy Cox, bass, Buddy Miles, drums) play at the Fillmore East. The live recording culled from the show is released as *Band of Gypsys*.

July 30, 1970

Hendrix plays at Rainbow Bridge in Hawaii.

September 17, 1970

Hendrix dies after chocking on his vomit while in a stupor from sleeping medication.

SELECT DISCOGRAPHY

Are You Experienced, 1967

Axis: Bold as Love, 1967

Electric Ladyland, 1968

The Cry of Love, 1971

The Jimi Hendrix Concerts,

Jimi Plays Monterey, 1986

First Rays of the New Rising Sun, 1997

NOTES

1. Mitch Mitchell, with John Platt, *Jimi Hendrix: Inside the Experience* (New York: Harmony Books, 1990), p. 18.
2. *New Musical Express*, March 11, 1967.

FURTHER READING

Cross, Charles R. *Room Full of Mirrors: A Biography of Jimi Hendrix*. New York: Hyperion, 2005.

Egan, Sean. *Jimi Hendrix and the Making of* Are You Experienced. Chicago: Chicago Review Press, 2002.

Mitchell, Mitch, with John Platt. *Jimi Hendrix: Inside the Experience*. New York: Harmony Books, 1990.

Murray, Charles Shaar. *Crosstown Traffic: Jimi Hendrix and the Rock 'n' Roll Revolution*. New York: St. Martin's Press, 1989.

About the Authors and Contributors

SCOTT SCHINDER is the author of several books about popular music and culture, including Rolling Stone's *Alt-Rock-A-Rama*. He has written for such publications as *Entertainment Weekly, Newsday,* and *Creem*.

ANDY SCHWARTZ is the former publisher and editor of punk/new wave music magazine *New York Rocker*. He also served as national director of editorial services for Epic Records (a division of Sony-BMG) and as a consulting researcher and archivist for the Rock & Roll Hall of Fame.

ALAN BISBORT has spent 25 years as a working journalist and writer. His writing has appeared in *Rolling Stone, Creem, The New York Times, Washington Post,* and *Vanity Fair*.

CHRIS COCKER is a freelance writer specializing in contemporary music.

SUSAN GODWIN is a freelance writer specializing in contemporary music.

JESSE JARNOW has written for the *London Times, Rolling Stone,* the Associated Press, and elsewhere. He blogs about books, b-sides, and baseball at jessejarnow.com.